ITALY IN THE SEVENTEENTH CENTURY

LONGMAN HISTORY OF ITALY

Italy in the Seventeenth Century

DOMENICO SELLA

LONGMAN
London and New York

Addison Wesley Longman Limited
Edinburgh Gate
Harlow, Essex CM20 2JE, United Kingdom
and Associated Companies throughout the world.

*Published in the United States of America
by Addison Wesley Longman, New York*

© Addison Wesley Longman Limited 1997

First published 1997

ISBN 0 582 03595 3 PPR
ISBN 0 582 03598 8 CSD

British Library Cataloguing-in-Publication Data
A catalogue record of this book is available from the British Library

Library of Congress Cataloging-in-Publication Data

Sella, Domenico.
Italy in the seventeenth century / Domenico Sella.
p. cm. -- (Longman history of Italy)
Includes bibliographical references and index.
ISBN 0-582-03598-8 (csd). -- ISBN 0-582-03595-3 (ppr)
1. Italy--History--17th century. I. Title. II. Series.
III. Series: Longman history of Italy (Unnumbered)
DG544.S45 1996
945'.07--dc20
96-44940
CIP

Transferred to digital print on demand 2001
Printed and bound by Antony Rowe Ltd, Eastbourne

Contents

Abbreviations

AISIG	*Annali dell'Istituto storico italo-germanico di Trento*
QS	*Quaderni storici*
SIE	*Storia d'Italia*, ed. Ruggiero Romano and Corrado Vivanti, 20 vols, Einaudi, Turin 1972–1986.
SSI	*Storia della società italiana*, ed. Giovanni Cherubini *et al.*, 25 vols, Teti, Milan 1981–1990.
T&C	*Timore e carità. I poveri nell'Italia moderna*, ed. Giorgio Politi *et al.*, Annali della Biblioteca statale e civica, Cremona 1982.

For Annamaria

Preface

From the days of the Enlightenment until quite recently, the seventeenth century has been the Cinderella of Italian historiography. Long viewed as a time of unrelieved decadence and gloom in sharp contrast to the splendours of the Renaissance on the one hand and to the rebirth of the nation's spirit in the eighteenth century on the other, the Seicento was dismissed as an almost embarrassing aberration in the trajectory of Italian history, an aberration that deserved but a fraction of the attention which scholars lavished on the centuries that preceded and followed it. In the last twenty years or so, however, the relative neglect in which the seventeenth century had been held for so long has given way to a remarkable surge of interest: a vast amount of research has been conducted on virtually every aspect of the nation's life, a wealth of new evidence has surfaced and, as a result, a new and profoundly different image of the period has begun to emerge. As a work of synthesis, this book is meant to provide an overview of the century in light of the revisions proposed by recent scholarship and of the lively debates those revisions have generated.

I am very grateful to my colleagues Robert M. Kingdon, David C. Lindberg, Johann Sommerville and John Tedeschi for generously agreeing to read portions of the manuscript in draft and for offering helpful comments, criticisms and suggestions on several points. I am also greatly indebted to my son Antonio for the expert, unfailing assistance he has provided in the preparation of the manuscript. My wife, to whom the book is dedicated, has helped me more than she probably realizes: not only have I benefited from her constant encouragement and support during the book's long gestation, but her comments and suggestions at various stages of the work have greatly contributed to bringing clarity to my thoughts and to my writing.

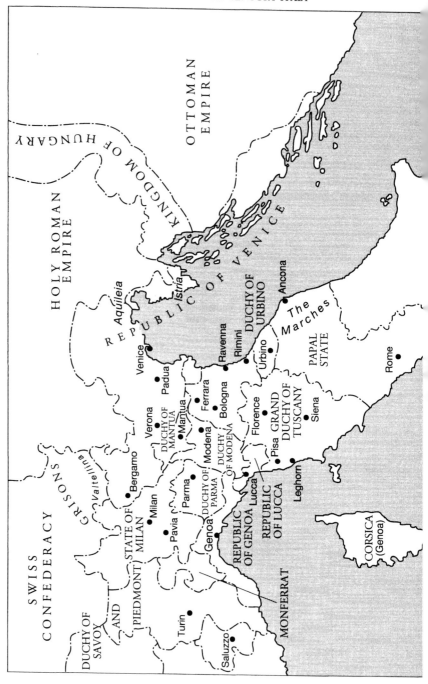

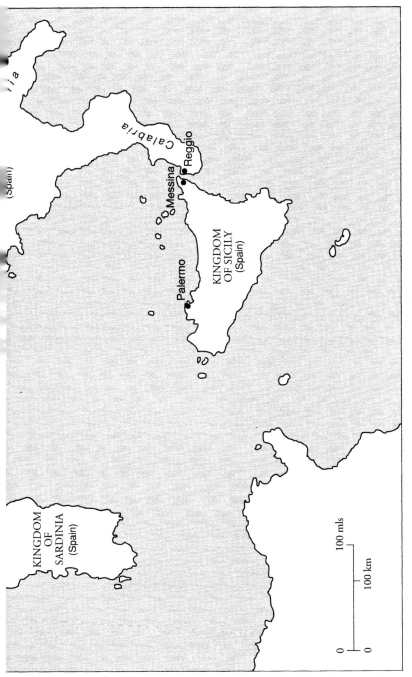

The Italian states in the seventeenth century

CHAPTER ONE

The system of Italian states

From 1559, the year of the Peace of Câteau Cambrésis between France and Spain, to the end of the century Italy enjoyed an exceptionally long period of peace, a period that stands in sharp contrast to the previous half century when the country had been turned into a battlefield on which the two major European powers had fought for supremacy. Câteau Cambrésis had not only restored peace and stability to a ravaged land and ushered in four decades of economic prosperity, it had also sealed the hegemony of Spain over Italy and had shaped the political map in a way that was to remain basically unchanged for the next 150 years.[1]

On that map Spanish possessions loomed the largest: over roughly the southern half of the peninsula (the Kingdom of Naples which the French kings had hoped to make their own earlier in the century) flew the standard of His Catholic Majesty who also held the island Kingdoms of Sicily and Sardinia; in the north the State of Milan too was under direct Spanish rule and represented, despite its relatively small size, a strategically vital component of the Spanish monarchy in that it guarded the access to Italy against any future French attempt at meddling in Italian affairs, besides providing an essential link between the dominions of the two branches of the Habsburg dynasty – the Spanish and the Austrian. The rest of the peninsula formed a mosaic of independent states: the Papal States stretching from Rome to the northern Adriatic (and, since 1598, to Ferrara), the Grand Duchy of Tuscany, the Venetian Republic with its dependencies on the Dalmatian coast, and the Duchy of Savoy seated astride the Alps and extending from Nice in the south

1. For the following discussion of political events I have heavily depended on the old but still authoritative accounts of Romolo Quazza, *Preponderanza spagnola (1559-1700)*, 2nd edn, Vallardi, Milan 1950; and of Vittorio De Caprariis, 'Il Seicento' in *Storia d'Italia*, vol. 2, ed. Franco Catalano *et al.*, UTET, Turin 1959, pp. 479–640. For the earlier period covered in this chapter see also the more recent work by Eric Cochrane, *Italy 1530–1630*, ed. Julius Kirshner, Longman 1988; for the later part of the century, Giorgio Spini, 'Italy after the Thirty Years War' in *New Cambridge Modern History*, vol. 5, ed. F.L. Carsten, Cambridge University Press 1961, pp. 458–73, is very useful.

to the shores of Lake Geneva in the north. The fragmentation of the political map was at its highest in an area roughly extending from Nice to the Adriatic and comprising the Marquisats of Saluzzo (contested by France and Savoy) and of Monferrato (then a possession of the dukes of Mantua), the Republic of Genoa, and the small Duchies of Parma, Modena and Mantua. Lastly, three other diminutive states – the Duchies of Urbino and of Castro in the Papal States and the Republic of Lucca – added to the bewildering complexity of the political map.

With roughly one half of the land under its direct rule and with the resources of its vast empire to back its policies, the Spanish monarchy was obviously in a position where it could make its influence felt on most Italian states, all the more easily so as some of them, although formally independent, were, in fact, beholden to Spain. One such state was Tuscany whose ruling dynasty (the Medici) originally owed its crown, to a large extent, to Habsburg largesse; besides, its Spanish patrons held five garrison towns along the Tuscan coast (the so-called Stato dei Presidi) from which Spanish forces could stage, if need be, a rapid military intervention. The duke of Savoy, whose dominions had been overrun by French forces in the early part of the century, had recovered them in 1559 in the wake of Habsburg victory and could hardly ignore the importance of Spanish support as a safeguard against future French claims. As for the Papacy it had little choice, in the face of the rise of Protestantism and as long as the religious future of France was in doubt, but to rely on the Habsburgs (both Spanish and Austrian) for the defence of the Catholic cause. Lastly, the fortunes of the Republic of Genoa, whose bankers were lending prodigious amounts of money to the Spanish government, were inextricably tied to those of their client.

It would be wrong to assume that the direct or indirect rule of Spain over much of the peninsula was necessarily perceived as an intolerable burden by Italians at the time. To be sure, at the beginning of the seventeenth century a few writers (Alessandro Tassoni, Traiano Boccalini, Fulvio Testi) denounced Spain as the source of all evils and called for all Italian states to join in a league in defence of Italian 'liberty'. Theirs, however, were isolated voices inspired more by nostalgia for a glorious but distant past than by a realistic assessment of present geopolitical conditions.[2] Most people no doubt accepted the Spanish presence as part of the normal order of things or as a 'lesser evil' (to use Tommaso Campanella's words) compared to the horrors of the first half of the century when Italy had been devastated by the Franco-Spanish contest.[3] Other views were even more favourable: Spain was sometimes praised as the guardian of the 'tranquillity of Italy' (*quiete d'Italia*): 'Italy', wrote the historian and political writer Scipione Ammirato in 1594 as he reflected on the calm and prosperity of the past forty years, 'has not felt as

2. Benedetto Croce, *Storia dell'età barocca in Italia*, 2nd edn, Laterza, Bari 1946, p. 480.
3. Quotation in Rosario Villari, *Ribelli e riformatori dal XVI al XVIII secolo*, Editori Riuniti, Rome 1983, p. 66.

2

oppressed [by Spanish rule] as had been feared, but for many years now has enjoyed greater happiness than ever before'.[4] It was a feeling, one might add, that was likely shared, in the regions under direct Spanish rule, by the social elites (whether feudal nobility or urban patriciates) inasmuch as Spain, as will be seen, made it a point to respect their privileged status and left them in nearly complete control of local affairs.[5]

THE END OF PAX HISPANICA

Peace and prosperity, however, were soon to come to an end. The new century ushered in a period of nearly sixty years during which war returned to the peninsula and brought back, in some areas, the instability and the devastations of the early sixteenth century. One main reason for this dramatic change was the revival of France as a great power after the wars of religion had come to a close in that country in 1598. Predictably, this meant that the two old rivals – France and Spain – would resume their contest for supremacy in Europe and that Italy would be, once again, one of the battlegrounds where the two powers would confront each other. It also meant that individual Italian states with a grudge or a claim against a neighbour might feel tempted to break the peace and to settle old scores by enlisting the support of one of the two superpowers. An early omen of things to come was provided by Piedmont-Savoy, then under the leadership of the ambitious, restless and somewhat reckless Duke Carlo Emanuele I (1580–1630). As early as 1588, taking advantage of the fact that France was in the throes of religious war, he had annexed the Marquisat of Saluzzo, the French enclave on the Italian side of the Alps that threatened the very heart of the duke's possessions in Piedmont. A war with France had followed with military operations unfolding mainly in Provence and Savoy rather than on Italian soil. After 1593, however, a revitalized France under the new Bourbon king Henry IV was able to contain the Savoyard forces and to demand that Carlo Emanuele restore Saluzzo to France (1598). As the duke refused, Henry IV marched his army into Savoy and occupied most of it (1600). In the event, papal mediation was able to arrange a compromise whereby Carlo Emanuele kept Saluzzo, but surrendered two small provinces on the French side of the Alps (Treaty of Lyons, 1601) – a trade-off that represented a success for the duke of Savoy in that, to use his own words, 'with Saluzzo in our hands, we

---

4. Quotation in De Caprariis, 'Il Seicento', p. 490. On the climate of opinion prevailing at the time see also Giuliano Procacci, *Storia degli Italiani*, Laterza, Bari 1968, vol. 1, p. 227 and Jean-Claude Waquet, 'Politique, institutions et société dans l'Italie du "Seicento"' in Yves-Marie Bercé *et al., L'Italie au XVIIe siècle*, Sedes, Paris 1989, pp. 32–4.
5. Waquet, 'Politique', pp. 58–9.

3

make it difficult for the French to march into Italy'.[6] Having thus eliminated, at a relatively small cost, a French salient in Piedmont, Carlo Emanuele drew closer to France and engaged in negotiations with other Italian states for the formation of a coalition or league which, with French support, would aim at driving the Spaniards out of north Italy: if successful, the ambitious plan would have enabled the duke of Savoy to annex a good portion of the neighbouring State of Milan. A formal treaty to that effect was signed with France at Bruzolo in 1609, but nothing came of it owing to Henry IV's assassination the following year. As for the Italian states whose help Carlo Emanuele had hoped to enlist against Spain, they quickly lost interest in his grand plan: whatever they may have thought of 'the liberty of Italy', they were highly suspicious of Carlo Emanuele's intention to expand into the State of Milan, for this would have substantially altered the balance of power in north Italy, an outcome no one cherished. As was said at the time, the several Italian rulers 'want an equal, not a superior' next door.[7] Nor did Carlo Emanuele do anything to assuage those suspicions: in 1608 he had married off his daughter Margherita to Francesco II Gonzaga, duke of Mantua and marquis of Monferrato, in the hope that the marriage might establish some future claim, if not to the entire Gonzaga inheritance, at least to Monferrato, a very small province, to be sure, but one that lay right in the middle of the duke of Savoy's Italian possessions. And in fact, when Francesco II died in 1612 without issue, Carlo Emanuele rushed to claim Monferrato for himself and, having received a polite refusal from the late duke's brother and heir, Ferdinando Gonzaga, in the spring of 1613 marched his army into Monferrato and easily conquered three of its major strongholds.

Predictably, his brutal aggression triggered a strong reaction: Spanish forces, supported by Austria, attacked from the State of Milan and managed to score some significant successes in Monferrato and to conquer the stronghold of Vercelli in northeastern Piedmont; Venice and Florence offered financial support to the beleaguered duke of Mantua; France itself (by now in a pro-Spanish mood under the regency of Henry's widow, Marie de' Medici) opened a second front on Carlo Emanuele's western flank. Between 1613 and 1617 war raged inconclusively all around Piedmont: two ceasefires mediated by the Papacy in 1614 and 1615 were broken as soon as they had been agreed on; on the battlefield Carlo Emanuele was able, if not to defeat his enemies, at least to hold his ground and to prove that his forces could stand up to those of Spain and its allies. In the end a stalemate was reached and both the Venetian Republic and France managed to persuade the duke of Savoy to surrender whatever land he had seized in Monferrato in return for Spain withdrawing from Vercelli. With this compromise, reluctantly accepted by Carlo Emanuele, the war over Monferrato – the first major war fought on

---

6. Quotation in Claudio Donati, 'Genova, Piemonte, Stato della Chiesa e Toscana nel Seicento' in *SSI*, vol. 11, p. 371; on pp. 371–2 Donati provides a succinct but excellent view of the duke's foreign policy.
7. Quotation in De Caprariis, 'Il Seicento', p. 488.

Italian soil since the settlement of 1559 – was brought to a close and Carlo Emanuele's ambitious plans for expansion were laid to rest, or so it seemed at the time.

ITALY AND THE THIRTY YEARS WAR

In 1618 the outbreak in Bohemia of what would one day be known as the Thirty Years War presented the restless duke with a fresh opportunity to resume his drive for aggrandisement and for getting even with the countries that had done so much to thwart his earlier plans, namely Spain and Austria. Accordingly, as soon as revolt broke out in Prague he dispatched 2,000 troops to assist the rebels and offered himself as a candidate to the elective crown of Bohemia. As his offer was ignored, he abandoned the rebels' cause and drew closer to the Austrian emperor, going so far as to offer him (in vain as it turned out) military support – an about-face that earned him at the time the unflattering epithet of 'chameleon'.[8]

The outbreak of the Thirty Years War impacted another small area in north Italy, namely the Valtelline, a narrow, rugged valley under the overlordship of the Grisons (but in fact largely autonomous) that ran from the northern tip of Lake Como to the Alpine pass of Spluga and thus provided a crucial link between the Spanish possessions in north Italy (the State of Milan) and the lands of the Austrian emperor and, beyond them, the Rhineland. The obvious strategic importance of the Valtelline was further enhanced in 1621 when war resumed in the Netherlands between Spain and the Dutch rebels: since the Atlantic sealanes had been virtually closed by the unremitting attacks of English and Dutch mariners, all Spanish troops and supplies intended for the Netherlands had to be funnelled through the Valtelline and the Rhineland if they were to reach their destination at all.[9] Whether this could be done or not ultimately depended on the goodwill of the Protestant Grisons, but with war in Germany pitting Catholics against Protestants such goodwill could hardly be expected. The Catholic population of the Valtelline, on its part, was inclined to support the Habsburg cause; as a result, clashes broke out between the two religious groups. After the Protestants attempted to crush Catholic opposition in the valley in 1619 the Catholics, prodded by the Spanish governor of Milan, responded by resorting to armed insurrection against their Protestant overlords, killing hundreds of them in what came to be known as the 'holy slaughter' (*sacro macello*) of 1620 and opening their gates to Spanish forces. Two years later the governor of Milan marched his

---

8. Ibid., p. 546.
9. The strategic importance of the Valtelline is fully discussed in Geoffrey Parker, *The Army of Flanders and the Spanish Road, 1567–1659. The Logistics of Spanish Victory and Defeat in the Low Countries War*, Cambridge University Press 1972, chs 2 and 3.

troops from the Valtelline all the way to Chur, the Grison capital, and forced its government to renounce all claims on the contested valley.

The Spanish occupation of the Valtelline was viewed as an alarming development by the Venetian Republic which had traditionally recruited mercenary troops in the Grisons and would not be able to do so as long as Spanish forces controlled the Valtelline. It was viewed with no less apprehension by France, for it greatly strengthened the position of its traditional enemy in north Italy. In 1620, however, neither Venice, still recovering from a short but costly war with Austria, nor France, faced as it was with a Huguenot uprising at home, could do anything to oppose the Spanish takeover. Only after order had been restored at home did France take the initiative of forming a coalition with Venice and Savoy against Spain. The latter responded in 1623 by offering a compromise: her troops would pull out of the valley and would be replaced by a papal garrison pending a final resolution of the whole issue. Three years later, secret negotiations between Richelieu and Olivares, the prime ministers of France and Spain respectively, led to the Treaty of Moncon whereby, unbeknownst to the Papacy and the other Italian states, the Valtelline was handed back to the Grisons, but with the stipulation that it would be demilitarized and that Catholics living in the valley would enjoy complete freedom of religion.

The dust had hardly settled in the Valtelline when Monferrato moved once again into the limelight. There were two reasons for this development: one was the impending extinction of the ruling house of Mantua and Monferrato as Duke Ferdinando Gonzaga died without male issue in 1626 and was succeeded by his ageing brother Vincenzo, himself with no children and no prospect of having any. Carlo Emanuele, needless to say, was only too ready to step forward with a claim to a share of the Gonzaga inheritance (the long-coveted Monferrato) on behalf of Mary, the daughter of the late duke and of Margaret of Savoy. His plans, however, were firmly resisted in Mantua by Duke Vincenzo who was determined to pass on all his dominions intact to Charles Gonzaga-Nevers, duke of Rethel, the scion of a collateral branch of the ducal family that had settled in France in 1549 and had achieved enormous wealth and considerable prominence there. To ensure a smooth transition while at the same time making his intentions unmistakeably clear, Duke Vincenzo had invited Nevers to take up residence in Mantua in 1625, there to be groomed for his future role as head of the Gonzaga state.

The looming conflict between the duke of Savoy and the duke of Nevers could have been nothing more than a local squabble between two Italian princelings were it not for the fact that, with war raging in Europe and with France increasingly stoking the fires of opposition to the two Habsburg monarchies, neither Spain nor Austria were prepared to tolerate, in the very heart of north Italy, a ruler who was notoriously a protégé of France. Under these circumstances the interests of Spain and of Savoy coincided, and in 1627 the two governments agreed to cooperate in preventing Nevers from succeeding to the throne of Mantua: the next duke would be a member of a collateral branch of the family, the Gonzaga-Guastalla who were friendly to

Spain; as for Monferrato, it would be partitioned between Spain and Savoy.

Upon the death of the old duke in 1627 the plan was set in motion: Savoyard troops invaded much of Monferrato in spite of the heroic resistance of the local forces, while Spanish troops from Milan laid siege to, but failed to conquer, Casale, the major stronghold in the region. As for Mantua, Spain's plans to instal a new duke of its choosing were blocked, ironically enough, by the Austrian emperor who reserved to himself the right of deciding the succession to a duchy that was, after all, an imperial fief. In 1628 the military situation was further complicated by the intervention of the French army and at once the whole issue of the Gonzaga succession took on a broader European dimension. Cardinal Richelieu, from the start, had watched developments in north Italy with growing concern, but had been unable to intervene as he was confronted with the Huguenot uprising at La Rochelle. He clearly sensed, however, that sooner or later France must support the duke of Nevers: Mantua and Monferrato in friendly hands would give France a strategic advantage over its enemies, for in that event the State of Milan would be caught between Mantua to the east and Monferrato to the west, and the Spanish supply lines running through it could be severed. In this way 'French hegemony in Italy would replace Spain's and Francis I's old dream would become reality'.[10]

As soon as order was restored at home a French army marched into Piedmont and conquered the town of Susa, 50 km west of the capital Turin, while Mantuan forces under the duke of Nevers opened a second front against the Spaniards in southern Lombardy. At that point, however, Carlo Emanuele did not hesitate to switch sides once again and to come to terms with France: in return for keeping portions of Monferrato (notably the towns of Alba and Trino), he put pressure on Spain to raise the siege of Casale; on its part, France twisted Nevers's arm so that he would gracefully consent to the loss of portions of Monferrato to the duke of Savoy.

Calm had thus apparently been restored when, in the spring of 1629, an imperial army of 30,000 foot and 6,000 horse descended into north Italy. Its goal was to take Mantua from the duke of Nevers. At the same time Spanish troops resumed the siege of Casale, now defended by a French garrison, as a first step to conquering Monferrato. Richelieu responded by dispatching a large army to Italy and, having failed to secure Carlo Emanuele's military cooperation, annexed the whole of Savoy as well as Saluzzo and Pinerolo in Piedmont. In 1630 Mantua surrendered to the imperial forces after the surrounding countryside had been systematically laid waste by the enemy and Venetian troops who had come to the rescue of the beleaguered city had been defeated in battle; Nevers went into exile and his wretched capital was subjected for three days to a sack the ferocity and savagery of which were appalling even by the standards of a violence-prone age. In Casale, on the other hand, the French held their ground against the Spaniards and this provided Richelieu with some leverage in his efforts to reach a settlement of the whole messy issue of the Mantuan succession – a settlement he urgently needed if he was to confront the Habsburgs

10. De Caprariis, 'Il Seicento', p. 556.

on the battlefields north of the Alps. After laborious negotiations a settlement was eventually reached at Cherasco in 1631, its conclusion no doubt facilitated by the fact that the previous year Gustavus Adolphus king of Sweden had landed in Germany, thus opening a new front against the Austrian emperor and forcing him to concentrate his forces and resources north of the Alps. At Cherasco it was agreed that Nevers would be reinstated as duke of Mantua, but with the proviso that he would formally profess his allegiance as vassal of the emperor; Vittorio Amedeo I, who had succeeded his father as the new duke of Savoy in 1630, was allowed to keep portions of Monferrato, but had to renounce any further claim to the Gonzaga inheritance; France kept Pinerolo, while all powers involved agreed to withdraw their troops from the Valtelline.

The Treaty of Cherasco no doubt represented a setback for the House of Savoy's policy of territorial consolidation and expansion on the Italian side of the Alps; by the same token it represented a major success for Richelieu in that it ensured a solid French presence on Italian soil – a direct one in Pinerolo, 'the gateway to Italy', and an indirect one in Mantua and in portions of Monferrato now firmly in the hands of a ruler friendly to France. But precisely to the extent that it placed France in a strategically strong position in Italy, Cherasco was bound to be a source of concern for the Italian states. Pope Urban VIII himself, in spite of the fact that he had favoured the French side in the negotiations leading to the treaty, was reported as ruefully commenting that 'it is certain that in this wretched Italy, if the Spaniards could be driven out, the French would establish their supremacy, which could be worse than the Spaniards' owing to the fecklessness, insatiable greed and capricious nature of that nation'.[11] Under the circumstances, it is understandable that the various proposals floated under French auspices in the 1630s to form a broad anti-Spanish coalition of Italian states met with a lukewarm reception and were quickly shelved: the fact of the matter seems to be that, as always, each state was primarily preoccupied with its own 'conservation' and the best hope to ensure the latter was to prevent either of two superpowers from achieving hegemony in the peninsula.[12]

In 1635 peace was shattered as France threw her army into the all-European mêlée in an attempt to break Habsburg power once and for all. Richelieu's main military thrust was directed at the Rhineland, but he also decided to open a second front in Italy. Having enlisted the support of the dukes of Savoy, Parma, Modena and Mantua, he dispatched through the Valtelline an army that was expected to attack the State of Milan from the northeast, while Savoyard troops attacked from the west and the other allies from the south. The encircling manoeuvre failed, however, as the duke of Modena defected to Spain and invaded the neighbouring Duchy of Parma. To make things worse for the French, in 1637 Vittorio Amedeo died and was succeeded by his son, Carlo Emanuele II, a four-year-old, sickly child. A

11. Quotation ibid., p. 561.
12. Ibid., p. 562.

regency government was thus inevitable, but the choice of a regent pitted the Francophile Duchess Dowager Christina against the late duke's brothers, Maurice and Thomas, both of them ardent supporters of Spain. Piedmont was thus turned into a battleground where a civil war raged for five years with the participation of French and Spanish forces, bringing devastation and untold misery to the land. Only in 1645 was the family quarrel brought to an end by the uneasy reconciliation between Christina and her in-laws: it was a reconciliation that reflected mutual exhaustion, but also the fact that France, now on the rise as the dominant military power after the battle of Rocroi (1643) and in control of much of Piedmont, was able to bring the two sides together and persuade them to compromise and cooperate.

THE PAPACY AND ITALIAN POLITICS

Throughout the tumultuous events of the 1620s and 1630s Pope Urban VIII (1623–44) had tried more than once to act as mediator and peacemaker between France and Spain as well as between the several Italian states. In doing so he had followed in the footsteps of his predecessor Clement VIII (1592–1605), the Roman pontiff who in 1595, in open defiance of Spanish protests, had taken the bold step of welcoming back into the Catholic fold the recently converted Henry IV king of France – a move intended to offset the hegemony of Spain in Catholic Europe and free the Papacy (and Italy) from the stifling embrace and tutelage of Madrid;[13] the pontiff also who had mediated the peace of Vervins between France and Spain in 1598. In pursuit of this policy of equilibrium Urban had gone so far as to encourage French intervention in Italian affairs, but at the same time, in his role as the head of the Catholic Church, he had provided moral and financial support to the Catholic forces in Germany led by the two Habsburg powers (Spain and Austria) at the very moment when France was opposing them. In the end, this difficult, not to say impossible, balancing act was bound to fail: not only did Urban's mediating efforts become less and less credible and effective, but the prestige of the Papacy was badly eroded – a far cry from where it had stood in the final stages of the Council of Trent (1543–65) or in subsequent decades when the Papacy had laid the groundwork for the great Christian victory over the Ottoman Empire at Lepanto (1571) or had played a decisive role in restoring peace between Spain and France. Other developments worked in the same direction. The annexation of the small Duchy of Urbino to the Papal

13. The behind-the-scene discussions that led to Clement VIII's decision and the key role played by Cardinal Baronius in persuading the pope are narrated by Cyriac K. Pullapilly, *Cardinal Baronius, Counter-Reformation Historian*, University of Notre Dame Press, Notre Dame, Ind. 1975; further details, especially on curial opposition to the decision, are provided by Agostino Borromeo, 'Il Cardinale Baronio e la corona spagnola' in *Baronio storico e la Controriforma*, Centro di Studi Sorani V. Patriarca, Sora 1982, pp. 69–84.

States in 1631 had created the perception of a Papacy bent on territorial expansion and, as such, representing a threat to the status quo (*conservazione*) so dear to the several Italian states, while the practice of nepotism which Urban VIII had raised to new levels as he lavished prodigious sums of money and lucrative sinecures on members of his family, the Barberini, could only generate disrespect for the papal office. The worst blow to his prestige, however, was possibly the ill-advised and, for the time being, failed attempt at annexing the Duchy of Castro, a small independent enclave just north of Rome that had been granted in fief to the Farnese family (the ruling house of Parma) in 1537 by another notorious nepotist pope, Paul III.[14]

Tensions between Rome and Parma had developed as early as 1635 when Duke Odoardo Farnese had joined a French-led coalition against Spain in the hope of being rewarded, in the event of victory, with the State of Milan – a hope Urban VIII, mindful of the dire consequences this would have had for the general stability of the peninsula, had strongly opposed. Tensions were further aggravated by Farnese's mismanagement of his finances in Castro and by the resulting outcry of his creditors who petitioned the pope to intervene. When Urban VIII ordered Farnese to honour his debts, he not only refused to comply, but defiantly poured arms and ammunition into Castro. In response, Urban excommunicated his rebellious vassal, stripped him of his title, and in October 1641 declared war on Parma. The war that followed saw Venice, Modena and Tuscany (concerned as they were with preserving the status quo in the face of what they perceived as papal expansionism) rush to Farnese's aid and their joint forces were able to inflict serious losses on the papal army, notably in the vicinity of Bologna and Ferrara. Once again, as in the case of the civil war in Piedmont, it was France that stepped in as peacemaker. In 1644 an agreement was cobbled together under French auspices whereby all enemy forces had to withdraw from papal territory and Farnese (after receiving absolution from the pope) was reinstated as the legitimate ruler of Castro. All in all, it was a return to the status quo, but it was also a humiliating experience for Urban VIII.[15]

The inconsequential war of Castro would be a mere footnote in the annals of Italian history were it not for the fact that it exposed the growing isolation and irrelevancy of the Papacy as a political force in international relations and revealed the commanding position France had achieved by then in Italian affairs.[16] The Peace of Westphalia that brought an end to the war in Germany

14. A full discussion of the Castro affair is in Quazza, *Preponderanza spagnola*, pp. 495–501; a shorter, vivid account in Jean Delumeau, *L'Italie de Botticelli à Bonaparte*, Colin, Paris 1974, pp. 200–1.
15. There was a tragic sequel to the War of Castro: in 1649, following the assassination of the bishop newly assigned to the town by Pope Innocent X, papal troops marched on Castro, conquered it and razed it to the ground.
16. On the declining international role of the Papacy resulting in part from the conflicting goals it was pursuing see Paolo Prodi, *The Papal Prince. One Body and Two Souls: The Papal Monarchy in Early Modern Europe*, transl. Susan Haskins, Cambridge University Press 1987, pp. 169, 177–9.

in 1648 fully confirmed both trends: the Papacy played no role in the final settlement and France clearly emerged as the dominant power in Europe. Which does not mean that Spain could be written off as the hollow relic of a once great power: although weakened by major uprisings in her own dominions, notably in Portugal, Catalonia, Naples and Palermo, Spain went on fighting its war against France until 1659 and proved to be a military power still to be reckoned with. In north Italy, in particular, Spanish forces managed to fend off a Franco-Modenese attempt to conquer Cremona in 1649 and three years later drove the French from Casale; in 1655 a joint effort by France and the duke of Savoy to capture Pavia (a mere 35 km south of Milan) failed in the face of Spanish resistance. In 1656 Franco-Modenese troops conquered the stronghold of Valenza in the southwestern corner of the State of Milan, but two years later the duke of Modena broke loose of the French alliance and returned his recent conquest to Spain. In 1659 the Treaty of the Pyrenees finally brought an end to the conflict that had pitted Madrid against Paris for nearly twenty-five years and, as far as Italy was concerned, it restored the status quo. Significantly, Pope Alexander VII (1655–67) was not invited to take part in the negotiations, a further sign of the decline of the Papacy as a player in international affairs.

VENICE AND THE TURKS

In all the vicissitudes of the first half of the century the Republic of Venice had been virtually absent, consistently refusing to take sides in the interminable conflict between France and Spain. The Republic had some very good reasons for keeping out of the fray. One was its preoccupation with preserving some kind of equilibrium between the two superpowers as the only way to safeguard the status quo in Italy; another reason was that Venice, as a maritime empire with significant possessions outside Italy (Dalmatia, the Ionian islands, Crete), had special problems to contend with, problems that were of little concern to her Italian neighbours.

Early in the century one such problem had been represented by Uskok depredations in the Adriatic Sea.[17] The Uskoks were Christian refugees who had fled before the Turkish conquest of the Balkans and had settled along the Dalmatian coast, notably in and around Segna (Senj). From there they had long engaged in acts of piracy against Turkish ships plying the Adriatic, much to the exasperation of the Venetian Republic which had traditionally claimed the Adriatic as its own territorial waters and, since making peace with the

17. In addition to the works cited in note 1 above, the following must be consulted on Venetian–Ottoman relations: Frederic C. Lane, *Venice. A Maritime Republic,* Johns Hopkins University Press, Baltimore 1973, pp. 398–400 and 409–11; and Gaetano Cozzi, 'Venezia nello scenario europeo (1517–1699)' in G. Cozzi, Michael Knapton and Giovanni Scarabello, *La Repubblica di Venezia nell'età moderna. Dal 1517 alla fine della Repubblica,* UTET, Turin 1992, pp. 99–102 and 117–27.

Ottoman Empire in 1573, had committed itself to ensure the safety of Turkish merchant ships in return for the Ottoman government's pledge to keep its own armed vessels out of the Adriatic. Keeping the Adriatic sealanes clear of pirates was thus essential if Venice was to remain on good terms with the Turks. This would have been a routine police action well within the capability of the Venetian navy, but, in fact, it proved a much more difficult enterprise in that the Uskoks were protected and supported by the Austrian government who saw in them a valuable pawn in its long-standing struggle against the Ottoman Empire. After negotiations between Vienna and Venice failed to resolve the issue, war broke out in 1615 and was bitterly, if inconclusively, fought on land and on sea with the intervention of Spanish warships on the Austrian side. In September 1617 the contenders finally came to an agreement over the Uskok issue as Vienna undertook to resettle the troublemakers inland.

Piracy drew Venice into war a second time thirty years later, but under quite different circumstances and with a profoundly different outcome. In 1644 some ships flying the flag of the Knights of Malta – the order of chivalry traditionally committed to the pursuit and capture of Muslim ships in the Mediterranean – attacked Turkish ships near the island of Rhodes and then sailed to the safety of the harbour of Candia (Heraklion) in the Venetian island of that name (also known as Crete). In retaliation the Ottoman government launched an amphibious expedition against the seaport of Canea (Khania) on Crete and captured it after a short siege – an exploit that exposed the total lack of readiness of the old republic whose navy had been allowed to decline to an all-time low since the glorious days of Lepanto and whose land forces in Crete had become seriously depleted in terms of both manpower and supplies. In vain did Venice appeal to Christian Europe for help in defending what it regarded, after the loss of Cyprus in 1570, as the last Christian bastion against the Infidel in the eastern Mediterranean: neither France nor Spain, then at war with each other, expressed much interest in the fate of a distant island; Spain could hardly spare a man or a gun from the European battlefield; as for France, it would not lightly deviate from its traditional friendship with the Ottoman Empire as the latter represented a valuable, if covert, ally against the Habsburg Empire. Only Pope Innocent X sent a number of warships to Crete and tried (in vain) to persuade other European governments to do the same. After the Peace of the Pyrenees in 1659, however, as news of the heroic and increasingly desperate resistance of the Venetian forces against the Turkish onslaught reached Europe, some belated military assistance came from France, Savoy and the Papacy, but to no avail. In 1669 the last Venetian garrison on the island surrendered with military honours and Crete, not unlike Cyprus a hundred years earlier, became part of the Ottoman Empire.

The Venetian Republic was to have her partial revenge twenty years later, but only because this time it would not confront the Turks alone, but as a member of a powerful coalition that included the Habsburg Empire, Poland and the Papacy. The coalition had formed in 1683 in response to a massive

Turkish drive against Austria; with Vienna itself under siege, Pope Innocent XI called for a Holy League against the Infidels, and Venice, after some hesitation, decided to join in January 1684 in the hope of recovering the islands of Cyprus and Crete. One of its finest naval commanders, Francesco Morosini, was placed at the head of a large fleet consisting of Venetian, Maltese, papal and Tuscan warships. Under Morosini naval operations went well and resulted in the Venetian reconquest of much of the Dalmatian coast and the Ionian islands that had earlier fallen to the enemy and in the conquest of the Morea (Peloponnesus). The next obvious step would have been an all-out assault on Crete and, in fact, such a move was in the planning stage after 1693. Nothing, however, came of it as the attention of Europe was increasingly drawn toward the issue of the Spanish Succession. In 1699 peace was signed with the Ottoman Empire at Carlowitz and Venice was able to retain its recent conquests in Dalmatia and the Morea, but the prospect of ever regaining Crete or Cyprus had vanished forever.

ITALY AND THE SUN KING

While for Venice the second half of the century was a time of high drama, grave challenges and heavy sacrifices of manpower and resources, for the rest of the peninsula, by contrast, it was a period of relative calm. No major changes (or attempted changes) in the political map or in the distribution of power among the Italian states occurred in this period, no major military campaigns or social upheavals, except for a failed conspiracy, abetted by the duke of Savoy, against the ruling oligarchy of Genoa in 1672 and a popular insurrection in Messina two years later.

To be sure, even in this uneventful period foreign meddling in Italian affairs was not entirely absent – and, not surprisingly, it was the work of the strongest and most aggressive power of the time, Louis XIV's France. In 1662 the somewhat extravagant claims of diplomatic immunity and extraterritoriality made by Louis's ambassador in Rome led to a confrontation with the Holy See, to the threat of a French military intervention in the Papal States, and to the actual invasion of the papal enclave of Avignon in southern France. A compromise was eventually worked out between the Papacy and the Sun King in 1664 and Avignon was evacuated, but tensions between the two resurfaced a few years later over the issue of the king's control over church appointments in France and of the French Church's claim of autonomy *vis-à-vis* the Roman pontiff. The quarrel dragged on with threats of military action on one side and of excommunication on the other until a settlement was reached in 1696.

More serious in the long run was Louis XIV's purchase in 1679 of the stronghold of Casale in Monferrato from the duke of Mantua then on the brink of bankruptcy. With Pinerolo already in French hands since the Cherasco Treaty of 1631, the acquisition of Casale not only turned Piedmont into a *de facto* French satellite, but it also provided Louis XIV with an invaluable springboard from which he could influence the course of Italian affairs. As a Venetian ambassador commented in 1681, 'Italy, long accustomed to bending her knee to Spain, has now shed any fear of that king and is turning her attention to the formidable power of France. Belatedly does she regret to have surrendered the gateway of Pinerolo and now trembles at the very thought of the consequences that the acquisition of Casale may produce at any time.'[18] In practice, there was very little anyone could do to remedy the situation: Venice had to worry about the Ottoman Empire; the Papacy, as we just saw, was embroiled in a bitter quarrel over its rights of jurisdiction over the French Church; Piedmont-Savoy was pretty much at Louis's mercy. And when Genoa tried to stand up to Louis's demands, it paid a terrible price for its courage. This happened in 1683 as the French king, now once again at war with Spain, demanded that no Genoese ships (albeit privately owned and already under contract) sail in the service of Spain. Better to make his point, in 1684 he dispatched a naval squadron to Genoa with an ultimatum and as the proud Republic refused to comply, the city was brutally shelled for five days by the French fleet. Spain did not lift a finger to help and the Genoese doge had no choice but to journey to Versailles to make a formal and humiliating apology for his audacity in resisting the Sun King's will and to sue for peace.

In Piedmont Louis was equally heavy-handed. In 1685, after depriving the French Protestants of the religious freedom they had enjoyed for nearly a century and after subjecting them to persecution, he demanded of Vittorio Amedeo II, the young and defenceless duke of Savoy, that he inflict the same treatment on the religious minority in his own dominions, the Waldensians. To make sure that his reluctant neighbour fully complied, in 1686 Louis sent an army over the Alps which, in conjunction with local forces, brought devastation and death to the Waldensian communities and forced thousands of their people to flee. Only in 1690, after he had joined the great coalition against France (the League of Augsburg), did Vittorio Amedeo reverse his policy and allow the Waldensians to return to their homes. But it was going to take six more years of warfare before Louis XIV agreed to leave the Duchy of Savoy alone. With the Treaty of Vigevano of 1696 Casale was handed back to the duke of Mantua and the French garrison withdrew from Pinerolo after sixty-five years of occupation.

INSTITUTIONAL STABILITY

For all the wars, shifting coalitions, attempted coups and foreign interventions, by 1700 the political map of Italy was very similar to what it had been a hundred years earlier. To be sure, there had been a few minor changes,

18. Quotation in De Caprariis, 'Il Seicento', p. 628.

notably in Monferrato and along the border between Piedmont and France, but the impression of overall long-term stability is inescapable. Much the same can be said of the form of government in individual Italian states. The native dynasties (*principi naturali* to use Machiavelli's term) who had ruled in 1600 (the Houses of Savoy, Gonzaga, Medici, Este, Farnese) were still in charge in 1700 and continued to rule their little dominions as (in theory) 'absolute' monarchs much as before. As for the Republics of Venice, Genoa and Lucca, in 1700 their traditional oligarchic structure was still basically intact in the sense that, as of old, a restricted urban nobility or patriciate monopolized all important government positions. Equally unchanged, from a strictly institutional standpoint, were the Papal States and the Spanish Kingdoms of Naples, Sicily and Sardinia. As Jean-Claude Waquet has rightly stressed, stability was the hallmark, the defining feature of the century.[19]

This overall pattern of stability is all the more remarkable in that during the seventeenth century the country was repeatedly touched not only by warfare, but also by events and forces (to be discussed in subsequent chapters) that could have had profoundly destabilizing consequences: three major famines (in 1628–29, 1648–50, and the 1690s); two devastating visitations of the bubonic plague (in 1630 in north and central Italy, in 1656 in the south) each of which caused a loss of lives in the order of 30–40 per cent; a rising and, in some areas, crippling burden of taxation; the unravelling of the urban economies; and a number of large-scale popular uprisings.

No one simple explanation can account for the fact that, in spite of all those adversities and calamities, the system of Italian states and their internal structure survived virtually intact from one end of the century to the other. To be sure, the overriding concern among Italian rulers, with the notable exception of Carlo Emanuele I and perhaps Urban VIII, was to preserve their inheritance and to join with others, if need be, to oppose anyone who attempted to alter the status quo. 'Peace and preservation', it has been said, was the ideal pursued by the Italian governments in the seventeenth century – a sharp departure from the goal of conquest and domination advocated by Machiavelli and pursued with abandon by Renaissance statesmen in the preceding century. The religious climate of the Counter-Reformation with its emphasis on tradition and stability may have played a role, but no doubt of greater importance was the clear, sober perception that any attempt at modifying the existing balance of power between Italian states could only spell disaster for all, as it had done in the previous century at the time of the Italian wars – unless perhaps a would-be aggressor could enlist the help of one of the two great European powers, Spain or France. But quite apart from the fact that past experience had shown that foreign intervention could have unforeseen and indeed tragic consequences, against such a risky strategy stood the hard reality that any meddling in Italian affairs by either one of those powers invariably caused the other to jump into the fray. Under the circumstances, the outcome would be far from certain, for even though

19. Waquet, 'Politique', p. 20.

France was on the ascendancy through much of the century, her foreign policy was often unpredictable and Spain was still a formidable contender. The failed French interventions in Naples in 1647 and in Messina in 1674, as will be seen, would be proof enough of this.

It is more difficult, however, to explain why, in the face of so many trials and tribulations, the internal structure of the Italian states exhibited as much stability as did their external borders. Part of the answer may be found in the fact that the second half of the sixteenth century had witnessed a remarkable process of institutional reconstruction and consolidation in most Italian states as they emerged from the turmoil and the devastations of the Italian wars. Whether in Piedmont-Savoy under Emanuele Filiberto, in Tuscany under Cosimo I, in the Papal States under Pius V and Sixtus V, or in the Spanish possessions under Philip II, state power had become more centralized and at the same time more pervasive, bureaucracies had been beefed up, uniform codes of law had been adopted, and the system of taxation had been overhauled in order to broaden the tax base and to provide some balance in the distribution of the tax burden between town and country. The upshot had been that seventeenth-century governments could draw on a solid institutional legacy that gave them the tools they needed to achieve their main goal of preserving the territorial integrity of their respective states as well as of maintaining law and order – and that legacy proved to be a remarkably enduring factor of stability.

Long-term stability characterized the economy and the social structure, too. The former demonstrated, as will be seen, an astonishing capacity for absorbing the shocks of a long, severe depression, with the result that by and large (but with the notable exceptions of Naples and Sicily) major dislocations and social upheavals were averted. As for society, with its rigid social stratification, its fragmentation into 'orders' or 'estates' each endowed with its own privileges, ethos and aspirations, it had a built-in resistance to change in that governments could play off one group against another and were unlikely to be confronted by any broadly based opposition. The institutional framework that had been put in place in the sixteenth century operated in the same direction: for all their centralizing efforts sixteenth-century governments had not erased the composite structure of their respective states. It was a structure that reflected (especially in north and central Italy) the long process whereby the several regional states had been cobbled together by the piecemeal absorption of independent city-states, feudal enclaves, free rural communities into the domain of a *signore*.[20] The process had involved,

20. For a general view see the seminal pages of Giorgio Chittolini, *La formazione dello Stato regionale e le istituzioni del contado, secoli XIV e XV*, Einaudi, Turin 1979, pp. 3–36. A provocative analysis of the historiography has been provided by Jean-Claude Waquet, *Le Grand-duché de Toscane sous les derniers Medicis. Essai sur le système des finances et la stabilité des institutions dans les anciens états italiens*, Ecole Francaise de Rome, Rome 1990, pp. 13–51. On specific regions see the recent works by: Giovanni Vigo, *Uno stato nell'impero. La difficile transizione al moderno nella Milano di età spagnola*, Guerini, Milan 1994, 111–15;

besides sheer military conquest, a good deal of negotiations leading to well-defined terms of surrender (*patti di dedizione*) that embodied a compromise between the conquering *signore* and the conquered communities and resulted in the recognition by the former of the institutional identity, legal traditions and administrative autonomy of the latter. In other words, incorporation into a larger 'regional state' (whether dynastic monarchy or aristocratic republic) had been based on a kind of contractual relationship between the new government and each individual community on terms that could not be modified, by and large, without fresh negotiations. The towns, in particular, had thus managed to retain much of their erstwhile autonomy as well as the right to lord it over the surrounding countryside (*contado*), notably in the area of judicial administration and the assessment of taxes – so long, of course, as they remained loyal to their new masters and produced a steady flow of revenue. Even where, as in the case of the Kingdom of Naples and the State of Milan, a territory had been subjected to the rule of an outside power, such as Spain, that presumably had the military force to sweep aside any obstacle that stood in the way of centralization – even there existing legal traditions, institutional structures, and a large measure of self-rule had been allowed to survive. The Spanish monarchs from Charles V on made it a point to respect and preserve the identity and the autonomy of their Italian possessions and, in a deliberate effort at winning the loyalty and the cooperation of their Italian subjects, left the day-to-day administration of the country to existing local elites, and dealt with each component of their dominions as a distinct entity with its own set of privileges and obligations. Under such conditions institutional change, however desirable in the abstract, would be hard to implement – a fact of which eighteenth-century reformers were keenly aware and which led them to view all those 'intermediate bodies' (orders, city councils, fiefs, guilds) as the greatest obstacle to change.

Institutional stability, however, did not mean total paralysis, let alone *immobilismo* in the sense of a blind refusal of change. For, in fact, under the pressure of necessity some changes were introduced in a number of Italian states in spite of fierce opposition from various centres of power, privilege and influence. Some of those changes will be discussed in later chapters, notably the new policies aimed at curbing the anarchical behaviour of the feudal nobility and the scourge of banditry that often went with it; at stripping towns of long-standing and jealously guarded tax privileges; at limiting the influence of the Church in the life of states. All those policies are evidence enough that, for all their weaknesses and for all the constraints imposed on them by external forces beyond their control, Italian governments of the seventeenth century were no mere historical fossils, but living organisms

---

Luca Mannori, *Il sovrano tutore. Pluralismo istituzionale e accentramento amministrativo nel Principato dei Medici (secoli XVI– XVIII)*, Giuffrè, Milan 1994, pp. 462–8; Villari, *Ribelli e riformatori*, pp. 271–3; and Ivana Pederzani, *Venezia e lo 'Stado de Terraferma'. Il governo delle comunità nel territorio bergamasco (secoli XV–XVIII)*, Vita e Pensiero, Milan 1992, ch. 1.

capable of responding to the challenges of their time. Admittedly, when it came to foreign policy, the room for manoeuvre was woefully limited and the Italian states' role was largely a passive one, for as long as the European stage was dominated by the contest between France and the two Habsburg monarchies, the diminutive Italian states could do little more than try to preserve their territorial integrity, indeed their very existence. Any plan for a league of Italian states aimed at 'liberating' the peninsula from foreign domination was bound to remain a pious dream of a few visionaries: quite aside from the difficulty of finding a common ground for states as different as the Venetian Republic, the Duchy of Savoy, or the Papal States, there was a sober realization that driving out Spain could be done only, if at all, with the help of France, and this, as contemporaries knew only too well, would merely replace one foreign master with another.

CHAPTER TWO

The economy

The fifty years of nearly uninterrupted peace the country enjoyed after Spanish hegemony had become firmly established in 1559 with the treaty of Câteau Cambrésis were also a period of vigorous economic expansion. The evidence for this is abundant and has led historians to discard the old view according to which the geographic discoveries of the late fifteenth century, the Italian wars of the early sixteenth century and, lastly, the coming of Spanish rule had destroyed the very foundations of the Italian economy and had ushered in an irreversible process of decline. We now know that, after the dislocations and destructions caused by war, the economy exhibited remarkable resilience.[1]

While population in general and urban population in particular made steady progress and by 1600 reached unprecedented levels, economic progress was being achieved along a broad front. In response to a rising demand for basic foodstuffs generated by demographic growth and manifesting itself in rising farm prices, a great deal of land was reclaimed from waste, swamp or forest throughout the peninsula, and in some areas, notably in the Veneto, in Piedmont and in the Tuscan Maremma, reclamation entailed large-scale investments in drainage or irrigation.[2] In Apulia, traditionally a

1. Gino Luzzatto, *Storia economica dell'età moderna e contemporanea*, 4th edn, vol. 1, Cedam, Padua 1955, pp. 117–23; Carlo M.Cipolla, *Before the Industrial Revolution, European Society and Economy, 1000–1700*, 2nd edn, Norton, New York–London 1980, pp. 255–6; Fernand Braudel, *The Mediterranean and the Mediterranean World in the Age of Philip II*, transl. Sian Reynolds, Harper and Row, New York 1973, vol. 1, pp. 387–94; Eric Cochrane, *Italy 1530–1630*, Longman 1988, pp. 171–83; Ruggiero Romano, 'L'economia' in *SIE Annali* 9 (1986), pp. 1895–1901; and Richard Goldthwaite, *Wealth and the Demand for Art in Italy, 1300–1600*, Johns Hopkins University Press, Baltimore and London 1993, pp. 13–67.
2. In addition to the classic study by Emilio Sereni, *Storia del paesaggio agrario italiano*, Laterza, Bari 1961, part VI, see Aldo De Maddalena, 'Il mondo rurale italiano nel Cinque e nel Seicento. Rassegna di studi recenti', *Rivista storica italiana* 76 (1964), pp. 354–75; A. Ventura, 'Le trasformazioni economiche nel Veneto tra Quattro e Ottocento', *Bollettino del Centro internazionale di studi di architettura Andrea Palladio* 18 (1976), pp. 132–3; Giorgio Borelli, *Città e campagna in età preindustriale, XVI–XVIII secolo*, Libreria Editrice Universitaria,

major supplier of raw wool, the number of sheep rose from 600,000 at the start of the sixteenth century to four times as many at the end.[3] The export of Calabrian raw silk more than doubled in the second half of the century in response to the growing demand generated by the manufacture of silk fabrics in Naples, Florence, Lucca, Venice and other northern towns.[4] That demand, however, was also responsible for the diffusion of the mulberry tree and the raising of silk worms in north Italy. The making of woollen cloth experienced sustained growth as well: in Venice the annual output of high-quality fabrics rose from about 10,000 pieces at mid-century to about 25,000 fifty years later; and the region around Bergamo could boast a similar increase in the production of less expensive fabrics. The Florentine woollen industry recovered quickly from the paralysis caused by the siege to which the city had been subjected in 1527, and by 1572 its annual output stood at roughly 30,000 pieces of high-quality cloth, possibly making Florence once again the largest textile centre in the peninsula, as it had been in the late Middle Ages. On a smaller scale progress was also taking place in the cloth manufactures of Milan and Como. Altogether the growth of the woollen industries stimulated the demand for alum, a key ingredient in the dyeing process and a major export item from the Papal States which had a virtual monopoly on its production. Other industries – from the making of armour in Milan to gunmaking in Brescia, to printing in Venice and Milan – tell much the same story and they all confirm the overall impression of a buoyant, expanding economy.[5]

Verona 1986, pp. 165–76 and 192–9; Salvatore Ciriacono, *Acqua e agricoltura: Venezia, l'Olanda e la bonifica europea in età moderna*, Franco Angeli, Milan 1994, pp. 89–113; and Enrico Stumpo, *Finanza e Stato moderno nel Piemonte del Seicento*, Istituto Storico Italiano, Rome 1979, p. 251.

3. John A. Marino, *Pastoral Economics in the Kingdom of Naples*, Johns Hopkins University Press, Baltimore 1988, p. 150.
4. Francesco Caracciolo, *Il Regno di Napoli nei secoli XVI e XVII. Economia e Società*, Università degli Studi, Messina 1966, pp. 122, 154–6.
5. Domenico Sella, 'The Rise and Fall of the Venetian Woollen Industry' in *Crisis and Change in the Venetian Economy in the Sixteenth and Seventeenth Centuries*, ed. Brian Pullan, Methuen 1968, pp. 106–26; Ruggiero Romano, 'A Florence au XVIIe siècle: Industries textiles et conjoncture', *Annales E.S.C.* 9 (1952), pp. 508–11; Bruno Caizzi, *Il Comasco sotto il dominio spagnolo. Saggio di storia economica e sociale*, Centro Lariano per gli studi economici, Como 1955, pp. 83–7; Giuseppe Aleati and Carlo M. Cipolla, 'Aspetti e problemi dell'economia milanese e lombarda nei secoli XVI e XVII' in *Storia di Milano*, Fondazione Treccani, Milan 1966, vol. 11, pp. 377–99; Stefano D'Amico, *Le contrade e la città. Sistema produttivo e spazio urbano fra Cinque e Seicento*, Franco Angeli, Milan 1994, pp. 64–79; Giovanni Vigo, *Uno stato nell'impero. La difficile transizione al moderno nella Milano di età spagnola*, Guerini, Milan 1994, pp. 63–9; Luigi De Rosa, 'De-industrialization in the Kingdom of Naples in the 16th and 17th Centuries' in *The Rise and Decline of Urban Industries in Italy and the Low Countries (Late Middle Ages–Early Modern Times)*, ed. Herman Van der Wee, Leuven University Press, Leuven 1988, pp. 121–9.

Not surprisingly trade and banking prospered along with the rest of the economy. From the early 1570s the small town of Leghorn on the coast of Tuscany was transformed by the Medici grand dukes into a major international harbour: the annual number of incoming ships went from about 350 in the 1570s to eight times as many by the opening of the next century, while the cosmopolitan population of the city rose tenfold in the same period. Although less spectacular, the growth of seaborne traffic in Venice was very substantial in terms of sheer numbers of incoming ships. No less important was the fact that in the 1560s and again in the 1590s the city of St Mark resumed her traditional role as the great clearing house of oriental spices, a role she had lost to the Portuguese at the opening of the sixteenth century. Her old rival, Genoa, did not fare quite so well as a commercial harbour; yet, even there, in spite of wide fluctuations, traffic did increase in the later part of the century and by 1600 had reached an all-time high.[6]

If Genoa could not quite match the performance of either Leghorn or Venice as a great international harbour, its people could take comfort in the fact that they (or rather a small elite in their midst) were second to none when it came to international finance. From 1575 Genoese financiers had replaced their German counterparts as bankers to the Spanish crown and for the next fifty years dominated the financial world by lending vast sums of money to a chronically indebted monarchy and by pocketing handsome profits (for themselves and for the countless small investors who entrusted their savings to their capable hands) when the loans plus interest were repaid with the silver and gold brought from the New World by the galleons of His Catholic Majesty.[7]

The impressive record of the Italian economy in the second half of the sixteenth century, however, was not without its costs and its casualties. While rising farm prices and land values must be credited with attracting a great deal of capital into agriculture in the form of both land acquisitions and large works of reclamation and irrigation, notably in the northern plain (the Po Valley), some areas took the short cut of overcropping and ended up with

6. Fernand Braudel and Ruggiero Romano, *Navires et marchandises a l'entrée du port de Livourne (1547–1611)*, Colin, Paris 1955, pp. 17–29, 109; Frederic C. Lane, 'La marine marchande et le trafic maritime de Venise à travers les siècles' in *Les sources de l'histoire maritime en Europe du Moyen Age au XVIIIe siècle*, ed. Michel Mollat, SEVPEN, Paris 1962, p. 28 and Lane, 'The Mediterranean Spice Trade: Its Revival in the Sixteenth Century', *American Historical Review* 45 (1940), pp. 581–90; Edoardo Grendi, 'Traffico portuale, naviglio mercantile e consolati genovesi nel Cinquecento', *Rivista storica italiana* 80 (1968), p. 599; and Claudio Costantini, *La Repubblica di Genova nell'età moderna*, UTET, Turin 1978, pp. 164–8.

7. Braudel, *The Mediterranean*, vol. 1, pp. 500–10; Giorgio Doria, 'Conoscenza del mercato e sistema informativo: il "know how" dei mercanti-finanzieri genovesi nei secoli XVI e XVII' in *La repubblica internazionale del denaro tra XV e XVII secolo*, ed. Aldo De Maddalena and Hermann Kellenbenz, Mulino, Bologna 1986, pp. 57–121.

serious problems of soil exhaustion. Moreover, the frenzy of land acquisitions by wealthy merchants and noblemen and the introduction of commercial crops was bound to have an unsettling impact on rural communities insofar as they eroded peasant ownership of the land, created a growing mass of landless peasants, and undermined the 'moral economy' of those communities by replacing the traditional priority given to local self-sufficiency with an emphasis on marketable crops.[8]

In the industrial sector, too, there were losers as well as winners. The astonishing success of the Venetian cloth industry, for instance, was in part at the expense of its Florentine rival: the latter failed to sustain its upward movement beyond the early 1570s and by 1600 its annual output had been virtually halved, the main cause of this downfall being, it would seem, Venetian competition in the Levant markets where both cities exported most of their high-quality fabrics.[9] Among the losers at that time one must also include shipping and shipbuilding. In late medieval times and even in the early decades of the sixteenth century both Venice and Genoa had boasted the two largest merchant fleets in the Mediterranean and their ships (built in their celebrated shipyards) had ensured most freight services between the inland sea and the Atlantic. In the second half of the sixteenth century, however, shipbuilding rapidly declined in both cities, apparently as a consequence of a timber shortage caused by massive deforestation in the Italian Alps; increasingly, seaborne trade headed for the two cities came to be handled by foreign ships – ships from Ragusa (Dubrovnik) at first and then from the Hanseatic towns, the Netherlands and, to a lesser extent, England. The upshot was that while, as late as the 1560s, three-quarters of the ships calling at Genoa had been Genoese built and owned, forty years later only one-quarter were, and the record of the Venetian shipping industry was no brighter.[10]

In spite of these losses, at the start of the seventeenth century Italy could boast a prosperous, vibrant economy that was fully integrated in the larger international context and enjoyed a commanding and enviable position in it.

8. Costantini, *La Repubblica di Genova*, pp. 173–89; Marco Cattini, *I contadini di San Felice. Metamorfosi di un mondo rurale nell'Emilia dell'età moderna*, Einaudi, Turin 1984, pp. 289–300.
9. Paolo Malanima, *La decadenza di un'economia cittadina. L'industria a Firenze nei secoli XVI–XVIII*, Mulino, Bologna 1982, p. 302; D. Sella, 'L'economia' in *Storia di Venezia*, vol. 6: *Dal Rinascimento al Barocco*, ed. Gaetano Cozzi and Paolo Prodi, Istituto della Enciclopedia Italiana, Rome and Venice 1994, p. 684.
10. Frederic C. Lane, 'Venetian Shipping during the Commercial Revolution' (1933) reprinted in *Crisis and Change in the Venetian Economy*, pp. 22–46; Braudel, *The Mediterranean*, vol. 1, pp. 628–40; Ruggiero Romano, 'La marine marchande vénitienne au XVIe siècle' in *Les sources de l'histoire maritime en Europe du Moyen Age au XVIIIe siècle*, pp. 33–68; Jean-Claude Hocquet, *Le sel et la fortune de Venise*, Publications de l'Université, Lille 1978, vol. 2, pp. 590, 609–10; and Ugo Tucci, 'Venetian Shipowners in the Sixteenth Century', *Journal of European Economic History* 16 (1987), pp. 277–96.

It was a position the country was not going to hold for long, however, for in the early years of the new century, and most certainly from the 1620s, the economy began to unravel.

AGRICULTURE: SETBACKS AND RECOVERY

In agriculture (by far the largest sector of the economy even in a country as rich in manufactures and as heavily urbanized as Italy was at the close of the sixteenth century) conditions began to deteriorate as early as the 1590s when a sequel of harvest failures brought skyrocketing prices, widespread famine and severe demographic losses in both town and country. A temporary return to normality in the first decade of the seventeenth century was soon shattered in the rich Lombard plain by the outbreak of the first war of Monferrato (1613–17) and even more seriously throughout much of north Italy by the war of the Mantuan succession (1627–31) and the terrifying epidemic of the bubonic plague that swept most of the peninsula north of Rome in 1630 and cut population totals by one-third. As a result, farm rents and land values plummeted and long stagnated at low levels, while much farmland was abandoned – a complete reversal of the conditions that had prevailed in the later part of the preceding century.[11] In the words of a 1634 document that reflected the views of the landed class in Cremona, 'due to the recent fall in the price of farm commodities, to the shortage of labourers and to their exorbitant demands a great many estates are now nearly worthless'.[12] And their lament was echoed a few years later by a Milanese nobleman who bemoaned the dwindling income he received from his lands and ruefully concluded: 'In these wretched times . . . I would be better off if I earned a living at some sort of trade.'[13]

The amount of land that was abandoned in the 1630s and allowed to revert to waste and wilderness is not known, but it must have been very substantial indeed if in 1639 Milanese authorities took the radical measure of declaring vacant farms forfeit to their owners and allowing anyone who was willing to resume cultivation to acquire full ownership.[14] To the west of the State of Milan Piedmont, too, experienced a sharp downturn as a consequence not

11. De Maddalena, 'Il mondo rurale', pp. 361–76; Romano, 'L'economia', pp. 1920–3; Luigi Faccini, *La Lombardia fra '600 e '700*, Franco Angeli, Milan 1988, pp. 87–8, 123–8; Gian Luigi Basini, *L'uomo e il pane. Risorse, consumi e carenze alimentari della popolazione modenese nel Cinque e nel Seicento*, Giuffrè, Milan 1970, pp. 65–76; and two essays in *The European Crisis of the 1590s. Essays in Comparative History*, ed. Peter Clark, Allen and Unwin 1985: one by N.S. Davidson on north Italy (pp. 157–76) and one on southern Italy by Peter Burke (pp. 177–90).
12. Quotation in Faccini, *La Lombardia*, p. 124.
13. Quotation in D. Sella, *Crisis and Continuity. The Economy of Spanish Lombardy in the Seventeenth Century*, Harvard University Press, Cambridge, Mass. 1979, p. 54.
14. Faccini, *La Lombardia*, p. 125.

only of the plague, but also of the savage civil war that was fought there from 1637 to 1642. The depopulation and the devastations of those years stood in sharp contrast to the prosperity of a not-too-distant past when Piedmontese agriculture had benefited from large-scale investments, notably in the form of an impressive network of irrigation canals.[15] Developments in the mainland possessions of the Venetian Republic (the Terraferma) tell a similar story of boom and bust. Whereas in the second half of the sixteenth century huge sums had been sunk into land reclamation, the drainage of swamp and bog, and the creation of irrigated fields for growing maize and rice (two highly profitable crops that were new to the region), the first half of the seventeenth century witnessed a dramatic downturn in investments and output.[16]

In the later part of the century, however, the agriculture of north Italy staged a strong recovery.[17] In the State of Milan signs of improvement are clearly discernible from the 1660s. As warfare ended after the Peace of the Pyrenees, population gradually moved back to its pre-plague level and as farm prices stabilized and even began to inch up, a good deal of capital was lured back into agriculture – the more easily so, it has been argued, as interest rates by then were at an all-time low. Not only was much land purchased at bargain-basement prices by wealthy townsmen from debt-ridden peasants who had borne the brunt of wartime taxation and military billets, but landowners old and new also undertook long-term projects aimed at raising the productivity and profitability of their estates, such as improving or repairing irrigation networks, increasing the size of dairy herds, expanding the cultivation of rice and maize and the planting of mulberry trees, and, more importantly, extending the practice of convertible husbandry with its elaborate system of crop rotation in which artificial grasses and fodder crops made it unnecessary to fallow the land. The result was that by the opening of the eighteenth century the Lombard plain had more than recovered lost ground and was well on its way to being the home of modern, progressive farming which nearly a century later was going to elicit the admiration of Arthur Young.[18]

15. Stumpo, *Finanza e Stato moderno*, pp. 251–2.
16. Ventura, 'Le trasformazioni', p. 137; Ciriacono, *Acque e agricoltura,* p. 108; Angelo Moioli, 'Una grande azienda del Bergamasco durante i secoli XVII e XVIII' in *Agricoltura e aziende agrarie nell'Italia centro-settentrionale,* ed. Gauro Coppola, Franco Angeli, Milan 1983, pp. 599–724; Marino Berengo, 'Patriziato e nobiltà: il caso Veronese' (1975) in *Potere e società negli stati regionali italiani fra '500 e '600,* ed. Elena Fasano Guarini, Mulino, Bologna 1978, pp. 200–6; Borelli, *Città e campagna,* pp. 209–10.
17. Dante Bolognesi, 'Le campagne dell'Italia padana nel Seicento', *Cheiron* 2 (1984), pp. 84–99 for an excellent survey of the literature. See also Maurice Aymard, 'La fragilità di un'economia avanzata: l'Italia e le trasformazioni dell'economia europea' in *Storia dell'economia italiana,* vol. 2, ed. Ruggiero Romano, Einaudi, Turin 1991, p. 85.
18. Faccini, *La Lombardia,* pp. 148–53, 159, 201–49; and Aldo De Maddalena, *Dalla città al borgo. Avvio di una metamorfosi economica e sociale nella Lombardia spagnola,* Franco Angeli, Milan 1982, pp. 183, 187–8.

In Piedmont, too, the 1660s mark the start of agricultural recovery: as land values began to rise capital flowed again into farming, new commercial crops such as rice and maize were introduced, and the production of silk entered an era of sustained growth. Agricultural recovery was especially vital to a region such as Piedmont where, as a contemporary observer had pointed out early in the century, 'the fertilitie of the soil rather than the craftsmanship of its people is the foundation of its wealth' and where, in the absence of significant manufactures, farm products formed the backbone of the export trade. A telling index of how much progress was achieved in the late seventeenth century is provided by data on the yield of the customs house in Susa, the gateway to the French market: between 1660 and 1680 revenue from that source jumped ninefold and one can safely assume that much of that rise reflected growing exports of silk, a commodity of which by then Piedmont had become a major producer. Nor was France the only outlet for Piedmontese silk: between 1680 and 1720 annual exports to England rose from 10,000 to 21,000 kg.[19] Land reclamation, irrigation works and the expansion of select commercial crops characterized agriculture in the Venetian mainland as well. It is worth noticing, however, that neither Piedmont nor the Terraferma, for all the progress they unquestionably achieved, adopted the more sophisticated system of convertible husbandry which in that very period was making headway in nearby Lombardy. Tuscany, on its part, followed a different path to recovery. There the dramatic expansion of cereal farming in the late sixteenth century had brought soil exhaustion and falling grain yields in its wake, making arable farming less and less profitable, and the sharp drop in prices that followed the epidemic of 1630 made a bad situation even worse. In the end, what saved Tuscan agriculture was a massive shift from arable farming to winegrowing: it was in the course of the seventeenth century that Tuscany's reputation as a major producer and exporter of wine became firmly established.[20]

In the South signs of trouble became visible in the early part of the century when the production of two commodities that had long loomed large in the export trade, namely raw wool and silk, fell abruptly and would not recover

19. Stuart J. Woolf, 'Sviluppo economico e struttura sociale in Piemonte da Emanuele Filiberto a Carlo Emanuele III', *Nuova Rivista Storica* 46 (1962), pp. 15–16; Stumpo, *Finanza e Stato*, pp. 62, 253–60.
20. Oscar Di Simplicio, 'Due secoli di produzione agraria in una fattoria del Senese, 1550–1751', *QS* 21 (1972), pp. 788–813. In the 1978 issue (no. 39) of the same journal are two other important articles on Tuscan agriculture: Giuseppe Pallanti, 'Rendimenti e produzione agricola nel contado fiorentino: i beni del Monastero di Santa Caterina, 1501–1689', pp. 849–52; Elsa Luttazzi Gregori, 'Un'azienda agricola in Toscana nell'età moderna: il Pino, fattoria dell'Ordine di Santo Stefano (secoli XVI–XVIII)', pp. 899–902. In Emilia recovery was sluggish with hardly any innovation in terms of either crops or methods of cultivation: Marco Cattini, 'In Emilia orientale: mezzadria cinquecentesca e mezzadria settecentesca. Continuita o frattura? Prime indagini', *QS* 39 (1978), pp. 868–9. On the role played by *mezzadria* (share tenancy) in holding back progress see Carlo Poni, *Fossi e cavedagne benedicon le campagne. Studi di storia rurale*, Mulino, Bologna 1982, pp. 15–96.

until the beginning of the next century. In Apulia the number of sheep which had peaked at 2.4 million around 1600 was cut in half during the exceptionally harsh winter of 1611–12. In subsequent years the size of the herd was further reduced and by mid-century was down to the half million mark and was going to stay at that level for the next fifty years. In nearby Calabria the chief casualty was raw silk, traditionally a vital component of the local economy and the mainstay of the region's export trade. Shipments of raw silk from Cosenza began to drop as early as the 1590s and by the middle of the next century were down to a mere fifth of what they had been earlier.[21]

The failure to rebuild the sheep population in Apulia after 1612 no doubt reflected to a considerable extent the crisis that affected, as will be seen, most Italian cloth manufactures during the seventeenth century. On the other hand, the dramatic slump in Calabrian silk production can be ascribed only in small part to a falling demand for silk in Italy, for the manufacture of silk fabric did not decline to the same extent as that of woollen cloth and, at any rate, the slack in Italian demand could have been picked up by countries, such as France, where silkmaking was on the rise. Of greater consequence in preventing a recovery was the expansion of sericulture in central and north Italy during that period: as new sources of supply emerged that were closer to the new silk manufactures north of the Alps, Calabrian silk producers must have found it harder and harder to compete.

Unlike wool and silk the staple crops that formed the core of the Mediterranean diet, namely wheat, olive oil and wine, do not seem to have been adversely affected in the first half of the century. For them the hard times came only later, in the wake of the great popular uprising of 1647 (the revolt of Masaniello) and of the widespread dislocations and destructions that accompanied it; then came the devastating epidemic of 1656 and the subsequent collapse of farm prices and land values. As in the North a generation earlier, vast expanses of land were allowed to return to waste and not until the 1690s did conditions begin to improve. Significantly, however, what recovery there was did not involve, as it did in the North, the shift to new crops, large works of irrigation or drainage, and the adoption of more advanced systems of farming. Rather, it was a mere return to traditional forms of cultivation with only limited shifts in the proportion of land allocated to various food crops in response to changes in relative commodity prices.[22]

21. Aurelio Lepre, 'La crisi del secolo XVII nel Mezzogiorno d'Italia', *Studi Storici* 22 (1981), pp. 59–61, 76; Aurelio Musi, 'La rivolta antispagnola a Napoli e in Sicilia' in *SSI*, vol. 11, pp. 321–2; Luigi De Rosa, *Il Mezzogiorno spagnolo tra crescita e decadenza*, Mondadori, Milan 1987, pp. 52–3; Marino, *Pastoral Economics*, p. 150; Antonio Calabria, *The Cost of Empire. The Finances of the Kingdom of Naples in the Time of Spanish Rule*, Cambridge University Press 1991, pp. 22–3.
22. Raul Merzario, *Signori e contadini di Calabria: Conigliano Calabro dal XVI al XIX secolo*, Giuffrè, Milan 1975, pp. 26–30; Aurelio Lepre, 'Rendite di monasteri nel Napoletano e crisi economica del Seicento', *QS* 15 (1970), pp. 853–65 and *Terra di Lavoro in età moderna*, Guida, Naples 1978, pp. 30–4; Maria Antonietta Visceglia, *Territorio, feudo e potere locale. Terra d'Otranto tra medioevo ed età moderna*,

The apparent inertia or rather conservatism exhibited by the southern landed classes, their reluctance to innovate and to improve, has been duly noticed and variously interpreted by students of the agrarian history of the Mezzogiorno. It has been pointed out, for instance, that restrictions on the free export of wheat, traditionally imposed by a government obsessed with ensuring an adequate supply of food to the city of Naples with its 300,000 souls, had a stifling effect on agriculture, especially in such bread baskets as Apulia whose grain production was largely preempted by government authorities (the office of the *Annona*) to feed the capital.[23] But no less important (and more pervasive) may have been the fact that in the Kingdom of Naples vast amounts of land were in the hands of feudatories who drew from a myriad of small tenants both rental income for the use of a plot of land and seignorial revenues generated by sundry fines and forfeitures imposed by the baronial court, as well as fees and tolls for the use of the roads, bridges, flour mills, oil and wine presses which, according to feudal law, belonged to the feudatories. Since in the South, unlike in the North of the peninsula, those feudal revenues loomed very large in a baron's total income,[24] it stands to

Guida, Naples 1988, pp. 132–5; Carla Russo, 'I redditi dei parroci nei casali di Napoli: struttura e dinamica (XVI–XVII secolo)', in *Per la storia sociale e religiosa del Mezzogiorno d'Italia*, ed. Giuseppe Galasso and Carla Russo, vol. 1, Guida, Naples 1980, p. 146. Also the following essays in *Problemi di storia delle campagne meridionali*, ed. Angelo Massafra, Dedalo, Bari 1981: Silvio Zotta, 'Rapporti di produzione e cicli produttivi in regime di autoconsumo e di produzione speculativa. Le vicende agrarie dello "Stato" di Melfi nel lungo periodo (1530–1730)', pp. 265–72; Giuseppe Galasso, 'Strutture sociali e produttive, assetti colturali e mercato dal secolo XVI all'Unità', pp. 168–9; Michele Benaiteau, 'L'agricoltura nella provincia di Principato Ultra nell'età moderna (secoli XVII e XVIII)', pp. 201–20; and Aurelio Musi, 'Il Principato Citeriore nella crisi agraria del secolo XVII', pp. 176 and 185. The contrasting record of agriculture in the North and in the South has been highlighted by Aymard, 'La fragilità di un'economia avanzata', pp. 99–114.

23. Giuseppe Coniglio, *Il Viceregno di Napoli nel secolo XVII*, Edizioni di Storia e Letteratura, Rome 1955, pp. 30, 42–3; Aurelio Lepre, 'Azienda feudale e azienda agraria nel Mezzogiorno continentale fra '500 e '600' in *Problemi di storia delle campagne*, p. 29; Zotta, 'Rapporti di produzione', p. 274. Corn exports were restricted in the Papal States, too, apparently with detrimental effects on production: Ivo Mattozzi, 'Per una ricerca sui rapporti tra comunità di Ravenna e poteri centrali nel Cinquecento. Appunti sulla questione annonaria' in *Persistenze feudali e autonomie comunitative in Stati padani fra Cinque e Seicento*, ed. Giovanni Tocci, CLUEB, Bologna 1988, pp. 222–46; Angela Maria Girelli, 'Il problema della feudalità nel Lazio tra XVII e XVIII secolo', *Studi Storici Luigi Simeoni* 36 (1986), p. 130.

24. Lepre, *Terra di Lavoro*, p. 30; Merzario, *Signori e contadini,* p. 16. Maria Antonietta Visceglia, 'L'azienda signorile in Terra d'Otranto nell'età moderna (secoli XVI–XVIII)' in *Problemi di storia delle campagne,* pp. 45–6, estimates seignorial revenues to have represented between 20 and 40 per cent of a feudal lord's total income. By contrast, in the Venetian mainland, in the Duchy of Urbino and in Spanish Lombardy seignorial revenues were generally considered negligible:

reason that for him it was easier to increase his income by enforcing more strictly existing feudal rights or by claiming new ones than by risking large sums in long-term investments such as expanding the size of herds, building drainage or irrigation canals or experimenting with new crops.

But, aside from the feudal class's aversion to risk and from the lucrative opportunities offered by a vast array of seignorial perquisites, there is little doubt that the inertia exhibited by agriculture (and, as will be seen, by industry as well) in the Kingdom of Naples also reflected a serious shortage of funds available for productive investment. For this the Spanish government bore a major responsibility: hard pressed for money, especially during the Thirty Years War, Madrid used the Kingdom of Naples as a seemingly inexhaustible source of revenue – as its 'richest and most dependable Peru', to use the words of a contemporary observer.[25] In fact, revenue from taxation rose fourfold in the first half of the century and in a time of relatively stable prices such an increase was real and meant that more and more resources were being diverted to unproductive uses.[26] But this was not the whole story, for even this rising tide of tax revenue fell short of the crown's needs and deficit spending on a prodigious scale had to be resorted to, so much so, in fact, that by the 1630s more than half of the entire government budget went to servicing a rapidly accumulating government debt. Under the circumstances, available private savings were bound to be attracted away from agriculture, trade and industry into government securities.[27] The negative effects of high taxation and deficit spending were further exacerbated by the fact that most government revenue was not spent in the Kingdom of Naples but found its way abroad either in the form of interest accruing to foreign (mainly Genoese) financiers who held large shares of the government debt or in the form of massive transfers of funds to whatever province of the Spanish

---

Giuseppe Gullino, 'Un problema aperto: Venezia e il tardo feudalesimo', *Studi veneziani* 7 (1983), p. 188; Bandino Giacomo Zenobi, *Tarda feudalità e reclutamento dele elites nello Stato pontificio (secoli XV–XVIII)*, Università degli Studi, Urbino 1983, pp. 28–9 and 51; Sella, *Crisis and Continuity*, p. 167. Even in Spanish Lombardy, however, feudal revenues could be substantial in some instances: they amounted to 12–18 per cent of the total income accruing to the marquess d'Adda from his vast estates east of Milan: De Maddalena, 'I bilanci dal 1600 al 1647 di un'azienda fondiaria lombarda. Testimonianze di una crisi economica' (1955) now reprinted in his *Dalla città al borgo*, p. 163.

25. Quotation from a 1675 anonymous report (in French) in Salvo Mastellone, *Francesco D'Andrea politico e giurista (1648–1698). L'ascesa del ceto civile*, Olschki, Florence 1969, p. 59. See also Giuseppe Galasso, *Il Mezzogiorno nella storia d'Italia*, LeMonnier, Florence 1977, p. 178.

26. De Rosa, *Il Mezzogiorno spagnolo*, p. 172.

27. Interest payments on the government debt rose threefold between 1595 and 1639 while the price level remained fairly stable: Giovanni Muto, ' "Decretos" e "medios generales": la gestione delle crisi finanziarie nell'Italia spagnola' in *La repubblica internazionale del denaro*, p. 287. See also De Rosa, *Il Mezzogiorno spagnolo*, pp. 28–34 and Calabria, *The Cost of Empire*, pp. 90–3.

monarchy where armies had to be paid and supplied. In the first half of the century a primary destination of those funds was the State of Milan in its dual role as battleground and as staging area for Spanish troops headed north of the Alps. The Milanese economy, it can be argued, was thus the beneficiary of a rising tide of government spending while the Kingdom of Naples was being inexorably stripped of resources.[28]

Sicily, too, had its share of troubles during the seventeenth century, but losses were not as severe as in Naples and the island's agriculture exhibited greater vitality and resilience. To be sure, the export of grain – traditionally a major item in the island's economy – dropped from 20,000 to 5,000 tonnes a year in the course of the century; on the other hand, the export of raw silk remained fairly stable around the half million pounds mark until 1674 when it was abruptly, but temporarily disrupted by the uprising in Messina of that year. The island also experienced a vast process of internal 'colonization' at the hands of the local nobility: in the first half of the century sixty new agricultural settlements were created in the sparsely inhabited interior of the island with wheat as their major crop; when demand for wheat began to fall in the wake of the great epidemics, landowners switched to more valuable crops such as wine grapes and citrus fruit. Thanks to these adaptations, it has been noted, Sicily 'does not seem to have been worse off at the end of the century than at the beginning'. The same, as we just saw, could not be said of the rest of the Italian South.[29]

INDUSTRIAL AND COMMERCIAL DECLINE

The trials and tribulations encountered by agriculture between 1620 and 1660 were paralleled and possibly surpassed by those affecting the other sectors of

28. On the role of Genoese bankers see Doria, 'Conoscenza del mercato', pp. 68–70 and Calabria, *The Cost of Empire,* pp. 118–19. Data on the huge transfers of government funds from Naples to the State of Milan especially between 1631 and 1648 in Mario Rizzo, 'Finanza pubblica, impero e amministrazione nella Lombardia spagnola: le "visitas generales"', in *Lombardia borromaica, Lombardia spagnola 1554–1659,* ed. Paolo Pissavino and Gianvittorio Signorotto, Bulzoni, Milan 1995, pp. 355–61 and pp. 323–5 on the likely impact of those transfers on the Lombard economy. See also De Rosa, *Il Mezzogiorno spagnolo,* pp. 167–8, 188.

29. Domenico Ligresti, 'Per un'interpretazione del Seicento siciliano', *Cheiron* 17–18 (1993), pp. 98–9. Internal colonization is discussed in two articles by Timothy Davies, 'Changes in the Structure of the Wheat Trade in Seventeenth-Century Sicily and the Building of New Villages', *Journal of European Economic History* 2 (1983), pp. 371–405, and 'La colonizzazione feudale della Sicilia feudale nella prima eta moderna' in *SIE Annali* 8 (1985), pp. 415–72. On silk, Maurice Aymard, 'Commerce et production de la soie sicilienne aux XVIe et XVIIe siècles', *Mélanges d'Archéologie et d'Histoire* 77 (1965), pp. 609–40; Carmelo Trasselli, 'Ricerche sulla seta siciliana', *Economia e Storia* 12 (1965), p. 215.

the Italian economy.[30] The earliest ominous signs of a downturn appeared in the cities of the North, such as Venice, Milan, Genoa and Florence – cities which in the previous century had epitomized Italy's prosperity and leading position in the European economy.

Starting around 1600 the number of ships calling at Venice began to drop and by 1620, if we are to judge from the receipts of the anchorage tax levied on all incoming (and by now mainly foreign) sails, had been cut in half – a drop that, not surprisingly, was matched by that of the receipts of the customs house. In those same years the spice trade which had revived so promisingly in the late sixteenth century came to an end as the Dutch East India Company established its trade monopoly in Southeast Asia, and this time Venice's loss was to prove irreversible. Nor were the woes of the city of St Mark at the dawn of the century confined to trade and shipping: the woollen industry, for a century the main source of exports to the Levant, saw its output plummet from an all-time high of 28,000 cloths in 1602 to half as many twenty years later and to a paltry 2,000 by end of century. The Venetian silk industry fared somewhat better, yet for it, too, the first decade of the century signalled a sharp downturn: by the mid-1620s production had shrunk by about 25 per cent and the slide continued to the end of the century when output was about a quarter of what it had been a hundred years earlier.[31] In Verona, another important centre of silkmaking in the sixteenth century, losses were even worse and by mid-century had resulted in the total extinction of a once flourishing industry.[32] The woollen industry of Florence was another major casualty in the industrial débâcle of the early seventeenth century: after the setbacks it had suffered, as will be recalled, in the 1570s at the hands of its Venetian rival, its output had stabilized around 15,000 cloths a year for the rest of the century, but by the 1620s it had dropped to half as much and by 1700 to a mere one-tenth.[33] In Milan the woollen industry faltered as early as the 1590s; a century later it was virtually extinct and silkmaking did not fare any better. Lesser textile centres such as Como, Cremona and Pavia suffered heavy losses, too, and we have reasons to believe that the crisis affected other industries as well, for the sharp drop after 1620 in the receipts of the excise that was levied on all goods entering or leaving the towns of the State of

30. Carlo M. Cipolla, 'The Economic Decline of Italy' (1952) in *Crisis and Change in the Venetian Economy*, pp. 127–45; Ruggiero Romano, 'L'Italia nella crisi del secolo XVII', *Studi Storici* 9 (1968), pp. 723–41; Giovanni Vigo, 'Manovre monetarie e crisi economica nello Stato di Milano (1619–1622)', *Studi Storici* 17 (1976), pp. 101–26; and Enrico Stumpo, 'La crisi del Seicento in Italia' in *La Storia. I grandi problemi dal Medioevo all'Età contemporanea*, ed. Nicola Tranfaglia and Massimo Firpo, vol. 5, UTET, Turin 1987, pp. 313–37.

31. In addition to the essays by F.C. Lane cited above in note 6, see Sella, 'L'economia', pp. 692–704.

32. Borelli, *Città e campagna*, pp. 282–3 and 305–9.

33. Romano, 'A Florence', pp. 508–11; Malanima, *La decadenza*, pp. 293–5.

Milan strongly suggests that the downfall of the textile industries was part of a more general, long-term depression that affected the entire economy.[34]

Hard times hit Genoa, too. Between 1620 and 1670 traffic in the harbour contracted sharply. In 1627 the Spanish government's bankruptcy (i.e. the repudiation of its debt) seriously hurt Genoese bankers and deprived them of their erstwhile commanding role in European finances. Genoa's silk industry ran into serious troubles as well: as against the 2,300 looms in operation in the city in the late sixteenth century only 500 were left a century later. As for the manufacture of silks in the countryside near Genoa, the picture is somewhat brighter, but not by much: in the course of the century the number of looms there went from over 5,000 to about 2,000.[35] Around Mantua a once prosperous knitting industry capable of processing 100,000 kg of wool a year had been virtually wiped out by the 1630s.[36] In and around the town of Salò on the western shore of Lake Garda, where papermaking had flourished in the sixteenth century and had supplied both the booming printing industry of Venice and the Turkish market, the number of papermills dropped from a peak of 160 in 1608 to merely 50 by mid-century.[37] And what few manufacturers had developed in the predominantly agricultural South were no more lucky than their northern counterparts. In Naples, for instance, silkmaking had enjoyed a long period of sustained growth in the course of the sixteenth century and by 1580 was reported as employing some 20,000 workers and as exporting much of its output to Spain – to the point that in the 1620s Madrid imposed restrictions on the importation of Neapolitan silks in order to protect Spanish manufacturers from the competition. A generation later, however, the silk industry in Naples no longer presented a threat, for it had collapsed under the impact of the 1647 uprising and had received the *coup de grâce* from the epidemic of 1656.[38]

34. Vigo, *Uno stato nell'impero*, pp. 69–87; a similar trend in Mantua: Aldo De Maddalena, 'L'industria tessile a Mantova nel '500 e agli inizi del '600' in *Studi in onore di Amintore Fanfani*, Giuffrè, Milan 1962, vol. 4, p. 652.

35. Edoardo Grendi, *La repubblica aristocratica dei Genovesi*, Mulino, Bologna 1987, pp. 339–49 (on shipping); on the silk industry, Gabriella Sivori, 'Il tramonto dell'industria serica genovese', *Rivista storica italiana* 84 (1972), pp. 897 and 937; and Paola Massa Piergiovanni, 'Social and Economic Consequences of Structural Changes in the Ligurian Silk-Weaving Industry from the Sixteenth to the Nineteenth Century', in *The Rise and Decline of Urban Industries*, pp. 17–39.

36. Carlo Marco Belfanti, 'Rural Manufactures and Rural Protoindustries in the "Italy of the Cities" from the Sixteenth through the Eighteenth Century', *Continuity and Change* 8 (1993), pp. 257–8.

37. Giovanni Zalin, 'Origini e sviluppo dell'industria cartaria nella "riviera" bresciana del Garda', *Archivio storico italiano* 133 (1985), pp. 595–610; Ivo Mattozzi, *Produzione e commercio della carta nello stato veneziano settecentesco. Lineamenti e problemi*, Università, Bologna 1975, pp. 7–8.

38. De Rosa, 'De-industrialization', pp. 131–3.

CAUSES AND SCAPEGOATS

The dismantling of so many industrial and trade centres that had once formed Italy's pride and had ensured the country's pre-eminence in the European economy has prompted historians to search for a general explanation of the entire dismal process.[39] Two such explanations were generally accepted in the past. One placed the blame on the coming of foreign domination in the early sixteenth century: the end of political 'liberty' was said to have 'prevented the Italian states from retaining the ground they once held or from acquiring new ground during the revolution created by the opening of new trade routes' resulting from geographic discoveries.[40] The other explanation identified the root cause of the economic downfall in the changing ethos of a once dynamic merchant class under the influence either of Renaissance humanism with its emphasis on learned leisure or of the aristocratic lifestyle introduced by the new foreign masters with its insistence on military prowess, courtly manners and the avoidance of the pursuit of profit; the Italian merchant class, it was argued, had betrayed its calling, had turned its back on the risks and the rewards of the marketplace, and had adopted the mores and the trappings of an idle aristocracy, squandering its wealth on landed estates, pageantry and the bucolic pleasures of a country villa. In the words of a nineteenth-century historian, 'Italians had been hard working and actively engaged in trade and industry . . . Then suddenly came those haughty Spaniards who told us that to attend to business is shameful and demeaning'; the result, as another writer put it at the time, was that 'vast sums of money previously invested in business were now sunk into land . . . and aristocratic ostentation . . . and meanwhile our wretched artisans, idled by lack of capital, died of plagues, famines and daily despair'.[41]

The first explanation must be discarded for we now know, as earlier historians did not, that the Italian economy prospered until the beginning of the seventeenth century even though Spanish domination had been in effect for half a century. Besides, when economic decline set in after 1600, it engulfed states (such as the Venetian Republic and the Papal States) that were not under Spanish rule no less than those that were. The coming of foreign

---

39. The relevant historiography on the causes of decline is discussed in: Luigi Bulferetti, 'Il problema della decadenza italiana' in *Nuove questioni di storia moderna*, vol. 2, Marzorati, Milan 1964, pp. 803–45; Guido Quazza, *La decadenza italiana nella storia europea. Saggi sul Sei-Settecento*, Einaudi, Turin 1971; Sergio Worms, 'Il problema della "decadenza" italiana nella recente storiografia', *Clio* 11 (1975), pp. 102–22; Judith M. Brown, 'Prosperity and Hard Times in Renaissance Italy?' *Renaissance Quarterly* 42 (1980), pp. 761–80; Stumpo, 'La crisi del Seicento'; and Aymard, 'Fragilità di un'economia avanzata', pp. 5–18.

40. Benedetto Croce, *Storia dell'età barocca in Italia,* 2nd edn, Laterza, Bari 1946, pp. 478–9.

41. Cesare Cantù, *La Lombardia nel secolo XVII. Ragionamenti,* Milan 1854, p. 66; Carlo Cattaneo, *Notizie naturali e civili sulla Lombardia*, Milan 1844, p. xci.

domination, however, has also been held responsible for the decline of the economy in that, it has been argued, it prevented the political unification of the peninsula and hence the formation of a large national market, such as the French or the English, capable of absorbing large quantities of manufactured goods under the protection, if necessary, of high tariff barriers.[42] But, quite aside from the fact that, with or without Spain, political unification is unlikely to have occurred in the sixteenth or seventeenth centuries, one can legitimately wonder whether it would have made a great deal of difference: not only was much of Italy's industrial output meant for export outside the peninsula rather than for the home market, but it is well to keep in mind that the economically most successful country in seventeenth-century Europe was the Dutch Republic, a country of two million people, roughly equal in size, that is, to the Papal States and the Venetian Republic and smaller, by a good million souls, than the Kingdom of Naples.

As for the explanation that stresses the changing mentality of the merchant class, it rests on the well-documented fact that many merchant families, after accumulating great wealth in trade or banking, withdrew from those activities and bought their way into the charmed circle of the landed nobility. The metamorphosis from entrepreneur to rentier, however, was not unique to Italy, but was a common feature of early modern European society: as John Hooker, the Elizabethan antiquary and county politician, put it when referring to his own country, merchants 'do attain to great wealth and riches, which for the most part they do employ to buy land and little by little they do creep and seek to be gentlemen'.[43] More importantly, it is a fallacy to assume that a merchant turned landowner or, for that matter, a landed nobleman, was invariably a lazy rentier, blissfully indifferent to the profit motive and loath to risk his money in the pursuit of gain. Often enough, the opposite seems to have been the case. Old and new aristocrats invested heavily not only in the acquisition of farmland, but in ambitious projects of land reclamation and improvement, and obviously did so with an eye on future profits. Nor were their investments confined to agriculture: in the seventeenth century Venetian patricians poured money into the construction of power-driven silk mills, the operation of stone quarries, loans to merchants and the wholesale trade of farm commodities; Genoese aristocrats, on their part, not only risked their capital in loans to the Spanish government, but also in the operation of ironworks and papermills in the surrounding countryside; in the Venetian Terraferma a number of feudatories judiciously diversified their portfolio by

42. Amintore Fanfani, *Storia del lavoro in Italia dalla fine del secolo XV agli inizi del XVIII*, 2nd edn, Giuffrè, Milan 1959, pp. 25, 40; Immanuel Wallerstein, *The Modern World-System. Capitalist Agriculture and the Origins of the European World-Economy in the Sixteenth Century*, Academic Press, New York 1974, pp. 216–20.

43. J.H. Hexter, *Reappraisals in History. New Views on History and Society in Early Modern Europe,* Harper, New York 1961, p. 114; Henry Kamen, *The Iron Century. Social Change in Europe 1550–1660*, Praeger, New York 1972, ch. 5. Hooker's quotation is in W.T. MacCaffrey, *Exeter 1540–1640. The Growth of an English Country Town,* Harvard University Press, Cambridge, Mass. 1958, p. 260.

acquiring fulling mills, iron furnaces and sundry industrial facilities; and wealthy Florentines, throughout the century, invested heavily in limited liability partnerships (*accomandite*) involved in the manufacture and trade of silks, leather goods and wine.[44]

Somewhat similar to the view that the Italian merchant class betrayed its traditional calling by moving into the ranks of the landed nobility is the view that from the late sixteenth century Italian society underwent a broad process of 'refeudalization' in the sense of a departure from the market economy and of its replacement with an economy dominated by privilege, by resort to compulsory labour services and by the merciless exploitation of the peasant masses at the hands of an arrogant feudal elite that held, legally or not so legally, both the levers of power and most of the country's resources. We will return to refeudalization as a social phenomenon in the next chapter and will argue that the concept rests on rather shaky foundations. At this point it will suffice to say that, even if refeudalization did occur, it is hard to see how it could seriously affect so many urban industries and shipping and commercial activities – unless one were to argue that refeudalization, insofar as it led to the immiseration of multitudes of consumers, deprived Italian manufacturers of their markets. This, however, was an unlikely outcome, for the masses allegedly victimized by feudal exploitation were peasants, and peasants most certainly were not and had never been buyers of Venetian high-quality cloth, Florentine silks, Milanese armour, high-grade Salò paper or oriental spices. All those goods, as will be recalled, were mostly intended for foreign markets whose import capacity was unaffected by whatever happened to the long-suffering Italian peasantry.

It has also been argued that Italy's economic prosperity had traditionally rested on the interdependence between an urbanized, industrial North and a

---

44. Daniele Beltrami, *La penetrazione dei Veneziani in Terraferma. Forze di lavoro e proprietà fondiaria nelle campagne venete nei secoli XVI e XVII*, Istituto per la collaborazione culturale, Venice and Rome, pp. 48–51; Berengo, 'Patriziato e nobiltà', p. 202; Ciriacono, *Acque e agricoltura*, p. 115; Carlo Poni, 'Archéologie de la fabrique. La diffusion des moulins à soie "alla bolognese" dans les Etats vénitiens du XVIe au XVIIIe siècle', *Annales E.S.C.* 27 (1972), p. 1490; Raffaello Vergani, 'I costi dell'estrazione: cave, frati e polvere da sparo nella Monselice del Settecento, *Archivio Veneto* 150 (1993), p. 149; Giuseppe Gullino, 'I patrizi veneziani e la mercatura negli ultimi tre secoli della Repubblica' in *Mercanti e vita economica nella Repubblica veneta (secoli XIII–XVIII)*, vol. 2, ed. Giorgio Borelli, Banca Popolare, Verona 1985, pp. 406, 421–6 and by the same author, 'Quando il mercante costruí la villa: la proprietà dei Veneziani in Terraferma' in *Storia di Venezia*, vol. 6, pp. 875–924; Manlio Calegari, 'Origini, insediamento, inerzia tecnologica nelle ricerche sulla siderurgia ligure d'antico regime', *QS* 46 (1981), p. 297; Costantini, *La Repubblica di Genova*, pp. 163, 395; Salvatore Ciriacono, 'Industria rurale e strutture feudali nella Terraferma veneta tra Sei e Settecento', *Studi Storici Luigi Simeoni* (1986), pp. 75–80; and R. Burr Litchfield, *Emergence of a Bureaucracy, The Florentine Patricians 1530–1790*, Princeton University Press, Princeton, N.J. 1986, pp. 205–15.

predominantly agricultural South, the former supplying manufactured goods and commercial and shipping services to the latter in return for foodstuffs and raw materials, such as wool and silk. As southern agriculture was disrupted by the crisis of the 1590s – so goes the argument – northern industries lost their best markets; the several regions of the peninsula then turned inward, each trying, as best it could, to achieve self-sufficiency. The outcome was the fragmentation of the country into separate regional economies and in each of them the ruling elite strove to control the food supply by acquiring more and more land and by imposing harsher terms on their tenants.[45] Admittedly, the nearly simultaneous decline of industry in the North and of the production of raw materials, notably wool and silk, in the South would seem to lend prima facie plausibility to this interpretation. Over against it, however, stands the fact, alluded to earlier, that most northern manufactured goods were exported not to the Mezzogiorno, but to non-Italian markets – silks to France and Germany, cloth and paper to the Ottoman Empire, glassware to England and France.

In the end, therefore, it is to those markets (as Carlo Cipolla argued long ago in a seminal essay)[46] that one must turn to find the key to Italy's economic woes. In some of them demand simply collapsed due to prolonged warfare or internal upheavals. The silk manufacturers of Genoa, for instance, attributed their misfortune to the loss of their German customers during the Thirty Years War.[47] The Venetians, on their part, had no doubts that plummeting sales of their high-quality cloth in the Levant were a direct consequence of the civil wars that plagued the Ottoman Empire in the first decade of the seventeenth century. As a Venetian consul ruefully reported from Syria in 1611, 'because of civil war the Turkish empire is so diminished in both population and wealth that it can buy but one third of what it used to' and he added that consumers increasingly switched from imported woollen cloth to locally produced cotton fabrics.[48] From other markets Italian goods were gradually excluded by mercantilist policies aimed at promoting the growth of local manufactures: French protectionist measures in support of the silk and mirror industries are a case in point, and so are those adopted by the English government as early as 1615 in favour of the nascent glass industry.[49] Lastly, even in the absence of newly erected protectionist barriers, Italian goods and services were driven out by less expensive or qualitatively

---

45. Maurice Aymard, 'La transizione dal feudalesimo al capitalismo', in *SIE Annali* 1 (1978), pp. 1179–90.

46. Cipolla, 'The Economic Decline of Italy', pp. 133–5.

47. Sivori, 'Il tramonto dell'industria serica', p. 939. The silk industry of Lucca, too, was affected: Rita Mazzei, *La società lucchese del Seicento*, Pacini, Lucca 1977, p. 30.

48. Sella, 'L'economia', p. 695. On the production of cheap cotton fabrics see Murat Cizakça, 'Incorporation of the Middle East into the European World Economy', *Review* 8 (1985), pp. 368–9. I am indebted to Professor Maureen Mazzaoui for this reference.

49. Luzzatto, *Storia economica*, vol. 1, p. 123.

more attractive foreign goods – and this seems to have been by far the most serious challenge.

In the course of the century competition on the international markets where Italy had long held a position of supremacy grew fierce. In the area of maritime transportation foreign competition, as will be recalled, had already taken its toll in the late sixteenth century. It intensified after England in 1604 and the Dutch Republic five years later made peace with Spain and their merchant ships could now sail undisturbed in Mediterranean waters. English and Dutch mariners, it was reported with a growing sense of alarm and envy in Venice, offered faster services and cheaper freight rates thanks to the better design of their ships, lower construction costs and lower rates of pay for their crews.[50] No wonder, then, if a growing share of the traffic in the harbours of Genoa, Venice and Leghorn came to be handled by ships from the North Atlantic. As for manufactured goods, notably textiles, which the English and the Dutch brought to the Levant, their success was achieved in spite of deteriorating market conditions in the region, because they were cheaper imitations of Italian articles and could thus appeal to consumers faced with a shrinking purchasing power.[51] Lower manufacturing prices, in turn, reflected the fact that the goods from northern Europe were generally shoddier and less durable imitations of the Italian goods they were displacing; but, if we are to believe Italian sources, lower labour costs in both England and Holland may have played a role as well.[52] Under the circumstances, the challenge confronting Italian producers was either to scale down the quality of their wares or to reduce the costs of production, or to try a combination of the two approaches. Yet, the decline of production in the major industrial and commercial centres of the peninsula clearly indicates that the challenge was not met – and the key question is why it was not.

As far as quality was concerned, Italy's urban guilds apparently continued to adhere to those high standards of workmanship that had made their reputation in the past and would thus seem to bear a major responsibility for the decline of their manufactures. Their determination not to water down the quality of their products, however, cannot be simply ascribed to benighted conservatism or sheer inertia. As Paolo Malanima has observed, as long as there was a market (albeit a shrinking one) for high-grade, expensive articles, it made sense 'to utilize in full a workmanship that still had admirers abroad and

50. Sella, 'L'economia', pp. 655–9 and the literature cited in note 10 above.
51. Richard T. Rapp, 'The Unmaking of the Mediterranean Trade Hegemony: International Trade Rivalry and the Commercial Revolution', *Journal of Economic History* 35 (1975), pp. 499–526.
52. Cipolla, 'The Economic Decline of Italy', p. 139. In a few instances lower production costs could also reflect the fact that Italy's competitors were ahead in terms of labour-saving technology: English hosiery produced on the stocking frame invented at the close of the sixteenth century undersold a once flourishing Italian manufacture in the course of the next century: see Carlo Marco Belfanti, 'Le calze a maglia: moda e innovazioni alle origini dell'industria della maglieria (secoli XVI–XVII)', *Società e Storia* 69 (1995), pp. 487–98.

to concentrate on high quality production, a production still in demand among those who had money to spend and were not deterred by high prices'.[53]

Adherence to high-quality standards, however, did not *per se* rule out a reduction of costs (and ultimately of prices) such as would make goods more affordable. And indeed the question of costs was very much on the mind of contemporaries – whether government officials, guildsmen or merchants – anxious to reverse the downward trend that afflicted so many industries. In document after document the argument was made that heavy taxation was to blame for industry's woes and that only a measure of tax relief could reverse the trend by making goods more competitive.[54] At first sight the argument seems to have a good deal of merit, for we know that in the course of the seventeenth century the burden of taxation increased in most Italian states: it apparently nearly doubled in the Papal States and in the Venetian Republic, more than doubled in the State of Milan, and rose fourfold in the Kingdom of Naples.[55] A closer look, however, ought to make us hesitant to accept at face value the loud complaints of merchants and guildsmen and their pleas for a measure of relief, because what few data are available on the incidence of taxation on the price of manufactured goods suggest that the tax collector's bite was rather modest. In the Genoese silk industry, for instance, taxes accounted for a mere 5–6 per cent of total costs; in Florence the government apparently levied only 1 per cent on the price of woollen cloth, in Milan perhaps 2 per cent.[56] Admittedly, in those three cities other duties may have been levied on incoming raw materials, but even so taxes do not seem to have been a major item of cost. Only in the case of Venice, where taxes represented a staggering 42 per cent of the price of high-quality cloth, can we say with confidence that drastically slashing taxes would have made the industry more competitive.[57] But, Venice excepted, there are other reasons for believing that taxes were not a decisive factor in undermining the competitiveness of Italian goods. The case of Milan is revealing on this point. There the government did from time to time grant tax reductions, and yet textile production failed to recover. Moreover, even the strongest advocates of

53. Malanima, *Decadenza*, p. 168.
54. Examples in Cipolla, 'The Economic Decline of Italy', pp. 138–9.
55. Fausto Piola Caselli, 'Crisi economica e finanza pubblica nello Stato Pontificio tra XVI e XVII secolo' in *La finanza pubblica in età di crisi*, ed. Antonio Di Vittorio, Cacucci, Bari 1992, pp. 174–5; Richard T. Rapp, *Industry and Economic Decline in Seventeenth-Century Venice*, Harvard University Press, Cambridge, Mass. 1976, p. 141; Faccini, *La Lombardia*, p. 91; Galasso, 'Economia e finanze', p. 63. Tuscany represented an exception: the tax burden remained virtually unchanged throughout the century: Enrico Stumpo, 'Finanza e ragion di Stato nella prima eta moderna. Due modelli diversi: Piemonte e Toscana, Savoia e Medici' in *Finanza e Ragion di Stato in Italia e in Germania nella prima Età moderna*, ed. Aldo De Maddalena and Hermann Kellenbenz, Mulino, Bologna 1984, pp. 215–16.
56. Sivori, 'Il tramonto dell'industria serica', pp. 921–5; Malanima, *Decadenza*, p. 171; Giovanni Vigo, *Finanza pubblica e pressione fiscale nello Stato di Milano durante il secolo XVI*, Banca Commerciale Italiana, Milan 1977, pp. 92–4.
57. Rapp, *Industry and Economic Decline*, p. 140.

tax relief as the panacea for industrial recovery also urged the government to impose a total ban on imported goods, thus implying that tax relief, however desirable, was no cure-all.[58]

If not taxes, then labour costs may have been the villain. And indeed tracts, petitions, legislative proposals, even denunciations of the 'insufferable burden of taxation' often included complaints about the excessive cost of labour: wage-rates were said to be higher than those prevailing abroad, with the result that Italian manufactures could not effectively stand up to Dutch and English goods on third markets and the same kind of complaint was voiced about labour costs in the shipbuilding and shipping industries. Seventeenth-century documents make it virtually impossible for us to measure and compare labour costs in different countries at the time, but the very fact that Italian goods and freight services were being undersold by foreign products and that labour costs were frequently singled out at the time as being responsible for the loss of market shares strongly suggests that here was, if not the Achilles' heel of the Italian economy, at least one of its chief weaknesses.[59]

As for what kept labour costs high, seventeenth-century sources often point a finger at the powerful and firmly entrenched craft guilds, alleging that they kept wages up either directly by setting and enforcing rigid wage-rates or indirectly by controlling (and, in fact, restricting) access to the crafts by dint of long apprenticeship requirements and stiff admission fees, with little regard for the long-term consequences of their actions.[60] In some instances those charges may well have been justified, but a sweeping indictment of the guilds does not seem warranted: in the case of the Florentine cloth industry it has been shown that the craft guilds, far from being able to dictate their own terms of employment and pay to the drapers who contracted work with them, were in fact fully at the mercy of the drapers' guild.[61] Not much is known about conditions in other towns, but what evidence we have on the social structure in general and on the operation of craft guilds in the construction industry points in the direction of labour markets in which artisans had little control over the level of pay.[62]

If this was the case, an explanation of the persistently high labour costs that seem to have afflicted Italian industries must be sought not so much in the allegedly strong bargaining power of the guilds, but rather in such long-term conditions of the labour market as would tend to sustain relatively high levels of pay in the towns even in the face of declining employment in a number of major industries. Most probably the key factor at play here was the

58. Sella, *Crisis and Continuity, pp. 70–4.*
59. Cipolla, 'The Economic Decline', p. 139; Fernand Braudel, 'L'Italia fuori d'Italia. Due secoli e tre Italie', in *SIE*, vol. 2 (1973), pp. 2226–46.
60. As, for instance, in Venice: Sella, 'The Rise and Fall', pp. 121–3.
61. Malanima, *Decadenza*, p. 160; Rapp, *Industry and Economic Decline*, p. 42.
62. Brian Pullan, 'Poveri, mendicanti e vagabondi (secoli XIV–XVII), in *SIE Annali* 1 (1978), p. 1032; D. Sella, *Salari e lavoro nell'edilizia lombarda durante il secolo XVII*, Fusi, Pavia 1968, pp. 44–8.

aggregate demand for labour remaining fairly stable over the course of the century as the urban economies continued to offer a broad range of employment opportunities in select luxury or artistic crafts, retail trade, and domestic service. That this was indeed the case is strongly suggested by the fact that neither Genoa, Milan, Venice nor Florence were turned into 'ghost towns' when their celebrated manufactures went under. Actually their population remained fairly stable over the course of the century, the huge void caused by the plague being quickly filled by immigrants from the countryside.[63] Nor have foreign visitors left us images of desolate cities teeming with masses of unemployed. Quite the contrary. In 1648 the Englishman John Raymond spoke of Milan's 'flourishing condition' and of its being 'thronged with Artisans of all sorts'; thirty years later an Italian visitor reported that the Milanese lived with 'splendore e decoro', that the local merchants were 'rich', and that the city boasted 1,586 horse-drawn coaches. 'There is great magnificence in Milan' echoed Bishop Burnet, an observer normally inclined to find fault with things Italian.[64] Venice made a favourable impression on its visitors, too. At mid-century John Evelyn was astonished by the shops he saw there overflowing with 'cloth of gold, rich damasks and other silks'; a few years later a French traveller wrote that Venice 'is replete of all things, not only those that are necessary for living, but also those needed for enjoying life'; in 1647 the papal nuncio noted in his report to the Curia that the city of St Mark appeared 'full of riches and luxuries'; and four decades later Burnet commented that 'although this Republick is much sunk from what it was, both by the great losses they have suffered in their wars with Turks and by the great decay of Trade, yet there is an incredible Wealth and a vast plenty of all things in this place'.[65] The image of opulence that Venice projected is confirmed by a close analysis of its economy: while its textile manufactures, its shipyards and its merchant marine were undoubtedly headed for virtual extinction, the labour force was gradually redeployed from those dying sectors to others, such as construction, artistic crafts and domestic service, with the result that the level of employment remained stable, and this would explain why no downward pressure was placed on wages.[66]

63. Carlo Marco Belfanti, 'Aspetti dell'evoluzione demografica italiana nel secolo XVII', *Cheiron* 2 (1984), pp. 101–32.
64. John Raymond, *Il Mercurio Italico communicating a Voyage* [. . .] *throughout Italy in the Years 1646 and 1647*, London 1648, p. 240; Galeazzo Gualdo Priorato, *Relatione della Città e Stato di Milano*, Milan 1675, p. 131; Gilbert Burnet, *Some letters containing an account of what seemed most remarkable in travelling through Switzerland, Italy* [. . .] *in the years 1685 and 1686*, 2nd edn, Rotterdam 1687, p. 95.
65. John Evelyn, *The Diary*, ed. E.S. De Beer, Oxford University Press 1955, p. 449; Grangier de Liverdys, *Journal d'un voyage de France et d'Italie*, Paris 1667, p. 820; and Burnet, *Some letters*, p. 127. The nuncio is quoted in Lucio Balestrieri, *Venezia presente e passato. Per un'interpretazione ideologica della storia*, Universitaria Venezia, Venice 1978, p. 111.
66. Rapp, *Industry and Economic Decline*, pp. 96–106, 164–7.

One way of avoiding the constraints of high labour costs would have been the adoption of labour-saving devices. To be sure, given the state of technology in the seventeenth century, options on this score were very limited, and yet some were available. The real obstacle to adopting them, however, were the guilds. In 1674, for instance, the Genoese government denied a request for permission to build a water-driven silk mill on the grounds that it would threaten the livelihood of the city's handspinners, and we can legitimately assume that the spinners' guild lobbied very actively to secure a ruling so favourable to its members. This is actually what the equivalent guild did in Florence and in that city, too, the water-driven mill was banned for several decades. In 1663 the handknitters' guild of Milan secured an injunction (not to be repealed until half a century later) against the introduction of the English stocking frame on the grounds that the new labour-saving device would have thrown 'thousands of women' out of work; in 1696 the goldleaf beaters' guild obtained a similar ruling against a new labour-saving device that would have mechanized the manufacture of gold thread.[67] Instances such as these are too few and far between to warrant any sweeping indictment of the guilds, for there are examples of guilds that were open to technological change and adaptation, or not strong enough to prevent the introduction of labour-saving technology.[68] The most one can say with any degree of confidence is that guild obstructionism did at times play a negative role and thus contributed to making some Italian products increasingly uncompetitive.

But possibly more common and equally serious was the guilds' reluctance to modify the quality or the design of their products in response to changing consumer tastes.[69] An instance of such conservative attitudes can be found in the Genoese silk manufacturers' refusal to respond to the changes in fashion emanating from France in the later part of the century: as a 1675 document puts it, 'new fashions and new products having been invented in our time by foreign nations, to want to continue as of old causes the utter ruin of [our] manufacture'.[70] The same problem plagued the once glorious silk industry of Lucca, a town where no one who wanted to introduce 'new inventions' was allowed to open shop lest 'he profit to the detriment of the rest'.[71] And in vain did a wool merchant suggest to Venetian weavers that they ought to produce 'cloths in the Dutch style . . . which have a good market in the Levant where the rich now prefer to dress in light cloth rather than in the heavier Venetian

67. Costantini, *La Repubblica di Genova*, p. 382; Malanima, *Decadenza*, p. 244; Sella, *Crisis and Continuity*, p. 103; and Belfanti, 'Le calze a maglia', pp. 489–90.
68. Rapp, *Industry and Economic Decline*, pp. 112–16; Malanima, *Decadenza*, p. 243; Richard Mackenney, *Tradesmen and Traders. The World of the Guilds in Venice and Europe c. 1250–c.1650*, Croom Helm 1987, p. 123. In Turin, Genoa and Venice the stocking frame was belatedly introduced in the 1660s and 1670s and the manufacture of silk stockings got off to a promising start (Belfanti, pp. 491–5).
69. Cipolla, 'The Economic Decline of Italy', pp. 137–8.
70. Quotation in Sivori, 'Il tramonto dell'industria serica', p. 940.
71. Quotation in Mazzei, *La società lucchese*, p. 26.

fabrics, even if these are of higher quality and more durable'.[72] In 1683 a Flemish clothmaker who had come to Venice to start the manufacture of textiles 'after the manner of Holland' had to give up his plans in the face of local guildsmen's hostility; only thirteen years later did he finally succeed in opening shop. In 1712 the Venetian Board of Trade commented on the decline of the city's woollen industry: 'the true source . . . of its decline is to be found in its reluctance to adapt to modern tastes, steeped as it is in the love of its old ways'.[73]

In the final analysis the decline of so many urban industries must be ascribed to the inability of Italian manufacturers to compete against the rising stars of northern Europe due to relatively high labour costs and, in some instances, to their resistance to technological change or quality innovation. High labour costs and conservatism in the workplace may well have been present in Italy long before the seventeenth century when things were going well, but as long as the country had been virtually the sole producer of certain high-quality goods and the chief supplier of sophisticated commercial and shipping services to much of Europe, neither of those features need have represented serious drawbacks.[74] In the seventeenth century, however, the international economic landscape had dramatically changed as emerging economies endowed with an abundant supply of cheap labour and less bound by tradition had caught up with and even surpassed Italy in a variety of fields. As a 1646 official report on the industrial decline of Milan put it, in other countries 'minds have greatly sharpened of late and our products are now being imitated with remarkable skill'. And these words were echoed by those of an obscure tax farmer that read like an epitaph on a glorious but bygone age: 'formerly only here were artificers to be found, but now they have spread all over the world'.[75]

INDUSTRIAL SURVIVAL AND GROWTH

Not all industries proved so vulnerable to foreign competition. Some, in fact, survived and even prospered, and new ones emerged even in the bleakest days of an ill-starred century. Among the survivors one finds, first of all, industries that depended on exquisite and still unsurpassed workmanship for producing luxury or artistic objects in which quality counted more than cost.

72. Quotation in Rita Mazzei, 'The Decline of the City Economies of Central and Northern Italy in the Seventeenth Century', *Journal of Italian History* 2 (1979), p. 203.

73. Sella, 'The Rise and Fall', p. 123; State Archives, Venice, *Cinque Savi alla Mercanzia* NS, busta 121, doc. of 3 March 1712.

74. Salvatore Ciriacono, 'Per una storia dell'industria di lusso in Francia: la concorrenza italiana nei secoli XVI e XVII', *Ricerche di storia sociale e religiosa* 14 (1978), pp. 181–202.

75. Quotations in Sella, *Crisis and Continuity*, pp. 79 and 104.

Such was violin-making in Cremona: it was in the seventeenth century that its unique reputation became firmly established throughout Europe, with no competitors in sight as yet. Another instance is provided by one branch of the Venetian silk industry. The industry as a whole, it will be recalled, lost much ground after 1600, but it was only the less expensive, plain fabrics that were adversely affected; by contrast, the output of expensive articles woven of silk and gold thread rose twofold in the course of the century.[76] Likewise the silkmakers of Milan managed to retain their reputation, if not for ordinary fabrics, at least for select luxury items such as 'embroideries in gold and silver' which an English visitor considered 'the best in the world'.[77]

In other industries the loss of traditional markets was offset by tapping new ones. The Murano (Venice) glassmakers, faced with newly erected protective barriers in France and England, responded by exporting their goblets, hand mirrors and coloured glass beads to Central Europe and North Africa.[78] For the silkmakers of Pisa, who had traditionally served the German market, the outbreak of the Thirty Years War nearly spelled disaster, but after mid-century they found new markets for their high-quality articles in the Spanish colonies and in Brazil. In addition to a resilient silk manufacture Pisa could also take pride in the survival of its oldest industry, leathermaking, an industry that continued to operate and to attract investment funds from some of the richest members of the Florentine patriciate throughout the century. Using primarily hides imported from North Africa and Muscovy via Leghorn, the industry prospered and although we have no data on aggregate output, we can be sure that it was no paltry business: at the end of the century the combined output of the four largest tanneries stood at about 350,000 lb (approximately 100 tonnes).[79]

The Florentine silk industry, as noted earlier, survived the seventeenth century virtually unscathed, with a steady output of about 10,000 cloths a year, and this in spite of the closing of the French market where it had made its fortune in the past. What rescued the industry from certain extinction was the tapping, mainly at the hands of the indefatigable merchants of Lucca, of a whole new market in Poland, a country where a landed aristocracy made rich by trading in grain and naval stores had developed an insatiable taste for fine brocats, satins and velvets apparently with little concern over prices. And if we are to judge from a few data on exports from Leghorn to London in the later part of the century, the English market, too, offered a significant new outlet for Florentine silks.[80]

76. Sella, *Commerci e industrie*, p. 131.
77. Richard Lassels, *The Voyage of Italy or a Compleat Journey through Italy*, Paris 1670, p. 130.
78. Astone Gasparetto, *Il vetro di Murano dalle origini ad oggi*, Neri Pozza, Venice 1958, p. 189.
79. Rita Mazzei, *Pisa medicea. L'economia cittadina da Ferdinando I a Cosimo III*, Olschki, Florence 1991, chs 3 and 6.
80. Malanima, *Decadenza*, pp. 263–4; Rita Mazzei, *Traffici e uomini d'affari italiani in Polonia nel Seicento*, Franco Angeli, Milan 1983; Ralph Davis, 'Influences de l'Angleterre sur le déclin de Venise' in *Aspetti e cause della decadenza economica veneziana nel secolo XVII*, Istituto per la collaborazione culturale, Venice 1961, p. 229.

But the strongest evidence of resilience and growth comes from industries located in the countryside, for these, inasmuch as they employed cheap peasant labour and were not subject to the jurisdiction of the guilds, did not have to contend as their urban counterparts did with either high labour costs or rigid quality controls and technological conservatism. Until recently the presence of rural industries in the Italian economy was largely ignored as the historians' attention was trained almost exclusively on the major towns, but now a growing body of evidence has surfaced that leaves no doubt as to their importance and their vitality.

Some rural industries had been in place long before 1600, their location being dictated, in large part, by the need to have easy access to raw materials and fuel, or to be in the vicinity of waterfalls. Mining and metallurgy are a case in point. The presence of large iron deposits and of forests in the mountains north of Brescia, for instance, obviously accounts for the formation since medieval times of an industrial region devoted not only to the extraction and smelting of local ores (at the tune, by the seventeenth century, of about 2,500 tonnes of pig iron a year), but also to the manufacture of metal goods, notably firearms. By the sixteenth century the gunmakers of Gardone Valtrompia had acquired a solid international reputation which they continued to enjoy through the next century and beyond. The seventeenth century, studded as it was with wars, brought plenty of business to the area: over and over again the gunmakers of Gardone were called upon to turn out at short notice tens of thousands of common service firearms not only for their own government (the Venetian Republic), but also for Spain, the Kingdom of Naples, and various German states. Not surprisingly under the circumstances, the number of blast furnaces in operation in the Brescia province showed no sign of decline over the entire century.[81] Another rural district in which metallurgy remained strong was the Apennine range north of Genoa where iron ores brought in from Isola d'Elba (a small island off the coast of Tuscany that was as rich in iron deposits as it was poor in timber) were smelted and turned into ordinary hardware by a peasant labour force which a seventeenth-century source describes as 'poor and cheap to hire' and which included women and children, the former being assigned the task of carrying loads of charcoal to the furnaces, the latter that of keeping the smith bellows going. Although no output figures are available, we know that here too, much as in the Brescia region, the number of furnaces in operation remained virtually constant over much of the century, implying a stable level of production.[82] Iron ores excavated in Elba also found their way to the ironworks strewn along the coast of Tuscany there to be smelted and turned into metal sheets, bars, rods and nails. Data on production are hard to come

81. Salvatore Ciriacono, 'Protoindustria, lavoro a domicilio e sviluppo economico nelle campagne venete in epoca moderna', *QS* 52 (1983), pp. 59–62; Belfanti, 'Rural Manufactures', pp. 261–2.
82. Calegari, 'Origini, insediamento', pp. 296–7; Costantini, *La Repubblica di Genova*, pp. 378–95; Edoardo Grendi, *Introduzione alla storia moderna della Repubblica di Genova*, Bozzi, Genoa 1973, pp. 106–7.

by, but those available for the period 1650–75 show a rise in pig iron output from about 700 to 1,000 tonnes a year.[83] Roughly in the same period the smaller, but not negligible iron production of Calabria recovered rapidly from the devastations wrought by the uprising of 1647 and the local ironmasters did a brisk business supplying cannon balls and sundry military hardware to the Spanish navy.[84] For metals other than iron the evidence is scarce, but at least in the case of copper mining in Val Iperina north of Venice we have one more instance of a growing industry, with annual output rising from 15 to 120 tonnes in the course of the century.[85]

A rural location also seems to have been the norm for the manufacture of paper, as the industry required both fast running streams for activating the papermills and an abundance of clean water for processing the linen rags. Two districts stand out in early modern Italy as chief suppliers of high-grade paper to the local as well as the international market: one was found at Salò on the shores of Lake Garda, the other around Voltri on the coast west of Genoa. Both apparently prospered in the sixteenth century, but their paths diverged in the next. The former, as mentioned earlier, suffered heavy losses as demand sharply fell in the Ottoman Empire, its traditional outlet; by contrast, for the Voltri papermakers the seventeenth century was a time of vigorous growth: the number of papermills in the area went from 40 around 1600 to 70 fifty years later, to 110 by end of century. No doubt the superior quality of the Voltri paper largely accounts for its success, but so does the fact that, unlike its Salò counterpart, it was exported to two expanding markets: one was Spain (and her American colonies) where as many as 200,000 reams were sold annually in the 1680s; the other was England, a country that in 1701 imported 80,000 reams of paper from Voltri as against a mere few thousands forty years earlier.[86]

Resilience and growth also characterized the woollen industry in the Alpine valleys north of Bergamo in the Venetian portion of Lombardy. With roots that went back to the late Middle Ages, its output had soared in the sixteenth century from 8,000 to 26,000 pieces of ordinary cloth, most of it intended for export to neighbouring Italian states and to Central Europe. From these high levels production had dropped sharply in the wake of the 1630 plague, but it later bounced back and by 1700, at a time when the woollen industries of

83. Roberta Morelli, 'Sullo "stato d'infanzia" della siderurgia secentesca: le ferriere e i forni di Follonica e Cornia (1640–1680)', *Ricerche storiche* 10 (1980), p. 492.
84. Antonio Di Vittorio, 'L'industria del ferro in Calabria nel Seicento' in *Wirtschaftskraefte und Wirtschaftswege. Festschrift für H. Kellenbenz,* ed. Jurgen Schneider, Klett-Cotta, Bamberg 1978, vol. 3, pp. 47–60.
85. Raffaello Vergani, 'Métallurgie pré-industrielle, pollution, vie rurale: le cas de la saute Italie', *Etudes rurales* 125–6 (1992), p. 72.
86. Manlio Calegari, *La manifattura genovese della carta (secoli XVI–XVIII),* ECIG, Genoa 1986, pp. 37, 57, 61, 118, 120. On exports to Spain, Albert Girard, *Le commerce francais à Séville et Cadix aux temps des Habsbourgs,* Boccard, Paris 1932, p. 385; and to England, D.C. Coleman, *The British Paper Industry 1495–1860. A Study in Industrial Growth,* Oxford University Press 1958, p. 21.

Florence, Venice and Milan had virtually ceased to exist, it reached a peak of 40,000 cloths a year.[87]

To the industries already in existence in rural areas new ones were added in the course of the century. The making of ordinary woollen cloth was introduced in the villages near Biella in Piedmont, in small rural communities on the shores of Lake Como, in the Venetian Terraferma, in Tuscany and in Abruzzi (Kingdom of Naples).[88] With the information now available it is not possible to gauge the size of those newcomers except in the case of Tuscany: by the 1660s the combined output of a number of villages and small towns (chief among them, Prato) was of about 10,000 cloths a year or roughly three times as many as were being turned out at the time by the moribund industry of Florence. The success achieved by the new rustic competitors elicited loud complaints from the Florentine guilds: 'cloth made in the contado is . . . free from all burdens', it was lamented, 'and less is spent on it for labour so that it can be offered at so low a price as to drive out most cloth made in Florence'.[89] The silkmakers of Venice must have harboured a similar grudge towards the new competitors who emerged in the countryside between Verona and Trent in the late sixteenth century and quickly asserted themselves as producers of plain silk fabrics (known as *ormesini da fodera*) mainly used by tailors for lining. As early as 1608 a Venetian source sounded the alarm as the new competition was driving the lower-grade fabrics of Venice from the market. Nor did this prove a passing threat: the new industry prospered well into the eighteenth century, long after its Venetian and Veronese counterparts had died out.[90] The manufacture of mixed fabrics of cotton and flax (fustians), too, was shifted from town to country. Once the pride of Cremona where in the late sixteenth century over 60,000 fustians had been produced annually, the industry had subsequently become extinct there only to find a new home in the countryside northwest of Milan: early in the seventeenth century it was reported as employing 'five to six thousand

87. D. Sella, 'Industrial Production in Seventeenth-Century Italy. A Reappraisal', *Explorations in Entrepreneurial History* NS 6 (1969), p. 238; Rapp, *Industry and Economic Decline*, p. 162.

88. Giuseppe Prato, *La vita economica in Piemonte a mezzo il secolo XVIII*, Società Tipografica Nazionale, Turin 1908, p. 236; Cipolla, 'The Economic Decline', pp. 132–3; Vittorio Beonio Brocchieri, 'La manifattura rurale nella "pars alpestris" dello Stato di Milano tra XVI e XVII secolo', *Archivio storico lombardo* 113 (1987), p. 19; Walter Panciera, *I lanifici dell'Alto Vicentino nel secolo XVIII*, Associazione Industriali, Vicenza 1988, p. 17; Marino, *Pastoral Economics*, p. 200.

89. Judith C. Brown, 'The Economic "Decline" of Tuscany: the Role of the Rural Economy' in *Florence and Milan: Comparisons and Relations*, ed. S. Bertelli, N. Rubinstein and C.H. Smyth, Nuova Italia, Florence 1989, p. 105; on Prato in particular see Paolo Malanima, 'Le attività industriali' in *Prato: storia di una città*, vol. 2, ed. Elena Fasano Guarini, Le Monnier, Prato 1986, pp. 232 and 251.

90. Ivana Pastori Bassetto, *Crescita e declino di un'area di frontiera. Sete e mercanti di Ala nel XVII e XVIII secolo*, Franco Angeli, Milan 1986, pp. 107–16.

people'; a century later its annual output was said to be of 100,000 fustians.[91]

The most dramatic instance of the ruralization of industry, however, was provided by silk throwing, the delicate process, that is, whereby several silk filaments are combined and twisted to form the yarn used as warp in high-quality fabrics and known as organzine. The main centre of production had long been Bologna where silk throwing had reached an unsurpassed level of perfection thanks to the use of hydraulic silk mills which an admiring writer described as 'large machines driven by a water stream and capable of spinning, combining and twisting four thousand filaments at one time, thus doing the work of four thousand spinners'.[92] Until about 1600, when it boasted 125 hydraulic silk mills capable of processing a million pounds of raw silk a year, Bologna had somehow managed to keep its wondrous technology shrouded in secrecy; but early in the seventeenth century the veil of secrecy had somehow been torn and 'silk mills Bologna style' began to spring up outside the old city, in rural rather urban locations, notably in the Venetian Terraferma. There, by the 1630s, the annual output of newly built mills was said to be sufficient to meet all the needs of the Venetian silk industry; by the 1680s the annual output of organzine in the Terraferma may have come close to 180,000 lb and most of it was being exported to France, Switzerland and the Netherlands where silk manufactures were rapidly multiplying. In the State of Milan, too, the countryside came to be dotted with hydraulic mills: 266 of them were in operation by 1679 much to the dismay of the handspinners of Milan who could hardly compete with the new labour-saving technology and with low-paid rural workers. In nearby Piedmont the Bolognese silk mills made their appearance only in the 1670s, but thirty years later 125 of them were employing nearly 7,000 workers and producing 685,000 lb of organzine a year. By the opening of the eighteenth century the proliferation of silk mills had made north Italy the chief supplier of high-grade organzine to the rest of Europe.[93]

A CHANGED ECONOMY

Given the mixed record of losses and gains that characterizes the Italian economic landscape in the seventeenth century, it is risky to formulate firm

91. Luigi Ferrario, *Busto Arsizio: Notizie storico-statistiche*, Busto Arsizio 1864, p. 54; Bruno Caizzi, *Industria, commercio e banca in Lombardia nel secolo XVIII*, Banca Commerciale Italiana, Milan 1968, pp. 33, 89.
92. [Pompeo Vizani], *Descrittione della città, contado, governo e altre cose notabili di Bologna*, Bologna 1602, p. 26.
93. Poni, 'Archéologie de la fabrique', pp. 1479–96 and 'Misura contro misura: come il filo di seta divenne sottile e rotondo', *QS* 47 (1981), pp. 385–422.; A.M. Trezzi, 'A Case Study of De-industrialization of the City: The Silk Mills of the City and Duchy of Milan from the Seventeenth to the Eighteenth Century' in *The Rise and Fall of Urban Industries*, pp. 139–51; Prato, *La vita economica*, p. 218.

conclusions as to the economy's overall performance. It should be clear, however, that the conventional picture of a whole economy sinking into unmitigated decay and settling down at levels of output and income that were dramatically lower than in the past is no longer tenable.[94] To be sure, for the decades between roughly 1620 and 1660 the preponderance of the evidence, whether on agriculture, trade or manufacturing, points to a general depression of major proportions that left but a few activities (such as the arms industry) unscathed and thus warrants the view that in those bleak decades the country declined not only in relative terms *vis-à-vis* other nations, but in absolute terms as well. The same, however, cannot be said of the last four decades of the century, when the recovery and the progress of agriculture (in the North), the resilience exhibited by rural industries, and the shift of old industries to the countryside compensated, at least in part, the irreversible economic losses suffered by the cities.

What one would wish to be able to determine is how the Italian gross domestic product around 1700 compared to that of a century earlier. Needless to say, no such rigorous comparison can be attempted with the kind of fragmented evidence available. Nonetheless, in view of all the new information that has surfaced in recent years, one can confidently say that the country did not sink into a state of unrelieved misery and economic backwardness. In this respect it is revealing that early in the eighteenth century Jacques Savary, the well-informed author of a massive compendium on world trade, did not think that it had so sunk, but viewed Italy as a country that was economically vibrant and worth doing business with.[95] And we saw that even the cities whose industries and commercial activities had suffered the heaviest losses did not experience depopulation and decay, but continued to project an image of prosperity.

Admittedly, the opulence of the cities need not be an infallible sign of the health of the economy as a whole, for it is conceivable that all the lavishly appointed mansions and the horse-drawn carriages that so much impressed foreign visitors merely reflected the wealth and the ostentatious tastes of a small social elite of landowners and government officials who lived in the cities off the income extracted from a wretched and oppressed peasantry; in other words it is possible that the concentration of enormous wealth at the top of society went hand in hand with deteriorating conditions at the bottom and that average per capita income was lower in 1700 than in 1600. Yet, there is some evidence that points to a different conclusion. For one thing, it is remarkable (albeit not conclusive) that seventeenth-century Italy was not especially afflicted (with the two major exceptions of a popular uprising in Naples in 1647 and of one in Messina in 1674) by the widespread social

94. Stumpo, 'La crisi', pp. 327–33. Aymard, 'Fragilità di un'economia avanzata', pp. 86–7, has persuasively argued that the economic decline of Italy, far from being a century-long, irreversible process, was a temporary setback covering the period 1620–50.

95. Carlo M. Cipolla, *Tre storie extra vaganti*, Mulino, Bologna 1994, p. 105.

unrest that a collapsing economy and deteriorating living standards would likely generate. Even more remarkable is the fact that whenever data on the real wages of ordinary workers have been assembled for the entire century (as they have been for five major cities), the resulting picture has been one of long-term stability – a finding that would be hard to reconcile with an economic débâcle.[96] As for levels of income in the countryside, the evidence is woefully scant and merely circumstantial, but what little there is seems to point in two opposite directions: there was deterioration in the South largely as a result of the growing burden of taxation and of seignorial dues that the peasantry and urban poor had to shoulder; in the North, by contrast, labour shortages after 1630 translated, for a time at least, into improving terms of employment for tenants and day labourers, while the diffusion of rural industries no doubt brought an additional source of income to a peasantry no longer solely dependent on farming for its livelihood.[97] In the end, therefore, it seems reasonable to conclude that at the close of the century at least the northern portion of the peninsula had made good most of the losses it had endured earlier on.

Recovery, however, was no mere return to the status quo, for by 1700 the economy was markedly different from what it had been a century earlier. For one thing, its centre of gravity had shifted from the towns to the countryside as more and more industries had died out in the former, while expanding or becoming newly established in the latter. Not surprisingly, the percentage of the population living in towns of more than 10,000 souls dropped from 15 to 13 per cent of the country's total, a drop that would not look especially significant were it not for the fact that it stands in sharp contrast to the trend toward urbanization that had characterized Italy in the sixteenth century and continued to characterize much of western Europe in the seventeenth. One must also bear in mind that the capitals of the several Italian states, nurtured as they were by the presence of a growing bureaucracy and a landed aristocracy anxious to bask in the reflected light of the court, managed to recover rather quickly from the devastations of the plague and from the decline of commercial and manufacturing activities. The real losers were a host of second-tier towns, such as Como, Cremona, Pavia and Ferrara, where de-industrialization was not offset, as it was in the state capitals, by government largesse and the conspicuous consumption of the aristocracy. In those lesser towns demographic losses were severe – in the order of 20 per cent (Pavia) and even 40 per cent (Cremona).[98] The shift to a less urbanized

96. Giovanni Vigo, 'Real Wages of the Working Class in Italy: Building Workers' Wages (14th to 18th Century)', *Journal of European Economic History* 3 (1974), pp. 378–99.
97. Faccini, *Lombardia*, pp. 137–9; Carlo Poni, 'Protoindustrializzazione: un commento', *QS* 51 (1982), p. 1109; Marco Cattini, 'In Emilia orientale: mezzadria cinquecentesca e mezzadria settecentesca. Continuità o frattura?', *QS* 39 (1978), p. 875.
98. Belfanti, 'Aspetti dell'evoluzione demografica', pp. 101–32; Renzo Paolo Corritore, 'Il processo di "ruralizzazione" in Italia nei secoli XVII–XVIII. Verso una regionalizzazione', *Rivista di storia economica* NS 10 (1993), pp. 370–4.

society should not necessarily be interpreted as a sign that industrial production came to represent a shrinking share of the economy. Rather, the shift reflected the ruralization of industry, a process that deserves special attention not only because it offset, in part at least, the industrial decline suffered by the cities, but also because the areas where rural industries took hold and prospered in the seventeenth century (northeastern Piedmont, the region northwest of Milan, the Bergamasque and Brescian valleys, the coastal region near Genoa) were also those where modern industrialization – the factory age – was to make its belated Italian debut two centuries later.

Another change that became discernible as the century wore on was the growing gap between North and South. The South did not witness a process of industrial ruralization comparable to the one that took place in the North, nor did southern agriculture exhibit a comparable dynamism in terms of new crops, improved infrastructure or new patterns of crop rotation. In other words, in the course of the century the two halves of the peninsula apparently moved further apart and the destiny of the southern half as an under-developed area may have been decided then. To be sure, long before the seventeenth century the southern economy had been overwhelmingly agricultural and had been geared to the export of grain, wool and silk to the urbanized North. But what was distinctive about the seventeenth century was, as we have seen, that those traditional exports dropped sharply, thus depriving the Mezzogiorno of much-needed sources of income.

But possibly the most important change undergone by the Italian economy from the age of Philip II to that of his last successor Carlos II had to do with its position or rank *vis-à-vis* other European nations. Even though, in absolute terms, the size of the economy may not have been appreciably smaller than what it had been a hundred years earlier, in relative terms it most certainly was. The Genoese bankers may not have ended up in the poorhouse after the Spanish bankruptcy of 1627, nor did they withdraw altogether from the world of international finance,[99] yet the days when they had dominated the financial markets and had managed colossal sums of money through the Piacenza fairs of exchange were forever gone. The harbour of Venice may not have fallen prey to complete paralysis or even lethargy after the downturn early in the century (as a matter of fact it remained quite active as a regional port for the rest of the century), yet the time when it was the hub of the Mediterranean trade was over, never to return. And so was Italy's erstwhile pre-eminence in manufacturing: in 1700 the country still exported rich silk fabrics, high-grade organzine, musical instruments, fine writing paper and artistic glassware, but it no longer enjoyed the clear supremacy it had had in the past; other nations had moved into fields where Italy had once been the front-runner and had pushed the former leader into the position of a minor, if still respectable, player in an expanding world economy.

99. Giuseppe Felloni, *Gli investimenti finanziari genovesi in Europa tra il Seicento e la Restaurazione*, Giuffre, Milan 1971.

CHAPTER THREE

Society

When looking at their own society, seventeenth-century Italian political writers saw it as being structured in 'orders' or 'estates'. Writing in 1634, a Neapolitan author identified three such groups: the nobility (or barons), the people (*popolo*) – a sort of middling order consisting of 'wealthy and virtuous individuals who live civil lives without engaging in base and mechanical trades' – and the plebs which he called 'the dregs of the commonwealth and, as such, inclined to seditions, to revolutions, to subverting laws and traditions'.[1] Likewise at mid-century the Florentine Donato Giannotti described Venetian society as consisting of 'three distinct orders': the *popolo* which, he added, 'we also call plebeians', the citizens, and the gentlemen.[2] Much the same typology held true in other parts of Italy: the labels applied to each order might differ from place to place, but the main tripartite division into orders remained the rule throughout the peninsula. Somewhat surprisingly, the clergy is never mentioned as a distinct order alongside the other three. The omission most certainly does not reflect the feeling that clerics did not represent a separate social and clearly identifiable social group (which of course they did, especially in the age of the Counter-Reformation when church authorities insisted more than ever that, in terms of training, dress code, and legal status, the clergy must be set apart from the laity[3]); rather, the omission reflects the fact that our sources were apparently concerned with how lay society was structured and took it for granted that the 'ecclesiastical order' stood as a group apart.

Historians have long debated and are still debating whether describing society as consisting of orders, that is to say as a hierarchy of social groups ranked on the basis of reputation, honour and birth, rather than of classes is, in fact, useful and realistic.[4] Some scholars have tended to dismiss the

1. Quotations in Giovanni Muto, 'Il Regno di Napoli sotto la dominazione spagnola' in *SSI*, vol. 11, pp. 230–2 and 252–3.
2. Corrado Vivanti, 'Lacerazioni e contrasti' in *SIE*, vol. 1 (1972), p. 907.
3. See ch. 4 below, p. 116.
4. On the debate see Peter Burke, 'The Language of Orders in Early Modern Europe' in *Social Orders and Social Classes in Europe since 1500. Studies in Social Stratification*, ed. M.L. Bush, Longman 1992, pp. 1–12.

typology based on orders as a mere cover for what, in fact, were 'classes' in the sense of groups that differed in terms of wealth or income as well as of their role in the economy. The problem with the concept of class, however, is that it fails to do justice to the way power and influence were distributed in early modern times: a Venetian gentleman or patrician who lived in poverty (and there were many such men) could sit and vote in the Great Council as even the richest *cittadino* could never hope to do; nor could a successful attorney or a rich financier expect to be allowed, merely by virtue of his wealth or reputation, to join the ranks of the Florentine or the Milanese patriciate. More often than not it took two or three generations in the upper echelons of the middling order before a family could hope to make it into the charmed circle of the aristocracy – unless, as sometimes happened, a government hard pressed for revenue decided to bestow a noble title on a commoner in return for a handsome contribution in cash.

This is not to deny that classes existed: especially in times of social conflict people could (and, as will be seen, sometimes did) ignore the rigid mould of orders and regroup along class lines, the haves against the have-nots. The point to remember, however, is that this kind of realignment was temporary and that, once conflict subsided, old distinctions based on status were promptly revived and individuals again identified themselves as members of an order. Such identification, one must add, was more than a question of mere perception or a simple formality, for it could actually affect individual lives in very tangible ways. Not only did rank meticulously dictate forms of address based on deference on one side and condescension on the other; not only did it play a crucial role in arranging marriages; it could also determine an individual's role in politics, top jobs in government being normally reserved for the aristocracy, or could seriously affect even a young man's education. The son of a wealthy Bergamasque merchant found that out when, in 1717, he applied for admission to the prestigious Collegio dei Nobili (a boarding school for scions of the aristocracy) in Siena. After being approved, his admission ran into trouble: as the embattled headmaster explained it, the mere prospect of a boy 'of lower condition' attending the school had generated 'universal outrage' among the Bergamasque noblemen who had children in the school; they viewed the admission of a commoner as a 'monstrosity' that would irreparably damage the reputation of the school.[5] A good century earlier, in Bologna, the local nobility had clashed with the reforming Archbishop Paleotti over his decision that all children without exception must attend the newly established Schools of Christian Doctrine: noble parents simply refused to comply on the grounds that their children 'are noble, have private tutors and [that] they [the parents] do not want them to be in the same school with plebeians'. To which the good archbishop replied (we do not know with what measure of success) that 'the Church makes no

---

5. Gian Paolo Brizzi, *La formazione della classe dirigente nel Sei-Settecento. I 'seminaria nobilium' nell'Italia centro-settentrionale*, Mulino, Bologna 1976, pp. 161–2.

distinction between nobles and ignobles' and that 'since the Church is common to all, it must be attended by all'.[6] A similar cleavage affected lay confraternities, too: while at first a good many of them had a socially mixed membership, in the course of time the trend was toward enrolling only individuals belonging to the same 'order'.[7]

THE ARISTOCRACY

In every Italian state the aristocracy included two distinct groups, each claiming to be part of the first order of society. One group traced its origins to a distant and often mythical feudal past and insisted on the deeds of military valour of its ancestors and on some remote imperial investiture to legitimize its present position; it still cultivated knightly or martial virtues and many of its members pursued careers in the armies of their sovereign, whether king of Spain, duke of Savoy or Venetian Republic. The power base of this feudal nobility or nobility of the sword lay primarily in the countryside where its fiefs were located and where their holders enjoyed, in addition to a sometimes large income derived from agriculture, a varying array of judicial and seignorial rights over the peasantry. The other aristocracy is better known to us as the patriciate, even though the term itself was not commonly used at the time. Its roots were urban and its claim to prominence and privilege rested on the family's long residence in a town and, above all, on several generations of the same family having held municipal office.[8] The feudal nobility was especially strong in the Kingdom of Naples. Although its 'barons' had lost much of their autonomous political power and their medieval habits of insubordination *vis-à-vis* the crown had been largely suppressed after Naples, in the early sixteenth century, had become part of a large monarchy as powerful as Spain, nonetheless with their huge country estates and with ample judicial and administrative authority over the peasantry, the barons still represented a major force in southern society, a force that not even as centralizing and determined a monarch as Philip II, dependent as he was on their loyalty for recruiting officers and soldiers for his army and for keeping a minimum of order in the countryside, could afford to antagonize. In Naples, however, another nobility had formed that was quite distinct from the

6. Adriano Prosperi, 'Intellettuali e Chiesa all'inizio dell'età moderna' in *SIE Annali* 4 (1981), pp. 246–7.
7. Christopher F. Black, *Italian Confraternities in the Sixteenth Century*, Cambridge University Press 1989, pp. 38–42; Louis Chatellier, *The Europe of the Devout: the Catholic Reformation and the Formation of a New Society*, transl. Jean Birrell, Cambridge University Press 1989, pp. 15–17.
8. The large body of literature produced in the 1960s and 1970s is surveyed in Cesare Mozzarelli, 'Stato, patriziato e organizzazione della società nell'Italia moderna', *AISIG* 2 (1976), pp. 421–512; see also *Patriziati e aristocrazie nobiliari*, ed. Cesare Mozzarelli and Pierangelo Schiera, Libera Università, Trent 1978.

baronage and rather similar to the patriciate of the north and centre of the peninsula. Known as *nobilta' di seggio* from the hall (*seggio*) where they met to transact matters pertaining to the administration of the city, this urban aristocracy held all the levers in the municipal government and was in charge, among other things, of that most sensitive task, the provisioning of a city with 300,000 inhabitants. Lesser towns (*università*) too had their own patriciates jealously guarding their inveterate right to run local affairs.[9]

In Venice the patriciate held a very special, not to say unique, position for it not only controlled the affairs of the city, but those of the entire state as well. Its 2,000 or so members formed a closed, hereditary caste and enjoyed the exclusive privilege of sitting in the Great Council and of being solely eligible to fill all major positions in government, from doge to senator, from ambassador to magistrate, from provincial governor to officer in the army or navy.[10] For all its enormous power inside and outside the city of St Mark, however, the Venetian patriciate cultivated the appearance of an urban, one is almost tempted to say bourgeois, elite. With no high-sounding titles, elaborate coats of arms or judicials rights over the peasantry; with no long trains of servants and invariably donning a plain black robe in public, Venetian noblemen stood in sharp contrast, according to an outside observer, to the flamboyant, ostentatious nobility of Naples who lived surrounded by 'pomp and magnificence' and always appeared in public with a retinue of 'grooms, butlers and servants'.[11] But the Venetian Republic had its feudal nobility too – if not in Venice itself, certainly in the mainland possessions it had conquered in the fourteenth and fifteenth centuries. Far from trying to suppress them, the Republic had coopted them and had won their loyalty by recognizing and confirming their feudal rights and perquisites so long as they did not conflict with its own laws and policies.

The duality of feudal nobility and urban patriciate existed, albeit with variations in the relative importance of the two groups, nearly everywhere in the pensinsula – in the Papal States as well as in the State of Milan, in the Grand Duchy of Tuscany no less than in the Duchy of Parma. In all of them the two aristocracies lived side by side, each with its own sphere of influence (the town in one case, the countryside in the other) and its own distinctive ethos and lifestyle. Yet, from the late sixteenth century there was a gradual blurring of the differences between the two groups, a blurring that was facilitated by intermarriage and by the fact that increasingly patrician families

9. Giuseppe Galasso, 'La feudalità napoletana nel secolo XVI' in *Potere e società negli Stati italiani fra Cinquecento e Seicento*, ed. Elena Fasano Guarini, Mulino, Bologna 1978, pp. 237–9; and Muto, 'Il Regno di Napoli', pp. 237–9.

10. James C. Davis, *The Decline of the Venetian Nobility as a Ruling Class*, Johns Hopkins University Press, Baltimore 1962, pp. 15–33; Gaetano Cozzi, 'Venezia nello scenario europeo' in G. Cozzi, Michael Knapton and Giovanni Scarabello, *La Repubblica di Venezia nell'età moderna*, UTET, Turin 1992, pp. 168–84; and M. Knapton, 'Tra Dominante e Dominio' in the same vol., pp. 497–502.

11. Quotation in Romolo Quazza, *Preponderanza spagnola (1559–1700)*, Vallardi, Milan 1950, p. 170.

invested in land and thus came to share common economic interests with the feudal nobility. Members of the urban elites began to sport the title of *gentiluomo* hitherto reserved to noblemen of the sword and in one town after another adopted stringent requirements aimed at defining ever more narrowly the conditions for access to their ranks, a primary although not absolute condition being birth in a socially prominent family with deep roots in the town's past, a record of civic service, and proof that no member of the family in the last two or three generations had engaged in 'base and mechanical trades'.[12] A process of 'aristocratic closure', in other words, got under way as the patriciate tended to become more exclusive and to ape the feudal nobility, adopting from the latter the notion that nobility is, first and foremost, determined by heredity rather than by education and service to the state as humanists had argued in an earlier age.[13]

Yet at the same time as the patriciate was adopting some of the trappings and the mores of the feudal nobility, the latter was increasingly led to conform to certain standards of civility and education that had long been typical of the urban elites. One reason for doing so was the lure of prestigious and often lucrative positions either in government or in the Church. As both the centralizing governments of the time, with their growing administrative and judicial apparatus, and the Counter-Reformation Church, with its expanding curial structure, offered more and more positions requiring an adequate literary and legal preparation as well as polished manners, it became advisable even for families of the feudal nobility to have their younger sons educated in a *collegio dei nobili* where they mixed with sons of the patriciate and acquired both the training and the social graces they would need in the future should they pursue a career in the administration or the courts of law.[14] It is perhaps no mere coincidence that the proliferation of boarding schools for noblemen was paralleled in the seventeenth century by a growing body of literature that revived, for the benefit of the feudal nobility, the humanist notion that true nobility finds its highest expression in 'virtuous' conduct and in a distinguished record of public service.[15]

Even as they were drawing somewhat closer, the two aristocracies still retained something of their distinctive cultural traditions – the feudal nobility, a strong sense of independence *vis-à-vis* the sovereign whom they continued to view, in the old spirit of chivalry, as but the first among his knightly peers;

12. Claudio Donati, *L'idea di nobiltà in Italia: secoli XIV–XVIII*, Laterza, Bari 1988, p. 62; on Tuscany in particular see Furio Diaz, *Il granducato di Toscana. I Medici*, UTET, Turin 1976, p. 243.
13. Examples abound: Giorgio Borelli, *Un patriziato della Terraferma veneta tra XVII e XVIII secolo. Ricerche sulla nobiltà veronese*, Giuffrè, Milan 1974, pp. 387–404; Giorgio Politi, *Aristocrazia e potere politico nella Cremona di Filippo II*, SugarCo, Milan 1976, pp. 33–47; Rita Mazzei, *La società lucchese del Seicento*, Pacini, Lucca 1977, pp. 3–6, 39–43; Donati, *L'idea di nobiltà*, pp. 52–5.
14. Giuseppe Galasso, 'Le forme del potere, classi e gerarchie sociali' in *SIE*, vol. 1 (1972), pp. 482–3; Brizzi, *La formazione della classe dirigente*, p. 207.
15. Donati, *L'idea di nobiltà*, pp. 274–8.

and the urban patriciates, a proud claim to self-government in their towns – and nothing better reveals those differences than the two aristocracies' response to the centralizing and increasingly intrusive policies of what, with some exaggeration, is generally referred to as the modern absolute state.[16] Whether those policies meant the closer supervision of and interference with urban administration, the limitation of feudal privilege in the countryside, or the assertion of the judicial supremacy of the crown, they all challenged the aristocracies' keen sense of group identity and autonomy. Urban patriciates found it relatively easy to adjust to those challenges, for they had a long tradition of administrative practice in their respective towns and many of their members had been trained in the law before entering a career of public service. So much so, in fact, that their rulers (whether the king of Spain in Milan, the pope in Rome, or the grand duke in Florence) gladly drew on their expertise as administrators, tax collectors or magistrates to run the country. As a quid pro quo for their loyalty, the rulers allowed the urban patriciate a great deal of leeway in the administration of their respective towns.[17] The patriciates, on their part, made every effort to consolidate their monopoly on municipal offices by adopting (with the consent of the government) strict rules aimed at restricting access to their ranks. As mentioned earlier, nearly everywhere in the late sixteenth and early seventeenth centuries increasingly stringent requirements ensured that only a select number of long established families would enjoy patrician status and hence access to office; new additions to the patriciate were not *per se* ruled out, but only after strict standards had been met, including, more often than not, a law degree.[18] Such an air-tight monopoly of power, one should add, did not always go unchallenged by the upper echelons of the lower orders who resented being excluded from office, and we shall see instances of such resentment later in this chapter. Suffice it to say at this point that by and large the patriciates managed to fend off any attempt at forcing them to share power with non-patricians and to the end of the century and even beyond retained their role as a kind of service nobility.

The Venetian patriciate represented a case apart, for it was never threatened by an encroaching monarch. Its total identification with the government of the Republic, its unquestioned right to be the only ruling elite, were so much part of the republican constitution as never to be seriously called in doubt. Which does not mean that the Venetian patriciate enjoyed in total peace and quiet its exalted position at the head of the state. In fact, it too had its problems, but they arose from divisions within rather than from

16. Giangiulio Ambrosini, 'Diritto e società' in *SIE*, vol. 1 (1972), p. 360.
17. Cesare Mozzarelli, 'Strutture sociali e formazioni statuali a Milano e a Napoli tra Cinquecento e Settecento', *Società e Storia* 2 (1978), pp. 433–6.
18. Cesare Mozzarelli, 'Il sistema patrizio' in *Patriziati e aristocrazie nobiliari*, pp. 50–1; Dante Zanetti, *La demografia del patriziato milanese nei secoli XVII, XVIII e XIX*, Università di Pavia, Pavia 1972, pp. 23–4; Maria Carla Zorzoli, *Università, dottori, giureconsulti. L'organizzazione della 'Facoltà legale' di Pavia nell'età spagnola*, Cedam, Padua 1986, pp. 365–71.

55

outside its own ranks. Those divisions pitted the less wealthy members of the patriciate against those among their peers who, thanks to their wealth, social prestige and shrewd manipulation of the electoral process, managed to fill all the important government offices, notably in the all-powerful Council of Ten, and in practice ran the government behind a veil of secrecy and intrigue. Opposition to that inner coterie had become especially vocal and widespread in the 1580s when a concerted effort by those excluded from office (known as 'the young') succeeded in driving out 'the old' by limiting the power of the Council of Ten – and the ensuing change in the leadership of the Republic had important implications not only for the composition of the ruling elite, but also, as will be seen, for the Republic's foreign policy, notably for its relations with Spain and the Papacy during the first decade of the century. Subsequently, however, the old guard recovered much lost ground and tensions built up once again within the patriciate and reached a peak between 1623 and 1629 when Ranier Zeno, a prominent patrician with a distinguished record of public service, raised the banner of opposition against the ruling establishment and openly accused the doge and his closest associates of abuse of power. His outspoken attacks struck a chord in many of the less prominent patricians and for a while Zeno became a hero in the eyes of all those (patricians or commoners) who had a grudge against the government. By 1627 the outcry against the status quo had reached such a pitch of intensity that the English ambassador in Venice felt justified in describing the situation as 'a kind of civil warre'. In the event, civil war never materialized, for by 1629, after minor and largely cosmetic modifications had been adopted in the way the Council of Ten operated, peace and normality were restored with government still firmly in the hands of the upper reaches of the patriciate.[19]

In the Republic of Genoa divisions within the patriciate ran deeper than in Venice. There, too, they grew out of widespread resentment against a small circle of the wealthiest families (also known as 'the old') which by the sixteenth century held a firm grip on government and excluded the majority of their fellow patricians ('the young') from it. By 1575 the tension between the two factions had reached breaking point and in the resulting clash 'the young', supported by the upper layers of the *popolo*, forced the ruling families out of the city. Within a year, however, a compromise had been struck whereby the two factions agreed to share power and to appease the wealthiest members of the *popolo* with the promise that every year a number of them would be admitted to the patriciate. The promise would not be kept: once firmly in control, 'the young' closed ranks with the old guard to keep the *popolo* out, and when the latter tried in the early part of the seventeenth century to force the door open by plotting against the government, repression

19. Gaetano Cozzi, *Il doge Nicolo Contarini. Ricerche sul patriziato veneziano agli inizi del Seicento*, Istituto per la collaborazione culturale, Venice and Rome 1958, pp. 2–22 (on the 'young') and pp. 229–77 (on the Zeno conspiracy); the quotation is on p. 247.

was swift and ruthless. Only in 1627 did the ruling elite relent somewhat and admit a substantial number of new families to its ranks. It did so in the face of a double crisis that seemed to threaten its very survival: on the one hand, in that year the Spanish crown repudiated its debt thus causing huge losses to the many patricians who had heavily invested in it; on the other, in that same year a plot against the Republic (the Vachero conspiracy) apparently instigated or at least encouraged by Spain was uncovered. Under the circumstances, the ruling elite needed all the help it could get – even from the despised *popolo*.[20]

For all the power and influence the urban patriciates wielded either as republican ruling elites or as high-ranking officials and magistrates in monarchical states, there was one area where they had to yield ground, namely their control over the surrounding countryside (*contado*) in matters of taxation. Traditionally, every major town's patriciate had claimed and exercised the right, once the government had decided how much tax revenue each district or province was expected to produce, to allocate the burden between the town and the *contado*. Not surprisingly, the heavier load had invariably been placed on the latter which was treated pretty much as a colonial dependency of the town and, as such, fair game for the tax collector. Nor had conditions improved for the *contado* after more and more patricians began to invest in landed estates as they did in the fifteenth and sixteenth centuries, for legislation had been enacted that taxed farmland belonging to townsmen at a lower rate than the rest, with the predictable result that rural landowners had to shoulder a growing tax burden. By the mid-sixteenth century the disparity between town and country had become so glaring as to be a major source of discontent among rural taxpayers and a cause of concern in government circles as more and more land came to enjoy a privileged tax status and thus contributed less and less to the treasury. To remedy the situation in the late sixteenth century the Spanish government established in the State of Milan the *congregazioni dei contadi*, elective bodies, that is, representing rural taxpayers and entitled to take part, alongside representatives of the city councils, in the periodical review of the tax rolls; it was further ruled that in the future no land newly acquired by townsmen would receive preferential tax treatment, and that both town and country would have to contribute their fair share toward the cost of quartering and provisioning troops, a cost traditionally borne only by the peasantry. Needless to say those reforms were resented by the towns' oligarchy and in 1604 an appeal was filed with the crown to have them repealed. Not only was the appeal denied by a government in dire need of revenue, but the erosion of urban privilege was pushed further in 1633 when the Spanish governor repealed the traditional exemption from military billets the towns had enjoyed

20. Claudio Costantini, *La Repubblica di Genova in età moderna*, UTET, Turin 1978, chs 8, 9 and 14; for a shorter account see Jean-Claude Waquet, 'Politique, institutions et societé dans l'Italie du "Seicento" in Yves-Marie Berce *et al.*, *L'Italie au XVIIe siècle*, SEDES, Paris 1989, pp. 86–9.

in the past.[21] Similar changes were adopted in the Venetian Republic, and for much the same reasons.[22] Genoa, on its part, took a different approach: in 1623 it established a new government agency with the specific task of closely monitoring the distribution of the tax burden between town and country and there, too, the intended result was to reduce the tax privileges enjoyed by townsmen in the past.[23] In Tuscany the Medici rulers went further than any other government in stripping the urban oligarchies of their authority over the *contado* and in placing the latter under the exclusive jurisdiction of a bureaucracy appointed by and solely answerable to them.[24]

The patriciates apparently offered little resistance to those changes even though they involved an erosion of their tax privileges and the partial loss of control over the *contado*. Rather, they seem to have settled without too much carping in the not uncomfortable role of city fathers with a broad measure of autonomy within the city walls. Besides, as experienced bureaucrats and trained lawyers, they provided an indispensable pool of talent from which the sovereign – whether the king of Spain in the State of Milan or the grand duke in Tuscany – recruited officials and magistrates for his own bureaucracy and for the bench.[25]

While urban patriciates, by and large, adapted themselves rather easily to the demands and the needs of the absolute state and contributed with their legal and administrative expertise to the smooth functioning of the bureaucratic machine, the same cannot be said of the feudal nobility whose relationship with the central government proved far more difficult and contentious. Tension between the two developed early on over the right traditionally claimed by

21. Giorgio Chittolini, 'Contadi e territori: qualche considerazione', *Studi bresciani* 12 (1983), pp. 35–48; Giovanni Vigo, *Uno stato nell'impero. La difficile transizione al moderno nella Milano di età spagnola*, Guerini, Milan 1994, pp. 121–31.
22. Knapton, 'Tra Dominante e Dominio', pp. 487–92; Luciano Pezzolo, 'Dal contado alla comunità. Finanze e prelievo fiscale nel Vicentino (secoli XVI–XVIII)' in *Dueville: storia e identificazione di una comunità del passato*, ed. Claudio Povolo, Neri Pozza, Vicenza 1985, pp. 384–97; Sergio Zamperetti, 'Per una storia delle istituzioni rurali nella Terraferma veneta: il contado vicentino nei secoli XVI–XVII' in *Stato, società e giustizia nella Repubblica veneta (secoli XV–XVIII)*, ed. Gaetano Cozzi, Jouvence, Rome 1985, pp. 69–86; Ivana Pederzani, *Venezia e lo 'Stado de Terraferma'. Il governo delle comunità nel territorio bergamasco (secoli XV–XVIII)*, Vita e Pensiero, Milan 1992, pp. 159–75, 301–24.
23. Costantini, *La Repubblica di Genova*, pp. 195–8. A similar development in Piedmont: Enrico Stumpo, *Finanze e Stato moderno nel Piemonte del Seicento*, Istituto Storico Italiano, Rome 1979, p. 170.
24. Diaz, *Il Granducato di Toscana*, pp. 103–6; and now more extensively in Luca Mannori, *Il sovrano tutore. Pluralismo istituzionale e accentramento amministrativo nel Principato dei Medici (secoli XVI–XVIII)*, Giuffrè, Milan 1994, pp. 55–74.
25. On Milan see Zorzoli, *Università, dottori, giureconsulti*, pp. 365–71; on Tuscany, Diaz, *Il Granducato di Toscana*, pp. 175–9 and R. Burr Litchfield, *Emergence of a Bureaucracy. The Florentine Patricians 1530–1790*, Princeton University Press, Princeton, N.J. 1986.

feudal noblemen to settle quarrels with their peers at the point of a sword rather than in a court of law like everybody else. Laws against the barbarous practice had been enacted in several Italian states as early as the 1540s, apparently with little effect. In 1563, however, the Council of Trent, in one of its concluding sessions, had issued a ringing and uncompromising condemnation of the 'abominable practice of the duel' under the penalty of excommunication for both those who engaged in it and for those who attended the bloody ritual.[26] Even though the Council's decree and government legislation failed to extirpate duelling completely, they certainly represented a serious challenge to the feudal nobility's claim of being above the law; they represented also a significant cultural shift away from private violence – a shift clearly visible in a growing body of literature that argued that a true knight need not resort to duelling to defend his honour, but must rely on the legal system instead.[27]

More threatening to the feudal nobility than the criminalization of duelling, however, was the policy adopted by governments hard-pressed for revenue of granting fiefs and the high-sounding titles attached to them to a growing number of wealthy commoners in return for a large contribution in hard cash. In the State of Milan, where twenty-five such grants had been made during Philip II's long reign (1556–98), four times as many were made during the equally long reign of Philip IV (1621–65); in the Kingdom of Naples the number of titled noblemen (*baroni*) rose from 110 to 434 between 1590 and 1675, most of the newly ennobled being rich financiers and tax farmers; in the small Duchy of Parma ennoblements rose from a total of merely thirteen in the second half of the sixteenth century to as many as 134 during the period 1641–80.[28] The upshot was not merely the numerical growth of the feudal nobility, but also the dilution of its prestige and influence, all the more so as sometimes, as happened in Piedmont, the government divided sizeable vacant fiefs into smaller and smaller fractions in order to accommodate a larger number of aspiring feudatories.[29] At the same time, as the newly ennobled upstarts could neither deny nor obliterate the fact that their fortune had been made in trade, money-lending or tax collection, in activities, that is, which the old aristocratic ethos had always considered 'base and ignoble', they went out of their way to argue that those activities were not at all incompatible with genuine nobility, provided they had been carried out discreetly. As a Milanese jurist put it, money-lending practiced in the public square was indeed demeaning, but ceased to be so if practiced on a large scale in the privacy of one's home – a concession that must have been horrifying to members of the old nobility of the sword, steeped as they were in the military ethos of chivalry.[30]

26. H. J. Schroeder, *Canons and Decrees of the Council of Trent. Original text with English translation*, Herder, St Louis, Mo. 1941, p. 251. See also Donati, *L'idea di nobiltà*, pp. 94–8, 102–9.
27. Giancarlo Angelozzi, 'Cultura dell'onore, codici di comportamento nobiliare e Stato nella Bologna pontificia: un'ipotesi di lavoro', *AISIG* 8 (1982), pp. 307–14.
28. Data are from Donati, *L'idea di nobiltà*, pp. 280–2.
29. Stumpo, *Finanza e Stato moderno*, p. 293.
30. Mozzarelli, 'Il sistema patrizio', pp. 60–1.

A third factor that contributed, in the long run, to the taming of the feudal nobility were state policies intended to assert the central government's direct control over all its subjects. In practice, this meant interposing government officials or magistrates between the feudal lords and the populace under their jurisdiction and to strip them of the right to keep private armies or bands of retainers. Predictably, the implementation of such policies varied a great deal from state to state. It was rather successful in the Papal States, especially after a series of energetic popes managed in the late sixteenth century to eliminate the scourge of banditry, a form of large-scale private violence that had long been abetted and even instigated by powerful feudatories, and gradually to turn the latter into loyal and more or less law-abiding vassals of the Holy See. In return, fiefholders were allowed to retain the right to administer justice (subject, however, to appeal in Rome) and to enjoy certain tax privileges.[31] The confrontation between the government and a violence-prone nobility was especially harsh in the small Duchy of Parma, a sixteenth-century creation of Pope Paul III for the benefit of his illegitimate son Pier Luigi Farnese. It was a state where a few feudal families (Pallavicino, Landi, Sanvitale) held vast fiefs which they ran as virtually independent states. It was therefore imperative for the Farnese to bring them into line if their newly acquired authority was to have any substance at all. But it was only during the reign of Ranuccio Farnese (1592–1622) that a systematic campaign was waged against the great feudatories: in the end they were forced to live in Parma under the duke's watchful eye and were deprived of most of their judicial authority; in the case of the most recalcitrant, their holdings were simply confiscated. Opposition to such stern measures was predictably strong and it led in 1610 to a plot to assassinate Ranuccio; the plot, however, was uncovered in time and seven noblemen were executed for *lèse-majesté*.[32]

The Venetian Republic, too, tried to curb feudal lawlessness in its mainland dominions and it too met with resistance. As one government inspector (*inquisitore*) specifically charged with enforcing the Republic's laws wrote from Bergamo in 1626, his efforts had brought him on a collision course with 'the gentlemen and knights' in the area and had earned him their 'hatred'.[33] Thirty years later the governor of the nearby province of Brescia had no easier time with the local nobility as he tried to curb their 'tyrannical arrogance'. Those over-bearing feudatories, he reported, surrounded themselves with 'cutthroats and criminals', barred government officials from their estates alleging feudal immunity, and 'openly flaunted' the authority of the Republic; nor would the victims of their outrages dare testify against them for fear of retaliation. Interestingly, the Venetian government, then fully engaged in the costly War of Candia and in desperate need of the military support of the nobility, proceeded rather

31. Angelozzi, 'Cultura dell'onore', pp. 322–4.
32. Giovanni Tocci, *Le terre traverse. Poteri e territori nei ducati di Parma e Piacenza tra Sei e Settecento*, Mulino, Bologna 1985, pp. 20–1, 58–66, 95–107; Quazza, *Preponderanza spagnola*, pp. 107–9.
33. State Archives, Venice, *Senato, dispacci rettori di Bergamo*, filza 20, doc. of 24 February 1626.

leniently against the perpetrators, limiting itself to summoning the worst offenders to come and spend some time in Venice and suspending them temporarily from public office.[34] In the later part of the century, as the Venetian Republic was no longer hampered by the pressing needs of war, leniency gave way to sterner measures ranging from banishment to the loss of noble rank, to prison terms, to (in a few cases) capital punishment.[35]

Genoa, too, had to contend with feudal anarchy, and possibly to an even greater extent than Venice, for its territory – a narrow strip of largely rugged land along the coast of Liguria that shared borders with six different foreign states – offered an ideal setting for armed bands of poverty-stricken mountaineers, fugitives from the law, smugglers and sundry other marginalized individuals who survived by dint of robberies, kidnappings and extortions and often operated with the connivance of high-ranking noblemen who hired them as retainers and used them in their unending quarrels with fellow noblemen. Against that scourge the Genoese authorities took drastic measures in the late sixteenth century, and these included the creation of a special agency with broad powers of summary justice and the use of the army in full-scale expeditions against the bandits and their patrons. In 1606 the radical step was taken of placing the rural communities that notoriously harboured outlaws under the control of a military officer (*capitano*) appointed by and solely answerable to the central government.[36]

We do not know how effective all those measures were in restoring a measure of order and legality in Genoese territory, but one is inclined to suspect that their success was modest at best. After all, the Apennine range north of Genoa continued to be a breeding ground for feudal violence for much of the seventeenth century and, besides, the notoriously fractious nature of the Genoese ruling elite may well have made it difficult to sustain the implementation of those measures in a consistent way. By contrast, the Venetian Republic, with its more stable, more cohesive ruling elite, seems to have been more successful in curbing lawlessness in its mainland dominions thanks to the creation, in the seventeenth century, of a new magistracy (the *Sindaci Inquisitori di Terraferma*) with broad discretionary powers to prosecute and convict bandits and their high-placed employers.[37]

34. Sergio Zamperetti, 'L'aria di Venezia. Sovranità statale e poteri particolaristici nel Bresciano del secondo Seicento' in *Studi veneti offerti a Gaetano Cozzi*, Cardo, Vicenza 1992, pp. 275–85.
35. Francesco Vecchiato, *Una signoria rurale nella Repubblica Veneta. I Pompei d'Illasi*, Libreria Universitaria Editrice, Verona 1986, pp. 94–5, 130, 147–8, 154–5. Instances of severe penalties inflicted on overbearing aristocrats in the Kingdom of Naples in Maria Sirago, 'Due esempi di ascensione signorile: i Vaaz di Mola e gli Acquaviva conti di Conversano tra Cinque e Seicento', *Studi Storici Luigi Simeoni* 36 (1986), pp. 175–6.
36. Coéstantini, *La Repubblica di Genova*, pp. 193–5, 197.
37. Gaetano Cozzi, *Republica di Venezia e Stati italiani. Politica e giustizia dal secolo XVI al XVIII*, Einaudi, Turin 1982, pp. 180, 189; Pederzani, *Venezia e lo 'Stado de Terraferma'*, p. 327.

From the mid-sixteenth century efforts aimed at curbing feudal insubordination were pursued in the Kingdom of Naples as well and they generated 'discontent' among the barons who complained that the presence of royal magistrates in the countryside had made their 'vassals [i.e. the people living in their fiefs] so bold as to be hard to keep in line'. It was further reported that 'the barons, being naturally proud, cannot tolerate being summoned, even for the slightest offence, before a court of law where, either in terms of legal procedures or in terms of the penalties meted out, no distinction is made between them [the barons] and the rest'.[38] This was probably a bit of an exaggeration and it is ironic that the barons who, after all, still enjoyed and would long enjoy enormous wealth, all kinds of privileges and considerable influence in high places, would portray themselves as innocent victims. Nonetheless, the words just quoted point to a growing feeling that under the new Spanish masters the feudal nobility's independence, its *de facto* immunity from royal jurisdiction, and the free hand it had traditionally had in dealing with the populace, were all being threatened by the king's magistrates. In response, after about 1600 the baronage resorted to hiring bands of armed retainers who, through violence and intimidation, imposed their will over a peasantry made increasingly restless by rising rents and ever-growing manorial obligations. Feudal violence proved successful in keeping the lid on peasant discontent until the uprising of 1647, but it also exposed the Spanish government's waning interest in bringing the barons to heel: as its needs for both revenue and manpower grew dramatically during the Thirty Years War, the government adopted a policy of conciliation rather than confrontation with the baronage.[39] Only in the second half of the century did Madrid find it possible to address the problem of feudal anarchy, notably the hiring of armed bands of retainers, the imposition of arbitrary road tolls and the practice of forcing local farmers to sell their crops to the feudatories at prices set by the feudatories themselves. Stringent measures were enacted especially in the 1680s by the energetic viceroy Marquess del Carpio, chief among them the authorization given to royal magistrates to proceed against perpetrators *ad modum belli*, that is to say with the use of military force without too much regard for legal niceties. Several prominent noblemen as well as their retainers were in fact apprehended and incarcerated; as a result, according to a 1689 tract, an 'inimical hatred' (*odio inimico*) against the Spaniards spread among the nobility especially (and here the prejudice typical of a society of orders showed itself) on account of 'the intolerable arrogance exhibited by the magistrates as they trample upon and show contempt for the Nobility'.[40]

38. Quotation in Muto, 'Il Regno di Napoli', pp. 230–1. Further evidence for the late seventeenth centruy in Salvo Mastellone, *Francesco d'Andrea politico e giurista (1648–98). L'ascesa del ceto civile*, Olschki, Florence 1969, pp. 102–3, 130.
39. Vittor Ivo Comparato, *Uffici e società a Napoli (1600–1647). Aspetti dell'ideologia del magistrato nell'età moderna*, Olshki, Florence 1974, pp. 388 and 418; Giuseppe Galasso, *Il Mezzogiorno nella storia d'Italia*, LeMonnier, Florence 1977, pp. 184–6; Rosario Villari, *Ribelli e riformatori dal XVI al XVIII secolo*, Editori Riuniti, Rome 1983, pp. 74–7, 96.
40. Mastellone, *Francesco d'Andrea*, pp. 76–88, 99–107.

REFEUDALIZATION?

The policies adopted by the various governments to curb feudal anarchy would seem to indicate that by the end of the century the feudal nobility had lost considerable ground as a semi-independent group that considered itself virtually above the law. This conclusion, however, runs counter to the notion of 'refeudalization' as a distinctive feature of Italian society in the seventeenth century – a notion that has achieved wide currency among Italian historians in the last thirty years or so. The term 'refeudalization' (or, more rarely, 'feudal restoration' or 'feudal offensive') has come into use to indicate 'the reappearance of a whole array of privileges, prerogatives, abuses, and shackles' in the countryside at the hands of the landed nobility with the result that 'peasant conditions experienced a slow, but continuous deterioration'. A further consequence, it has been claimed, was that a once dynamic economy driven by a progressive middle class was increasingly 'smothered' and underwent a 'process of involution' at the end of which the feudal nobility had secured a commanding position in both economic and social terms. Refeudalization has thus been presented as the key to the economic decline of Italy from the heights of the Renaissance to the doldrums of the Baroque age.[41]

As regards economic decline, we saw in the previous chapter that it can be accounted for with other and more plausible causes. We also saw that it affected the towns more than the countryside. In the latter (especially in the

41. The relevant historiography is reviewed in two articles in *Studi Storici Luigi Simeoni* 36 (1986): Giorgio Borelli, 'Alcuni problemi in tema di rifeudalizzazione', pp. 7–9 and Giovanni Muto, 'La feudalità meridionale tra crisi economica e ripresa politica', pp. 29–55. Early statements of the refeudalization thesis are in three essays by Ruggiero Romano: 'Tra XVI e XVII secolo. Una crisi economica: 1619–1622', *Rivista Storica Italiana* 74 (1962), p. 511; 'L'Italia nella crisi del secolo XVII', *Studi storici* 9 (1968), p. 736; and 'Una tipologia economica' in *SIE*, vol. 1 (1972), pp. 256–304; and in Rosario Villari, *The Revolt of Naples* (1967) transl. James Nowell with the assistance of John Marino, Polity Press 1993, pp. 101–22; Salvatore Romano, *Le classi sociali in Italia dal Medioevo all'età contemporanea*, Einaudi, Turin 1965, p. 29; Francesco Caracciolo, *Il Regno di Napoli nei secoli XVI e XVII. Economia e società*, Università degli Studi, Messina 1966, pp. 215–36; Emilio Sereni, 'Agricoltura e mondo rurale' in *SIE*, vol. 1 (1972), pp. 207–8. Reservations or criticisms have been expressed by Elena Fasano Guarini, 'Introduzione' to *Potere e società negli Stati regionali italiani fra Cinquecento e Seicento*, Mulino, Bologna 1978, p. 34; Domenico Sella, *Crisis and Continuity. The Economy of Spanish Lombardy in the Seventeenth Century*, Harvard University Press, Cambridge, Mass. 1979, pp. 148–73; in three articles in *Studi Storici Luigi Simeoni* 36 (1986): Giorgio Chittolini, 'Feudatari e comunità rurali nell'Italia centro-settentrionale (secoli XV–XVII)', p. 28; Salvatore Ciriacono, 'Industria rurale e strutture feudali nella Terraferma veneta fra Sei e Settecento', pp. 77–8; and Enrico Stumpo, 'A proposito di rifeudalizzazione: il caso del Piemonte', pp. 57–65. See also Stumpo, 'La crisi del Seicento' in *La Storia. I grandi problemi dal Medioevo all'Età contemporanea*, ed. Nicola Tranfaglia and Massimo Firpo, vol. 3, UTET, Turin 1987, pp. 329–34.

North) agriculture proved resilient and manufactures survived and even prospered during the seventeenth century. This would be a paradoxical outcome if refeudalization had indeed had such a stifling influence on the economy, for by definition feudal lords held sway in the countryside and it is there that their rule (or misrule) should have had its most crippling effects.

It is still conceivable that refeudalization, while not adversely affecting the economy as a whole, did result in an increasingly skewed and inequitable income distribution and in worsening economic conditions for the rural masses as they were being mercilessly exploited by a feudal nobility unrestrained by the law of the state. This is what the proponents of refeudalization have also argued. The evidence they have marshalled in support of their interpretation includes the proliferation of new feudal investitures; the enfeoffment of more and more rural communities which had previously been 'free from the feudal yoke'; the strenuous efforts mounted by many such communities to avoid being turned into fiefs by offering to pay, as the law allowed them to do under certain circumstances, a large ransom (known as the 'price of redemption') into the government's coffers; sundry instances of outrages perpetrated by feudal lords against their 'subjects'; and, lastly, outbreaks of peasant rebellion. Separately or in combination all these facts have been taken as evidence that feudalism enjoyed a new lease of life and that Italian rural society was forced back into a mould from which it had broken loose in the late Middle Ages when the rise and triumph of the city-states, the emergence of the bourgeoisie, the inroads of the market economy into the countryside had spelled the decline, if not the total disappearance, of the feudal system. But whether, in fact, one can speak of a resurgence of feudalism in the seventeenth century has been actively debated in the last twenty years or so. In the course of the debate new evidence has been brought out by the careful study of individual communities or regions and, not surprisingly, what has emerged is that conditions varied widely from one Italian state to the next and that, even within one same state, sweeping generalizations are risky. Moreover, it has become increasingly clear that superficially similar phenomena occurring in different parts of the peninsula can conceal quite different realities.

Consider the proliferation of feudal investitures, the creation, that is, of new counts, marquesses and dukes to each of whom the sovereign granted (in fact, sold) a fief, large or small, with (at least on paper) broad judicial powers and the right to impose certain fees and fines on the local people. This 'inflation of honours' occurred, as will be recalled, in several Italian states, but did not necessarily mean the same thing in each of them. In the Kingdom of Naples, for instance, fiefs often encompassed vast territories and brought with them broad judicial powers over the local peasantry;[42] in Piedmont-Savoy, by contrast, the sovereign accommodated the growing

---

42. Giuseppe Coniglio, *Il Viceregno di Napoli nel secolo XVII*, Edizioni di Storia e Letteratura, Rome 1955, pp. 71–3; Villari, *The Revolt of Naples*, pp. 5, 108; Muto, 'Il Regno di Napoli', pp. 265–6.

number of new feudatories by granting to each a fraction of a vacant fief, to the point that one same community might have several lords who took turns in exercising their newly found authority. In Piedmont, by the way, that authority amounted to very little: the right to administer justice was narrowly defined to cover only minor crimes and misdemeanours, all decisions handed down in a feudal court could be appealed in state courts, and the judge chosen by a feudal lord had to be approved by the Senate in Turin.[43] Nor was Piedmont's case unique: both in Spanish-ruled Milan and in the Grand Duchy of Tuscany feudal authority was similarly restricted in spite of the high-sounding formulas found in the investiture charter.[44] Wide regional variations have also emerged in the percentage of the population subject to feudal rule: a mere 4 per cent in Tuscany over against possibly 50 per cent in the Kingdom of Naples and the State of Milan. For the Papal States partial data present a very diverse picture: in the region closest to Rome between 35 and 60 per cent of the people lived on feudal land; in the Marches only 3 per cent and in Umbria 6 per cent.[45] Clearly, any generalization applicable to the entire peninsula is highly suspect.

And so is the view, which is at the heart of the refeudalization thesis, that feudal power increased (whether legally or not so legally) in the course of the century and that rural communities were prepared to make painful financial sacrifices to remain free. Here again the record is mixed. Superficially similar actions conceal different realities and in some instances what sounds like the voice of the oppressed turns out, on closer scrutiny, to be something altogether different.

For the Kingdom of Naples there is abundant evidence of growing peasant exploitation at the hands of the baronage: higher and higher rents, the introduction of new manorial obligations or the resumption of old ones, the resort to coercion or intimidation to force peasants to work the land on terms unilaterally laid down by their masters. There is also evidence of rural communities and small towns struggling to put together the large ransom needed to acquire or retain their freedom or even rioting to fend off a dreaded enfeoffment.[46] But recent research has also revealed instances of an opposite reaction to the issue of 'redemption' from feudal rule: in 1635, in a number of villages in the vicinity of Naples peasants expressed their opposition 'to removing themselves from the baron's power' and to return under the direct authority of the crown on grounds that this would be too costly ('these poor petitioners cannot afford new burdens'); they also argued

43. Stumpo, *Finanza e Stato moderno*, pp. 290–4.
44. Sella, *Crisis and Continuity*, pp. 164–9; Diaz, *Il Granducato di Toscana*, pp. 342–4; and Litchfield, *Emergence of a Bureaucracy*, pp. 7, 35, 118.
45. Chittolini, 'Feudatari e comunita', pp. 17–18; Caracciolo, *Il Regno di Napoli*, p. 107; Bandino Giacomo Zenobi, *Tarda feudalitàa e reclutamento delle elites nello Stato pontificio (secoli XV–XVIII)*, Università degli Studi, Urbino 1983, pp. 10–11; Giuseppe Pansini, 'Per una storia del feudalesimo nel Granducato di Toscana durante il periodo mediceo', *QS* 19 (1972), pp. 183–5.
46. Caracciolo, *Il Regno di Napoli*, pp. 212–18.

that 'at present they consider themselves well treated and protected by their baron who, with so much charity and affection, loves them as his own children'. This last statement sounds a bit melodramatic and smacks of adulation. And yet, that same peasant petition contains a revealing bit of information that gives it credence: the initiative to free the village from feudal rule is said to have originated with 'a few individuals who want to lord it over the poor' and not with the majority of the villagers; and these 'few individuals' turn out to have been *maggiorenti*, that is to say men of property who had everything to gain were the community to rid itself of the presence of a nobleman who outranked them and might limit their own power over the rest of the villagers.[47] Other instances of a rural community splitting over the issue of enfeoffment, with the poor supporting it and the better off opposing it, have been documented for other parts of Italy as well. In 1643 a legal battle broke out between the town of Chieri in Piedmont and the feudal lords of the large village of Santena nearby: Chieri claimed that Santena ought to fall under its own jurisdiction and contribute its share of taxes to the town rather than enjoying separate fiscal status as part of a fief. Interestingly, twenty farmers with some property in Santena sided with Chieri, while tenants and day labourers supported the feudal lords' position.[48]

Such a split within the village community illustrates the danger of portraying rural society as an undifferentiated mass of downtrodden peasants labouring under the harsh rule of the nobility. It also raises the question of why the lowest layers of the peasantry would want to remain under that rule. Was it because of pressure or intimidation exerted by their masters? This is possible, but evidence from the State of Milan suggests another alternative. A study of twenty-five cases in which villages were faced with the choice between enfeoffment and 'redemption' has revealed a fairly constant pattern: opposition to enfeoffment did not come from the peasantry, but from local non-noble landowners; on their part, the peasants, when asked for their opinion, expressed either indifference to, mild satisfaction with, or outright support for the prospect of their community either remaining under feudal rule or being turned into a fief; in no case did they oppose enfeoffment. Such an attitude on the part of the peasantry would be paradoxical if feudal rule invariably meant unchecked exploitation and oppression. But, in fact, in the State of Milan the feudal lords' authority was narrowly circumscribed and their conduct closely monitored by the Senate and, when it came to taxes and other obligations, enfeoffment hardly introduced any change in the life of a village, except that now tax revenue accrued to the feudatory rather than to the royal treasury. Redemption from feudal rule, on the other hand, always implied the payment of a ransom, and to put the hefty sum together new

47. Muto, 'Il Regno di Napoli', p. 315. Caracciolo, *Il Regno di Napoli*, p. 351, too, stresses the fact that local landowners were often the most vocal opponents of feudal rule, and so does Coniglio, *Il Viceregno di Napoli*, pp. 27, 152.
48. Giovanni Levi, *Inheriting Power: The Story of an Exorcist*, transl. Lydia Cochrane, University of Chicago Press 1988, pp. 103–7.

levies would have to be imposed on the village. This would explain in part the reluctance expressed by some villagers when asked how they felt about freeing themselves from feudal rule. But another reason may have been on their minds when they expressed outright support for feudal rule as did the Neapolitan peasants quoted above. Lombard peasants occasionally provide a clue to what they had in mind, for some of them asserted that a feudal lord would 'dispense generous alms' or, more frequently, 'give them protection'. The last point is worth noticing, for it sheds some light on one aspect of feudalism that has been generally neglected in favour of other, less palatable features, such as arrogance and coercion, namely the bonds of reciprocity that could be established between a loyal peasantry and a benevolent, paternalistic lord. What those bonds actually were is not always easy to know, but we catch glimpses of them in those few instances where our sources are more explicit than in most. The feudal lord of Melzo near Milan, for instance, was mourned at his death in 1678 because, it was said, 'he has assisted the community in every possible way, notably by securing for it exemption from the excise'. Twenty years earlier the small town of Gallarate had welcomed the prospect of being enfeoffed to the Marquess Visconti di Cislago, because from him 'we can expect constant favours, protection and assistance in the matter of military billets'.[49] In the large fief of Ariccia in the Papal States, on the other hand, the lord won a measure of gratitude from his subjects because he closely monitored the proceedings of the feudal court and frequently reduced its sentences. And similar instances have been documented for the Kingdom of Naples.[50]

To be sure, not all rural communities were as lucky as the ones just mentioned and quite a few feudatories are on record as flagrantly abusing their power, not only in the South where noble misconduct seems to have been especially common, but in the North as well, notably in the Venetian province of Verona where the feudal nobility was firmly entrenched and apparently rode roughshod over the peasantry,[51] or in the fiefs ensconced in the Apennine mountains north of Genoa where the feudal lords ruthlessly used their police and judicial powers to squeeze their tenants and were so much feared that, as one man put it, 'nobody dares to quarrel with our lord the Count, for he is so powerful that he can ruin anyone in no time'.[52]

49. Sella, *Crisis and Continuity*, pp. 155–64; also Cristina Stefanini, 'Fiscalità e tensione sociale in una comunità lombarda del Seicento', *Studi bresciani* 12 (1983), pp. 7–31.
50. Angela Maria Girelli, 'Il problema della feudalità nel Lazio tra XVII e XVIII secolo', *Studi Storici Luigi Simeoni* 36 (1986), pp. 117–18. Likewise in some fiefs near Parma: Maria Teresa Bobbioni, 'Conflittualità e amministrazione della giustizia in un feudo padano tra la fine del '500 e il primo trentennio del '600' in *Persistenze feudali*, ed. Giovanni Tocci, CLUEB, Bologna 1988, pp. 151–66. For the Kindom of Naples, see Caracciolo, *Il Regno di Napoli*, pp. 130–1.
51. Vecchiato, *Una signoria rurale*.
52. Giorgio Doria, *Uomini e terre di un borgo collinare dal XVI al XVIII secolo*, Giuffrè, Milan 1968, pp. 265–86. Quotation in Sella, *Crisis and Continuity*, p. 166.

Not everywhere were rural folks so intimidated and defenceless. In 1576, when the lord of Anguillara in the Papal States arbitrarily raised by 30 per cent the rent in kind on all peasant land within his fief, the community loudly protested and forced him to rescind his decision.[53] In Venetian territory, too, some rural communities could raise their voices against feudal abuse and be heard. Mel was one such community: in 1654 riots broke out when the feudatory, Count Zorzi, announced that he would sharply limit the authority of the elected village council especially in matters pertaining to the use of the surrounding woods by the villagers, in spite of the fact that these had always been considered common property and that the right to cut timber in them had traditionally been assigned to individuals by the village council. As Count Zorzi would not back down Mel appealed to Venice for redress, and won. It is worth noticing that here too the count's most active opponents were not the landless peasants, but the small owners (a group comprising about half the population and controlling half the land) who feared that the count wanted to exclude them from the profitable · timber business.[54] A confrontation of a more serious nature and with more serious consequences for the feudatory occurred in another village of the Venetian mainland, Valmareno, in 1670: accused by his peasant 'subjects' of trying to revive obsolete and onerous manorial obligations and of using intimidation and even violence to stop them from suing him in a Venetian court of law, the lord of Valmareno, Guido Brandolini, was eventually tried before the dreaded Council of Ten, found guilty, heavily fined and, for good measure, banished from his lands for ten years. The sentence, one might add, proved salutary, for after his return in 1681 and until his death twelve years later Brandolini proved himself a model administrator and a dynamic, progressive landowner.[55]

In light of the evidence now available the notion that from the late sixteenth century Italian society as a whole was forced into the straitjacket of a resurgent feudalism can no longer be maintained. What can be said with a degree of confidence is, first of all, that in the South feudalism was a major and pervasive aspect of society in the seventeenth century and that the demands placed on the peasantry by the landed nobility grew heavier, at least in the first half of the century. Whether this worsening of peasant conditions justifies the use of the term 'refeudalization' is, however, open to question, for, as Giuseppe Galasso has pointed out, the term itself assumes that feudalism had largely receded from southern society before the sixteenth century and was then reintroduced – an assumption that is clearly unfounded for the Kingdom of Naples where feudal institutions had never ceased to exist

53. Girelli, 'Il problema della feudalità', pp. 129–30.
54. Nerina Ranon, 'La comunità di Mel nel Seicento. Fra rivendicazione signorile e conflitto interno', *Studi veneziani* NS 20 (1990), pp. 87–131.
55. Danilo Gasparini, 'Signori e contadini nella contea di Valmareno, secoli XVI–XVII' in *Stato, società e giustizia nella Repubblica veneta*, ed. Gaetano Cozzi, Jouvence, Rome 1985, vol. 2, pp. 174–87.

and thrive.[56] The second point that can be made is that in central and north Italy the proliferation of feudal investitures is no proof of a revival, let alone a strengthening, of the feudal system; rather, it reflects the governments' needs for additional revenue and their ability to do so by exploiting the vanity of social upstarts who were anxious to enhance the prestige of their families with a high-sounding but largely hollow title and were willing to pay for it with their newly acquired wealth.[57]

THE MIDDLING ORDER

One notch below the aristocracy stood a social group variously known as *cittadini* (citizens) in Venice, *popolo* or *ceto civile* in Naples, *popolo grosso* (people of substance) in Genoa and sometimes referred to as 'those of the middling sort' (*quelli della sorte mediocre*). It was a group whose members often could equal or even surpass their social superiors in wealth and yet one that was separated from the aristocracy by a wide social and cultural gap. We saw earlier how alarmed, indeed outraged, the Bergamasque nobility had been when the son of a rich merchant had been admitted to the exclusive boarding school their children attended. Their reaction is not surprising in a society of orders where differences in rank and 'honour' were all important, but one is also inclined to suspect that the Bergamasque nobles at the time felt threatened by (and therefore wanted more than ever to keep their distance from) social inferiors who, as our sources attest, were often much better off than they were.

In Italy the middling order was a mixed group. In Naples, for instance, it was understood to include, according to a mid-century source, 'three sorts of people: those who enjoy an independent income; those who work in the courts of law; and merchants and craftsmen who are especially esteemed' such as goldsmiths, printers, physicians, architects, but also secretaries and butlers.[58] Much the same could be said for other parts of Italy, although in each the relative importance of specific professions or trades varied, reflecting different economic, social and political conditions. In a provincial town such as Bergamo, located as it was at the centre of a rich manufacturing region, merchants held a prominent position next to the nobility,[59] as they also did in cities like Milan or Genoa. In Piedmont and in the South where agriculture was the mainstay of the economy, the merchant class did not loom as large;

---

56. Giuseppe Galasso, 'La feudalità napoletana nel secolo XVI' in *Potere e società*, pp. 254–5; Guido Quazza, *La decadenza italiana nella storia europea. Saggi sul Sei-Settecento*, Einaudi, Turin 1971, pp. 70–1.

57. See ch. 2, p. 27n above.

58. Quotation in Claudia Petraccone, 'Fonti e prime ricerche sui mestieri a Napoli alla vigilia della rivolta antispagnola', *QS* 26 (1974), p. 504.

59. *Relazioni dei Rettori veneti in Terraferma*, vol. 12, *Podestaria e Capitanato di Bergamo*, ed. B. Polese, Giuffrè, Milan 1978, pp. 28, 345.

rather, it was government service that offered the best opportunities for social advancement to ambitious commoners willing to serve as magistrates, tax farmers, or customs inspectors. In the first half of the century the dukes of Savoy employed in high-level positions ten times as many commoners as noblemen, for, as a contemporary put it, 'individuals of low birth are totally devoted to the sovereign's will, whereas noblemen and the wealthy have the means for resisting it and can raise obstacles to his supreme commands'.[60] The same reliance on the middling order as a nursery of bureaucrats held, on a grander scale, in the Kingdom of Naples where positions in the central administration came to be increasingly filled by commoners, much to the chagrin of the Neapolitan patriciate (nobilta' di seggio) who felt excluded from the responsibilities and the rewards of office. From the mid-sixteenth century lawyers, in particular, rose to such prominence in all departments of the royal administration as to be accused of being 'absolute masters' of the realm. In the process they developed a strong sense of corporate identity as 'men of the robe' (togati) clearly distinct from both the nobility and the ceto civile (merchants, tax farmers, and professionals) from which they had emerged.[61] Their rise to high office and their ubiquitous presence in all government agencies generated jealousy, but also respect. By the end of the century, we are told, even the nobility 'treated them with the highest respect and invited them not only to ride in their carriages but into their homes as well'.[62] As for the togati themselves, their sense of identity and pride was well expressed by one of the most distinguished and successful members of the profession, Francesco D'Andrea, when he wrote, possibly with a touch of hyperbole: 'Having travelled through various parts of Italy and observed the people and the customs of other cities, I dare say that there is no city in the world where merit is more recognized and where a man who has no other asset than his own worth can rise to high office and great wealth ... without having to depend on either birth or money to get there ... '.[63]

It is no mere coincidence that the rise of commoners to high office through the legal profession occurred especially in the Duchy of Savoy and the Kingdom of Naples, in states, that is, where the tradition of municipal autonomy going back to the medieval city-states was weaker than in the State of Milan or in Tuscany and where, as a consequence, the urban patriciate was less prominent as an elite with long administrative experience. In its absence the government had little choice but to create such an elite from scratch as it

---

60. Stumpo, Finanza e Stato, pp. 162–3, 214, 231, 270.
61. In addition to the classic work by Comparato, Uffici e società a Napoli, now see Roberto Mantelli, Il pubblico impiego nell'economia del Regno di Napoli: retribuzioni, reclutamento e ricambio sociale nell'epoca spagnola (secoli XVI–XVII), Istituto italiani per gli Studi filosofici, Naples 1986, pp. 315–16, 320, 328; Muto, 'Il Regno di Napoli', p. 308.
62. Quotation in Pasquale Lopez, Riforma cattolica e vita religiosa e culturale a Napoli dalla fine del Cinquecento ai primi anni del Settecento, Istituto Editoriale del Mezzogiorno, Naples and Rome 1964, p. 201.
63. Quotation in Muto, 'Il Regno di Napoli', p. 248.

were, and this could be done only by recruiting future bureaucrats from the top layers of the middling order. The old nobility had neither the expertise nor the inclination to assume the burden of running the law courts, monitoring the food supply or collecting taxes: such mundane tasks they probably regarded as below their dignity and as basically unattractive – all the more so as in a century studded with wars military commands still offered to them, as they did not to commoners, more desirable outlets for their ambition.

Historians have long debated whether or not the rise of individuals of 'the middling sort' to high positions in the central administration and the legal system of the Kingdom of Naples represented the emergence of a new progressive social force capable of challenging the basic structure and the values of a society in which feudal power and the aristocratic ethos continued to loom large. Historians have also wondered whether the men of the robe were able to articulate a different, one is tempted to say bourgeois, ideology based on the abolition of privilege, equality of all before the law, the suppression of baronial anarchy and of all barriers that stood in the way of social mobility, freedom of expression and freedom of trade.[64] After much debate the answer seems to be that, while the new elite and their kin and allies in the middling order were able, toward the end of the century, to formulate new ideas of reform and, for a time, found in the Marquess Del Carpio (1683–87) a viceroy willing to implement them, in the end not much changed and the existing regime remained pretty much intact. The men of the robe have been blamed for that and with some justification, because, for all their interest in reform, they were still mesmerized by the prestige and the trappings of the aristocracy and indeed many of them, as soon as they could afford to do so, purchased a fief and joined ranks of the feudal nobility, thus 'betraying' their historical mission as heralds of reform.[65] The charge of betrayal, however, is only partly warranted. For one thing, we ought to remember that throughout Europe noble rank was still a virtually irresistible magnet for upwardly mobile commoners: in this respect Neapolitan magistrates and government officials were no exception.[66] For another thing, and perhaps more importantly, it is unrealistic and anachronistic to imagine that in the seventeenth century any group, no matter how enlightened and determined, could radically transform the existing regime without the full support of the government – and Spanish authorities, a few remarkable viceroys excepted, were unlikely to promote any sweeping programme of reform that might have caused unrest, dislocations and strife in their Italian dominions.

---

64. Quazza, *La decadenza italiana*, pp. 80–2. On the ideology of the *ceto civile* see also Mastellone, *Francesco d'Andrea*, pp. 121–3, 147.
65. Mastellone, *Francesco d'Andrea*, pp. 137, 139, 157, 181, and Mozzarelli, 'Strutture sociali e formazioni statuali', p. 456.
66. Muto, 'Il regno di Napoli', pp. 256–7. A similar process was at work in Piedmont (Stumpo, *Finanza e Stato*, pp. 109–11) and in Europe (Henry Kamen, *The Iron Century. Social Change in Europe 1550–1650*, Praeger, New York 1972, ch. 5).

In those Italian states where the urban patriciate had long been and continued to be deeply involved in administration and the judiciary there was less need and less room for members of the middling order. The Grand Duchy of Tuscany is a case in point. There, as elsewhere in Italy, in the sixteenth and seventeenth centuries the growth of the centralizing, bureaucratic state meant the replacement of the old system of government typical of the medieval city-state, based on the rotation of offices among patricians chosen by election, with a system that depended on permanent office-holders appointed by the grand duke himself. In the new system commoners were eligible for and were often appointed to office, yet over two centuries patricians, despite their relatively small numbers, secured about half of all important positions in the administration, transforming themselves in the process from a municipal and highly independent oligarchy into a loyal service nobility.[67]

In Venice the needs of the early modern state were met in a different way. There, as will be recalled, it was never a question of creating a new administrative elite as in Piedmont-Savoy or Naples, not even after the conquest of the Terraferma had made the machinery of government more extensive and complex: all key posts, whether in Venice itself or in its dominions, continued to be filled by patricians on a rotating basis. This would have presented serious problems of continuity in policy-making had not the Republic called upon the second order of society (the *cittadini*) to provide a more permanent, if subordinate, administrative apparatus. At this point it is well to recall that the *cittadini* of Venice, although by no means a closed hereditary caste like the patriciate, still formed a clearly defined and privileged status group or rather a three-layered group representing about one-tenth of the city's population.[68] At the bottom were the *cittadini de intus*, individuals who had settled in the city for at least fifteen years and had achieved a certain level of affluence in trade or the liberal professions. Their main privilege was that of being allowed to engage in trade and manufacturing in Venice itself. Next came the citizens *de intus et de extra* who, on account of a longer residence in the city, were entitled to engage in trade with foreign countries. Finally, those individuals whose fathers and grandfathers had enjoyed the status of citizens could ask to be recognized as *cittadini originari*; as such, they enjoyed two additional privileges, that of filling key positions in the large charitable institutions of the city known as *Scuole grandi* and, more importantly, that of serving as 'secretaries' in all major government departments, from the Senate to the Council of Ten to embassies abroad. The top layer of the citizenry thus represented an influential elite in Venetian society, one notch below the patriciate. Not only did the management of the *Scuole grandi*, with their huge endowment and a membership that ran into the thousands, raise them to the level of major civic figures; their long-term

67. Litchfield, *Emergence of a Bureaucracy*, especially Part II.
68. Daniele Beltrami, *Storia della popolazione di Venezia dalla fine del secolo XVI alla caduta della Repubblica*, Cedam, Padua 1954, p. 72.

appointment to some 500 secretarial positions in various departments meant that, unlike their rotating patrician superiors, they acquired a unique knowledge of the ins and outs of government and could quietly influence the decision-making process.[69] 'They hold all secretarial positions in their hands', wrote Giovanni Botero, the political theorist, in 1605, 'so that by attending committee meetings and accompanying ambassadors [on their mission] they take part in all the secrets and deliberations of the Republic' and 'seeing themselves so close to the gentlemen and so similar to their lords, they feel they are participants in both government and liberty'; and he concluded by saying that, 'being satisfied and contented, they do not worry about anything else'.[70] The last comment deserves attention, for here Botero echoes a view commonly held at the time, namely that by dangling before the middling order the prospect of social advancement and by entrusting to its upper layer considerable, if subordinate, civic and governmental responsibilities, Venice managed to preserve the social peace within and to safeguard its 'liberty' vis-à-vis the outside world. And its legendary stability and liberty may have been strengthened from the 1640s onwards as the Republic, faced with mounting military expenditures, relaxed the rigid rule that allowed only cittadini originari to have access to government jobs and offered a plethora of lesser offices for sale to other members of the middling order and even to members of the popolo.[71]

Towns in the Venetian Terraferma were less liberal than the capital when it came to integrating the lower orders into the machinery of government and were thus the stage of frictions and even open conflict. In Verona, a town where the old nobility had a firm grip on municipal administration, it was reported in the 1570s that 'there is great hatred ... between merchants and noblemen. The people sides with merchants [and] the cause of the quarrel is ... that the merchants have been excluded from the government.' And again ten years later: 'there is resentment over the fact that judicial affairs are in the hands of the nobility without anybody else's participation'.[72] In Brescia the quarrel was between the patrician oligarchy and a group of over seventy

69. On the cittadini see Brian Pullan, *Rich and Poor in Renaissance Venice. The Social Institutions of a Catholic State to 1620*, Harvard University Press, Cambridge, Mass. 1971, pp. 99–113; Andrea Zannini, 'Un ceto di funzionari amministrativi: i cittadini originari veneziani, 1569–1730', *Studi veneziani* NS 23 (1992), pp. 1312–45; and Giuseppe Trebbi, 'La società veneziana' in *Storia di Venezia*, vol. 6: *Dal Rinascimento al Barocco*, ed. Gaetano Cozzi and Paolo Prodi, Istituto della Enciclopedia Italiana, Rome 1994, pp. 163–82.

70. Quotation in Donati, *L'idea di nobiltà*, p. 202. A similar admiring assessment of the role of the cittadini was expressed by a papal nuncio in 1581: see Aldo Stella, *Chiesa e Stato nelle relazioni dei nunzi pontifici a Venezia. Ricerche sul giurisdizionalismo veneziano dal XVI al XVIII secolo*, Biblioteca Apostolica Vaticana, Vatican City 1964, pp. 167–8, 174.

71. Zannini, 'Un ceto di funzionari', p. 141.

72. Biblioteca Marciana, Venice, *Cod.ital VII*, 1187, 'Memorie e osservazioni sullo stato della Signoria di Venezia in Terraferma', pp. 14, 23.

well-to-do lawyers, physicians and merchants. Since the late fifteenth century the patriciate had managed, through strict eligibility requirements (no practice of 'mechanical arts' for three generations) and the cooptation of new members from a small pool of friends and kin, to control the common council; this gave them a free hand in the assessment of taxes, in the sale of public land, in managing the municipal debt and (it was alleged) in lining their pockets in the process. The resentment of those excluded was exacerbated in the 1640s by increasing taxation and by the economic depression then sweeping the entire peninsula; a climax was reached in 1644 in what a contemporary source called 'the revolution of the seditious discontents against the nobility and council of Brescia'. 'This', its most recent historian has written, 'was not simply an anti-tax protest . . . nor was it a revolt of the have-nots against the haves: no significant difference in economic circumstances existed between them and the ruling oligarchy as both belonged to the top 10 per cent of the tax rolls'. Rather it was a confrontation of two status groups as the excluded one demanded to gain membership in the city council, to have a say in city government, and to achieve a measure of prestige commensurate to its economic standing. As a 'seditious revolution', one might add, it was a rather tame affair involving as it did a good deal of recriminations and influence peddling as well as drafting a formal petition to the Venetian authorities asking them to redress the injustice of oligarchic rule. A petition signed by seventy-two prominent citizens, however, was sufficiently alarming for Venice to intervene and order the city council to open its ranks to the petitioners – only to reverse itself a year later after the oligarchs successfully lobbied for a return to the status quo.[73]

Things got more serious in Genoa. Although similar to Venice in many respects, notably in the fact that its prosperity (and that of its ruling oligarchy) had been built on trade and shipping, Genoa unlike its rival had failed to develop a solid and finely balanced institutional framework in which political power ultimately belonged to a closed hereditary elite, but in which some limited outlets had been provided for the middling order of the *cittadini*. In Genoa the ruling elite had been much more fluid and unstable until the coup of 1528 when the oldest and wealthiest families (Doria, Spinola, Grimaldi, Fieschi) had taken the lead in establishing an oligarchic form of government, while at the same time leaving the door ajar for ten wealthy families of the middling order (*popolo grasso*) to be admitted to noble rank every year. The new dispensation, as will be recalled, had produced more resentment than harmony as the nobility refused to share power with the newcomers and made it difficult for other non-nobles to join. In 1575 civil war broke out between rival factions, with the 'new nobles' gaining the upper hand and driving the old guard out of the city. Only the mediation of the Papacy and of Spain had succeeded in reconciling the two sides on the basis of a

73. Joanne Ferraro, 'Oligarchs, Protesters and the Republic of Venice: the "Revolution of the Discontents" in Brescia, 1644–45', *Journal of Modern History* 60 (1988), pp. 627–53.

compromise that sanctioned the full equality of nobles old and new, while retaining the provision that ten *popolo* families would be admitted to the patriciate every year. On this basis calm prevailed for the next half century (a time of great prosperity for Genoa), but tensions persisted under the surface, all the more so as the patriciate adopted stricter and stricter criteria for the admissions of new members and, by declaring that the professions of lawyer, notary, physician, broker and money-changer were, just like manual trades, incompatible with noble status, managed to prevent the admission of new men to the inner sanctum of government. In 1628, taking advantage of the disarray created in the financial market by the recent Spanish bankruptcy as well as by an invading Savoyard army, a conspiracy headed by Giulio Cesare Vachero was organized with the covert support of the duke of Savoy, its aim being the physical destruction of the ruling nobility and the overturning of the existing form of oligarchic government in favour of one dominated by well-to-do commoners. Uncovered in time, the conspiracy was nipped in the bud, four of its leaders were executed (in spite of the duke of Savoy's intercession on their behalf) and the patrician regime emerged stronger and more exclusive than ever, not to be seriously challenged for the rest of the century.[74]

THE PLEBS

When early modern writers addressed the subject of the people who did not belong either to the nobility or to the middling order, they did so only briefly, lumping together what probably represented 80 per cent of the population under the label of 'plebs' and often referring contemptuously to that large human mass as 'the dregs of the commonwealth'.[75] If they took the trouble of acknowledging in passing that society needed artisans, journeymen, day labourers, and domestic servants for its survival and wellbeing, they did not recognize them as true members of the commonwealth, as true citizens, but took it for granted that they were merely 'servants' who, being propertyless, had no stake in society and should not, therefore, have any political role whatsoever: as a contemporary source bluntly put it, 'it is not fitting that those who have no land should make laws for those who do'.[76] On their part, historians in the past have paid scant attention to the lowest layers of society and, while eschewing contempt or condescension toward them, they too have tended to dismiss them as a large undifferentiated mass that played but a passive and silent role in history except on the rare occasions when they rose

74. Costantini, *La Repubblica di Genova*, pp. 101–22, 245–66.
75. On the contempt for and fear of the plebs, see Comparato, *Uffici e società a Napoli*, pp. 408–12 and Gino Benzoni, *Gli affanni della cultura. Intellettuali e potere nell'Italia della Controriforma e barocca*, Feltrinelli, Milan 1978, pp. 121–3.
76. Quotation in Cristina Stefanini, 'Fiscalità e tensione sociale in una comunità lombarda del Seicento: il caso di Maleo', *Studi bresciani* 4 (1983), p. 18.

in armed rebellion and tried, mostly in vain, to overturn the power structure which excluded and oppressed them. Only in recent years has the historians' attention been trained on the plebs and, not surprisingly, has found it far more differentiated, far less passive and, one might add, far more interesting than had been generally assumed in the past.

In the countryside the oversimplified picture of a society consisting of a few powerful landed nobles on one side and of an exploited peasantry on the other has given way to one that is more complex. More often than not below the nobility stood a thin layer of middling farmers who owned some land, a sort of rural bourgeoisie sometimes referred to in the sources as *maggiori estimati* (literally, 'more highly assessed'), followed by numerous small owners and a few large tenants who owned, if not land, at least draught animals and farm implements, and by a handful of shopkeepers, craftsmen and an occasional notary or schoolteacher. At the bottom were the landless peasants who eked out a precarious living working for wages as day labourers (*braccianti*) on somebody else's land. The study of rural society has also revealed that villages were not mere clusters of peasant families passively enduring the rule of the landlords, but rather communities in which an assembly of heads of family elected officers to discharge such tasks as the assessment of taxes, the upkeep of roads, the apprehension of criminals; an assembly also that served as a forum where the villagers' views could be aired and, within narrow limits, collective action could be taken to uphold the customary rights of the community through legal channels.[77]

It has been said that in early modern Italy the law represented for the lower classes 'an inaccessible language', that it meant only 'expropriation . . . by individuals belonging to the higher classes'.[78] In actual fact, rural communities seem to have known fairly well what the law said and what it could do for them. The village of Suno in Piedmont, for one, fought a legal battle that stretched for nearly a century against the local marquess over the issue of whether or not a newly introduced crop (maize) ought to be subject to a feudal levy like traditional crops. The villagers' perseverance paid off in the end, for in 1676 the courts found in favour of the village.[79] At about the same time the villagers of Anguillara near Rome sued their feudal lord before the high papal court, the Sacra Rota, to defend their right to graze cattle on the stubble, and won.[80] At mid-century, as will be recalled, the community of

77. Examples in Carlo Ginzburg, *The Cheese and the Worms. The Cosmos of a Sixteenth-Century Miller*, transl. John and Ann Tedeschi, Penguin 1982, pp. 14–15; Stefanini, 'Fiscalita e tensione sociale', pp. 14–18; Gasparini, 'Signori e contadini nella contea di Valmareno', pp. 165, 169; Ranon, 'La comunità di Mel', pp. 87–131; Faccini, *La Lombardia*, pp. 134–5, 179, 224; and Annibale Zambarbieri, *La traccia dell'uomo. Maleo: il fiume, il prato, la comunità*, Cassa rurale e artigiana del Basso Lodigiano, Meleto 1986, pp. 284–7.
78. Ambrosini, 'Diritto e societa', p. 308.
79. Giovanni Levi, 'Innovazione tecnica e resistenza contadina: il mais nel Piemonte del Seicento', *QS* 42 (1979), pp. 1095–6.
80. Girelli, 'Il problema della feudalità', p. 130.

Mel appealed to Venetian authorities against the feudatory's attempt to limit their right to assemble and to have a say about the assessment of taxes, and scored a victory. And so did the village of Illasi mentioned earlier. What is striking in these and similar instances,[81] it has been noted, is 'the knowledge and the experience rural communities had of judicial procedures and their ability to shoulder substantial [legal] costs' in defence of their rights.[82]

In the towns the plebs did not form an undifferentiated and hopelessly passive mass either. One kind of distinction was based on privilege, whether legal or *de facto*, in the sense that small groups of artisans organized in guilds managed to assert their sole right to a certain type of work and to restrict access to their guild, thus making it virtually impossible for any non-member to open his or her workshop. A vivid example of this practice and of the ensuing cleavage within the workforce between a labour elite and a disenfranchised mass of dependent wage earners is provided in a 1615 petition submitted to Venetian authorities by the journeymen who worked for the local cloth shearers (*cimadori*) against their employers. The petition accused them of barring even the oldest and most experienced journeymen from joining the guild as full-fledged masters; in this way, it was alleged, a small clique kept under its thumb a large and low-paid workforce, while at the same time enhancing its bargaining power *vis-à-vis* the drapers who had unfinished cloth to shear and had no choice but to turn to the shearers' guild.[83] A somewhat similar situation held in the Milan construction industry. In theory, to be a mason or stonecutter one had first to serve an apprenticeship of several years before being admitted to the rank of master in the guild; as a master of his craft he was then considered a small independent contractor entitled to hire his own journeymen and apprentices and to deal directly with clients. In practice, things were different: above the mass of master masons (several hundred of them in a city of about 100,000 souls) stood a dozen 'headmasters' (*capomaestri*) who ran the affairs of the guild and acted as building contractors *vis-à-vis* their clients, recruiting as many masters and journeymen as were needed for a specific construction job. As a result, the construction industry had a three-layered structure *de facto* dominated by a few contractors.[84]

Even in the absence of guilds sharp divisions could develop on the basis of skill and specialization, thus imparting a hierarchical structure to the workplace.[85] In the blast furnaces along the coast of Tuscany where the iron

81. As, for instance, in the State of Milan: Faccini, *La Lombardia*, pp. 130–1, 140.
82. Gasparini, 'Signori e contadini', p. 188.
83. Brian Pullan, 'Poveri, mendicanti e vagabondi (secoli XIV–XVII)' in *SIE Annali 1* (1978), p. 1032. A similar polarization has been documented for the Lucca silk industry in Marino Berengo, *Nobili e mercanti nella Lucca del Cinquecento*, Einaudi, Turin 1965, p. 256.
84. Domenico Sella, *Salari e lavoro nell'edilizia lombarda durante il secolo XVII*, Fusi, Pavia 1968, pp. 32–44.
85. The point is discussed by Stuart Woolf, 'Order, Class and the Urban Poor' in *Social Orders and Social Classes in Europe since 1500*, pp. 188–94.

ore from Elba was processed, an iron master was in charge of both recruiting his own workers and supervising the smelting process, and he was paid four times as much as the men, some of them highly skilled, who worked under him. Further downstream, in the forges and rolling mills where pig iron was turned into sundry iron articles, one finds a stratification of forge masters, journeymen, charcoal makers and carters each paid at different rates.[86] A rather complex labour hierarchy characterized other industries too, such as textiles and papermaking,[87] but nowhere was it as complex as in ship-building, if we are to judge from the Venetian Arsenal, the huge state-owned shipyard employing 1,000–2,000 workers. There a number of government-appointed officials, mainly drawn from the order of the *cittadini,* were in charge of the overall management of the facility and were responsible for assigning work to gangs or teams of craftsmen (shipwrights, caulkers, oarmakers, sawyers); but the teams themselves worked under the direction of foremen, known as *capi d'opera,* who, in addition to monitoring the actual execution of a given phase of construction, also had broad discretion in selecting, hiring, and firing the workers under their command. Needless to say, those foremen represented a kind of labour aristocracy and earned substantially more than the rest of the workers.[88] Xenophobia could, then as now, create further divisions among workers – witness Mantua where the local wine porters' and shoemakers' guilds fought a running (and ultimately, it would seem, unsuccessful) battle against seasonal immigrants from the Alpine valleys who spent winters in the city and challenged the guilds' supposed monopoly by offering to work for less.[89]

With the exception of the upper stratum of *capomaestri* and *capi d'opera,* seventeenth-century workers had one thing in common, albeit in varying degrees, and that was their grinding poverty. If employed fairly regularly, a master mason with a wife and two young children had to earmark a good 30 per cent of his annual earnings just to buy bread – a clear indication of wretched living standards. For a journeyman whose rate of pay was nearly half that of a master, feeding a family would seem to have been virtually impossible. Admittedly, wages earned on the construction site did not necessarily represent the entire family income as wives more often than not

86. Roberta Morelli, 'Men of Iron: Masters of the Iron Industry in Sixteenth-Century Tuscany' in *The Workplace Before the Factory. Artisans and Proletarians 1500–1800,* ed. Thomas M. Safely and Leonard N. Rosenband, Cornell University Press, Ithaca 1993, pp. 153–6.
87. On the textile industry see Stefano D'Amico, *Le contrade e la città. Sistema produttivo e spazio urbano a Milano fra Cinque e Seicento,* Franco Angeli, Milan 1994, pp. 101–32; on the paper industry, Manlio Calegari, *La manifattura genovese della carta (secoli XVI–XVIII),* ECIG, Genoa 1986, ch. 5.
88. Robert C. Davis, *Shipbuilders of the Venetian Arsenal. Workers and the Workplace in the Preindustrial City,* Johns Hopkins University Press, Baltimore 1991, pp. 55, 59–60.
89. Carlo Marco Belfanti, 'Le corporazioni e i forestieri (Mantova, secoli XVII–XVIII)', *Studi Storici Luigi Simeoni* 41 (1991), pp. 85–102.

worked as domestic servants or at the spinning wheel, while children could bring home a few pennies working at casual jobs. Still, one cannot escape the conclusion that most of the 'plebs' lived close to sheer subsistence. And in the event of prolonged unemployment or of a dearth that caused food prices to soar, they were likely to fall into utter destitution and to face severe malnutrition and even starvation.[90]

For all that, the working poor were not the worst off members of the plebs, for a notch below them was a mass of marginalized individuals (vagrants, beggars, the permanently disabled) who had no marketable skill and hence no prospect of employment, and survived by dint of mendicity or petty larceny, sometimes banding together in recognized associations or guilds (complete with membership rosters and elected officials) in order to protect their turf against other equally destitute people. One such organization was the Compagnia della Visitazione founded in Rome in 1613: membership was restricted to the blind and the lame, the latter serving as guides to the former, and they enjoyed in exclusivity the right to beg outside church doors. Aptly referred to in modern historiography as the 'structural poor', those lifelong beggars and vagrants may have represented between 4 and 8 per cent of the urban population, but the actual number of those who roamed the streets in search of alms was no doubt larger as at any one time there were artisans and journeymen temporarily out of work who, for lack of savings to draw on, were forced into mendicity. Their number has been estimated at possibly 10 per cent of the population – a stark reminder of the precarious economic conditions working people lived in.[91]

It is much harder to venture even the crudest estimate of the percentage of poor in the countryside, but we have little difficulty in assuming that conditions there were no better than in the towns. In fact, endemic poverty was largely, although not solely, responsible for a major social problem that sixteenth- and seventeenth-century governments endlessly wrestled with: the problem of bandits, of individuals who, in the words of a document from

90. On real wages and living standards see Dante Zanetti, *Problemi alimentari di una economia preindustriale. Cereali a Pavia dal 1398 al 1700*, Boringhieri, Turin 1964, pp. 60–2, 84–8; Sella, *Salari e lavoro*, pp. 19–26; Marzio Achille Romani, *Nella spirale di una crisi. Popolazione, mercato e prezzi a Parma tra Cinque e Seicento*, Giuffre, Milan 1975, pp. 234–8; Carlo M. Cipolla, 'Economic Fluctuations, the Poor and Public Policy (Italy, 16th and 17th Centuries)' in *Aspects of Poverty in Early Modern Europe*, ed. Thomas Riis, Sijthoff, Alphen 1981, pp. 65–77; Davis, *Shipbuilders*, pp. 102–3. On the basis of evidence from several Italian towns, Pullan, 'Poveri, mendicanti e vagabondi', p. 996, has concluded that 'about two thirds of heads of households, even in the prosperous Italian towns, could be considered in some sense "poor" and susceptible, sometime during their lifetime, to become dependent on charitable organizations or on public assistance'. Conditions were no less precarious in other European countries: Jean-Pierre Gutton, *La societé et les pauvres en Europe (XVIe–XVIIIe siècles)*, PUF, Paris 1974, pp. 72–9.
91. Pullan, 'Poveri, mendicanti e vagabondi', pp. 955, 988–9, 1014.

Lucca, 'totally oblivious of their conditions as peasants and day labourers, have no other occupation than that of thugs [and] always armed with all sorts of weapons . . . live mostly by robberies . . . They are almost always very poor, never do any work [and yet] always manage to eat in taverns and to dress well above their station in life.'[92] The widespread presence of bandits, especially in the mountainous areas of the Papal States and the Kingdom of Naples, no doubt reflected a variety of factors – population pressure, the rebelliousness of rural communities against the tax collector and the press gang, the chance of finding employment as retainers of a local feudatory – but underlying it all was rural poverty, the uncertainty of employment facing day labourers, the utter ruin that the loss of a plot of land to the usurer or the tax collector could bring to a peasant family.[93]

A world, both urban and rural, so deeply marked by social and economic disparities; a world in which the rich few lived in stately mansions, drove in sumptuous carriages and engaged in Gargantuan feats of overeating while the vast majority of their fellow countrymen and women lived close to sheer subsistence and, at times, in utter destitution, would seem to be one in which open, violent conflicts between rich and poor were bound to occur with some frequency. And occur they did, as will be seen in the coming pages. What is remarkable, however, is that those conflicts were relatively rare; what needs explaining, in other words, is how the social peace was maintained most of the time in spite of conditions that seemed to invite social warfare.

Part of the answer is to be found in the brutality and indeed the savagery of repression that was visited on the leaders of any riot or revolt: we shall see instances of this and we have no difficulty in assuming that the prospect of harsh retribution had a deterrent effect on the populace. At the same time it would be simplistic to portray the plebs as being constantly kept in line solely or even primarily by fear. Other things were no doubt at work that either fostered a sense of acceptance of existing social and economic inequalities or that mitigated those inequalities by providing a 'safety net' for at least some of the poor some of the time.

The culture of the time, for one thing, incessantly reminded the have-nots of their obligation to respect and to show deference to their social superiors with carefully differentiated forms of address tailored to every social rank and with a plethora of unwritten rules dictating who should have precedence over whom and what attire and bearing was appropriate at each rung of the social ladder. At the same time obedience to the powers that be was a theme that the clergy, in Counter-Reformation Italy no less than in other European

---

92. Mazzei, *La società lucchese*, pp. 144–5.
93. On banditry see Quazza, *Preponderanza spagnola*, pp. 141–3; Fernand Braudel, *The Mediterranean and the Mediterranean World in the Age of Philip II*, transl. Sian Reynolds, Harper and Row, New York 1973, vol. 2, pp. 734–56; Berengo, *Nobili e mercanti*, pp. 346–56; Vivanti, 'Lacerazioni e contrasti', pp. 920–1; and Paolo Preto, 'Gli emarginati' in *Mentalità, comportamenti ed istituzioni tra Rinascimento e decadenza 1500–1700*, ed. Giuseppe Galasso, Electa, Milan 1988, pp. 162–3.

countries whether Catholic or Protestant, never ceased to preach. The relationship between social superiors and inferiors, however, was never merely a one-way street. Not only did preachers routinely admonish and exhort the rich and powerful about their moral duty to be just and charitable,[94] but the bonds between different social groups involved protection and benevolence from above as well as deference and submission from below; no less importantly, the sense of paternalistic obligation, of *noblesse oblige*, at the top was paralleled at the bottom by the expectation that the rich and powerful must help the poor and the downtrodden. As is often the case in highly polarized, yet stable societies, elements of reciprocity ran through the social fabric and helped hold it together in spite of its built-in potential for conflict. We saw examples of this in some villages where the peasants welcomed the prospect of coming under the rule of a feudatory precisely because they saw in him a patron who would shield their village from the demands of the tax collector and the quartermaster or from the arrogance of local landowners. Reliance on a patron also played a role in the lives of those Venetian shipwrights who, having forged bonds of friendship with patrician navy officers while serving on warships, later in life cultivated those bonds by arranging for their patrician friend to be the god-father of their children and sought his help for rising in the Arsenal's labour hierarchy.[95]

Social stability and public tranquillity also depended on the fact that the 'popular classes', divided as they were into a galaxy of isolated rural communities and, in the towns, into many separate guilds each with its own collective identity, could seldom share and formulate common goals, let alone agree on a joint plan of action against either the central government or the local ruling elite. What a French parish priest said of the villagers under his care at the close of the seventeenth century – 'they love their own pays [and] are quite detached from everything that happens in the rest of the world'[96] – could have been said just as well of their Italian counterparts. Local problems of taxation, feudal obligations, the upkeep of roads and bridges, the size of

94. Benzoni, *Gli affanni della cultura*, p. 125 provides examples of what he calls 'the hailstorm of terrorist preaching' that was intended to frighten the poor into accepting their wretched condition without protest and the rich into giving alms, and interprets these admonitions merely as a form of social control aimed at preserving the status quo. In the context of an age in which religious values loomed large this is an oversimplification. Pullan, 'Poveri, mendicanti e vagabondi', pp. 1034–7, on the other hand, while not denying the concern for preserving the social peace, provides a more balanced view by taking into account the genuinely religious and moral motivations that stood behind many acts of charity. Those motivations were perhaps best expressed by one preacher when he said that 'while the poor receive life from the rich, the rich receive salvation from the poor' (quotation in Achille Erba, 'Pauperismo e assistenza in Piemonte nel secolo XVII' in *T&C*, p. 223).

95. Davis, *Shipbuilders*, pp. 70–1.

96. Quotation in Peter Burke, *Popular Culture in Early Modern Europe*, Harper, New York 1978, p. 50.

the harvest were the narrow but overriding concerns of the rural community and it was over these that the villagers worried and argued most of the time. In the towns the political horizon of the plebs was not much broader and probably did not go beyond the town's ramparts or even the boundaries of the neighbourhood. Within the town the workers' focus of attention was probably restricted to the affairs and the interests of the guild with its web of rules and regulations, its jealously guarded privileges, and its social and charitable functions. It is thus not surprising that governments valued the guilds not only as regulatory agencies in a strictly economic sense, but also as outlets for the 'political' instincts of at least the most ambitious among the working poor. As an eighteenth-century Venetian magistrate put it,

the permanent tranquility of our republic . . . comes from the fact that we have allowed and granted to the people a semblance of government. The meetings [of guildsmen], the election of officers, the assignment of responsibilities, the introduction of new by-laws, the free debate among members of the same guild, are all things that create, as it were, small republics among the people and with these they satisfy their ambitions.[97]

WELFARE

The likelihood of social conflict inherent in a society so deeply marked by inequality was further reduced by informal arrangements or by institutional structures that provided some assistance, if certainly not to all those in need, at least to substantial numbers of individuals who fell, either temporarily or permanently, into destitution – a not uncommon occurrence at a time when more than half of the population lived close to the subsistence level and, as such, was vulnerable to a sudden rise in food prices or to a spell of unemployment.

A buffer against hard times was no doubt provided by kinship ties, at least for those individuals who were fortunate enough to have relations who could help them. Familial assistance in the face of hardships is hard to document as its informal nature has left few traces in archival sources, but that it was deeply rooted in the culture of the time can be inferred by what little we know about the role kinship ties played in early modern society. A few examples will suffice. In rural Piedmont, we are told, peasants found a measure of support among kinsmen that went well beyond the boundaries of the immediate family: even though most of them lived in nuclear households, they could expect the assistance of even distant blood relations. In practice, clusters of separate but related households recognized the authority of one

97. Quotation in Giuseppe Morazzoni, *Il mobile veneziano del Settecento*, Gorlich, Milan 1952, p. 34.

capofamiglia, a sort of leader of the entire parentage who designed marriage strategies, helped his kindred find tenancies and advised them on the sale or purchase of plots of land. Solidarity beween kinsmen could go to astonishing lengths. The analysis of transactions involving small, even minuscule parcels of land in the village of Santena has revealed an incredible range of prices for roughly similar plots; it has also revealed that prices were lowest when the buyer happened to be a stranger and highest when he was closely related to the seller. The explanation for this seemingly perverse behaviour of the land market is to be found in the fact that people parted with their land only out of extreme necessity and that, whenever possible, even distant relations came to the seller's rescue, as a stranger would not, by offering an inflated price.[98] Family solidarity and cohesion could take other forms, too: in villages near Lake Como marriages were normally arranged between individuals as closely related by blood as canon law would allow. The practice reflected in part the diminutive size of those communities where inevitably a good many individuals were somehow related to fellow villagers and where, as a consequence, finding a mate outside the extended family might prove difficult; but it often reflected a deliberate strategy as when a man married a female cousin too poor to afford even the modest dowry that would have been indispensable for attracting a suitor from outside the family; it reflected, that is, the strength of family solidarity and we can safely assume that the latter was not confined to marriage arrangements.[99] All of which supports G. Delille's view that in early modern society the truly poor 'are not those who have nothing whatsoever, but those who are outside any network of solidarity', those, in particular, without family relations.[100]

To the latter partial relief could come from private almsgiving or, in the case of nubile women, from private charitable endowments (known in the South as *monti di maritaggio*) the income of which went to provide modest dowries.[101] More commonly, the urban poor who were fortunate enough to belong to a guild could hope to receive small amounts of cash from the guild itself in the event of an illness, a disabling accident or old age, while some guilds went so far as to support vocational boarding schools for the children of indigent members. The purpose of these forms of assistance was to spare the victims of misfortune or old age the humiliation and hardship of 'being forced into mendicity'.[102] Where the guilds could not or would not reach, some measure of assistance was sometimes provided by charitable lay organizations known as confraternities which, building on a strong medieval tradition, multiplied and expanded their scope in the age of the

98. Levi, *Inheriting Power,* pp. 38, 47, 84–97.
99. Raul Merzario, *Il paese stretto. Strategie matrimoniali nella diocesi di Como, secoli XVI–XVIII*, Einaudi, Turin 1981, pp. 13–16.
100. Gerard Delille, 'Un esempio di assistenza privata: i Monti di maritaggio nel Regno di Napoli (secoli XVI–XVIII)' in *T&C*, p. 279.
101. Ibid., p. 276.
102. Giovanni Muto, 'Forme e contenuti dell'assistenza nel Mezzogiorno moderno: il caso di Napoli' in *T&C*, pp. 244–7.

Counter-Reformation. To confraternities we shall return in a later chapter. Right now it will suffice to say that from the late sixteenth century they addressed an impressive range of human needs – from the care of the sick to the distribution of alms, from the rehabilitation of 'fallen women' and the education of poor children to providing legal assistance *pro bono* to defendants too poor to afford the cost of an attorney's services.

Governments or, more precisely, civic authorities did play some role in providing relief to the poor: in Mantua, for instance, from the late sixteenth century a permanent agency was established that raised poor rates from the nobility and the merchants and distributed the money to the unemployed.[103] Similarly in Bergamo, a town of 22,000 souls, its chief public welfare agency (the Misericordia) could feed in a normal year as many as 7,000 indigent people who were identified on the basis of periodical surveys.[104] But the towns' most important function was that of operating costly welfare institutions such as hospitals, homes for foundlings, nursing homes for the old or, more commonly, institutions that combined all of these services. In fact, Italian towns could boast a long tradition in this area dating back to the early fifteenth century when the celebrated Ospedale degli Innocenti was founded in Florence, the general hospital known as Ca' Granda was built in Milan and similar institutions sprang up in Parma, Venice, Rome and Naples making Italy the object of admiration and emulation throughout Europe all the way to the eighteenth century.[105] During his journey to Rome Martin Luther, for one, had been impressed by the hospitals he had visited and had reported, perhaps with some exaggeration, that 'they consist of royal buildings [where] excellent food and drink are available to all, servants are very diligent, physicians very learned and beds and clothes very clean'.[106] Later visitors were equally impressed, although their comments were somewhat more restrained than Luther's. The English traveller Fynes Moryson, writing in the 1590s, singled out the Florentine hospital of Santa Maria Nuova as the best in Italy, but he had also words of praise for the hospital of San Lazzaro in Venice where, he said, '400 or 500 paupers' are fed. Nearly twenty years later Thomas Coryate noted that in the Milan Ca' Granda 'are an hundred and twelve chambers and foure thousand poore people are relieved'. At mid-century, in his *Description of Italy*, Richard Lassels admiringly listed all the hospitals and poorhouses supported by the guilds of Rome. On his part, his contemporary John Evelyn, after visiting the chief hospital in Rome (Ospedale di Santo Spirito), stated that ' 'tis altogether one of the most pious and worthy Foundations that I ever saw', notably on account of the fact that in it 'are forty Nurses who give suck

---

103. Roberto Navarrini and Carlo Marco Belfanti, 'Il problema della povertà nel Ducato di Mantova: aspetti istituzionali e problemi sociali (secoli XIV–XVI)' in *T&C*, p. 31.
104. Pullan, 'Poveri, mendicanti e vagabondi', p. 994.
105. Black, *Italian Confraternities*, p. 201.
106. Quotation in Paolo Simoncelli, 'Note sul sistema assistenziale a Roma nel XVI secolo' in *T&C*, p. 137.

to such children as are accidentally found exposed and abandoned'; he also noticed the 'children of bigger growth 450 in number who are taught letters'; and he went on to praise the hospital for being 'exquisitevely neate' and for providing separate rooms 'for such as are sick of maladies of a more rare and difficult cure'. Bishop Gilbert Burnet, no friend of things Catholic, wrote of the Annunziata hospital in Naples that 'it is the greatest hospital in the world' and described in some detail 'the spacious and convenient layout of its wards', while another foreign visitor estimated at 2,000 the number of its patients and at 800 that of 'children of the poorer sort' who were being 'instructed in letters and art [i.e. crafts] according to their inclination till they become great'.[107] In Perugia the hospital, jointly funded and managed by the city, the confraternities and the bishop, had 800 beds in its medical wards. In any given year the several hospitals of Venice harboured an estimated 4,000 'perpetual poor' or nearly 3 per cent of the city's population, and similar percentages obtained in seventeenth-century Florence.[108] Nor was outpatient care totally neglected, at least in Naples where the municipal government had on its payroll nine physicians charged with visiting the sick in their homes.[109] All in all, it is safe to say that, relative to the rest of Europe, Italy was in the forefront in terms of welfare. The admiring observations made by seventeenth-century travellers suggest this much and they were echoed in the mid-eighteenth century by a member of the Royal Society who, after conducting a comparative survey of hospitals and other relief institutions throughout Europe, concluded that 'no country in the world equals Italy in the care of the poor and sick'.[110]

Admittedly, the impressions reported by visitors of any large welfare institution should not always be taken at face value as they may well err on the side of optimism: those visitors most likely spent but a few hours touring the premises and their hosts may have made every effort to show only the best side of their institution and to project an image of tidiness and contentment, while discreetly hiding from their eyes and ears the harsher aspects of the hospitals' daily routine and the true sentiments of the inmates – and those sentiments seldom found their ways into written documents. Even so, it seems undeniable that in most Italian towns the old and the sick could count on at least a measure of relief and assistance which, by the standards of the time, was uncommonly good.

The same cannot be said of another welfare institution, the poorhouse, where beggars and orphans and other down-and-outs were confined against their will and subjected to a stern regimen of work and indoctrination. We

107. Quotations in Edward P. de G. Chaney, 'Giudizi inglesi su ospedali italiani, 1545–1789' in *T&C*, pp. 87–100. On the Annunziata see Aurelio Musi, 'Pauperismo e pensiero giuridico a Napoli nella prima metà del secolo XVII' in *T&C*, pp. 261–2.

108. Black, *Italian Confraternities*, pp. 196–9; and Pullan, 'Poveri, mendicanti e vagabondi', p. 991.

109. Muto, 'Forme e contenuti', p. 240.

110. Chaney, 'Giudizi inglesi', p. 100.

catch a glimpse of what conditions may have been there in a petition submitted to the Genoese civic authorities in 1668 by the inmates of the local poorhouse. It reads:

We, poor and unhappy men and women who are forced to live in this hell ... constantly subjected to punishments of jail, beatings, shackles, shaving of hair and flogging worse than galley slaves, ... cry out for mercy before Jesus Christ and Your Lordships, for we are desperate [and ready] to jump from a window and to turn a knife onto ourselves so as to put an end once and for all to this misery.[111]

We have no way of deciding how accurate a description this was of conditions in the Genoa poorhouse, but neither do we have serious reasons for dismissing it out of hand as one more example of Baroque hyperbole. At the same time one should not draw from it broad conclusions applicable to the treatment of the poor in the rest of Italy. In Genoa commitment to the poorhouse was compulsory and, as such, likely to result in harsh discipline and even brutal treatment, but few other cities, as will be seen shortly, followed Genoa's example of the forcible internment of their poor.

In some respects Italy's welfare system may have been ahead of its time, but it was still woefully inadequate to meet all or even most of the needs of the poor. In the late sixteenth and through much of the sevententh centuries a recurrent theme in government circles was the danger that hordes of beggars, vagrants, 'rogues and vagabonds' posed to the public peace and to personal safety – a clear indication that the existing system failed to cover all those in need. The view of the poor as socially dangerous was, of course, widespread in Europe at the time and reflected in part the rapid pace of urbanization under way since the sixteenth century and the long depression in the central decades of the seventeenth century. But it may also have reflected a less charitable, less tolerant attitude toward the poor as well as a determination on the part of the increasingly centralized state to adopt stringent measures for the elimination of a pool of potential troublemakers and of the unseemly sight of poor wretches 'who roam[ed] the streets like brute animals with no other concern than to find food' and thus detracted from the decorum and stateliness of cities that were being transformed by architects and urban planners to reflect new splendour on their rulers. There was also at work a new concern that not all beggars and vagabonds deserved to be supported by charity, but that many of them chose to live on the dole because they preferred a life of sloth and thievery to the hard but morally uplifting discipline of the workplace. In such cases, it was argued, almsgiving could do more harm than good, for 'to give them alms ... makes the plebs lazy and deters them from work; therefore, the most fruitful charity is to make them earn their bread by their own labour'.[112]

111. Quotation in Edoardo Grendi, 'Ideologia della carità e società indisciplinata: la costruzione del sistema assistenziale genovese (1470–1670)' in *T&C*, p. 74.
112. On changing attitudes toward poverty and mendicity in Europe in general see Gutton, *La societé et les pauvres*, pp. 95–115. For Italy see Pullan, 'Poveri,

Faced with a multitude of problems that existing welfare institutions and private charity could alleviate but not resolve, seventeenth-century governments and civic authorities tried a variety of approaches. One was to stockpile grain at public expense for sale at an artificially low price in times of scarcity;[113] another was to offer grain to the indigent from a public granary (*monte frumentario*) in the form of a loan which the recipient was expected to repay in kind after the next harvest.[114] Another approach focused on employment rather than consumption: a government would subsidize private employers during a recession if they agreed to hire or retain workers – as was done in Florence in 1621 when as many as 800 unemployed weavers were so hired. Alternatively, a government could finance public works, such as the repair of the city ramparts, the construction of new roads or the draining of marshlands.[115] At times city authorities resorted to inhumane measures to cope with teeming masses of indigents: they inflicted or threatened to inflict harsh physical punishment on the 'undeserving poor' who 'while pretending to be sick, spend their time loitering, playing dice, blaspheming, and sleeping in the streets'; or they simply drove the undesirable out of town.[116]

These and similar measures were all short-term in nature and were adopted mainly during emergencies. A long-term approach, however, was also considered, namely the forcible internment of the poor in workhouses, an approach that appealed to several European governments, notably in the Dutch Republic and in France, during the seventeenth century as the panacea for curing both the social evil of disorder and the moral evil of sloth.[117] It was a harsh, indeed brutal approach as the Genoese inmates' petition quoted above makes only too clear, for it amounted to the incarceration of the poor and to inflicting savage punishment on the recalcitrant and the laggards. In Italy the policy of 'putting the rabble behind bars', as a Sienese document

mendicanti e vagabondi', pp. 1014–15 and the following essays in *T&C*: Irene Polverini Fusi, 'Pauperismo ed assistenza a Siena durante il Principato mediceo', p. 157; Muto, 'Forme e contenuti', p. 255; Navarrini and Belfanti, 'Il problema della povertà', pp. 128–30; and Daniele Lombardi, 'Poveri a Firenze. Programmi e realizzazioni della politica assistenziale dei Medici tra Cinque e Seicento', p. 175.

113. Black, *Italian Confraternities*, pp. 159–62.

114. Yves-Marie Bercé, 'Troubles frumentaires et pouvoir centralisateur: l'émeute de Fermo dans les Marches (1648)', *Mélanges d'Archéologie et d'Histoire de l'Ecole Francaise de Rome* 73 (1961), pp. 492–3.

115. Alessandro Pastore, 'Strutture assistenziali fra Chiesa e Stato nell'Italia della Controriforma', in *SIE Annali* 4 (1981), p. 448; Lombardi, 'Poveri a Firenze', pp. 174–5; and Cipolla, 'Economic Fluctuations', pp. 74–5.

116. Lombardi, 'Poveri a Firenze', pp. 169, 171; Navarrini and Belfanti, 'Il problema della povertà', p. 130; and Bronislaw Geremek, 'Renfermement des pauvres en Italie (XVe–XVIIe siècles). Remarques préliminaires' in *Mélanges en l'honneur de Fernand Braudel. Histoire économique du monde méditerranéen 1450–1650*, Privat, Toulouse 1973, pp. 208–13.

117. Gutton, *La societé et les pauvres*, pp. 123–35; Pullan, 'Poveri, mendicanti e vagabondi', pp. 1018–20; Pastore, 'Strutture assistenziali', pp. 444–7.

bluntly put it, had been attempted in town after town since the fifteenth century if not earlier, but, if we are to judge from the recurrent complaints about the presence of swarms of beggars in the streets of most towns over the next two centuries, enclosing the poor proved beyond the financial and/or the organizational ability of the authorities.[118] The case of Rome is especially revealing, for here was a city where the problem of pauperism seems to have been especially acute both because the city itself harboured no large manufacturing activities capable of absorbing a high number of unemployed and because the notorious poverty of the surrounding countryside produced a steady flow of destitute immigrants. In 1581 Pope Gregory XIII ordered all beggars off the streets and confined them to a vacant monastery there to be housed, fed, put to work and trained, but within two years the project had to be abandoned for lack of funds. Sixtus V had no more luck six years later when he tried to revive the project, nor, for that matter, had Innocent XII a century later.[119] Elsewhere in the peninsula the record of success was no better than in Rome: in most major cities compulsory workhouses were established at one time or another, but often enough the experiment had to be discontinued either for lack of funds or because the very notion of forcible internment was highly unpopular.[120]

If internment failed, better and certainly more humane results were achieved, as will be seen, by the many private agencies that came into being in the wake of the religious revival under way since the late sixteenth century and that strove to target the needs of clearly identified groups – abandoned children, abused women, prostitutes, former convicts – with an eye not only at short-term assistance, but also at more lasting solutions. In the end, however, neither public welfare programmes nor private charities could hope to solve the problem of poverty, for the early modern economy, with its low levels of productivity, poor communications, vulnerability to the vagaries of weather and harvest, and with over half the people living at bare subsistence levels, was in no position to ensure either steady employment or a decent livelihood to the masses.[121] Nor did the early modern state have the means to create, support and operate a welfare system capable of ensuring even a minimal safety net to those in need – a fact of which the authors of the various utopias written at the time seem to have been aware as they proposed

118. Contrary to what Geremek, 'Renfermement des pauvres', p. 213, asserts.
119. Black, *Italian Confraternities*, pp. 214–16; Simoncelli, 'Note sul sistema assistenziale', pp. 145–7.
120. Such was the case in Florence (Lombardi, 'Poveri a Firenze', pp. 179–81); in Prato (Giuliano Pinto and Ivan Tognarini, 'Povertà e assistenza' in *Storia di Prato* vol. 2, pp. 437–8) and in Naples (Muto, 'Forme e contenuti', pp. 255–8). Siena considered, but in the end rejected, the idea of enclosing the poor (Polverini Fosi, 'Pauperismo ed assistenza', pp. 158–60). On hostility to internment see Black, *Italian Confraternities*, p. 136 and Lombardi's 'Poveri a Firenze'.
121. On the underlying causes of widespread poverty in preindustrial societies see Gutton, *La societé et les pauvres*, p. 198; Pullan, 'Poveri, mendicanti e vagabondi', pp. 1027–31.

a total transformation of the economy and of society rather than *ad hoc*, partial reforms as the only way to resolve the economic and social problems of their time.

There was one problem, however, that the state could neither ignore nor approach in a piecemeal, limited manner, namely epidemic disease and specifically the plague, a devastating scourge that was visited on north Italy in 1630 and on the South in 1656 wiping out a third of the entire population. The magnitude of the devastation, the memory of past outbreaks, and the terror that the mere prospect of a return of the disease generated in people's minds prompted city and state governments to take sweeping measures intended to keep the disease at bay at the first signs of an outbreak and to cope with its terrifying consequences once it spread. Since the mid-sixteenth century in all major north Italian towns permanent boards of health were in place that were charged with gathering all available information from other towns or countries about local outbreaks of the plague; increasingly state governments, too, supervised and coordinated the works of those boards and, in the event of the plague being detected in a neighbouring country, issued stringent preventive measures ranging from a total embargo on trade with the infected country to the posting of guards at the borders to form a sanitary cordon against people, animals and goods that might carry the disease, to imposing quarantines on incoming ships. Once the plague had struck, city authorities saw to it that the sick and those known to have had contact with them were committed to a pesthouse while their homes were boarded up and their clothes and furnishings were burned. The city also had to ensure a minimum of food to the inmates of the pesthouse, to recruit and pay physicians and surgeons willing to serve the sick as well as large numbers of gravediggers. What is remarkable in all this is the high degree of organization both before and during a plague: to be sure, the measures taken (with the exception of the sanitary cordon and the quarantine), based as they were on total ignorance of the real causes and remedies of the disease, were of little avail and sometimes even compounded the problem (as when all dogs and cats were ordered slaughtered), but there is little doubt that government agencies tried their best and allocated huge sums of money in their struggle against 'an invisible enemy', even though their efforts often generated more resentment than gratitude as merchants objected to the trade embargo, workers complained of the unemployment caused by the embargo, and many people complained about the commitment of family members to the misery and the horrors of the pesthouse.[122]

---

122. On this, see Carlo M. Cipolla, *Cristofano and the Plague. A Study in the History of Public Health in the Age of Galileo,* Collins 1973, and *Fighting the Plague in Seventeenth-Century Italy,* University of Wisconsin Press, Madison 1981.

REVOLTS

A society as polarized between the rich few and a wretchedly poor majority as Italian society was in the seventeenth century would seem to be a prime candidate for bitter and bloody social conflict. In fact, however, open rebellion against the status quo, violent upheavals by the disenfranchised masses against the ruling elite were relatively rare and, with one major exception, were of a local nature. Although no systematic count of popular uprisings is available, it is safe to say that during the entire century most Italian states and towns experienced no major outbreaks of violent protest and that those few that did experienced them but once: Milan, for instance, was the stage of serious riots in 1628, but remained quiet for the rest of the century; Fermo and the surrounding countryside were racked by popular revolt in 1648, but saw no repetition of the upheaval thereafter; Naples, which had witnessed a major revolt in 1585, remained relatively calm for the next sixty years and again, after the revolt of 1647, enjoyed another half century of tranquillity; and in Piedmont the popular masses did not stir until the 1680s.

The infrequency of popular revolts can be ascribed, as we have seen, to several causes such as the fear of repression, the narrow, parochial outlook that kept people focused on their community or guild, the existence of bonds of reciprocity that made social disparities more tolerable, and finally the presence of welfare institutions, inadequate though they may have been, that could somehow soften at least some of the blows of misfortune. One should add that the division of society into orders and the divisions existing within each order made it difficult for a broadly based sense of solidarity to develop capable of rallying large numbers to the banner of rebellion. As J.H. Elliott has observed, 'the ordering of society in early modern Europe tended to militate against class solidarity. A society grouped into corporations, divided into orders, and linked vertically by powerful ties of kinship and clientage cannot be expected to behave in the same way as a society divided into classes.'[123] Such, as we have seen, was the case with Italian society in the seventeenth century: accordingly, what is surprising is not so much that revolts occurred so infrequently and were invariably local in scope, but that they occurred at all.

What was needed for rallying large numbers behind a common cause and for triggering a concerted, violent mass movement was a crisis of such proportions as would seriously affect the lives of the multitude, make them temporarily oblivious of their habitual differences and divisions, and provide a common target for their discontent. Such had been the case in Naples in 1585 when a severe dearth and skyrocketing food prices had triggered riots in the course of which the official (*eletto del popolo*) responsible for provisioning the city was murdered by an enraged mob. Repression had quickly followed and

---

123. J.H. Elliott, 'Revolution and Continuity in Early Modern Europe' (1969) now in his *Spain and Its World 1500–1700. Selected Essays*, Yale University Press, New Haven 1989, p. 99. See also Burke, *Popular Culture*, p. 176.

thirty-one rioters had been executed.[124] In 1628 it was Milan's turn to witness a major outbreak of mob violence. As famine struck following a crop failure in the region and as conditions deteriorated even further as a result of the military operations connected with the War of the Mantuan Succession, on Martinmas hungry crowds took out their rage on the bakers and plundered their shops – the more eagerly so as it was rumoured that the bakers, in complicity with the city authorities, were holding back large supplies of flour in the expectation of further price increases. Interestingly enough, the Spanish governor would have opted for price controls and rationing as the best way for restoring calm in the city, but the city council, speaking with the voice of the patriciate, persuaded him to resort to force instead, and the Martinmas bread riot was crushed by the army after its alleged ringleaders had been apprehended and executed.[125] Even more serious was the uprising that broke out in Fermo and spread to the Marches in the Papal States in 1648 at the time, that is, of one of the worst famines of the century when grain prices rose threefold in Rome and more than doubled in Milan. Unlike in Milan where twenty years earlier the patriciate had stood squarely against the plebs, in Fermo the patriciate closed ranks with the crowd in opposing the papal governor on grounds that he had ordered all grain produced in the region to be brought to the municipal warehouse allegedly for distribution to the hungry populace, but in fact for shipment to Rome in response to the frantic requests of the papal government anxious to provide a minimum of food to the beleaguered capital. Prodded by the local patriciate, the people of Fermo staged loud demonstrations against the governor and, confronted with his decision to bring in troops to restore order, took up arms and forced him to barricade himself in the local prison. Whereupon the mob ransacked his palace, stormed the prison and murdered him in cold blood. Rome responded by despatching a new governor with 1,200 foot and 300 horse, and an uneasy calm was quickly restored. An investigation got under way, arrests were made and eventually harsh sentences were handed down: six persons (two of them noblemen) were executed, while ten others were sentenced to the galleys.[126]

The different attitude of the patriciate in Milan and in Fermo in the face of a popular uprising is puzzling at first sight, but it can be accounted for by the fact that the Milan patriciate owned large country estates and, as such, had everything to gain from rising grain prices, whereas its Fermo counterpart owned little land, but owed its fortune primarily to the grain trade and was thus opposed to a governor who, by arranging grain shipments to Rome, had bypassed them altogether.

Neither Milan nor Fermo, one might note, saw a repetition of the upheavals of 1628 and 1648, not even during the serious food crisis of the 1690s. In a

124. Villari, The Revolt of Naples, pp. 19–33.
125. Fausto Nicolini, 'Il tumulto di San Martino e la carestia del 1629' in his Aspetti della vita italo-spagnola nel Cinquecento e nel Seicento, Guida, Naples 1934, pp. 127–288.
126. Bercé, 'Troubles frumentaires', Mélanges d'Archéologie et d'Histoire 74 (1962), pp. 759–87.

general way, one must also note the fact that serious bread riots were rather rare occurrences even though food shortages most certainly were not. The reason for this may have been that food shortages *per se* were not enough to touch off a riot, let alone an armed insurrection. Seventeenth-century people were fully aware that shortages were ultimately caused by the vagaries of the weather and therefore had to be patiently endured until the next harvest. What was needed to arouse a hungry populace to violent action was the perception that some individuals were hoarding food in order to take advantage of rising prices. This was seen as a violation of the unwritten code of decency and reciprocity, the 'moral economy', which was supposed to undergird the relationship between rulers and ruled, between rich and poor.[127] The bakers of Milan and the city fathers who stood by them had violated that code by hoarding desperately needed food, and so had the governor of Fermo. In both cases popular fury had been unleashed against the perpetrators.

The famine that swept much of the peninsula in the late 1640s also affected Sicily, an island which in normal years was a net exporter of grain to continental Italy and to Spain.[128] Riots broke out in Palermo in 1647 and were triggered not by hunger as such, but by the decision of municipal authorities to require bakers to reduce the weight of the standard loaf of bread while keeping its price unchanged – a not uncommon, but highly unpopular form of rationing in those days. The mob engaged in widespread arson and pillage; it also stormed the city jail freeing its 600 inmates. What is remarkable about the Palermo revolt is that it soon turned from a bread riot not unlike Fermo's into a full-scale taxpayers' rebellion. While clamouring for more bread, the insurgents also turned their ire against the tax collector's office and demanded the abolition of the excise tax (*gabella*) levied on the basic commodities that went into the people's diet (flour, olive oil, wine, fish and cheese); they also demanded the right to elect to the city council two representatives of their own choosing. These last two demands, which had more to do with the growing burden of taxation all Spanish possessions had to shoulder in the final stages of the Thirty Years War than with the food shortage, were promptly accepted by a frightened Spanish viceroy, the Marquess of Los Velez. Interestingly, they had been jointly formulated by the local craft guilds

---

127. The point is stressed by Oscar Di Simplicio, 'Sopravvivenze e declino dell'economia urbana' in *SSI*, vol. 10 (1987), pp. 60–1. A good analysis of E.P. Thompson's concept of 'moral economy' is by John Stevenson, 'The "Moral Economy" of the English Crowd: Myth and Reality' in *Order and Disorder in Early Modern England,* ed. Anthony Fletcher and John Stevenson, Cambridge University Press 1985, pp. 218–38.

128. The account that follows is based on H.L. Koenigsberger, 'The Revolt of Palermo in 1647' (1943) now in his *Estates and Revolutions. Essays in Early Modern European History,* Cornell University Press, Ithaca 1971, pp. 253–77 and on Giuseppe Giarrizzo, 'La Sicilia dal Cinquecento all'Unità d'Italia' in Vincenzo D'Alessandro and Giuseppe Giarrizzo, *La Sicilia dal Vespro all'Unità d'Italia,* UTET, Turin 1979, pp. 311–21.

and the liberal professions. Having thus achieved a measure of participation in government, these two well-organized groups then proceeded to reform the fiscal system, notably by replacing the obnoxious gabelle with a tax on luxuries such as horse-drawn carriages, expensive bottled wine, and stately mansions – all measures clearly meant to shift the tax burden onto the wealthier members of society. The revolt, however, did not stop at this point, but was pushed further by the guilds, especially after news came that in Naples too an insurrection had broken out. Under the leadership of Giuseppe Alesi, a master goldbeater, the guildsmen armed themselves, took control of the city ramparts, and even envisaged the possibility of overthrowing Spanish rule, while the viceroy escaped to the safety of a well-armed galley at anchor in the Palermo harbour. Alesi, on his part, quietly tried to find a compromise with him and in the event was able to win his approval of forty-nine *Capitoli* or terms which, in addition to confirming the abolition of the gabelle, reduced house rents by 25 per cent, gave the *popolo* equal representation with the patriciate in the municipal government, and entrusted to the guilds both the provisioning of the city and the responsibility for keeping law and order; in return, Alesi had to surrender command of the rebel forces to the viceroy, retaining only a measure of authority in civil matters. Whatever that authority was, he did not exercise it for very long: on 22 August he was assassinated by a band of noblemen. His murder and the 'white terror' that followed triggered new outbreaks of violence in the streets, but by then the tide had clearly turned against the guilds. Without a strong leader, with no real experience in government affairs, often at loggerheads with one another, unable to secure either French military intervention or the support of other Sicilian towns, and faced with the prospect of municipal bankruptcy, the guilds lost control of events and made it relatively easy for a new energetic viceroy, Cardinal Teodoro Trivulzio, to bring Palermo to its knees and to restore the status quo. The next viceroy, Don John of Austria, consolidated his predecessor's work by entrusting to the local Inquisition the task of investigating all future candidates to public office in order to assess their loyalty to the crown and their 'devotion to the public good'.

One reason why in August 1647 Viceroy Los Velez had so promptly acceded even to the most radical demands of the Palermo insurgents was that a month earlier revolt had erupted in Naples and, as a consequence, neither money nor military reinforcements could be expected from that quarter. Nor could they be expected from other parts of the Spanish monarchy, for Madrid was fully engaged at the time in the final stages of the war in Germany as well as in suppressing revolts in Portugal and Catalonia. Moreover, to the Spanish crown events in Naples were of greater concern than events in Palermo: the Kingdom of Naples, as will be recalled, was a chief source of revenue and of manpower to the Spanish monarchy as well as the indispensable foundation of its hegemony over the whole of Italy.

The revolt of Naples in 1647, besides drawing the full attention of Madrid, had a vast resonance throughout western Europe at the time: it was closely monitored by the English Parliament and provided inspiration to the Paris insurgents during the Fronde.[129] It has also attracted, especially in our century, the attention of historians and has been the subject of spirited debates about its nature, causes and results.[130] All this interest in what, at first glance, looks nothing more than a taxpayer revolt similar to, and no more successful than, the one in Palermo can be explained only in small part by the colourful and tragic figure of Masaniello, the illiterate fisherman who for ten dramatic days was at the head of the revolt and demonstrated an astonishing ability both as a political and as a military leader. As Cardinal Filomarino, the archbishop of Naples, put it in a dispatch to Rome, 'this Masaniello has risen to such heights of authority, respect and obedience that he has caused the whole city to tremble at his commands which his followers carry out with the utmost diligence and precision; he has demonstrated prudence, good judgment and moderation; in short, he has become a king in this city and the most glorious and triumphant king the world has ever seen'.[131] But the unusual interest elicited by the revolt in Naples has to do with more than just Masaniello. It has to do with the fact that it occurred in the largest city in Europe at the time; with the fact also that from an urban riot it quickly developed into a peasant uprising engulfing much of southern Italy; and finally with the range and diversity of the social forces involved and the radicalism of some of their actions, culminating in the proclamation of an independent republic.

The spark that caused the insurrection on 7 July 1647 was the imposition of a new tax on the sale of fresh fruit, on items, that is, that loomed large in the people's diet. That spark, however, would not have ignited as large a firestorm as it did had not the Kingdom of Naples been in the throes of a major crisis. As alluded to in another chapter, after the Spanish monarchy had become involved in the Thirty Years War, its southern Italian dominions had been subjected to relentless and growing fiscal pressure with most of the revenue being funnelled toward the State of Milan and other theatres of war. The enormous demands placed on the Kindom of Naples had hit the lower classes especially hard as the Spanish crown had resorted to taxing an ever-wider range of consumer goods in the towns and to raising heavier and heavier land and poll taxes in the countryside. Popular discontent had reached such levels that four years before the revolt broke out the highest magistracy in Naples had warned the Spanish viceroy that 'the people are driven to such state of despair that they are fleeing the country and . . . what is most deplorable some have gone to live in the State of the Turks'.[132] In

129. Rosario Villari, *Elogio della dissimulazione. La lotta politica nel Seicento*, Laterza, Bari 1987, pp. 66–77.
130. Rosario Villari, 'Masaniello: Contemporary and Recent Interpretations', *Past and Present* 108 (1985), pp. 117–32; Pier Luigi Rovito, 'La rivoluzione costituzionale a Napoli (1647–48)', *Rivista Storica Italiana* 98 (1986), pp. 367–8; and Waquet, 'Politique, Institutions', pp. 74–82.
131. Quotation in Aurelio Musi, 'La rivolta antispagnola a Napoli e in Sicilia' in *SSI*, vol. 11, p. 29. I have heavily relied on this excellent essay for what follows.
132. Quotation in Luigi De Rosa, *Il Mezzogiorno spagnolo tra crescita e decadenza*, Mondadori, Milan 1987, p. 187.

94

Naples itself the taxpayers' resentment had been exacerbated by the knowledge that a number of aristocrats and financiers were amassing huge fortunes either as tax farmers or by lending money at outrageous rates to a government desperate for revenue. In the countryside, the taxpayers' plight was made worse by the often illegal forms of exploitation the baronage increasingly inflicted on the peasantry in order to recoup from the ravages of the land tax, while the authorities, anxious to retain the barons' loyalty, looked the other way. At the same time, discontent was rife among the lawyers, if for different reasons: their grievances reflected the growing sense of alienation the *togati* felt in the face of the ascendancy of the great financiers and the resurgence of baronial power in the top echelons of government; it reflected as well their outrage in the face of financial chaos and fiscal irresponsibility.[133]

On 7 July the announcement of a new tax on fresh fruit was met by the vendors' refusal to comply, a refusal that at once elicited widespread support not only from the popular masses, but also from members of the legal profession. The crowd took to the streets, the prisons were stormed to secure arms, a militia quickly formed that included many veterans who had served abroad in the Spanish army, and a revolutionary committee was established with Masaniello at its head. Behind him, or rather at his side, was another and quite different leader who coached the youthful and inexperienced fisherman in his new role and provided the insurgents with a political programme. This 'grey eminence' of the revolution was Giulio Genoino, then eighty years of age: he had held high office in Naples a quarter century before and in 1620 had made a name for himself as the architect of a plan of constitutional reform that would have given the middling order, and the legal profession in particular, a larger role in the government of the Kingdom of Naples at the expense of the nobility. The plan had been fully endorsed by the then viceroy duke of Osuna, but had been flatly rejected in Madrid by a government opposed to any reduction in the powers of the nobility; Osuna had been recalled and Genoino locked up in a fortress where he was to languish for the next eighteen years.[134] In 1647 he re-emerged as the chief spokesman of a disgruntled middling order just as Masaniello emerged as the leader of the urban masses. It was Genoino's intuition that this time far-reaching changes could be achieved only if the two main social forces, the *popolo* and the plebs, would work together.

On 9 and 10 July the urban masses turned their anger against and set fire to the homes of some of the great financiers and tax farmers – men like Felice Basile who, according to a contemporary chronicle, 'had risen from [being a]

---

133. On the background of the revolt, besides the classic analysis by Villari, *The Revolt of Naples*, see Vittor Ivo Comparato, 'Toward the Revolt of 1647' in *Good Government in Spanish Naples*, ed. Antonio Calabria and John A. Marino, Peter Lang, New York 1990, pp. 275–316; and Rovito, 'La rivoluzione costituzionale', pp. 373–5.
134. A full discussion of the failed attempt at constitutional reform, in Comparato, *Uffici e società a Napoli*, pp. 259–324.

lowly baker ... to enormous wealth through tax farming and loans to the state', or like a Cesare Lubrano who, by much the same means, 'had gone from mere stevedore to being worth 300,000 scudi'.[135] The leaders of the insurgents quickly put together a fairly coherent military organization and began to formulate their demands for reform, while the mob engaged in widespread arson and looting. On 13 July, however, it looked as if a resolution of the conflict might be at hand: thanks in part to the mediation of Cardinal Filomarino (the only member of the establishment enjoying the respect of both sides) the viceroy swore to a set of terms drafted by Genoino which, in addition to repealing the gabelle and allowing the insurgents to keep their weapons, granted elected representatives of the *popolo* the right to share power with the patriciate on an equal basis.

In actual fact, in making those concessions the viceroy was merely marking time, waiting for instructions and, hopefully, military reinforcements from Spain. Meanwhile, he tried to drive a wedge between the more radical, popular forces led by Masaniello and the more moderate ones led by Genoino. But in the end he listened to those in his entourage who advocated getting rid of Masaniello, and on 16 July the charismatic fisherman was murdered during a service in the cathedral in spite of Cardinal Filomarino's attempt to save his life. The three assassins were subsequently handsomely rewarded by the crown with money, a noble title and a lucrative government position. Genoino, on the other hand, was raised to high office.

If the viceroy had hoped that Masaniello's brutal murder would restore law and order, he was quickly disappointed: Naples did not lay down arms and the insurrection spread to the countryside where it pitted the peasantry against the feudal nobility. In Naples, however, the unity that, for a mere ten days, had seen the poorest proletariat join forces with the guilds and the *togati* began to unravel, each group pushing its own agenda in spite of Genoino's strenuous efforts at keeping them united. Eventually, Genoino himself was ousted and replaced by a triumvirate consisting of a nobleman, a lawyer and a representative of the *popolo*. The new leadership submitted new terms to the viceroy (notably the exclusion of the nobility from high office and the replacement of government-appointed officials with men chosen by the triumvirate) only to be turned down by a viceroy who by now had received instructions from Madrid and who knew that a military showdown was imminent.

At the beginning of October a large Spanish squadron sailed into the Bay of Naples under the command of Don John of Austria, the Spanish king's half-brother, and subjected the city to heavy shelling from its 3,000 guns. Undaunted, the insurgents at this point burned all bridges and declared Naples to be a free republic under the protection of Spain's archenemy, the king of France. Their bold but hasty decision, however, assumed all too readily that France would indeed rush to their rescue; besides, it left

135. Quotation in Aurelio Lepre, 'La crisi del XVII secolo nel Mezzogiorno d'Italia', *Studi Storici* 22 (1981), p. 69.

unanswered the question of what the new republic would be like. That assumption proved wrong and the constitutional question turned out to be highly divisive: France failed to provide military help and in Naples three mutually exclusive views collided regarding the shape the republic was to take. The patriciate rallied behind Henry of Lorraine, duke of Guise, a French prince who offered to serve as head of an oligarchic state modelled after the Dutch Republic; the popular forces called for a more broadly based constitution closer to the Swiss model; and between those two extremes stood a moderate faction headed by the distinguished and highly respected jurist Vincenzo D'Andrea whose goal was a republican government run by 'virtuous men', that is to say by individuals deemed worthy of exercising authority on account of their administrative competence, their record of public service and their legal expertise.[136]

In a deeply divided city none of the three factions could hope to assume power and to give the fledgling republic a chance. Besides, as anarchy spread in the provinces and all attempts at formulating a joint plan of action agreeable to both Naples and the provinces failed, it became clear that the new republic could not long survive both its internal divisions and the naval blockade. Accordingly, steps were taken (especially by D'Andrea) toward a negotiated settlement. This was completed on 6 April 1648: in addition to abolishing certain taxes and providing compensation for the destruction caused by the naval bombardment, it granted greater representation in the city administration to the *popolo* and a general pardon to the insurgents. Thereupon Don John of Austria and his Spanish troops made a carefully staged, triumphant re-entry and the curtain fell on the revolt of Naples, while in the provinces the peasant insurrection either petered out or was savagely put down by the joint forces of the government and a vindictive nobility.

Much has been written about the causes of the defeat of the insurgents a mere nine months after they had raised the banner of revolt and even of outright independence from Spain. There is now considerable agreement among scholars that a major factor was represented by the deep divisions within Neapolitan society as well as the gulf that separated the city from the rest of the kingdom in terms of interests, grievances and aspirations.[137] A further source of the insurgents' weakness has been found in the fact that, unlike in the Netherlands, the aristocracy (both the urban patriciate and the feudal nobility) threw in its lot with Spain, thus depriving the rebels of the leadership that only the most prestigious order of society could provide.[138] As for the long-term consequences of the revolt, it would be a mistake to assume, as was often done in the past, that its defeat simply meant a return to the status quo. The failed revolt, in fact, resulted in some significant, if limited,

---

136. On the ideological divisions within the rebels' ranks see Rovito, 'La rivoluzione costituzionale', pp. 403–6, 426–34 and 443.
137. Rosario Villari, 'Appunti sul Seicento', *Studi Storici* 23 (1982), p. 751.
138. Elliott, 'Revolution and Continuity', pp. 109–10 and 112.

changes.[139] Not only did the Spanish crown grant a measure of tax relief to its Neapolitan subjects, but in Naples the middling order, the *popolo*, came to play a somewhat larger political role than before: after 1648 the Spanish viceroys made it a point to consult with representatives of the *popolo* before introducing changes in the fiscal system; with the help of officials recruited from among the *togati* they worked at recovering crown revenues that had been alienated or usurped in the past; and they often filled some of the highest slots in the administration with members of the legal profession rather than with noblemen as had been done before the revolt. In this limited sense the revolt can be said to have been 'a step on the road to the modern state' and to have paved the way to the reform movement of the next century,[140] for the legal profession, now in the ascendancy, was by training sensitive to the need of asserting the authority of the crown over aristocratic or corporate privilege, and proved the more willing to do so as it came into contact with and avidly absorbed the new intellectual currents and political theories then being debated in the rest of Europe. Changes in the central administration of the kingdom and in the governance of the city of Naples did not, at first, reach very far into the countryside where the feudal nobility continued to lord it over the peasantry as of old. Only in the last decade of the century did the Spanish authorities, with a stronger bureaucratic apparatus at their command, gradually make their presence felt, as will be recalled, by engaging in a running battle against private bands of retainers and by curbing the worst manifestations of feudal lawlessness and arrogance. But it would still be a long time before the modern state could be fully in control there.

In 1647, when famine had struck, Messina, Sicily's largest city and Palermo's rival for pre-eminence in the island, had not revolted. Messina had remained relatively calm, except for a quickly suppressed bread riot; in fact, in order to curry favours with the viceroy, the city had contributed money to help put down the Palermo rebels. Some twenty-five years later, on the other hand, it was Messina's turn to stage a major revolt, indeed two revolts in a row, while Palermo hardly stirred and instead urged the Spanish authorities to crush the insurgents. Nothing better illustrates the profound differences and rivalries that separated the two Sicilian cities and ultimately facilitated Spain's control over the restless island than the staggered chronology of their revolts.[141]

139. The old view of the utter futility of the revolt as expressed by Michelangelo Schipa, *Masaniello*, Laterza, Bari 1925, p. 177 and by Benedetto Croce, *History of the Kingdom of Naples* (1925) transl. Francis Frenaye, University of Chicago Press 1970, p. 127 is no longer generally accepted. The consensus now seems to be that the revolt did produce some changes: Galasso, *Il Mezzogiorno*, pp. 204–6; Villari, *Ribelli e riformatori*, p. 84 and 'Masaniello', p. 106; and Rovito, 'La rivoluzione costituzionale', pp. 368, 446–50, 452.
140. Villari, *Ribelli e riformatori*, pp. 8, 84.
141. The account that follows is based on Denis Mack Smith, *A History of Sicily. Medieval Sicily 800–1713*, Chatto and Windus 1968, ch. 22, and on Giarrizzo, 'La Sicilia dal Cinquecento', pp. 328–45.

In Sicily troubles began in the autumn of 1671 after the harvest had failed two years in a row and famine swept the island taking thousands of lives. In Palermo and in other towns there was relatively little agitation, possibly because memories of the repression of 1647 were still alive; by contrast, in Messina the plebs went on a rampage, looting and torching the houses of the rich, notably those of the merchant oligarchy who had traditionally controlled the city's government. The Spanish governor of Messina, Don Luis Del Hoyo, however, was able to restore the public peace rather quickly not only by rushing in emergency food supplies, but also, and more importantly, by effecting a 'bloodless revolution': the Messina Senate, traditionally the preserve of a small oligarchy of silk merchants and landed noblemen, was reformed so that from now on half the seats would be filled by elected representatives of the *popolo* (mainly the artisans organized in the craft guilds); other municipal agencies were similarly thrown open to the *popolo*.

The restoration of calm, however, proved to be but a pause: the city oligarchy was not prepared to accept the drastic curtailment of its power and, in fact, was readying itself for a counter-attack. In July it refused entrance to Spanish troops into the city and executed some leaders of the *popolo*, thus igniting Messina's second revolt – this one an overtly aristocratic revolt or counter-revolution. *Per se* the odds would have been clearly against the rebels had not Spain (and her ally, the Dutch Republic) been at war with France (supported by England): this meant that the rebels could seek and indeed received help from Louis XIV in the form of an expeditionary force that landed in Messina, while a French naval squadron protected the city from the Spanish navy. But even though the French monarch offered Sicily its independence 'under a king of its own', the rest of the island remained loyal to Spain. On his part, Louis XIV did not stage an all-out military campaign and in 1678 withdrew his forces. With the French gone, the aristocratic rebellion collapsed and before the end of the year Spanish troops re-entered the city amidst cheering crowds. The following year the Senate was abolished, the town hall razed, a fortress built to watch over the city, the rebels' property confiscated and Messina, much to Palermo's delight, was stripped of its ancient monopoly over the silk trade and its commercial prosperity destroyed.

The late seventeenth century witnessed one final uprising of major proportions in the Duchy of Savoy, and precisely in the area of Mondoví in southern Piedmont near the Genoese border.[142] Known as the 'salt war' (*guerra del sale*), it was a bloody, long-drawn-out insurrection that unfolded in three stages (1680–82, 1684–86, and 1697–99) with a ferocity that has no parallel in the annals of seventeenth-century Italy. Yet, in spite of its long duration, the seriousness of the challenge it presented to an absolute state in the making, and the size of the military forces deployed to crush it, the 'salt war' has not received in the past the kind of attention that the revolts in

142. A detailed reconstruction of events in Geoffrey Symcox, *Victor Amadeus II. Absolutism in the Savoyard State 1675–1730*, Thames and Hudson 1983, pp. 82–93, 132–3.

Naples and Messina have, possibly because, occurring as it did in the dominions of the House of Savoy rather than in those of Spain, it was viewed as an embarrassment by historians imbued with nationalist fervour and all too often inclined to emphasize the more constructive, more flattering aspects of a dynasty that seemed predestined to achieve one day the unification of Italy.

The salt war was a taxpayers' revolt triggered by the imposition of an onerous tax on salt on a region which, unlike the rest of the Savoyard dominions, had been exempt from it since 1396 when it had accepted to submit to the rule of the House of Savoy. Pressing financial needs had led the government to repeal the exemption, thus not only imposing a fresh burden on the district and threatening the profitable business of smuggling into other parts of Piedmont salt imported from Genoa, but also, and perhaps more importantly, infringing on what the local people considered their ancient 'liberty'. The salt war, in short, represented 'the collision between the expanding authority of the state and the tradition of local autonomy in a region more strongly attached to its ancient independence than perhaps any other in Piedmont'.[143]

In Mondoví, the capital of the district, government forces had a relatively easy time restoring order and collecting the new tax, for the local oligarchy had little taste for a prolonged fight and by 1681 had in fact come to terms with ducal authorities. In the countryside, by contrast, rebellion went on and in the summer of that year the insurgents closed in on Mondoví and, venting their pent-up resentment against a town that had traditionally lorded it over them, looted the houses of the rich. Unable to control the situation, the government granted a full pardon to the rebels in the spring of 1682 and repealed the salt tax. Unrest and violence did not subside, however, for the revolt against the tax now turned into a fratricidal war of country versus town. Nor did an attempt by Duke Vittorio Amedeo II to restore peace with a force of 3,000 men meet with success, for in 1686 his troops had to be diverted to fight the Waldensians further north. Only a decade later was the duke free to mount an all-out campaign against the rebellious district. In 1699 an army 10,000 strong finally managed to defeat the rebels in battle. Repression followed with a ferocity reminiscent of that visited on the Waldensians a few years before: forty-nine rebel leaders were executed, a number of villages were razed to the ground and their inhabitants (nearly 2,500 of them) were deported to the ricefields around Vercelli. Moreover, all traces of local autonomy were erased, the salt tax was collected, and a high-ranking government official was put in charge. Relying on superior military force and exploiting local divisions and ancient hatreds, the absolute state had won in the end.

143. Symcox, p. 83.

CHAPTER FOUR

Religion

Students of seventeenth-century Italy generally agree that Catholicism was a major influence in shaping the lives of the Italian people in nearly all aspects – religious, cultural, social and even political. And as the seventeenth century encompassed much of the period of church history known as the Counter-Reformation or Catholic Reform, it has become widely accepted that in that century the latter left a deep mark on the country. Traditionally, the prevailing view has been that this was to the country's detriment. Writing in the late nineteenth century, in the heady days of nationalism and liberalism, Francesco De Sanctis, in his celebrated *History of Italian Literature* (1870), stigmatized Italian culture in that period as being permeated by hypocrisy, by a taste for hollow appearances and by a servile respect for authority, and he did not hesitate to lay most of the blame for this sorry state of affairs at the doorsteps of the Catholic Church as it had emerged from the Council of Trent (1545–63) – a Church, as he saw it, whose chief concern was to oppose Protestantism and repress all forms of dissidence; a Church whose main goal was to instil in its members a sense of passive, unquestioning obedience to papal authority, and whose key weapons were the Inquisition and the censorship of books. Nor did De Sanctis have to go far to find notorious examples of intolerance: the burning of Giordano Bruno at the stake in 1600, Tommaso Campanella's long incarceration, the condemnation of Galileo in 1633 were all facts that spoke for themselves and seemed to provide a satisfactory explanation for Italy's failure from the late sixteenth to the end of the seventeenth century to produce any poet, historian or political thinker who could remotely compare with the giants of an earlier age – Dante, Petrarch, Ariosto, Machiavelli and Guicciardini.[1]

1. Francesco De Sanctis, *History of Italian Literature*, transl. Joan Redfern, Basic Books, New York 1959, vol. 2, pp. 622–5. In his *Preponderanze straniere*, Vallardi, Milan 1895, p. 111, the distinguished political historian Ettore Callegari used even harsher terms to denounce what he regarded as 'the disastrous consequences' the Counter-Reformation – as epitomized by the papal Inquisition – had on the nation: 'Deprived of any freedom to write, to speak and even to think . . . Italy was turned into the least and the most wretched of all western nations.'

Even though it was limited to culture in general, De Sanctis's assessment of the baneful influence of the Counter-Reformation on the Italian nation is representative of the climate of opinion that prevailed among Italian intellectuals of the nineteenth century. Yet, with qualifications, this negative view has been shared by most scholars in the first half of our century and is still held by some. To be sure, in his masterful *Storia dell'eta' barocca in Italia* (1935) Benedetto Croce provided a more balanced assessment of the period than any of his predecessors would have been willing to countenance. He acknowledged, for instance, that the Church of Rome was no more intolerant than most Protestant churches and that the works of Catholic theologians, church historians and biblical scholars were in no way inferior to those of their opponents. He also recognized the presence in the ranks of Italian Catholicism of large numbers of 'upright men, heroic missionaries, blameless and generous souls' deserving of our admiration; and he had words of praise for the many charitable institutions that the Church founded or promoted; as an Italian, he even expressed gratitude toward the Church and toward the Jesuit order in particular for having quenched the sparks of religious division, thus sparing the country the horrors of religious warfare. For all that, however, Croce's assessment of the Counter-Reformation was hardly more benign than De Sanctis's: in his view the Counter-Reformation was no great spiritual movement comparable to the Renaissance or the Reformation. Rather, it was a sad deviation in the history of the human spirit, for ultimately the Counter-Reformation 'merely defended an institution, the Catholic Church'; as such, it could not have 'the greatness . . . of an eternal spiritual and moral moment' in history. 'No matter how hard one tries', he wrote, 'one cannot find in the Counter-Reformation any other idea but this: that the Catholic Church is a highly salutary institution and is therefore worth preserving and strengthening.' A consequence of this was, in his view, that the Counter-Reformation was essentially 'political' in the sense that it involved a relentless search for whatever means (cultural, religious or political) were best suited to safeguard and buttress the Church as an institution. And this, Croce asserted, explains 'the intellectual and moral poverty inherent in the Counter-Reformation . . . No great book . . . was inspired by it; no great poet, . . . no artist'; all cultural expressions were turned into mere instruments for serving the Church and, as a result, they all withered or rang hollow. In the end, he concluded, 'the orthodoxy of the Counter-Reformation paralleled and fostered Italy's decadence and was in itself an orthodoxy of decadence'.[2]

This negative assessment still has its supporters and seventeenth-century Italy has recently been portrayed as a nation 'humiliated, depressed, sunk in darkness and polluted by hypocrisy', as a nation guided by a Church that 'lacked a prophetic voice capable of confronting the powers that be with the genuine transcendence of otherwordly values';[3] or as a nation in which

2. Benedetto Croce, *Storia dell'età barocca in Italia. Pensiero, poesia e letteratura, vita morale,* 2nd edn, Laterza, Bari 1946, pp. 10, 11, 14, 17, 72, 485.
3. Gino Benzoni, 'Intellettuali e Controriforma', in *SSI*, vol. 11, pp. 130–1.

'religion . . . degenerated into contrived devotional practices' and 'morality . . . into caviling casuistry'[4] with dire consequences on all aspects of life, ranging from the destruction of the glorious legacy of Renaissance humanism to stifling all aspirations for a genuine religious reform, even to killing the spirit of capitalism and hence the economic prosperity of the country.[5]

Since the 1940s, however, voices have been raised against these remorseless indictments of the Counter-Reformation as the chief cause of Italy's woes. A work of revision has been under way ever since which, while neither ignoring nor minimizing the repressive aspects of the Counter-Reformation and their negative impact on Italian life, has brought to light other and more positive aspects, has shown that much of what passes for typical of or unique to Italy in that period was, in fact, common to other countries, both Catholic and Protestant; and, lastly, that the programme pursued by the Church of Rome was neither so pervasive nor so successful as has generally been assumed, but ran into all kinds of obstacles that severely limited its implementation and hence its overall impact on the life of the country.

The work of revision can be said to have first been inspired by Hubert Jedin with the publication in 1946 of a small, but seminal book, *Katholische Reformation oder Gegenreformation?*,[6] in which he persuasively argued that in the history of Catholicism during the sixteenth and seventeenth centuries one must distinguish two separate strands: one was the movement toward the internal 'reform' of the Catholic Church, a movement that preceded the rise of Protestantism (and continued thereafter) and should be properly labeled 'Catholic Reformation'; the other (the Counter-Reformation) was the Church's response to the rise of Protestantism and involved repressive measures and even the resort to force. While, especially after the Council of Trent, the two strands were often intertwined with one same church leader or ecclesiastical agency at times taking part in both, the two strands, Jedin argued, must be kept conceptually distinct if we are fully to understand the course of events. On his part, in 1951 H.O. Evennett presented the Counter-Reformation as 'first and foremost a powerful religious movement' and stated that recognizing it as

---

4. Luigi Firpo, 'The Flowering and Withering of Speculative Italian Philosophy and the Counter-Reformation: the Condemnation of Francesco Patrizi' in *The Late Renaissance 1525–1630*, ed. Eric Cochrane, Harper, New York 1970, p. 270.

5. The large body of literature denouncing the Counter-Reformation as the source of Italy's woes has been critically reviewed by Eric Cochrane, 'Counter-Reformation or Tridentine Reformation? Italy in the Age of Carlo Borromeo' in *San Carlo Borromeo: Catholic Reform and Ecclesiastical Politics in the Second Half of the Sixteenth Century*, ed. John M. Headley and John B. Tomaro, Folger Books, Washington 1988, pp. 31–46.

6. An expanded and updated English version is in *History of the Church*, ed. Hubert Jedin and John Dolan, vol. 5, Burns and Oates 1980, pp. 431–574. On the influence of Jedin's approach on the study of the Italian Church see Susanna Peyronel Rambaldi, 'La Controriforma' in *SSI*, vol. 11, p. 56.

such was 'the first condition of a fruitful approach to its study'.[7] Some twenty years later Jean Delumeau placed the history of early modern Catholicism in a broader European context and saw the Catholic Reform/Counter-Reformation as part of a general religious revival that swept western Europe in the sixteenth century and extended well into the next century: at the heart of that revival, in both Protestant and Catholic versions, was the goal of 'Christianization' of the popular masses who, behind a façade of adherence to the teachings and the rituals of the Church, had in fact a minimal understanding of those teachings and often mixed church rituals with belief in magic and superstition. Nor was that revival, according to Delumeau, merely an attempt by the elite to indoctrinate the uneducated masses: on both sides of the religious divide the revival was also a response by the Churches to a widespread yearning for a more intimate, more personal form of religion. In short, for Delumeau 'the two Reformations, Luther's and Rome's, were two processes which apparently competed, but in actual fact converged, by which the masses were christianized and religion [was] spiritualized'.[8] The same concept of two parallel processes – a Catholic and a Protestant one – was also adopted, albeit from a quite different perspective, by Wolfgang Reinhard in the early 1980s. He rejected the conventional view of the Protestant Reformation as a 'progressive action' and the Catholic Counter-Reformation as a 'reactionary reaction'. He stressed that both movements, after an early spontaneous phase, came under the control of conservative church authorities who strove until the close of the seventeenth century to impose, with the assistance of the state, religious conformity, and to consolidate their identity vis-à-vis rival churches with the formulation of 'confessions of faith', the adoption of a uniform liturgy, the publication of a catechism, the creation of new schools with an overt confessional slant, the censorship of books, the repression of dissent, and a heavy reliance on the power of the state. These two parallel processes he called 'confessionalization'.[9] This is a label that, by stressing the similarities between Catholicism and Protestantism in terms of institutions and strategies, runs the risk of ignoring or at least underestimating the profound doctrinal differences between the two, but has the distinct merit of reminding us that most of the features we traditionally associate with the Counter-Reformation were not uniquely Catholic, let alone uniquely Italian.

7. H.O. Evennett, *The Spirit of the Counter-Reformation*, ed. with a postscript by John Bossy, University of Notre Dame Press, Notre Dame, Ind. 1970, pp. 21–4.
8. Jean Delumeau, *Catholicism between Luther and Voltaire. A New View of the Counter-Reformation*, transl. Jeremy Moiser, Burns and Oates 1977, pp. 1, 28, 154–61. Delumeau's interpretation has been endorsed by A.D. Wright, *The Counter-Reformation: Catholic Europe and the Non-Christian World*, St Martin's Press, New York 1982, pp. 1–6.
9. Wolfgang Reinhard, 'Reformation, Counter-Reformation and the Early Modern State. A Reassessment', *Catholic Historical Review* 75 (1989), pp. 383–404; and more fully in his recent essay, 'Was ist katholische Konfessionalisierung?', *Reformationsgeschichtliche Studien unde Texte* 135 (1995), pp. 419–52.

Given these new perspectives, in the last thirty years or so historians have increasingly trained their attention not only, as their predecessors had done, on the repressive, coercive measures adopted by the Catholic Church (in its Counter-Reformation mode), but also on the efforts aimed at instilling in the faithful a more demanding, more personal, yet accessible, form of spirituality, at improving the level of education and the moral conduct of the clergy, and at encouraging all kinds of charitable initiatives on the part of the laity. Thanks to all this new research we now know far more than before about the various facets of the religious history of Italy and we have a better appreciation of the fact that the leading figures of the Counter-Reformation were not merely concerned (as Croce would have it) with the preservation of the institutional Church (although they no doubt were concerned with that, too), but also with the quality of religion as preached by the clergy and as practiced by their flock. Uppermost on the minds of at least the best among them was a new sense of their responsibilities as shepherds of souls, a heightened sense of mission that required of them not only that they shield the flock from the danger of heresy, but also that they combat religious ignorance, the practice of magic and all kinds of superstitious beliefs. But we also know more about how difficult the implementation of those goals proved to be; how much even the best intentions ran into walls of inertia or of outright opposition; and how, by the end of the century, actual results fell far short of expectations. This being the case, the image of the Counter-Reformation Church as a monolithic, all-powerful institution capable of controlling and reshaping all aspects of Italian life appears less and less convincing.[10]

At the heart of the programme of Christianization was the notion that the Church must be 'reformed', that is to say purged of clerical abuses, such as simony, pluralism, non-residence, and concubinage; that religious life, at all levels, must be made to conform to higher standards of spirituality; and that the Christian message must be felt throughout society.[11] It is revealing, in this respect, that what is considered one of the earliest and in the long run most influential expressions of the Catholic Reform movement in Italy, namely the Schools of Christian Doctrine founded in Milan in 1539, was originally named Compagnia della Reformatione Christiana and that its by-laws, as revised in

10. The view that the Counter-Reformation Church was primarily concerned with 'controlling' each and every aspect of Italian society and culture and the implication that it was largely successful in doing so is at the heart of Adriano Prosperi, 'Intellettuali e Chiesa all'inizio dell'età moderna' in *SIE Annali* 4 (1981), pp. 161–252, where the word '*controllo*' appears nearly on every page. In the same volume Piero Camporesi, 'Cultura popolare e cultura d'elite fra Medioevo ed eta moderna', p. 128, speaks of the Church's 'strategy of uncompromising and hegemonic control' over all social classes.

11. On the medieval antecedents of the concept of 'reform' see Konrad Burdach, *Riforma, Rinascimento, Umanesimo, Due dissertazioni sui fondamenti della cultura e dell'arte della parola moderne* (1918) transl. Delio Cantimori, Sansoni, Florence 1935, pp. 11–48.

1585, expressed its main goal with these words: 'Teaching children well is to reform the world toward a true Christian life'.[12] In a similar vein Ignatius Loyola, the founder of the Jesuit order, in encouraging the formation of lay congregations, had set as their goal 'the reform of the world'.[13] In this ambitious perspective, all individuals – high born and low born, young and old, clergy and laity – and all social groups must be remoulded according to the Christian paradigm. Nor did this grand programme remain the property of a few isolated individuals. Under the shock produced by the Protestant Reformation and within the parameters set by the Council of Trent, it became a wide-ranging and to some extent a centrally coordinated plan of which Italy, due to the presence of the Papacy on its soil, was likely to be the main beneficiary – or, as its detractors would say, its chief victim.

To implement this programme one of the earliest steps was the publication of a catechism in which the principles of Catholic dogma and ethics were presented in terms accessible even to the uneducated masses; on their part, reform-minded bishops, preachers and parish priests strove to drive home to their flock the importance of 'purifying' their lives, of availing themselves of sacraments and devotional practices as aids to a more Christian conduct, of avoiding not only major sins such as blasphemy, usury, fornication and drunkenness, but also popular forms of entertainment like dancing, dicing, the carnival, which they considered as conducive to immorality. At the same time a more demanding code of behaviour, a 'daily ascetism' was urged (as it was at the time by the Protestant reformers) that stressed diligence, frugality, self-control, and the performance of 'works of mercy' toward the poor and the sick.[14]

REFORMING THE CLERGY

To carry out its vast programme of Christianization of the masses the Tridentine Church needed, first of all, a dedicated, disciplined and

12. Miriam Turrini, ' "Riformare il mondo a vera vita christiana": le scuole di catechismo nell'Italia del Cinquecento', *AISIG* 8 (1962), pp. 407 and 435.
13. Louis Chatellier, *The Europe of the Devout. The Catholic Reformation and the Formation of a New Society*, transl. Jean Birrell, Cambridge University Press 1989, p. 11.
14. On self-discipline in the workplace and the mutual obligations of employers and employees as advocated by Carlo Borromeo see Albano Biondi, 'Aspetti della cultura cattolica post-tridentina. Religione e controllo sociale' in *SIE Annali* 4 (1981), p. 264; on efforts at suppressing popular forms of entertainment, Peter Burke, *Popular Culture in Early Modern Europe*, Harper, New York 1978, pp. 208ff.; and Elide Casali, ' "Economica" e "Creanza" cristiana', *QS* 41 (1979), pp. 555–83, on religious literature intended to remind landowners of their duty to combat superstition and foster piety and high moral standards among their tenants.

well-trained clergy capable of leading their flock and of serving as exemplars for them to follow, and, in fact, the Council of Trent had given a great deal of attention to clerical 'reform' and had formulated directives to that effect, notably as regards the qualifications and the responsibilities of church leaders, the bishops. The ideal bishop, as envisaged by the Council, was to be first and foremost a 'good shepherd' with the care of souls (*cura animarum*) as his primary duty.[15] As such, he was expected to reside in his diocese (and this implied the end of the lucrative practice of pluralism whereby one same prelate held title to more than one diocese); he was also expected to visit periodically all the parish churches under his jurisdiction, to hold annual meetings (synods) of the clergy of the diocese, and to inspect at regular intervals the monasteries and convents located in it in order to ensure that monks, friars and nuns lived blameless lives. Bishops were also required to come periodically to Rome and report to the pope in person (*ad limina* visits), to keep Rome regularly informed of conditions in their dioceses, and to carry out all instructions and directives emanating from the Curia.

In the half century or so after the closing of the Council, the blueprint of the ideal bishop found concrete expression in a number of outstanding churchmen, whose example was to remain normative for generations to come. The most famous of them all was Carlo Borromeo, archbishop of Milan from 1565 to 1584, but there were others in his generation with an exemplary record as bishops – men like Gabriele Paleotti in Bologna, Ippolito de' Rossi in Pavia, Alfonso Carafa and Burali d'Arezzo in Naples. They all shared an unquestionable, although never servile, loyalty to the Holy See, an intense piety, and a strong commitment to work for the spiritual welfare of their flock, to relieve poverty, and to raise the quality of the clergy. This unusual cluster of remarkable church leaders and the relative success of their work of reform apparently did not have its equivalent in the first half of the seventeenth century:[16] few names of bishops stand out in that period (Federico Borromeo of Milan was one of them) and the implementation of the Tridentine programme seems to have slowed down. This is not surprising given the tragic sequel of wars, popular uprisings, famines and epidemics that struck Italy between 1610 and 1656; moreover, the Papacy's involvement in the politics of the Thirty Years War no doubt diverted its attention from the work of reform. By contrast, in the second half of the century, in what has been called the 'Tridentine revival', one encounters several names of outstanding bishops, from Stefano Durazzo in Genoa and Gregorio Barbarigo in Venice to the three distinguished Neapolitan archbishops Innico Caracciolo, Antonio Pignatelli and Giacomo Cantelmo Stuart.[17]

15. Hubert Jedin, *Il tipo ideale di vescovo secondo la Riforma cattolica*, transl. E. Durini, Morcelliana, Brescia 1950, pp. 81–110; Delumeau, *Catholicism*, pp. 18–19.
16. Peyronel Rambaldi, 'La Controriforma', p. 68.
17. The expression 'Tridentine revival' (*regain tridentin*) is in Jean-Michel Sallmann, 'Le catholicisme triomphant en Italie au XVIIe siècle' in Yves-Marie Bercé *et al.*, *L'Italie au XVIIe siècle*, Sedes, Paris 1989, p. 239. On late seventeenth-century

It would be wrong, however, to assume that even when the Italian Church was graced with outstanding leaders as it was in the late sixteenth and again in the late seventeenth century, the Tridentine programme of reform was fully implemented and that religious conditions in general improved dramatically. And it would be misleading to draw sweeping conclusions from the achievements of a few exceptional bishops while ignoring the failures or the inaction of the many among their peers who shared neither their vision nor their zeal. One must also bear in mind that, regardless of the personalities of individual bishops, the Tridentine programme ran against formidable obstacles and constraints that stood in the way of its implementation.

Ironically, one type of constraint came, at times, from the Roman Curia itself, specifically from the Congregation of the Council, the central agency, that is, that was charged with interpreting the Tridentine decrees and scrutinizing any initiative taken by the bishops at the local level. Control from the centre was probably a necessity if reform was to spread to the whole Catholic Church and if the Papacy was to counter the influence of the modern centralizing state over church affairs; but it could also thwart the efforts or dampen the zeal of even the most dedicated prelate by requiring that all their decisions and plans be scrutinized and, if need be, amended in Rome before they were enacted. This could lead to exasperating delays at best or to a bishop's directives being blocked by a curial veto at worst – something even as loyal and highly respected a prelate as Carlo Borromeo lamented when he wrote: 'Bishops know very well what measures are necessary or useful for the good administration of their flock; [this point is] something that is beyond the understanding of those who are far away and who, by and large, have never had the experience of running a local church.'[18]

No less serious was the problem presented by the large number of dioceses in Italy (315 of them as opposed to 130 in France, a country much larger than Italy), some of them diminutive in size and lacking an adequate financial base;[19] one consequence of this fragmentation was, as will be seen, that many of them found it economically impossible to establish and support a seminary as mandated by the Council of Trent. The problem could be compounded by the fact that a good many dioceses were burdened by so-called 'pensions', in the sense that part of their revenues were earmarked for

bishops, Gregorio Penco, *Storia della Chiesa in Italia*, vol. 2: *Dal Concilio di Trento ai nostri giorni*, Jaca Book, Milan 1976, pp. 28–30, and Romeo De Maio, *Società e vita religiosa a Napoli nell'età moderna (1656–1799)*, Edizioni Scientifiche Italiane, Naples 1971, pp. 23–7.

18. Quotation in Peyronel Rambaldi, 'La Controriforma', p. 67. On the curia's interference see also Achille Erba, *La Chiesa sabauda tra Cinque e Seicento: ortodossia tridentina, gallicanesimo savoiardo e assolutismo ducale (1580–1630)*, Herder, Rome 1979, pp. 86–7.

19. Joseph Bergin, 'Between Estate and Profession: the Catholic Parish Clergy of Early Modern Western Europe' in *Social Orders and Social Classes in Europe since 1500: Studies in Social Stratification*, ed. M.L. Bush, Longman 1992, p. 67.

other prelates, notably for officials in the Roman Curia or for the pope's nephews. This was especially true of the Kingdom of Naples where nearly a quarter of all episcopal revenues was absorbed by pensions. Although openly recognized as an evil, the system of pensions could not be easily eradicated because on it depended the livelihood of large numbers of curial prelates who could not have been supported out of the chronically depleted papal treasury.[20]

What a lack of resources and the burden of pensions could mean in the life of a diocese was dramatically exposed by a close advisor to the reform-minded Pope Innocent XI (1676–89):

a wretched bishop cannot assist the poor who are his children; he cannot provide stipends for good clerics . . .; oftentimes he is tempted to commit abuses and confer holy orders for a price in an attempt to find enough money for paying the pension . . . The most suitable candidates refuse to serve in a diocese that is burdened with pensions and in the end the [vacant] position goes to some foolish man full of ambition or to some discontented friar. [Forced to raise money] the bishop makes himself detested to his clergy and to his flock by charging heavy fees for [religious] services that normally ought to be provided at no charge or at a more moderate rate.[21]

Innocent XI, by the way, took steps to remedy the situation and in 1677 (a good century after the Council of Trent) substantially reduced the number of pensions thus providing at least partial relief to beleaguered bishops, and his reforms were vigorously pursued by Innocent XII two decades later.

Pensions, however, were not the only drain on diocesan resources. To an extent that varied from state to state, governments too made claims on church revenues and added to the bishops' woes,[22] making it difficult and often impossible for them to set up a seminary or to provide adequate financial assistance to those among their clergy (and there were many of them especially in rural areas) who lived in utter poverty and often made ends meet by engaging in secular activities, in clear violation of canon law and to the obvious detriment of the care of souls. 'Let no priest', thundered the arch-bishop of Turin in 1625, 'work as physician or surgeon, or as attorney in a

20. Mario Rosa, 'Curia romana e pensioni ecclesiastiche: fiscalità pontificia nel Mezzogiorno (secoli XVI–XVIII), QS 42 (1979), pp. 1030–4 and 'La Chiesa meridionale nell'età della Controriforma' in SIE Annali 9 (1986), pp. 299–309. The cost of nepotism reached its highest levels between 1623 and 1676 during the pontificates of Urban VIII, Alexander VII and Clement X as documented by Fausto Piola Caselli, 'Crisi economica e finanza pubblica nello Stato Pontificio tra XVI e XVII secolo' in La finanza pubblica in età di crisi, ed. Antonio Di Vittorio, Cacucci, Bari 1992, p. 173.
21. Claudio Donati, 'La Chiesa di Roma tra antico regime e riforme settecentesche (1675–1760), in SIE Annali 9 (1986), pp. 721–6; the quotation appears on p. 723. Further relief was provided by Innocent XII (1691–1700): Piola Caselli, 'Crisi economica', p. 153.
22. Enrico Stumpo, 'Il consolidamento della grande proprietà ecclesiastica nell'età della Controriforma' in SIE Annali 9, pp. 288–9.

secular court or as notary in private transactions. Let them abstain from trade
. . . and from teaching women how to read, write, sing or play an instrument . . . '.[23]

To speak of bishops in financial straits and of parish priests living in
poverty may sound paradoxical in light of the fact that the Italian Church as a
whole owned vast amounts of land as well as government securities and
actually saw its holdings steadily increase in the course of the century as
bequests and donations from pious men and women poured in, especially in
the wake of the great epidemics of 1630 and 1656.[24] The problem, however,
was not only that ecclesiastical wealth was unevenly distributed and that
glaring disparities existed between dioceses, but also, and more importantly,
that much of that wealth was in the hands of the great monastic houses or
abbeys which lay outside the bishops' jurisdiction and for the most part
showed little inclination to come to the assistance of poor dioceses and
parishes; the less so as they were often held *in commenda* in the sense that,
in spite of the directives of the Council of Trent, the titular abbot was an
absentee prelate who held a position in the Roman Curia or even in a secular
government and thus considered the abbey merely a source of income to
support himself and his entourage.[25] Given this state of affairs, it is hardly
surprising that a good many abbeys were far from being beacons of 'reform'
and were denounced by the saintly bishop Francis of Sales in 1618 as dens of
'crass ignorance, stenching immorality, greed and intolerable arrogance'.[26]

The maldistribution and the misuse of church revenues was thus a major
obstacle to the programme of regeneration launched at Trent and failure to
remove that obstacle represented one of the most serious limitations affecting
a Church that is often portrayed as an efficient, well-disciplined, all-powerful
organization capable of controlling every aspect of Italian life. And there were
other, equally serious obstacles, notably the way bishops were selected. In
this respect, even the most zealous and dedicated pope had his hands largely
tied, for by the early sixteenth century most Italian (and European) states had
secured from a weak Papacy the right to nominate to a number of church
positions, subject only to papal confirmation. On this score conditions varied
a good deal from state to state, the governments of the Republics of Genoa
and Lucca, the Duchies of Savoy, Parma, and Modena, and the Grand Duchy
of Tuscany enjoying a nearly total control over episcopal appointments, while
in the State of Milan, the Venetian Republic, the Kingdoms of Naples and of
Sicily, and, of course, the Papal States a majority of episcopal sees were fully

23. On clerical poverty see Erba, *La Chiesa sabauda*, pp. 178 and 194–6 (quotation
    on p. 195); Paolo Preto, 'Benefici parrocchiali e altari dotati dopo il Tridentino a
    Padova' *QS* 15 (1970), pp. 795–813; Carla Russo, 'I redditi dei parroci nei casali di
    Napoli: struttura e dinamica (XVI–XVIII secolo)' in *Per la storia sociale e religiosa
    del Mezzogiorno d'Italia*, ed. Giuseppe Galasso and Carla Russo, vol. 1, Guida,
    Naples 1980, pp. 145–60; and Sallmann, 'Le catholicisme triomphant', pp. 252–7.
24. Stumpo, 'Il consolidamento', pp. 268–9 and Luigi Faccini, *La Lombardia fra
    Seicento e Settecento*, Franco Angeli, Milan 1988, pp. 144–6.
25. Delumeau, *Catholicism*, p. 27; Erba, *La Chiesa sabauda*, pp. 208–11.
26. Quotation in Erba, *La Chiesa sabauda*, p. 372.

in the pope's gift.[27] Altogether, secular authorities probably controlled a majority of appointments in the country and, predictably, made them on the basis of political as much as of religious considerations.[28] This did not necessarily exclude exemplary clerics from the episcopate, but it stands to reason that, by and large, the selection of bishops was heavily influenced by political considerations that had little to do with the care of souls.

Secular interference was even more pervasive at the level of lesser ecclesiastical offices or 'benefices', such as cathedral canonries, parishes, chaplaincies, abbeys and so on. It would appear that over half of them throughout Italy were controlled by laymen in the sense that the latter – whether heads of state, feudal lords, city councils, or wealthy families – enjoyed the right of lay patronage (giuspatronato): the right, that is, to nominate a cleric of their choice, the role of church authorities being merely that of ensuring that the nominee met the minimal requirements (holy orders) for the office. The system obviously gave secular governments ample opportunities for rewarding loyal servants or supporters without dipping into the public treasury; to influential families with one or more ecclesiastical positions in their gift it provided a valuable means for securing a livelihood for younger sons. At the same time the system undermined the bishop's authority both because he had little say in the choice of candidates and because, once a man received the benefice from his lay patron, he enjoyed, for all practical purposes, tenure for life.

That lay patronage was recognized as a major obstacle to effective reform is borne out by the fact that at Trent a draft proposal on 'the reform of the princes' had been introduced by the papal legates that was aimed at eliminating virtually all forms of lay patronage. But the proposed legislation, which would have dealt 'a mortal blow' to the whole system, had to be shelved in the face of the dogged opposition of several governments. The withdrawal of the 'reform of princes' was a major defeat for the forces of reform and for the next two hundred years the Papacy would try in vain to recover from it.[29]

In the Kingdom of Naples lay control over the clergy took two other forms, both equally resented by reformist bishops. In the towns, notably in Naples itself, a large number (possibly half) of churches were run by vestries (mastrie) composed of laymen: although their authority was per se limited to the administration of the church's temporal affairs, vestries often played a major role in the appointment of a new pastor and treated him, in the words of a bishop writing in the 1590s, as 'a mercenary and subordinate'.[30] In the

27. Wolfgang Reinhard, 'Finanza pontificia, sistema beneficiale e finanza statale nell'età confessionale' in Fisco, religione, stato nell'età confessionale, ed. Hermann Kellenbenz and Paolo Prodi, Mulino, Bologna 1989, pp. 479–81.
28. Erba, La Chiesa sabauda, pp. 264–74.
29. What precedes is based mainly on Gaetano Greco, 'I giuspatronati laicali nell'età moderna' in SIE Annali 9 (1986), pp. 553–72.
30. Carla Russo, 'Parrocchie, fabbricerie e comunita nell'area suburbana della diocesi di Napoli (XVI–XVIII secolo)' in Per la storia sociale e religiosa del Mezzogiorno, pp. 9–79.

countryside, on the other hand, probably three-quarters of all parishes were *chiese ricettizie*. In the eyes of the law these were autonomous corporations each with its own endowment of farmland donated in times past by members of the community and each entitled to recruit its priests from among men born in the community itself. The drawbacks of the system are obvious enough: not only did the bishop have little say in the selection of new clergy and no control at all on how parish revenues were spent, but recruiting priests exclusively within small communities and under the influence of the local landed families was not likely to produce an especially zealous and inspired clergy. As such, the system found its harshest critics among the bishops who distinguished themselves for their piety and for their commitment to reform, and its staunchest supporters among government officials who were only too glad to preserve a system that shackled episcopal authority so effectively. Paradoxically, Rome must share some of the blame for perpetuating the system, for it chose not to back up the reforming bishops in their efforts to dismantle the *ricettizie*, apparently for fear that any all-out attempt to do so would have led to a major confrontation with Spanish authorities and would have likely resulted in a humiliating defeat for the Holy See. And so the *ricettizie* survived and no doubt impeded the progress of reform.[31]

In the South clerics who owed their position to lay patrons or were firmly ensconced in parishes that were legally and economically autonomous were but one of the problems bishops had to contend with. Another and no less serious problem was represented by a growing number of footloose clerics (known as *chierici selvaggi* or wild clerics) who had neither a definite ecclesiastical assignment nor a firm source of income and, as ·such, were clearly redundant and difficult to subject to the discipline and decorum envisaged by the Council of Trent. And there were more and more of them. It is estimated that between the closing of the Council and the mid-eighteenth century the number of Italian ecclesiastics, whether priests or clerics who received minor orders but stopped short of being ordained to the priesthood, increased dramatically. While the increase was especially large in the South (which by mid-century had proportionately three to four times as many clerics as the North), it affected the entire peninsula. Behind the trend several causes were at work, but it is unlikely that a rise in genuine religious vocations was among them. As a church official writing from Rome to the papal nuncio in Naples in 1626 lamented, 'many individuals receive the tonsure and minor orders, in order to escape the jurisdiction of the civil courts and to claim the immunity [from taxation] enjoyed by clerics and not because they have an inclination to religious life'. For those who chose to be ordained to the priesthood an incentive to do so was provided, in the absence of a true

31. On the origins of *ricettizie* see Fiorenzo Romita, 'Ricettizie, chiese' in *Enciclopedia Cattolica*, vol. 10, p. 876; as obstacles to the reform of the clergy: Gabriele De Rosa, *Chiesa e religione popolare nel Mezzogiorno*, Laterza, Bari 1978, pp. 27–33, 57–65.

commitment to the ministry, by the growing number of pious bequests intended to pay for masses for the deceased; an unattached priest could thus hope to earn a modest living from small stipends without ever concerning himself with the care of souls.[32] An eighteenth-century churchman described those unattached clerics as follows: 'One sees priests who run wherever the stipend for the celebration of masses is highest, notably at funerals . . . just like artisans and wage labourers who seek to be hired at the highest possible rate.'[33]

But possibly of greater importance in directing young men to the ministry was family pressure in that a career, however modest, in the Church was seen as a way of taking care of younger sons while leaving the family estate intact for the oldest son to inherit. Conscientious bishops were well aware of the problem and of the harm 'forced vocations' did to the individuals involved as well as to the reputation of the Church. Wrote a bishop toward the end of the century:

Surrounded by their numerous sons and daughters, [parents] pick and choose among them as one would do with fish or apples, deciding without appeal that one must become a priest, another a nun, another yet a friar, and that this one should marry . . . Fathers and mothers without shame, all you want is for your children to double [the size of] your estate . . . for out of the five children you have you force two daughters and two sons to become nuns and friars so as to save money and to increase the pile of money or the properties intended for the remaining son who, by marrying, will carry on the memory of your name and the reputation of the family.[34]

Ordinations to the priesthood based on self-interest rather than on a true vocation would not have been so common had future priests been required to spend years of rigorous training in a seminary and had they been carefully screened by their bishop and questioned about their true intentions before being admitted to holy orders. This is what the Council of Trent had envisaged for them, but in actual fact those requirements were not generally enforced. Not only, as will be seen, did most dioceses fail to set up a seminary, but even the screening procedure could be circumvented either by the candidate dissimulating his true intention or by a bishop who, presumably in order to accommodate the wishes of an influential family, was willing to ordain a young man without asking too many questions. Unscrupulous prelates could evade another requirement set by the Council, namely that no one should be ordained unless there was a vacant position (a benefice or living) waiting for him. Cardinal Innico Caracciolo, the austere and reforming archbishop of Naples who worked strenuously to recruit to the priesthood only genuinely committed men, deplored in 1683 the unsavoury practice followed by a fellow bishop: 'I know that in a poor diocese near Naples one of the canonries is called the canonry of ordinations. Anyone, even a total

32. Xenio Toscani, 'Il reclutamento del clero (secoli XVI–XIX)' in *SIE Annali* 9 (1986), pp. 577–91 (quotation on p. 586).
33. Quotation in De Rosa, *Chiesa e religione popolare*, p. 25.
34. Quotation in Toscani, 'Il reclutamento del clero', p. 588.

stranger, who wanted to be ordained simply applied to receive it; he was then duly ordained and shortly after resigned his office as canon and left the diocese so that the same canonry could be used again for others.'[35] Possibly out of charity, Caracciolo did not specify whether the obliging prelate performed those ordinations for a fee, but one is inclined to think that he did.

Clerics who did not go beyond minor orders could not, of course, expect to earn a living by saying masses for the dead or by officiating at weddings and funerals, and thus had to find other sources of income. Their number, one should point out, was far from negligible at least in some parts of the country: around 1640 in Calabria out of a total of about 8,000 clerics only a third were priests. Calabria may have been an extreme case, but nearby Apulia, with only half its clergy consisting of priests, had no cause for rejoicing. To earn a living this plethora of minor clerics often served as secretaries, tenants, handymen or guards on ecclesiastical or lay estates, when they did not join groups of bandits. Their immunity from taxation and from the jurisdiction of civil courts made them especially attractive as employees, but, as responsible church leaders never tired to lament, their presence cast discredit on the Church as a whole.[36]

The problems created by lay patronage, family pressure and the casual ordination of unqualified candidates by easy-going bishops would have been mitigated, if not entirely resolved, had all candidates to the priesthood been required to go through years of rigorous intellectual training and a strict regimen of devotional practices in established and closely monitored schools. Little wonder, then, that the Council of Trent had urged (although, for practical reasons, not formally required) bishops to set up schools to be known as 'seminaries' (literally 'nurseries') and in doing so had departed from the long-standing practice whereby the training of future priests was either handled by the universities or more commonly by older priests who informally instructed their pupils in a sort of apprenticeship.[37] The traditional

---

35. Quotation ibid., p. 590.
36. Pasquale Lopez, *Riforma cattolica e vita religiosa a Napoli dalla fine del Cinquecento ai primi anni del Settecento*, Istituto Editoriale del Mezzogiorno, Naples and Rome 1964, pp. 32–8; Rosario Villari, *Ribelli e riformatori dal XVI al XVIII secolo*, Editori Riuniti, Rome 1983, pp. 91–4; Rosa, 'La Chiesa meridionale', pp. 315–21; Aurelio Musi, 'Fisco, religione e stato nel Mezzogiorno d'Italia (secoli XVI–XVII)' in *Fisco, religione, stato nell'età confessionale*, pp. 449–50.
37. Maurilio Guasco, 'La formazione del clero: i seminari' in *SIE Annali* 9 (1986), pp. 634–9. Since Italian universities did not have a faculty of theology, the few clerics who attended them enrolled in the law faculty (Elena Brambilla, 'Società ecclesiastica e società civile: aspetti della formazione del clero dal Cinquecento alla Restaurazione', *Società e Storia* 12 (1981), pp. 308–29) with the result that the Italian secular clergy was notoriously weak in terms of theological preparation (Giancarlo Angelozzi, 'L'insegnamento dei casi di coscienza nella pratica educativa della Compagnia di Gesù' in *La "Ratio studiorum". Modelli culturali e pratiche educative dei Gesuiti in Italia tra Cinque e Seicento*, ed. G.P. Brizzi, Bulzoni, Rome 1981, pp. 146–7).

practice, needless to say, had produced mixed results, to put it mildly: while the Church had always had some competent clergy, one of the most frequent complaints levelled at the diocesan clergy in the sixteenth century had been that most of them were abysmally ignorant (*imperitissimi viri* a 1536 document called them) to the point of near illiteracy and that there was little in the moral conduct and demeanour of many parish priests that would distinguish them from their flock, especially when it came to hunting, drinking, gambling and consorting with women of dubious reputation. To those who advocated reform, the institution of seminaries thus looked like a first crucial step toward a better educated, more disciplined and more conscientious clergy. As Cardinal Sforza Pallavicino, the author of the official history of the Council of Trent published in 1656–57, put it, at the Council 'the institution of seminaries was especially praised, many [bishops] going so far as to say that if nothing else had come out of the Council, this decision alone would have been recompense enough for all their labours and inconveniences'.[38]

As was often the case with other aspects of the Catholic reform programme, however, the gap between good intentions and their implementation proved to be very wide indeed, so much so, in fact, that not until the beginning of the twentieth century, that is to say a good three centuries after Trent, were all Italian priests trained in seminaries. Not that the Council's call for the establishment of seminaries fell on deaf ears. In fact it was answered in earnest by those bishops who were committed to the renewal of religious life – men such as Borromeo in Milan, Paleotti in Bologna, Bollani in Brescia, Carafa in Naples, Morone in Macerata to name but a few – and in the closing decades of the sixteenth century seminaries opened their doors in a good number (albeit a minority) of Italian dioceses. This promising trend, however, slowed down in the first half of the next century when few new seminaries were created and some that were already in operation had to be closed. There was a slight improvement after 1660 at the time of the Tridentine revival, but by the end of the century a majority of Italian dioceses were still without a seminary.[39] The main reason behind this rather modest record of achievement was economic as a large number of dioceses simply lacked the resources to open a seminary or to keep it going after it had been opened. Such was the case at Lecce in Apulia at the start of the century, where the bishop tried to establish a seminary, but had to drop his plans for lack of funds; or in Pozzuoli near Naples where one did open in 1587, but had to be closed within a few years for the same reason; nor did a second attempt in 1624 prove more successful. And the same dismal record of failed attempts

38. Quotations in Guasco, 'La formazione del clero', pp. 630 and 639.
39. Luciano Allegra, 'Il parroco: un mediatore fra alta e bassa cultura' in *SIE Annali* 4 (1981), pp. 902–4 (on late sixteenth-century seminaries); Guasco, 'La formazione del clero', pp. 648 and 656 identifies sixty-four seminaries being created between 1552 and 1564 as against forty-five between 1600 and 1650.

prevailed in Piedmont, too.[40] Even where, as in Naples, a seminary managed to remain in operation from the time of its foundation in 1568, its existence was precarious and its educational standards were rather low as it had to struggle against severe financial constraints. Only from the 1670s, under the leadership of archbishops Caracciolo and Cantelmo, did the Naples seminary find a more solid economic basis and achieve higher intellectual and spiritual standards.[41]

Although few in numbers, the seminaries that came into existence did make an impact on the quality of at least part of the clergy. 'There was a marked contrast', it has been said, 'between the few clerics who had been trained in the seminaries and the many who had not and who lived on the fringes of the institutional Church.'[42] The reason for the contrast is easily understood, if one bears in mind how seminarians were trained. Following the example set by Carlo Borromeo in the seminary he established in Milan in 1565, the new institutions aimed at turning out priests who, in terms of education, piety, moral conduct and outward decorum would stand as models of Christian living and exude the high dignity and the distinct nature of the clerical status. To that end Borromeo had insisted, in the rules he laid down for his seminary, not only on rigorous intellectual training and an austere lifestyle, but also on a strict code of dress and manners: seminarians must wear the cassock, always behave with 'gravity', and avoid the use of titles of nobility when addressing fellow seminarians of genteel extraction – all these rules being meant to drive home the fact that, as future priests, they were all peers who were about to join a group clearly distinct from lay society. The awareness of being members of a separate 'estate' was reinforced in the literature intended for the edification of future priests by the insistence that they should never tolerate the arrogance of overbearing laymen and should be ready 'to resist anyone, including princes, whenever the independence, the dignity and the property of the Church were at stake'.[43]

Where seminaries did not exist or could train but a fraction of future priests other channels became available through which the Tridentine model of the priest could make inroads, however slowly. In the State of Milan and in Piedmont one such channel was provided by the periodical meetings (congregazioni) which the rural clergy of a given district (pieve) were required to attend, there to be instructed by visiting theologians on matters of dogma and ethics.[44] In the Kingdom of Naples a similar role came to be played after 1668 by the Priests of the Mission (also known as Lazarists), an

40. Mario Rosa, *Religione e società nel Mezzogiorno tra Cinque e Seicento*, Di Donato, Bari 1976, p. 56 (on Lecce); Lopez, *Riforma cattolica*, p. 120 (on Pozzuoli); Erba, *La Chiesa sabauda*, pp. 312–22 (on Piedmont).

41. Lopez, *Riforma cattolica*, pp. 126–34.

42. Rosa, 'La Chiesa meridionale', p. 324.

43. Prosperi, 'Intellettuali e chiesa', pp. 225–6; Allegra, 'Il parroco', pp. 922–4.

44. Danilo Zardin, 'L'ultimo periodo spagnolo (1631–1712). Da Cesare Monti a Giuseppe Archinto' in *Storia religiosa della Lombardia*, vol. 10: *Diocesi di Milano*, La Scuola, Brescia 1990, p. 582; Erba, *La Chiesa sabauda*, pp. 349 and 352.

order founded in France in 1628 by St Vincent de Paul specifically to minister to the intellectual and spiritual needs of the parish clergy.[45] It was thanks to agencies such as these that, even where a seminary did not exist, the quality of the clergy slowly but noticeably improved especially in the later part of the century. Other factors helped too, notably the new spiritual climate (the Tridentine revival) that prevailed among the higher echelons of the Church in the last quarter of the century. In Rome two austere popes, Innocent XI (1676–89) and Innocent XII (1691–1700), first imposed strict limits to and ultimately dismantled the system of pensions and put an end to the practice of nepotism in which some of their predecessors had engaged with abandon. From Innocent XI also came new directives aimed at curbing the lavish lifestyle of many prelates and at ensuring that bishops would reside in their dioceses.[46] At the diocesan level the main focus was on the quality of the clergy. Greater attention was devoted to the selection of candidates to the priesthood and to their training, if not in a seminary, at least in a school run by a religious order or in a university. Results were especially dramatic in Naples where the succession of three archbishops committed to reform (Caracciolo, Pignatelli and Cantelmo) between 1667 and 1702 led to noticeable improvement in the intellectual calibre of the clerics as shown by the growing number of university graduates in their ranks (20 per cent by the end of the century as against a mere 3 per cent in the first half) as well as by the presence of clergy in the buoyant cultural life of the city, notably in the Accademia degli Investiganti which, as will be seen, did so much to revitalize intellectual life in that period.[47]

A contribution to raising standards of clerical education and conduct was also made by the bishops' periodic visitations to the parishes of their dioceses. Although mandated by the Council of Trent, visitations had long remained rather sporadic events until about 1660, largely due to the unsettled conditions of the country in the preceding four decades. After that date the visitation became a normal feature in the life of a parish, and it was no mere formality surrounded by pomp and ceremony, for in the course of a visitation a bishop could interview not only the local pastor, but a number of parishioners as well, and if we are to judge from the few records that have survived and have been studied, those parishioners could be quite outspoken in exposing their pastor's failings and faults, thus providing the bishop with the information he needed to correct them.[48]

45. De Maio, *Società e vita religiosa*, p. 11; Sallmann, 'Le catholicisme triomphant', pp. 257–8; Guasco, 'La formazione del clero', pp. 658–68.
46. Donati, 'La Chiesa di Roma', pp. 726–8 and 733; Sallmann, 'Le catholicisme triomphant', pp. 238–9.
47. Giacomo Garzya, 'Reclutamento e sacerdotalizzazione del clero secolare nella diocesi di Napoli. Dinamica di una nuova politica pastorale nella seconda metà del Seicento' in *Per la storia sociale e religiosa*, vol. 2, pp. 128 and 157; De Maio, *Società e vita religiosa*, pp. 22–3, 44–6 and 69–73.
48. A vivid instance is provided by Laura Megna, 'Vita religiosa e pietà di popolo in una comunità rurale vicentina d'ancien regime: Lisiera e centri limitrofi nell'età

The inadequacies of the parish clergy deriving from a lack of resources, poor training and lay interference in the selection process were alleviated in part by the religious orders, both those of late medieval vintage such as the Franciscan and Dominican orders of mendicant friars and those (Jesuits, Barnabites, Somaschi and Theatines) that were founded in the first half of the sixteenth century. As orders of 'clerics regular', the new creations represented a departure from traditional practice in that they were intended as communities of priests who were largely free from such traditional monastic obligations as the long hours devoted to choir service and a life of relative isolation from the outside world. Rather, they were meant to serve in the world, setting an example of priestly virtue, teaching the catechism, preaching, hearing confessions, caring for orphans and other people in need and occasionally, where no seminary was in existence, training future priests in their schools. Unlike the mendicants, communities of clerics regular were allowed to own property and thus did not have to solicit alms for supporting themselves.

The religious orders, old and new, unquestionably played a major and growing role in ministering to the Italian people and in many ways, as will be seen, compensated for the inadequacies of the parish clergy. But they, too, were beset by problems, some of them caused by their own successes. The administration of the large farming estates donated or bequeathed by pious lay men and women for the support of their churches, shrines and schools sometimes became an end in itself and thus diverted the orders' attention from their mission, the care of souls – witness the repeated reprimands addressed by the superior general of the Jesuits to those among his brethren who neglected their religious duties for the lucrative trade in wine produced on the order's estates.[49] The very growth in membership experienced by the new religious orders also resulted in the proliferation of small convents which, in order to survive, either attracted worshippers (and their donations) with sometimes extravagant claims as to the miraculous powers of relics or icons preserved in their churches, or engaged in lucrative activities that had little to do with religion. The problem was confronted head-on by Innocent X in 1649 with the establishment of a special commission charged with the task of taking a census of all existing religious houses in Italy: those that had fewer than twelve members or were too oblivious of the decorum and the mission expected of clerics would be closed and their endowment and revenues would then be assigned in part to the creation of new seminaries and schools and in part to the support of poor parishes. The commission reported that in the peninsula as a whole the number of religious establishments as well as their membership had soared since 1580 and now stood at nearly 6,000 with

---

moderna' in *Lisiera: immagini e documenti per la storia e cultura di una comunita veneta*, ed. Claudio Povolo, vol. 1, Neri Pozza, Vicenza 1981, pp. 177–8. On the impact visitations had on the clergy in general see Allegra, 'Il parroco', pp. 912–14.

49. De Maio, *Società e vita religiosa*, pp. 112–14.

some 70,000 clerics within their walls. The commission also ordered as many as 1,500 small convents closed, their inmates reassigned to larger ones where they could be more closely monitored, and their revenues reallocated. In the event, however, Innocent X's sweeping plan was carried out only partially as 25 per cent of the convents that were supposed to be closed down did in fact survive thanks to the relentless lobbying efforts in Rome of their respective orders, influential lay patrons, or the communities where the convents and their shrines were located. Still, thirty-two new seminaries and an un-determined number of parishes were endowed with the properties of those convents that did not escape the papal axe.[50]

The same tension between reform and the inertia of ingrained habits and vested interests is discernible in the case of religious orders of women. For them too the Council of Trent had provided a blueprint of reform aimed at eradicating two kinds of abuses that had become deeply entrenched. Even though there still were, and continued to be, convents with an impeccable record of piety and austerity, in others a flagrant disregard of monastic rules had crept in: the strict rule of enclosure whereby no outsider was allowed to set foot in the cloister was often flaunted and nuns entertained guests in their quarters; a frivolous social life was tolerated and could easily lead to immorality; leadership positions were often assigned on the basis of social rank rather than merit; and a convent's economic resources were used for the benefit of the nuns' families rather than of the convent itself. To all those sources of scandal, and in fact at the root of many of them, was the practice of families forcing young women to take the veil simply for the sake of saving the cost of a marriage portion. All these blatant abuses had been addressed in the Council's decree on religious orders. In it the rule of enclosure was reaffirmed, strict administrative controls were placed on the convents' finances, and the procedures for electing the mother superior or abbess were made more stringent in the hope of eliminating any outside interference. Lastly, the principle that no woman ought to be forced to enter the cloister against her will was spelled out in unmistakeable terms, excommunication was threatened for its violators, and it was ruled that any prospective candidate to the convent must be closely questioned by the bishop or by his deputy in order to ascertain 'whether she is being forced, whether she is being deceived, whether she knows what she is doing' (*an coacta, an seducta sit, an sciat quod agat*).

---

50. Rosa, *Religione e società*, pp. 281–4; Stumpo, 'Il consolidamento della grande proprietà ecclesiastica', pp. 272–80; Sallmann, 'Le catholicisme triomphant', pp. 242–50. Misconduct and abuses persisted in some monasteries in the second half of the century. In 1666 Alfonso Litta, archbishop of Milan, denounced to Rome monks and friars who 'absolved any sin as long as a donation was made', 'greedily' went after pious bequests to expand and beautify their churches and encouraged the cult of allegedly miraculous icons (Enrico Cattaneo, 'La religione a Milano nell'età della Controriforma' in *Storia di Milano*, vol. 11, Fondazione Treccani, Milan 1958, p. 311).

As with many of the Council's directives, those applying to nuns, too, proved difficult to implement in the face of strong opposition. The rule of enclosure, for instance, was denounced by Venetian authorities in 1580 on the grounds that 'should women's convents be reformed or brought to stricter standards daughters of the nobility who even before entered the cloister only reluctantly, after the reform will simply refuse to do so'. In 1629, the patriarch (archbishop) of Venice himself conceded that he had allowed all possible accommodations 'within the boundaries of decency and good example' to the rules of discipline and the dress code in order to make life in the cloister more tolerable to women who 'are confined within those walls not for reasons of devotion, but because their families have so decided' – a clear admission that nearly seventy years after the closing of the Council of Trent forced vocations were still the norm, at least in Venice.[51]

Restoring a measure of discipline and decorum in the cloisters took a long time and only in the second half of the century are there clear signs that the Council's directives were taking hold.[52] Respecting a woman's freedom to enter the convent or not, on the other hand, proved a more elusive goal, for on this point the Tridentine reforms ran counter to entrenched family interests and patrimonial strategies and challenged (as did the Tridentine decree on marriage with its insistence on the spouses' free consent) deeply ingrained notions of parental authority. Commenting in the mid-sixteenth century on a ruling then being contemplated by church authorities 'to prevent virgins to be sent to a monastery against their will either by force or by deceit', a Bolognese notary wrote that the ruling would have disastrous consequences on well-to-do families: there were too many nubile girls, he said, relative to the number of eligible bachelors, dowries were prohibitively high, and a father might have to marry off his daughter to a man of lower social rank 'for lack of a suitable dowry'. In Modena a contemporary of his put it more bluntly: 'our townsmen, in order to provide a handsome dowry to one daughter, throw the rest into a convent' and then added that those women

51. What precedes is based on Gabriella Zarri, 'Monasteri femminili e città (secoli XVI–XVIII)' in *SIE Annali* 9 (1986), pp. 387–403; the quotations appear on pp. 404 and 414. See also Ginevra Conti Odorisio, *Donna e società nel Seicento. Lucrezia Marinelli e Arcangela Tarabotti*, Bulzoni, Rome 1979, pp. 194–214, for a discussion of the writings of an early seventeenth-century Venetian nun (Tarabotti) who denounced the 'monastic hell' to which many young women were condemned by their families. It should be noted that female religious communities are one of the few aspects of Italian women's history that have been the subject of systematic investigation. To appreciate the range and depth of the new research see the important collection of essays in Lucetta Scaraffia and Gabriella Zarri, eds, *Donne e fede. Santità e vita religiosa in Italia*, Laterza, Rome and Bari 1994.

52. De Maio, *Società e vita religiosa*, pp. 115, 119 and 123; Mario Rosa, 'Organizzazione ecclesiastica e vita religiosa in Lombardia dall'età dei Borromei al periodo napoleonico' in *Problemi di storia religiosa lombarda*, Cairoli, Como 1972, p. 180.

'once they are locked up in a convent . . . curse the day and the hour when they were forced in and turn into raging rather than blessed creatures'.[53] Those words were written before the Tridentine decree on women religious was enacted in 1563, but even after its passage the evil of forced vocations did not disappear. In a 1581 report to his superiors in Rome, the nuncio in Venice denounced in dramatic terms the resistance opposed by the Venetian government to the requirement that, before admitting a young woman to the cloister, a determination must be made as to whether 'she decides to shut herself forever inside four walls for reasons of true devotion and of service to God, or whether she is pushed by fear of her father who has forced her with threats to consent verbally, separating her tongue from her heart, simply because he does not have enough money to marry her off to a man of equal standing'. The consequence of this abuse, the nuncio went on to say, was that the wretched woman found 'the yoke of monastic obedience' intolerable and eventually 'her father's unjust and vicious decision' led her to 'despair'.[54]

The practice of forced vocations apparently went on unabated and may even have grown worse in the seventeenth century. Such at least seems to have been the case in Florentine patrician families: whereas in the sixteenth century 28 per cent of their daughters entered the convent, in the following century 50 per cent did, and we can reasonably suspect that the increase did not entirely reflect a surge in devotion.[55] It seems more likely that deteriorating economic conditions, notably falling land values and rents, in the central decades of the century gave the landed patriciate a greater incentive to avoid the cost of dowries for their daughters. No comparable data are available for the Milanese patriciate until the seventeenth century: in its first half 50 per cent of all patrician daughters became nuns just as in Florence, but only 30 per cent did in the second half.[56] Whether the decline in 'vocations' reflected declining religious fervour among young women, greater respect for their wishes on the part of their parents, or a more conscientious and honest screening process by church authorities it is hard to say. One can legitimately suppose that the Tridentine revival in the later part of the century saw a more rigorous application of the Council's decree and thus contributed to reducing the number of forced vocations.

53. Quotations in Zarri, 'Monasteri femminili', pp. 361, 365 and 414.
54. Quotation in Aldo Stella, *Chiesa e Stato nelle relazioni dei nunzi pontifici a Venezia. Ricerche sul giurisdizionalismo veneziano dal XVI al XVIII secolo*, Biblioteca Apostolica Vaticana, Vatican City 1964, p. 192.
55. R. Burr Litchfield, 'Demographic Characteristics of Florentine Patrician Families. Sixteenth to Nineteenth Centuries', *Journal of Economic History* 29 (1969), pp. 197 and 203.
56. Dante E. Zanetti, *La demografia del patriziato milanese nei secoli XVII, XVIII, XIX con un'Appendice genealogica di Franco Arese*, Università di Pavia 1972, pp. 60 and 83.

CHRISTIANIZATION

All the inadequacies and sundry forms of misconduct that plagued the Italian clergy in the seventeenth century should not obscure the fact that in its ranks (most notably within the new religious orders) there was a large and probably growing number of individuals who approached the work of spiritual and moral reform in earnest, devoted to it prodigious efforts and devised new ways of bringing religious education to and arousing religious fervour in their flock.

Devotional literature intended for pious souls was one such way. Its main thrust was that a genuine religion, with its demanding moral code and its intense regimen of prayer and meditation, was meant not just for the few select souls who embraced the life of 'perfection' in the cloister, but for ordinary people as well.[57] The spirituality known as Devotio Moderna that had been formulated in the late fourteenth and fifteenth centuries and more recently the spirituality of Loyola's *Spiritual Exercises* had to be popularized so that, ideally, they would become accessible to any devout lay man or woman. It is thus not surprising that the age of the Counter-Reformation saw an outpouring of devotional books addressed not only to monks and nuns, but to all devout souls regardless of their station in life or level of education; their titles (*The Spiritual ABC, The Prayer of the Heart Made Easy, The Short Compendium of Christian Perfection,* to name but a few) clearly suggest their practical and popularizing intent.[58]

Some of the new devotional literature came to seventeenth-century Italy from abroad, notably the works of Francis de Sales (1567–1622), titular bishop of Geneva, whose writings addressed to people who lived 'in the world' were translated into Italian and became quite popular. But possibly the most widely read book of the genre was *The Spiritual Combat* by Lorenzo Scupoli (1530–1610), a member of the newly founded Theatine order. Originally published in 1589, it went through 254 editions in the next century and a half. What makes the book remarkable is the way it downplayed all the ascetic practices and the long hours spent in church that were traditionally associated with genuine religious commitment. Answering the question of 'what constitutes a true and genuine spiritual life', Scupoli noted that:

many people have identified it in a harsh regimen of mortification of the flesh, hairshirts, scourging, fasting, long vigils and the like. Others (especially women) delude themselves that they have attained it when they recite many prayers, attend many Masses, visit churches and receive Communion frequently. Many more (and these include quite a few monks) . . . have come to believe that everything depends on conscientious attendance in the choir and in observing silence, solitude and rules and regulations.

57. Evennett, *The Spirit of the Counter-Reformation,* pp. 32–5 and Delumeau, *Catholicism,* p. 8.
58. Mario Bendiscioli, *La riforma cattolica,* Studium, Rome 1958, pp. 132–4.

'But this is not so', Scupoli went on to say. While not denying the usefulness of external devotions and penances performed in moderation, he turned the light on the innermost recesses of the soul where the 'spiritual combat' between the ego and God's will must unfold and he indicated four steps on the way to 'the heights of perfection', namely self-denial, total confidence in God, the surrender of one's will and silent prayer to a God of love.[59] Clearly, here was a spiritual roadmap that, *per se*, anyone, layperson or cleric, could travel, although it would be obviously wrong to assume that the spiritual message proposed by Scupoli and many other spiritual masters of his time became daily fare for the masses. The latter, as will be seen presently, found other ways to express their religiosity. Yet, in the light of Scupoli's popularity and of the plethora of devotional books that proposed a similar type of piety, one can only conclude that many devout souls must have been attracted by a spirituality that was personal and intimate, but at the same time accessible.

The new spirituality centred on the importance of the interior life and on the intimate dialogue of the soul with its Maker was paralleled, in theological quarters, by a growing attention to and respect for the individual conscience. We see this in the Council of Trent's condemnation of the conventional view that for a marriage to be valid it had to be approved by the spouses' families; now its validity was made to depend only on the spouses' free consent – a concept that was opposed or only reluctantly accepted by the laity at the time for it was perceived as a grave threat to parental authority.[60] Likewise, the Council had denounced and condemned in the strongest terms the widespread practice of forcing young women to become nuns against their will. Moral theologians also began to discuss, as had not been done in the past, the duties of parents towards their offspring in sharp contrast to the traditional emphasis on the obligations children have toward their parents. In the same spirit, confessors' manuals of the Counter-Reformation devoted greater attention to the moral duties of masters toward their servants, notably the obligation not to tempt them into immorality, to care for them in an illness, not to strike them in anger, and so on.[61]

The more personal approach to religion was also responsible for the greater place the sacrament of penance or confession came to have in the spirituality of the time. Although the Council of Trent had merely reaffirmed the long-standing obligation of annual confession, people were now urged to confess to a priest more frequently, preferably on a monthly basis, and to engage regularly in the introspective practice known as 'examination of conscience', while the confessor's role was increasingly seen not only as that of a church official

59. Quotations in *Riforma cattolica. Antologia di documenti*, ed. Mario Bendiscioli and Massimo Marcocchi, Studium, Rome 1963, p. 277.
60. Jean-Louis Flandrin, *Families in Former Times. Kinship, Household and Sexuality in Early Modern France*, transl. Richard Southern, Cambridge University Press 1979, pp. 131–5; Maria Luigia Ruggiero, 'Bellarmino e la donna' in *Bellarmino e la Controriforma*, ed. Romeo De Maio *et al.*, Centro di Studi Sorani 'V. Patriarca', Sora 1990, pp. 905–6, 915–16.
61. Flandrin, *Families in Former Times*, pp. 137–40, 143.

authorized to absolve the repentant sinner, but also as a spiritual counsellor, especially in cases in which the penitent was struggling with doubts as to the morality of an action and needed guidance or reassurance. There was also a growing emphasis on the need for at least the most pious souls to find a 'spiritual director' who could advise and guide them on the path of a more intense devotional life. The new emphasis on confession gave rise to a vast literature intended either for confessors or for penitents: a recent study has identified nearly 500 titles coming out of the Italian presses in the second half of the sixteenth century and nearly as many in the next fifty years that addressed various aspects of confession and spiritual direction.[62]

The emphasis on religion as an intimate, highly personal experience which, as we have seen, loomed large in Counter-Reformation spirituality took an extreme and, in the eyes of church authorities, aberrant form in the current of spirituality known as Quietism. Although it never involved more than small circles of mystics and spiritual virtuosi, Italian Quietism deserves a mention, for it embodied, albeit in an extreme and even outlandish form, the widespread aspiration for a more intense, more personal type of religion in the age of the Counter-Reformation.[63] Quietism flourished in the second half of the seventeenth century, but it is generally agreed that its main tenets were foreshadowed in the *Short Compendium of Christian Perfection* written by the Jesuit Achille Gagliardi, probably in collaboration with the mystic Isabella Cristina Bellinzaga, and first published in 1647. Inspired by Loyola's *Spiritual Exercises*, but going beyond its teachings, Gagliardi proposed three stages on the road to perfection: denying the self to the point of 'annihilating' all the pious feelings that feed the ego, including the sense of spiritual comfort that comes from the performance of 'good works'; a complete surrender to God's will to the point where the soul becomes 'God's prey' and the totally passive recipient of His promptings; and, finally, the complete 'identification' or 'deification' of the soul resulting from silent 'mental prayer' and 'acquired contemplation' in the sense that the individual, without uttering words or performing any outward act of devotion, simply rests in the divine presence. Other writers elaborated and pushed to extremes Gagliardi's mysticism arguing, for instance, that mental prayer is the only valid form of prayer, thus spurning all external devotions and even the liturgy and the sacraments of the Church; arguing also that a life of virtue and mortification is irrelevant to the contemplative soul and may be even dangerous insofar as it conflicts with the passivity and total abandon required of the true mystic; that one must be indifferent to the question of one's own salvation or damnation, because the only thing that really matters is the will of God; that the person

62. Evennett, *The Spirit of the Counter-Reformation*, p. 37; Miriam Turrini, *La coscienza e le leggi. Morale e diritto nei testi per la confessione nella prima età moderna*, Mulino, Bologna 1991, pp. 66, 192, 205–6, 221.
63. The standard work on the subject is still Massimo Petrocchi, *Il Quietismo italiano del Seicento*, Edizioni di Storia e Letteratura, Rome 1948 and I have mainly drawn on it for what follows. On Pelagini now see Gianvittorio Signorotto, *Inquisitori e mistici nel Seicento italiano. L'eresia di Santa Pelagia*, Mulino, Bologna 1989.

who has reached contemplation can no longer sin; and, lastly, that reason, knowledge, understanding have no place in contemplation, for all the mystic can say is that God exists and is utterly incomprehensible.

By its very nature Quietism could not appeal to a large public. It is significant, however, that small circles of Quietists sprang up all over Italy and in the most diverse milieux. For a time Quietism found sympathizers (including Pope Innocent XI) in the Roman Curia; a cardinal, Pier Matteo Petrucci (1636–1701) bishop of Jesi, was one of his chief theorists; Franciscan friars such as Sisto de Cucchi and Paolo Monasseri spread the Quietist message with their writings; laymen, too, such as Count Maurizio Scarampi, actively promoted the diffusion of the new spirituality in Piedmont and Liguria, and so did Laura, duchess of Mantua, in her dominions. In Naples Quietism drew a large following in the 1670s, possibly as a reaction to the theatrical excesses of popular devotion. What is most striking is that, in the 1650s and 1660s it enjoyed considerable popularity among the peasants of Valcamonica, a rugged valley north of Brescia. In 1652 Giacomo Casolo, an illiterate layman from Milan widely admired for his piety and for his charitable activities, had spent some time in the valley and founded a number of 'oratories' or conventicles dedicated to St Pelagia (hence the label *pelagini* pinned on Casolo's followers) in which lay men and women gathered to practice mental prayer and to seek spiritual 'perfection'. Although Casolo himself cannot properly be called a Quietist in view of his relentless work among the poor and the sick, of his devotion to the Eucharist, and of the harsh regimen of mortification to which he subjected himself, his Valcamonica followers (at least if we are to believe their critics) seem to have veered toward Quietist positions and to have espoused the notion that 'no one can be saved unless one practices mental prayer' and that attending Mass and receiving the sacraments are not necessary for salvation.

Quietism was formally condemned by the Catholic Church in 1687, nearly half a century after it had made its first appearance in Italy. The timing and the motives of the condemnation are still the subject of debate. It has been argued that Louis XIV brought pressure to bear on Rome to condemn a movement which, by then, was rife in France and threatened the monolithic character of the French Church at the very time the Sun King, with the Revocation of the Edict of Nantes (1685), prided himself with having eliminated all forms of religious dissent from French soil. Yet one cannot overlook the fact that Quietism, especially after it had achieved visibility and influence in Rome itself at the hands of the Spanish priest and mystic Miguel de Molinos, was bound to be viewed as a serious threat to Catholic orthodoxy, for it denied or at least downplayed the need for the sacraments and the devotions sanctioned by the Church as well as the importance of 'good works' for attaining salvation. French lobbying may have hastened the condemnation, but so did the disturbing allegations that Molinos, the high priest of the sect, condoned moral laxity in his followers and that his own private conduct was not above reproach. Whatever the exact cause or cluster of causes of the condemnation may have been, it is difficult to see how church authorities could have long looked the other way when confronted with a religious movement that questioned the validity of the sacramental system and the importance of expressing one's commitment to the faith through charitable works. The strange thing is that the official repudiation of Quietism came as late as it did.

By their very nature, Quietism and even the spirituality advocated by Scupoli were bound to have but a limited following. In order to reach the mass of ordinary and often illiterate men and women other approaches were called for. One especially favoured by the new religious orders (Capuchins, Theatines, Priests of the apostolic Missions and, above all, Jesuits) were the 'missions'. These were religious events lasting several days in which a team of especially trained priests came to a town or village for an intense round of sermons followed by confessions, penitential processions, the burning of playing cards, obscene books and magic amulets, home visits to the sick and the public reconciliation of enemies, the whole event culminating in a solemn Mass which the entire community was expected to attend.[64] Missions have been called 'the most distinctive and important phenomenon in the religious history of Italy during the seventeenth century' in that they represented the most conspicuous form of encounter between the new 'reformed' religion of the clerical establishment and the traditional religion as practiced by the popular masses as well as the systematic effort of raising the latter to the level of the former.[65] And since missions, more often than not, were held in the countryside – in areas, that is, that had remained relatively isolated from and had often been neglected by church authorities in the past – they came to represent a bridge between two worlds (town and country, literate elites and illiterate masses) that had traditionally been separated from each other. The missions thus paved the way to that growing presence of the Church in the rural world that was to remain typical of Italy in the next three centuries. Originally intended to counter the inroads of heresy in a few regions of the peninsula (such as Piedmont and Calabria in the 1560s and the Valtelline in the early seventeenth century), mission preachers soon turned to disseminating religious instruction, revitalizing spiritual life and raising moral standards, especially in remote rural areas of the South which to the missionaries looked culturally and religiously backward and hardly more Christian than 'the Indies' where their confrères were evangelizing the heathen.[66]

64. Vivid descriptions of non-Jesuit missions in Maria Gabriella Rienzo, 'Il processo di cristianizzazione e le missioni popolari nel Mezzogiorno. Aspetti istituzionali e socio-religiosi' in *Per la storia sociale e religiosa del Mezzogiorno*, vol. 1, pp. 441–81; and of Jesuit missions in Elisa Novi Chavarria, 'L'attività missionaria dei Gesuiti nel Mezzogiorno d'Italia tra XVI e XVIII secolo' in the same work, vol. 2 (1982), pp. 159–85.
65. Carlo Ginzburg, 'Folklore, magia, religione' in *SIE*, vol. 1 (1972), p. 656.
66. Roberto Rusconi, 'Predicatori e predicazione (secoli IX–XVIII)' in *SIE Annali* 4 (1981), p. 1006; Peyronel Rambaldi, 'La Controriforma', p. 94.

The first task facing the preachers was to overcome the seemingly abysmal ignorance of their audience as regards even the basic principles of the faith. On this point we have the well-known and possibly a bit overdrawn testimony of the Jesuits who at mid-century conducted missions in the South and reported that the local peasants had but the faintest knowledge of Catholic doctrine to the point that they could not even decide how many gods there are.[67] And the level of religious instruction was apparently not much higher in the mountains near Lucca: there, according to lay authorities, people 'go nearly a whole year without attending Mass and without sacraments . . . and since virtually none of their priests teaches Christian doctrine to them, there are many adults who know nothing of our holy Faith'.[68] Equally unsettling to the preachers was the discovery that the religion practiced by the peasantry was often inextricably mixed with magic and superstition. This should have come as no surprise to them, for what is now commonly referred to as 'popular religion' had been around for centuries. It had, however, been either ignored or tolerated by the medieval church establishment on the somewhat condescending assumption that the uneducated masses, so long as they did not rebel against ecclesiastical authorities, would be saved in the end, in spite of their crass ignorance and errant ways, thanks to their good intentions and the prayers of the clergy. This benign neglect was now to be replaced by aggressive proselytizing that would Christianize the masses and close the large gap separating popular religion from the official teachings of the Church.[69]

Instances of the gap are as numerous as they are diverse. They include fertility cults such as the one that was practiced by the *benandanti* of Friuli in the sixteenth century and was aimed at protecting the harvest and the people themselves against witches' spells.[70] They include also the practice, denounced in an *Index superstitionum* compiled in 1576 at the request of Carlo Borromeo, archbishop of Milan, of dropping ashes in the shape of a cross at the four corners of a field the day after Christmas as a way of warding off spring storms. The Index also condemned the placing of a missal under the pillow of an infertile married couple in order to restore their ability to procreate which, it was believed, had been lost as a result of a curse.[71] The same mixture of Christian rituals or sacred objects with (possibly)

67. Ginzburg, 'Folklore, magia, religione', pp. 657–9.
68. Rita Mazzei, *La società lucchese del Seicento*, Pacini, Lucca 1977, p. 147.
69. Jean Delumeau, 'Prescription and Reality' in *Conscience and Casuistry in Early Modern Europe*, ed. Edmund Leites, Cambridge University Press and Maison des Sciences de l'Homme, Paris 1988, pp. 144–5. An excellent survey and critical analysis of the literature devoted to popular religion is provided in David Gentilcore, 'Methods and Approaches in the Social History of the Counter-Reformation in Italy', *Social History* 17 (1992), pp. 73–98.
70. Carlo Ginzburg, *Night Battles. Witchcraft and Agrarian Cults in the Sixteenth and Seventeenth Centuries*, transl. John and Anne Tedeschi, 2nd edn, Penguin Books 1985.
71. Attilio Agnoletto, 'L'interpretazione cattolica' in *La 'religione popolare'. Tre interpretazioni: la cattolica, la protestante, la sociologica*, ed. A. Agnoletto, Istituto Propaganda Libraria, Milan 1991, pp. 72–81.

pre-Christian magical elements (and that mixture was the essence of superstition as defined by theologians at the time) was present in various forms of love magic that seem to have been widely practiced in the countryside, sometimes with the assistance of the local priest. In 1586 one such priest was charged by the Inquisition with advising an unsuccessful suitor that he could win the affection of the woman he wanted simply by touching her arm with holy oil (duly supplied by the priest himself) while whispering: 'Those whom God has joined let no man put asunder.'[72] The same goal could be achieved by using a magnet that had been 'baptized' with holy water by the priest, or by the recitation on nine successive mornings of nine Pater Nosters and nine Ave Marias followed by a very unorthodox prayer to St Martha requesting that all sorts of misfortunes and sufferings be visited on the object of unrequited love until he acquiesced.[73] In Tuscany an official of the Inquisition denounced the practice of applying five drops of molten wax from a duly blessed candle to the body of a woman in labour in order to facilitate delivery; and the official also reported the widespread fear of evil witches (*maliarde*) deemed capable of harming babies in the womb with their curse.[74] As late as 1681 in the countryside near Udine some women claimed to be able, with special prayers and for a modest fee, to resuscitate for a brief moment still-born babies whom they would quickly baptize prior to a Christian burial. The fraudulent ritual, which was based on the theologically dubious premise that all unbaptized babies are destined to hell and which preyed on the parents' fear and credulity, was ordered discontinued by the Inquisition, but to no avail: the ritual continued to be performed in the region until the nineteenth century.[75]

The worship of religious images or icons and the attribution to them of magic properties was another area of concern for the reformers. In 1563 the Council of Trent had formulated in clear terms the official position of the Church on the subject against the popular inclination to use religious images as talismans or charms:

The images of Christ, the Virgin Mother of God and other saints ... must be held in due respect and venerated certainly not because one believes that there is in them some divinity or power, ... nor because one should ask favours of them or place one's trust in them as pagans used to do of old ... but because the honour we give those images is intended for the prototypes they represent. Through those images ... we adore Christ and venerate the saints whose likeness they convey to us.[76]

72. De Rosa, *Chiesa e religione popolare*, p. 39.
73. Mary O'Neil, 'Magical Healing, Love Magic and the Inquisition in Late Sixteenth-Century Modena' in *Inquisition and Society in Early Modern Europe*, ed. Stephen Haliczer, Croom Helm 1987, p. 102.
74. Adriano Prosperi, 'Vicari dell'Inquisizione fiorentina alla metà del Seicento. Note d'archivio', *AISIG* 8 (1982), pp. 283 and 303.
75. Silvano Cavazza, 'La doppia morte: resurrezione e battesimo in un rito del Seicento', *QS* 50 (1982), pp. 551–82.
76. Quotation in Agnoletto, 'L'interpretazione cattolica', p. 53.

To what extent this orthodox approach to icons was accepted and internalized by the average Italian believer is impossible to determine with precision, but if we are to judge from the recurrent efforts by Roman authorities and local bishops to restrain or suppress the excessive or unauthorized worship of religious images, those efforts do not seem to have been very successful. Ironically, some of the blame can be pinned on the lower clergy itself – unscrupulous mission preachers eager to achieve quick results by exploiting popular credulity or local parish clergy who were unwilling to oppose the religious sentiments of their flock.[77]

Much has been written in recent years about the clash between the official religion advocated by reform-minded, educated churchmen and popular religion; between an elite religion centred on personal piety, on the internalization of a strict and demanding moral code, on the rejection of superstition and magic, and a religion that was more easy-going, less discriminating in its choice of rituals and in which elements of the official teaching freely mixed with proscribed or, at best, tolerated elements of magic and folklore. In particular, the campaign waged by church authorities to purify or suppress some expressions of popular religiosity has been portrayed by some scholars as a vast programme of cultural domination, even of 'enslavement', of the masses engineered by an elite that was determined to establish its control over the plebs by obliterating a rich cultural heritage in a grand 'totalitarian' strategy.[78] One problem with this interpretation is that it assumes as incontrovertible that church authorities were mainly motivated by a drive for power for power's sake (the defence and strengthening of the Church as an institution, as Croce would have it) and it fails even to consider the possibility that other and nobler motivations (such as the education of the masses and the raising of moral standards) were at play. Another problem is that the proponents of the 'cultural domination' theory never make clear what alternative course the Church ought to have pursued. Leave the illiterate masses alone with their magic and superstitions and reserve the true faith as it had emerged from centuries of theological speculations and debates to a small educated elite? Interestingly enough, this rather patronizing alternative had been discussed in Italy in the early sixteenth century at a time when, under the humanists' influence and in response to their call for a more genuine religion grounded in Scripture, popular superstitions and devotional practices had come under fire as being incompatible with the true faith. At that time some members of the Church establishment had advocated the separation of the religion of the educated few from that of the many who lived in ignorance – a separation, it has been said, that 'might have avoided the vertical break

77. De Maio, *Società e vita religiosa*, pp. 106, 143–8 and 153; De Rosa, *Chiesa e religione popolare*, pp. 142–3.
78. Ginzburg, 'Folklore, magia, religione', p. 650 writes of the 'systematic smothering of any alternative religious manifestations'; Camporesi, 'Cultura popolare e cultura d'elite', p. 111 portrays the Counter-Reformation as 'doggedly determined to obliterate . . . popular culture' and as pursuing 'the enslavement (*asservimento*) of the popular masses' (p. 127).

between Churches, but only at the price of a deep horizontal break [within the Church] between different levels of religious truth'. The idea was rejected thanks especially to the opposition of some of the most distinguished members of the reformist wing of the Church on the eve of the Council of Trent: they argued forcefully and, as it turned out, successfully that the doctrinal content of religion is one and that any separation between the religion of the learned and the religion of the crowd would be inadmissible in light of the universality of the Christian message.[79] Catholicism thus opted for one religion for both the elite and the rank-and-file. While allowing for different shades of spirituality and varying levels of instruction in different layers of society, it upheld the existence of a doctrinal core that every believer must know and subscribe to. Having made this choice, the Catholic Church (and, for that matter, the mainline Protestant Churches) was committed to trying to present that core in such a way that it would be accessible to the uneducated. Hence the Schools of Christian Doctrine, the catechisms, the missions, the efforts expended on the training of future priests, the new emphasis on the care of souls.

But even assuming that church leaders were indeed inspired by a desire to dominate and control the masses in order to make them conform to a predetermined, rigid pattern of beliefs, the question still remains of how far they succeeded in implementing their 'totalitarian' plan. In the light of what we have just seen, the answer seems to be that their efforts had but limited success. One can legitimately wonder, for instance, how lasting a mark a sporadic mission could have on a village community. It has been pointed out that missions were, by their very nature, short-lived events, 'spiritual raids' as it were, that resulted in spectacular surges of collective devotion, but could not establish solid foundations for the future, the less so as all too often, as we have seen, the local parish clergy was too poorly educated and motivated to be able to build on the work of the missionaries.[80] Nor can one overlook the fact that throughout the century bishops and inquisitors, like their Protestant counterparts, continued to denounce superstitious beliefs and practices – a clear indication that the old popular ways persisted even a century after Trent and in spite of all the efforts at eradicating them.[81] Finally and no less significantly, recent research has convincingly shown that church authorities often had to accommodate their views and their policies to the lived experience and to the emotions of the people they were trying to reform or had to tolerate expressions of popular religiosity they could not suppress; in other words, the encounter of the two religious cultures did not result in the clear-cut victory of one over the other; rather it involved a 'two-way

79. Prosperi, 'Intellettuali e chiesa', pp. 177, 184–8 and 215–16 (quotation on p. 187); and Alberto Asor Rosa, *Il Seicento. La nuova scienza e la crisi del Barocco*, vol. 1, Laterza, Bari 1974, pp. 32–3.
80. Peyronel Rambaldi, 'La Controriforma', p. 96. De Rosa, *Chiesa e religione popolare*, pp. 118–19 and 211 provides instances of the persistence of popular religion in spite of the Church's efforts to suppress them.
81. Delumeau, 'Prescription and reality', p. 145.

exchange' as 'the official teaching could be influenced, modified and invigorated by the beliefs and practices of the commonality'.[82]

One instance of how the church leadership could be influenced by popular tastes and sentiments is provided by the tendency, so conspicuous in the age of the Baroque, toward theatricality, a tendency that contrasts with the call for an intimate, introspective piety found in so much devotional literature of the period, and yet was encouraged and even stage-managed by some members of the clergy with an eye on popular taste. The English diarist John Evelyn, writing in 1645, has left us a vivid picture of what he observed in Rome on Good Friday, notably 'the procession of several people that most lamentably whipped themselves till all the blood stained their clothes . . . at every three or four steps dashing the knotted and ravelled whipcord over their shoulders as hard as they could lay it on, whilst some of the religious orders and fraternities sang in a dismal tone, the lights and Crosses going before, which shewed very horrible and indeed a heathenish pomp'.[83] Colourful pageantry and sombre theatricality were also the stock-in-trade of some mission preachers who no doubt knew what their audience wanted. Following a carefully planned script, they walked into the village square at dusk carrying a large cross in a candlelight procession; they or their assistants held a skull in their hands or wore a crown of thorns on their head while uttering 'terrifying screams' so that 'hearts could more easily turn to repentance'.[84] And their sermons, too, played on the imagination of the audience with fire-and-brimstone tales of how God could punish sinners followed by comforting tales of forgiveness often obtained through the intercession of the Virgin Mary and the saints.[85] This kind of preaching coupled with rituals that smacked of superstition could at times reach such excesses as to earn the reprimands of some of the most conscientious and level-headed bishops who tried, probably in vain, to put an end to what they considered to be sheer exploitation of popular fears and anxieties.[86] Celebrations in honour of the local patron saint, too, could be the occasion for astonishing feats of pageantry, and the massive response of the public suggests that they were carefully staged with a clear perception of what the public expected. A good example is the festival that took place in May 1609 in Perugia to celebrate the transfer of some relics from their old repository to a new and more fitting one. All the churches in the town were decked in tapestries and silk cloth; three triumphal arches were built at the town's expense featuring sculptures and epigrams; the houses

---

82. Christopher F. Black, *Italian Confraternities in the Sixteenth Century*, Cambridge University Press 1989, p. 75; Gentilcore, 'Methods and Approaches', pp. 75 and 81.
83. Quotation in Black, *Italian Confraternities*, p. 2.
84. Peyronel Rambaldi, 'La Controriforma', p. 95.
85. De Maio, *Società e vita religiosa*, p. 61.
86. This was so in Lombardy as shown by Angelo Majo, *Storia della Chiesa ambrosiana*, vol. 2, Nuove Edizioni Duomo, Milan 1983, pp. 72 and 83; and by Zardin, 'L'ultimo periodo spagnolo', pp. 588, 596 and 600–1. Likewise in the Kingdom of Naples: De Maio, *Società e vita religiosa*, pp. 59, 105–7 and 141.

along the procession route were lavishly decorated and four fountains provided free wine (courtesy of the confraternities) for the participants in the procession. The festival must have been a resounding success, if not necessarily in strictly spiritual terms, certainly as popular theatre: well advertised in advance, it reportedly drew between 40,000 and 60,000 spectators.[87]

Another, albeit quite different, instance of how popular sentiment could influence religious practice is provided by the evolution of one of the most popular devotions in the seventeenth century, namely the Rosary, that is to say the recitation of fifteen Our Fathers and 150 Hail Marys interspersed with silent meditations on the main events in the lives of Christ and the Virgin Mary. Probably dating back to the twelfth century, the devotion of the Rosary had originally been intended as a private form of prayer and meditation and, as such, had been very much part of the spiritual climate generated by the Devotio Moderna with its emphasis on the cultivation of the interior life and on an intensely personal spirituality. Brought to Venice by German merchants around 1500, it later enjoyed the support of religious leaders such as Carlo Borromeo and became widespread throughout Italy during the pontificates of Pius V (1566–72) and Gregory XIII (1572–85). But as the Rosary gained in popularity it lost much of its original character as a private devotion; especially from the 1620s recitation of the Rosary turned more and more into a public ritual in which the prayers were spoken out loud by the entire congregation. With this accommodation the Rosary presumably became more accessible and attractive to people who felt little inclination for long silent prayers and meditations.[88]

The veneration of saints was another area where the dialectic between elite and popular religion was at play. Although no invention of the Counter-Reformation, the cult of saints intensified in that period: pilgrimages to local shrines became ever more popular and here and there new 'saints' were added to the official roster by popular acclaim: these were individuals who in their lifetime had achieved a local reputation for their holiness and, more importantly, for their alleged ability to perform miracles. Faced with the proliferation of new cults, Rome responded in the 1620s by ruling that no public cult of a saint would be tolerated unless the new saint had been duly recognized ('canonized') by the Papacy after a lengthy and exhaustive investigation of the candidate's alleged virtues and miracles.[89] As for pilgrimages, church authorities tried to avoid the obvious risk of superstition involved in them by making the celebration of a solemn Mass and the sermon on the life of the saint the centrepiece of the pilgrimage, but, as Carla Russo has pointed out, there are good reasons for assuming that what continued to attract the pilgrims was the chance of making contact with a sacred object, whether drinking from a miraculous spring at the site of the shrine, rubbing

87. Black, *Italian Confraternities*, p. 111.
88. Rosa, *Religione e società*, pp. 218–33.
89. Sallmann, 'Le catholicisme triomphant', pp. 295–7.

against the saint's statue, or even taking with them a chip from the statue itself.[90] The Church also tried (we do not know with what measure of success) to curb the activity of 'holy men' who performed unauthorized exorcisms or miraculous cures or prophesized the impending end of the world. Prayers and processions intended to ensure a bountiful harvest or to end a drought (the so-called 'Rogations') could also reveal differences in perception between church authorities and the faithful: to the former they were a form of petitioning God; to the latter, a magic ritual which, if properly performed, would automatically produce the desired outcome.[91]

The tension between an elite and a popular religion; the persistence of practices and beliefs that were typical of the latter; the concessions the Church had to make to the sentiments and needs of the populace – all of this ought to serve as an antidote to the view that the Counter-Reformation imposed an alien religion *en bloc* on the Italian people and, in the process, obliterated the genuine, spontaneous expressions of their religiosity. The fact of the matter seems to be that the acculturation of the rural masses was only partial and that, in the end, the religion of the majority was a blend of directives from above and deeply rooted emotional needs from below.

As regards the urban masses, the record is rather different, not only because the gap between what Catholic reformers proposed and what the urban masses believed was not so wide as in the countryside, but also because in the towns the goal of Christianization could be pursued more systematically and with more permanent results by establishing various levels of schools intended for the laity. One of the earliest and most successful examples of this was the Confraternity of Christian Doctrine, alluded to earlier, 'for teaching children on Sundays and holy days the Christian way of life, good habits and how to read and write, at no charge'. In Milan, by 1600, the Confraternity's Sunday schools enrolled 20,000 pupils and boasted 700 lay teachers; at that time in Bologna (a city half the size of Milan) 600 teachers instructed 3,000–4,000 children or about 70 per cent of the population under fourteen; while in Rome in 1611 the Confraternity operated 78 schools with an enrolment of about 10,000 boys and girls. The impact of those schools on the urban masses is difficult to assess, but it is safe to assume that they played a decisive role in bringing church doctrine as formulated in the Tridentine catechism to a wide audience; they also no doubt contributed to raising the level of literacy among the plebs, for attendance was compulsory and the goal was to reach all children, but especially the children of the poor. Of those schools it has been said that they represented a first, partial step toward a

90. Carla Russo, 'Mentalità e comportamenti religiosi nell'Europa cattolica' in *La Storia. I grandi problemi dal medioevo all'età contemporanea*, cd. Nicola Tranfaglia e Massimo Firpo, vol. 3/1, UTET, Turin 1987, pp. 91–8 (on how the Church tried to restrain, but in the end tolerated, the superstitious cult of saints) and p. 99 (on pilgrimages).
91. As, for instance, in Piedmont: Erba, *La Chiesa sabauda*, pp. 431–5. For a case study see Giovanni Levi, *Inheriting Power. The Story of an Exorcist*, transl. Lydia C. Cochrane, University of Chicago Press 1988.

modern educational system – obligatory, directed to the masses, and aimed at the socialization of children according to a precise blueprint.[92]

Elementary schools operating on weekdays rather than just on Sundays and feast days were certainly not so common in spite of the directive emanating from Rome that all parishes hire a 'teacher of grammar' who would instruct children both in the catechism and in reading and writing.[93] In rural communities, in particular, such teachers may have been the exception rather than the rule. Yet, they were not totally absent, and we have no reason to assume that the case of the countryside around Grosseto in Tuscany was unique: there a survey of 54 villages conducted in 1676 indicated that 46 of them had a schoolteacher on their payroll.[94] Towns, however, were no doubt more fortunate in that respect both because of a long tradition of public elementary schools and because of new initiatives which, in the spirit of the Catholic Reform movement, expanded the scope of public education and addressed specific educational needs that had presumably been neglected in the past. In Rome a schoolmaster, Leonardo Cerusi, opened a boarding school for street urchins in 1582; after his death in 1595 responsibility for the school was taken over by the famed church historian Cardinal Baronius and enrolment reached the 150 mark. From 1607 Mantua had a boarding school where indigent girls were taught reading and writing – a very unusual form of schooling for young females at the time. In Turin an *Albergo di virtù* (literally, a 'hostel of virtue'), originally established by the lay confraternity of St Paul, imparted vocational training to poor boys. Likewise in seventeeenth-century Naples a number of charitable endowments (*monti*) supported boarding schools (*conservatori*) where children and adolescents were taught 'grammar and the abacus'. Incidentally, *conservatori* were created in Naples to address other needs as well: in addition to five such institutions for boys and ten for girls, there came into existence eleven for adult women, one for the aged, and twelve for the sick. Together, the *conservatori* came to harbour as many as 5,000 people. In Rome near the close of the century an Apostolic Hospice was founded by a priest to house the homeless, but also to provide them with vocational

---

92. Turrini, 'Riformare il mondo', pp. 287 and 411–30; Paul Grendler, 'Borromeo and the Schools of Christian Doctrine' in *San Carlo Borromeo: Catholic Reform and Ecclesiastical Politics*, pp. 165–7; Black, *Italian Confraternities*, pp. 226–7; Alessandro Pastore, 'Strutture assistenziali fra Chiesa e Stati nell'Italia della Controriforma' in *SIE Annali* 4 (1981), pp. 458–9. The official *Catechismus ex decreto Concilii Tridentini*, published in 1566, ran to over 400 pages and was explicitly addressed to pastors (*ad parochos*); it was structured in four parts (Creed, sacraments, Ten Commandments and prayer); much shorter versions using a question-and-answer format for easy memorization by children were subsequently produced (notably by Cardinal Bellarmine) and adopted in the Schools of Christian Doctrine (Celestino Testori, 'Catechismo', in *Enciclopedia cattolica*, vol. 3, Vatican City 1949, pp. 1123–4.
93. Erba, *La Chiesa sabauda*, p. 287.
94. Ildebrando Imberciadori, 'Spedale, scuola e chiesa in popolazioni rurali dei secoli XVI–XVIII', *Economia e Storia* 6 (1959), p. 436.

training. Siena may have been late in confronting the educational needs of the poor, but in 1698 its archbishop, in cooperation with two noblemen, established a boarding school for indigent boys between the age of seven and eighteen. According to its founders, who had been strongly influenced by the new ideas on welfare advocated at the time by French Jesuits, the main goal of the new school was 'to combat the idleness of the poor by having them work at an honest and godly trade', probably some craft. Although no one was forced to enroll, those who did but later proved impervious to the work ethic imparted there faced expulsion from the town – an early instance perhaps of a new harsher attitude toward the structural unemployed.[95]

It was, however, the religious orders that contributed most to the creation of full-time schools, for they could more easily provide the required space and teaching staff. Soon after its foundation in the mid-sixteenth century the Somaschi order achieved a reputation for educating the children of poor families so that they could become good artisans and even go on to become clerics. No less respected and successful was the order of Pious Schools (Scolopians): their schools multiplied in the course of the seventeenth century, especially in the South, and always retained a 'popular' character in that they focused primarily on elementary education, with tuition being charged only to families that could afford to pay.[96] The philosophy underlying these and similar endeavours was clearly articulated by Silvio Antoniano, the humanist author of a book on Christian education written in 1584 at Carlo Borromeo's request. In terms that have a modern ring about them, he stressed the need for good teachers capable of educating not just the wellborn, but 'ordinary people' (*cittadini di piu' comune stato*) as well and at no charge if necessary as prescribed by the Council of Trent. Children of whatever extraction, 'even very low', he wrote, must be taught at least 'how to read, write and count' because these things are 'useful for the rest of one's life'. When it came to female education, Antoniano, as we would expect, was far less modern: 'as for girls, he wrote, those of low and poor condition do not even need to learn how to read'; noble women, on the other hand, should have at least some familiarity with reading, writing and arithmetic.[97]

While Somaschi and Scolopians concentrated their efforts on elementary and vocational education for the children of the lower classes, other orders,

95. Black, *Italian Confraternities*, p. 205 (for Rome); Wright, *The Counter-Reformation*, p. 261 (for Modena); Sandra Cavallo, *Charity and Power in Early Modern Italy. Benefactors and their Motives in Turin 1541–1789*, Cambridge University Press 1995; Muto, 'Forme e contenuti', p. 252 (for Naples); Penco, *Storia della Chiesa in Italia*, vol. 2, p. 42 (for Rome); Irene Polverini Fosi, 'Pauperismo ed assistenza a Siena durante il Principato mediceo', in *T&C*, pp. 160–1.

96. On the Somaschi see Brian Pullan, *Rich and Poor in Venice. The Social Institutions of a Catholic State, to 1620*, Harvard University Press, Cambridge, Mass. 1971, pp. 259–63; on the Scolopi, Penco, *Storia della Chiesa in Italia*, vol. 2, pp. 54–5.

97. Quotation in Biondi, 'Aspetti della cultura cattolica', pp. 270–1.

most notably the Jesuits, made it their specialty to train the future members of the elite, the children of noble and middling families from which government officials, magistrates, military officers, lawyers and other professionals were recruited. The proliferation of Jesuit 'colleges' (boarding schools) from 1574, when their first school for young noblemen was founded in Milan, to the end of the seventeenth century was truly remarkable: forty-nine such colleges were in existence in 1600, eighty in 1630, ninety-seven in 1661 when their total enrolment was about 5,000, and their number was probably even higher by the close of the century. In those institutions the curriculum was traditional and centred on the humanities, that is to say on the study of Latin grammar, literature and rhetoric in the early years and on mathematics, scholastic philosophy and the law in the final years of schooling. To these traditional subjects were added, near the end of the century, more 'modern' ones such as algebra, geography and military engineering. Academic subjects, however, were but one aspect of a Jesuit education. The colleges' enormous reputation both in Italy and abroad rested not only on the quality and range of the academic curriculum, but also on the fact that they were run under a strict code of discipline, that they stressed the religious and moral formation of their students and last, but for the students' families probably not least, that they attached great importance to teaching social graces, from music to dancing, from acting to fencing and horsemanship – all the things which, in the words of a 1640 document, 'are useful to the making of a perfect gentleman'. This last remark is revealing of what Jesuit education was trying to achieve, namely shaping the future ruling elite in a Catholic mould. 'Pupils', reads a seventeenth-century source, 'are the stuff out of which bishops, cardinals, governors, royal councillors and other high officials are made, and for this glory and honour be to God our Lord.'[98] In our own time and in a more critical vein, Jesuit education has been portrayed as being driven by an overriding concern and ambition: that of 'controlling the ruling elite and through it of controlling politics'.[99] Which is probably correct, provided one does not demonize the Jesuits as being driven by a thirst for power for power's sake. Even though some Jesuits may have made the attainment of power or at least of influence an end in itself, it is likely that the overall pedagogical strategy of the Jesuit order was inspired by a nobler intent: that of promoting the cause of the Catholic faith and the 'reform' of society in a Christian mould by ensuring that future leaders would be intellectually and morally grounded in that faith. In a confessional age, when a country's religious future depended so heavily on the religious choices of its rulers, this was not an unreasonable, let alone contemptible strategy.

98. Gian Paolo Brizzi, *La formazione della classe dirigente nel Sei-Settecento. I 'seminaria nobilium' nell'Italia centro-settentrionale*, Mulino, Bologna 1976, pp. 9, 95, 155, 209–38 (the quotation appears on p. 95). On Jesuit schools see also Brambilla, 'Società ecclesiastica e società civile', pp. 305–29.

99. Bendiscioli, *La Riforma cattolica*, p. 161.

For all their success and popularity, Jesuit colleges did not escape criticism and actually generated opposition even in the seventeenth century. Other religious orders apparently resented the competition of a body that was better funded and enjoyed greater favour by the powers that be. Old universities (Bologna, Padua, Messina) felt threatened by the Jesuits' policy of opening their own colleges in their very backyard, not only as preparatory schools, but as full-fledged institutions of higher education. This kind of opposition against a new, dynamic and indeed aggressive organization should not surprise and, in fact, could have been expected, all the more so as Italian universities were at the time in a state of crisis with much of the best work being done outside their walls, notably, as will be seen, in the so-called academies. More serious was the criticism directed at the quality of education imparted in Jesuit schools, namely that, catering as it primarily did to the needs of the aristocracy, it was too elitist; that it emphasized literary skills at the expense of the sciences and rhetoric over content; and that it was irreparably conservative in outlook. Although, as will be seen, the accusation of ignoring the sciences is certainly unjustified, there is a good deal of truth in the other charges of elitism and conservatism. Because of these flaws Jesuit education began to lose much of its prestige as the century drew to a close.[100]

THE RESPONSE OF THE LAITY

All the various facets of the Italian Church surveyed so far – the reform of the clergy, the emergence of new religious orders, the efforts aimed at reaching the masses through preaching and education – represented so many attempts by the church hierarchy to implement the programme of renewal that lay at the heart of the Catholic reform movement. As such, they all tell us a great deal about what the hierarchy intended to accomplish (and also what kind of obstacles stood in its way), but shed little light on the question of how effective those efforts were in producing a genuine religious response among the laity. To gauge that response, to assess, that is, the level of true commitment as opposed to mere compliance to church rules (such as attendance at Mass on Sundays or the annual confession of one's sins) is notoriously one of the most difficult tasks confronting the student of religion in times past. The difficulty, however, is partly mitigated by what is known about the many voluntary religious associations (confraternities) of lay men or women: precisely because they were voluntary, their number, membership and goals are good indicators of lay participation in the religious revival and of what lay people (or at least the most committed among them) considered most important in expressing their religiosity.

100. The reputation of Italian Jesuit schools among the European Catholic nobility is discussed by Gian Paolo Brizzi, 'La pratica del viaggio d'istruzione in Italia nel Sei-Settecento', *AISIG* 2 (1976), pp. 203–13; contemporary criticisms of the Jesuit curriculum in Brizzi, *La formazione della classe dirigente*, pp. 52–3.

Confraternities were no invention of the Counter-Reformation, for, in fact, they had a long pedigree behind them going back to the late Middle Ages when the mendicant orders (Franciscans and Dominicans) had strongly encouraged their formation as the best way of fostering piety among the laity and of shielding them against the possible threats of heretical ideas. The emphasis had been on devotional practices (harsh penance, prayers and pilgrimages), but also on almsgiving, settling family feuds, and the restoration of peace in towns rent by factional strife. In the sixteenth century the medieval tradition had been kept alive, and, if we are to judge from the number of newly created confraternities, had exhibited renewed vitality.[101] The city of Rome saw the foundation of eighty new confraternities in the sixteenth century and of thirty-four in the next century; around 1600 Assisi, a town of only 14,000 souls, boasted eleven confraternities and the surrounding countryside twenty-eight; in Perugia at about the same time an estimated 10 per cent of the entire population belonged to confraternities; in Venice, on the eve of the plague of 1576, 5,000–6,000 people were enrolled in the major lay confraternities known as the *Scuole Grandi* and an undetermined number in the lesser ones. In those same years the Neapolitan Confraternity of the Holy Spirit, with 6,000 members, supported a boarding school for 400 indigent girls. The list could be prolonged, but it would only confirm the overall impression of massive lay involvement in charitable and devotional organizations from the late sixteenth century and lend credence to the view that in any Italian town a quarter of the adult male population were enrolled.[102] At any rate, the whole phenomenon was sufficiently conspicuous for the Council of Trent to have taken notice of this surge of lay fervour and to have laid down some ground rules for the drafting of by-laws, the selection of officers, and the proper management of whatever financial resources or properties a confraternity might control; in addition, the Council mandated that the local pastor should closely monitor their activities within the parish. The new legislation was clearly aimed at preventing the mismanagement of resources at the hands of unscrupulous or inept officers as well as any possible deviation from orthodox doctrine and practice or the excesses of conviviality that were not uncommon on the feast of the patron saint.[103]

101. Broad overviews in Roberto Rusconi, 'Confraternite, compagnie e devozioni' in *SIE Annali* 9 (1986), pp. 471–82, and Danilo Zardin, 'Le confraternite in Italia settentrionale fra XV e XVIII secolo', *Società e Storia* 35 (1987), pp. 81–137. On this subject I have greatly benefited from my daughter Barbara's comments and suggestions.
102. Black, *Italian Confraternities*, pp. 50–5 and 270. Although primarily the responsibility of religious orders, schools, notably vocational schools, for poor children were occasionally established and operated by lay confraternities as in Mantua (Wright, *The Counter-Reformation*, p. 261), in Turin (Erba, 'Pauperismo e assistenza', p. 24), and in Naples (Lopez, *Riforma cattolica e vita religiosa*, p. 86 and Muto, 'Forme e contenuti', p. 252).
103. Black, *Italian Confraternities*, pp. 62–3 and Allegra, 'Il parroco', pp. 925–8. Allegra's view that the Church's supervision of confraternities was 'intended to

As in the past, one main function of confraternities was to foster the spiritual life of their members and to raise it a notch or two above what was expected of ordinary Catholics. This involved the daily recitation of specified prayers, receiving the sacraments of confession and communion at regular intervals, and attending a meeting of the membership every week. But increasingly, in the climate of activism that characterized the Counter-Reformation Church,[104] charitable activities were viewed as inseparable from genuine piety and became the confraternities' main focus and *raison d'être*. None better embodied the theme that was at the core of the Catholic reform movement – 'to reform the world toward a true Christian life' – than the Marian Congregation founded in Rome in 1563 by the Jesuit Jean Leunis.[105] It was designed as a gathering of lay students of the Collegio Romano who combined devotional practices inspired by Loyola's *Spiritual Exercises* with the defence of the Church against all enemies, with proselytizing in their social milieu, and with charitable works such as visiting the sick, providing meals to the hungry, loans to the poor, and shelters for repentant prostitutes. Within a few years Marian Congregations had sprung up in major European cities, from Naples to Paris, to Antwerp and were acclaimed as 'nurseries of a very holy life'. Although each congregation was closely supervised by a Jesuit priest, it was and remained a lay organization headed by laymen (prefects) and open to individuals from all walks of life – students, noblemen, merchants, artisans and, in the early years, women as well. The goal was to embrace the entire society without distinction of rank, income or gender. It did not take long, however, before this egalitarian approach had to bow before the deeply rooted assumptions and prejudices of a highly stratified 'society of orders': not only were women excluded, but separate Marian Congregations came into existence for different social groups. By the 1590s, for instance, Naples had several separate congregations, one for noblemen with 200 members, one for lawyers with 80, one for artisans with 500. In this way, it was felt, each segment of society could be better served and 'converted'.

Marian Congregations experienced an enormous success throughout Catholic Europe in the seventeenth century, and Italy was no exception: by the end of the century Naples and the surrounding region alone had 135 and their presence was felt at all levels of society. Predictably, the success of so ubiquitous, highly disciplined and zealous an organization raised the

---

smother their religious life ... through regimentation' (p. 926) is unconvincing and calls for corroboration. Two instances of episcopal intervention aimed at correcting flagrant administrative abuses rather than dampening religious fervour (Black, p. 198) suggest a different conclusion.

104. Activism or social concern as defining features of the Counter-Reformation have been stressed by Bendiscioli, *La Riforma cattolica*, p. 107; A.G. Dickens, *The Counter-Reformation*, Norton, New York 1968, p. 200; Evennett, *The Spirit of the Counter-Reformation*, pp. 86–8; and Delumeau, *Catholicism*, p. 161.

105. For what follows see Chatellier, *Europe of the Devout*, pp. 3, 5, 16–18, 22–5, 45, 89–108, 129–32.

suspicion that the 'devout' formed some kind of sinister fifth column working for the Papacy and, as such, potentially disloyal to the state. But, curiously enough, it was also feared that Marian Congregations could undermine the social fabric. As a worried observer of those 'secret conventicles' put it in 1596, 'the separation of the people from the nobility threatens to ruin the social peace and the union of the republic'.[106] What had him so worried was probably the fact of artisans and journeymen meeting on their own without the presence and the supervision of a representative of the ruling elite: this might foster in them a sense of group identity and, who knows, encourage them some day to formulate and voice grievances or, worst still, to take concerted action in the social arena. It is possible that this is precisely what they did in Naples at the time of the Masaniello uprising: when the crowd of craftsmen and journeymen stormed and looted the palace of the duke of Andria while sparing the Jesuit college nearby, it was suspected that behind their action there was careful planning – as there certainly was, after the revolt, in the artisans' decision to set up a fund for assisting their fellow workers who had been thrown in jail.[107]

It is one of the glories of Italian Catholicism in early modern times to have inspired a wealth of initiatives aimed at mitigating the dire effects of the calamities (famines, epidemics, wars) that afflicted the country in the sixteenth and seventeenth centuries. What is remarkable about those initiatives is that most of them were launched and carried out by lay confraternities and involved primarily lay men and women, albeit with the encouragement and some supervision of church authorities.[108] This point is worth stressing, for it can serve as an antidote to the cliché according to which the laity in the age of the Counter-Reformation were passive executors of orders and directives handed down by the hierarchy. No amount of prodding, directives or even admonitions from fire-and-brimstone preachers could have induced countless men and women to devote themselves to assisting the sick, visiting prison inmates, or teaching children for free had there not been a widespread yearning for a more committed, more evangelical type of religion. To be sure, one cannot rule out the possibility, indeed the likelihood, that some individuals joined a confraternity primarily out of a need for socializing or in order to impress their neighbours with their godliness. We now know that in Turin reasons of social prestige were behind a good many large contributions made to confraternities, hospitals and orphanages by members of the professional and merchant elite as a way of achieving recognition and winning acceptance among the aristocracy.[109] This was certainly not the first time, nor would it be the last, when philanthropy was used as a means of

---

106. Quotation in Chatellier, *Europe of the Devout*, p. 119.
107. Chatellier, *Europe of the Devout*, pp. 122–4.
108. Such was the case in Milan where, in the 1640s, Archbishop Monti promoted a variety of charitable institutions run by lay men or women (Signorotto, *Inquisitori e mistici*, pp. 44–5).
109. Cavallo, *Charity and Power*, pp. 129 and 134.

social advancement. It is, however, revealing of the climate of opinion of the Counter-Reformation that generosity toward the afflicted rather than some other form of munificence or ostentation was viewed as a primary mark of social prestige.

Yet, after making due allowance for ulterior motives in the minds of some benefactors, the fact remains that the record of charitable initiatives in the Counter-Reformation is quite impressive in terms both of sheer numbers and the range of needs that was being addressed.[110] A prime example is that of the care of the sick and the disabled. In the second half of the sixteenth century Rome saw the creation of six new hospitals; their operation heavily relied on a number of newly founded lay confraternities that complemented the work of the full-time hospital staff and of the new religious order founded by Camillo de Lellis with the exclusive task of ministering to the sick. In Naples a confraternity of women came into existence in the 1590s for the purpose of visiting and assisting patients in the several hospitals that had opened in recent years. In the same city lay initiative remained strong in the next century: in 1607 a layman endowed a nursing home for the old; the following year another founded a shelter for the blind; and in 1655 a hospital was founded for the disabled (*poveri cionchi*). In Milan the celebrated hospital known as Ca' Granda received a grandiose addition, courtesy of a wealthy merchant.[111]

Another area of philanthropy in which laymen were increasingly active was poor relief. In Naples the Oratorian order promoted the creation of three new confraternities (one open to noblemen, one to merchants, and one to craftsmen) that were responsible for distributing bread to the hungry every Sunday; in the 1660s a shelter for the homeless was set up in which over 800 people, half of them women and children, were housed and trained in various crafts. Throughout the South *monti frumentari* were erected, that is to say warehouses where stocks of grain were stored for distribution in time of dearth.[112] In Turin a lay confraternity (the Compagnia di S Paolo) was established in 1563 for the purpose of converting heretics and encouraging piety among its members. Its record was rather undistinguished until 1605 when, on the Jesuits' advice, it shifted its focus and soon became one of the main centres of philanthropy in the city. The Compagnia (whose membership consisted predominantly of lawyers, magistrates, financiers and government officials) provided dowries to indigent women and established an agency (Ufficio Pio) for assisting the shamefaced poor (*poveri vergognosi*), that is, members of the nobility or of the middling order, who had fallen on hard times and were ashamed of begging in the street. It also ran a shelter for

110. For a survey, see Alessandro Pastore, 'Strutture assistenziali fra Chiesa e Stati nell'Italia della Controriforma' in *SIE Annali* 9 (1986), pp. 433–65.
111. On Rome, Black, *Italian Confraternities*, p. 190; on Naples, Lopez, *Riforma cattolica*, p. 76 and Muto, 'Forme e contenuti', pp. 251 and 254; on Milan, Majo, *Storia della Chiesa ambrosiana*, vol. 2, p. 75.
112. Lopez, *Riforma cattolica*, pp. 76–7 and 93; De Majo, *Società e vita religiosa*, p. 135. On 'monti frumentari', see De Rosa, *Chiesa e religione popolare*, p. 130.

orphan girls and another for married women who had been abandoned or were being abused by their husbands. At mid-century when Turin lay devastated by civil war, the Compagnia was instrumental in persuading the government to open a shelter where at any given time several hundred beggars could be housed and fed. And, lastly, it established a credit office (*Monte*) for making loans to the poor at low interest rates.[113] The latter, by the way, was no isolated institution nor was it the first of its kind. *Monti di pieta'* had sprung up in the fifteenth century in order to shield the needy from the prohibitively high interest rates charged by professional money-lenders. In the course of the next two centuries they proliferated, especially in north Italy, and no doubt helped to tide over many a 'deserving poor' in an emergency. In the long run they also contributed to the acceptance of the notion that (except in the case of loan sharks) lending money at (moderate) interest is a legitimate and socially useful economic activity.[114]

The rehabilitation of women who, due to poverty, had turned to or had been forced into prostitution as well as the preventive sheltering of girls at risk of becoming prostitutes were two areas where confraternities were involved: one approach favoured by Marian Congregations and other confraternities was to ransom women from the procurers for whom they worked and then provide them with temporary lodgings and vocational training prior to their return to a normal life. In Bologna an institution known as Casa del Soccorso di S. Paolo and operated by a confraternity harboured repentant prostitutes, rape victims and single women who had 'lost their honour' in the eyes of society and sought their rehabilitation: no matter how disreputable her past had been, it was assumed that, if a woman voluntarily entered the house and adapted for a year or so to its strict devotional and work discipline, she would be considered 'redeemed' and her honour fully restored; the confraternity would vouch for that and would provide her, if need be, with a small dowry to help her find a husband.[115]

Prison inmates were another target of confraternal philanthropy. At this point one must bear in mind that in early modern Italy a prison sentence was not one of the possible punishments inflicted on convicted felons (except in cases adjudicated by church courts): fines, flogging, banishment, service in the galleys and, in extreme cases, the death penalty were the options available to the criminal justice system; incarceration, on the other hand, was used mainly

113. Cavallo, *Charity and Power*, pp. 109–15.
114. Paolo Prodi, 'La nascita dei Monti di Pietà: tra solidarismo cristiano e logica del profitto', *AISIG* 8 (1982), pp. 215 and 222–3.
115. Chatellier, *Europe of the Devout*, pp. 45 and 132; Lucia Ferrante, 'L'onore ritrovato. Donne nella Casa del Soccorso di S. Paolo a Bologna (secoli XVI–XVIII)', *QS* 53 (1983), pp. 499–527. Similar institutions came into existence in Naples in the mid-seventeenth century (Pasquale Lopez, *Clero, eresia e magia nella Napoli del Viceregno*, Gallina, Naples 1984, p. 148); in Milan (Majo, *Storia dela Chiesa ambrosiana*, vol. 2, pp. 75–6); and in Mantua (Roberto Navarrini and Carlo Marco Belfanti, 'Il problema della povertà nel Ducato di Mantova: aspetti istituzionali e problemi sociali (secoli XIV–XVI)' in *T&C*, p. 135).

prior to or during trial or for delinquent debtors until their obligation had been paid. One of the main objects pursued by confraternities such as that of S. Croce in Milan, the Pieta' in Rome, or the SS. Annunziata in Lecce was, therefore, not only to provide religious and material comfort to inmates awaiting trial, but also to secure the release of debtors from jail by offering to reimburse their creditors. Additional assistance took the form of food and clothes to former convicts until they found work. Some congregations specialized in the spiritual assistance of criminals awaiting the death sentence and often enough enjoyed the privilege of requesting one or more pardons every year. In Perugia this meant that on average one out of four criminals escaped execution thanks to the intercession of a confraternity. In Faenza, we are told, the same privilege was generally used to rescue prisoners who had been unable to afford a good defence attorney or had no previous criminal record.[116]

Other instances of charitable activities in a wide range of fields could be enumerated, for virtually every town had its panoply of confraternities, but hopefully enough has been said so far to suggest that Counter-Reformation Italy witnessed an impressive surge of lay activism. Nor did those confraternities limit themselves to dispensing alms to the beggar in the street. As we have just seen, they also tried to help the poor and the victims of abuse to be reintegrated into society, so much so, in fact, that confraternities in that period have been viewed as precursors of modern professional welfare agencies.[117] One reason behind this growing professionalism was no doubt the ideal of 'reforming the world toward true Christian living', for this could be construed to mean that a truly Christian world ought to be free of beggars, abandoned children and vagabonds; the more so as all those poor wretches, living as they did in destitution and ignorance, were in grave danger of losing their souls in lives of crime and immorality, unless they were rehabilitated. Poverty and ignorance, in other words, came to be seen as festering grounds of immorality; as such, they had to be eradicated from the Christian commonwealth.[118]

Another and no less important reason behind the professionalization of charity, and one that does not exclude but rather complements the other, may have been the sheer magnitude and visibility of the social problems that confronted religious reformers and committed laymen at the time. In the sixteenth century Italy, like the rest of Europe, experienced rapid population growth and a dramatic process of urbanization with all the problems of

116. Black, *Italian Confraternities*, pp. 217–22; Alessandro Parisini, 'Pratiche extragiudiziali di amministrazione della giustizia: la "liberazione dalla morte" a Faenza tra Cinquecento e Settecento', *QS* 67 (1988), pp. 147–68. Vincenzo Paglia, *'La pietà dei carcerati'. Confraternite e società a Roma nei secoli XVI–XVIII*, Edizioni di Storia e Letteratura, Rome 1980, provides the most detailed analysis of this kind of philanthropy as practiced in Rome.
117. As suggested by John Bossy in his 'Introduction' to Delumeau, *Catholicism*, p. 5.
118. For an excellent discussion of this see Brian Pullan, 'The Old Catholicism, the New Catholicism and the Poor' in *T&C*, pp. 14–23.

congestion and inadequate housing that went with it; food prices rose for much of the century and reached a peak in the 1590s when the peninsula suffered from famine. The next century had its own hardships and dislocations: while demographic pressure eased and prices levelled off, renewed warfare on Italian soil, major crop failures in 1628 and 1649, the devastating epidemics of 1630 and 1656, the popular uprisings of 1647, and economic depression between 1620 and 1660, all caused widespread suffering and despair. Charity thus had to respond, as best it could, to all those challenges and, if it was to be even minimally effective, had to adopt more professional, more targeted strategies.

COERCION AND REPRESSION

Writing in 1580 to one of his closest associates, Carlo Borromeo, the austere archbishop of Milan, observed that 'if [he] could fulfill his duties . . . only with sweetness and love, this would be quite pleasing to him . . . but oftentimes it is necessary to use the rod'.[119] In saying so Borromeo expressed a view that to him as well as to most of his contemporaries, Catholic and Protestant alike, must have seemed self-evident, namely that any serious programme of reform involved not just pastoral care, proselytizing and education, but also a measure of discipline and coercion – in Jedin's terminology, 'reform' could not be disjointed from 'counter-reformation'. It is essential, therefore, that after discussing the reform aspect of Italian religious history in the seventeenth century, we turn to the record of coercion of recalcitrant souls and of repression of ideas and practices that were considered incompatible with the true faith.

Coercion and repression are words that, in the context of early modern Catholicism, conjure up at once the memory of the Holy Office of the Roman Inquisition, the centralized agency established by the Papacy in 1542 for the defence of orthodoxy and the prosecution of error with the use of force, if necessary. In theory its jurisdiction extended over the whole Catholic world, but, in fact, it held no sway in Spain and most of the Spanish possessions where a separate agency, fully under the control of the crown, had been in charge since the late fifteenth century, while in France its powers were restricted by and had to be shared with the highest secular court, the Parlement. On the other hand, the Italian peninsula, fragmented as it was into several states, none of which could muster quite the same autonomy vis-à-vis the Papacy as larger nations could, offered less resistance to the activity of the Inquisition and would thus seem to represent a chosen field where the latter could operate effectively. Even in Italy, however, there existed regional

119. Quotation in Paolo Prodi, 'San Carlo Borromeo e le trattative fra Gregorio XIII e Filippo II sulla giurisdizione ecclesiastica', *Rivista di Storia dela Chiesa in Italia* 11 (1957), p. 226.

variations. Sicily and Sardinia fell under the jurisdiction of the Spanish rather than the Roman Inquisition; in the Kingdom of Naples, where repeated attempts to introduce the Spanish Inquisition failed in the face of popular opposition, the responsibility for prosecuting heresy traditionally belonged to the local bishops, and only special cases could be tried, at Rome's request, by a representative of the Holy Office. In the small Republic of Lucca, too, the task of prosecuting heresy was the local bishop's prerogative, but the bishop himself had to be assisted in his work by a lay magistrate; in Venice and in Genoa, on the other hand, judges of the Roman Inquisition were in charge, but had to work side by side with government-appointed lay magistrates. But even with these variations and limitations (and with the exceptions of Sicily and Sardinia) there is no doubt that from the mid-sixteenth century the Roman Inquisition could exert greater influence in Italy than in any other Catholic country at the time.[120]

In the light of this it is not surprising that since the eighteenth century the Inquisition has loomed large in Italian historiography and, at the hands of writers of the Enlightenment first and then of historians reared in the liberal, anticlerical tradition of the nineteenth century, has been the *bête noire* of early modern Italian history, held to be largely responsible for the decline of Italian culture from the dazzling heights of the Renaissance to the doldrums of the Baroque age; its most illustrious victims (Giordano Bruno executed in Rome, Tommaso Campanella kept in prison for nearly a quarter century, Galileo forced to recant) were celebrated as 'martyrs' of free thought. There is some truth in this view as will be seen later in this book and no scholar today (not even the most conservative Catholic apologist) would be prepared to defend the Inquisition and its use of force. Recent scholarship, however, has done two things: first, it has placed the Inquisition in the European context of its time and, second, it has corrected the image of the Inquisition as that of a bloodthirsty, fanatical institution bent on smothering any minimal sign of dissent by dint of torture and the stake.[121]

The European context was one of intolerance. To be sure, a few isolated voices were raised in the sixteenth and seventeenth centuries to denounce the use of force as a means of suppressing dissent; yet the general assumption, shared by church and secular authorities alike in both Catholic and Protestant

120. Adriano Prosperi, 'Per la storia dell'Inquisizione romana' in *L'Inquisizione romana in Italia nell'eta moderna: archivi, problemi di metodo e nuove ricerche*, Ministero per i Beni culturali e ambientali, Rome 1991, pp. 44–64.

121. The literature is surveyed by Adriano Prosperi, 'Studi recenti sulla storia dell'Inquisizione nella prima età moderna', *Rosary College Italian Studies* 3 (1989), pp. 178–9 and 192; and two essays by Agostino Borromeo: 'Contributo allo studio dell'Inquisizione e dei suoi rapporti con il potere episcopale nell'Italia spagnola del Cinquecento', *Annuario dell'Istituto Storico Italiano per l'età moderna e contemporanea* 29–30 (1977–78), pp. 219–76, and 'The Inquisition and Inquisitorial Censorship' in *Catholicism in Early Modern History. A Guide to Research*, ed. John W. O'Malley S.J., Center for Reformation Research, St Louis 1988, pp. 253–72.

countries, was that doctrinal error has no rights and must be suppressed, and that any form of moral or religious conduct that in the eyes of the authorities deviated from the norm must be punished either by the state or by the Church, or more commonly by both, as a threat to both. Virtually everywhere in Europe church and state, Consistory or Inquisition and magistrates worked hand in hand to ensure conformity to the established faith and to punish ungodly conduct. The targets of intolerance – Lutherans and Anabaptists in Catholic Italy, Anabaptists and Catholics in Lutheran Germany, Arminians and Catholics in Calvinist Holland, Recusants and Quakers in Anglican Britain, Jews and Muslims in Spain – all fell victim to the same belief that religious dissent, being an affront to the true faith and therefore an obstacle to salvation, has no place in a Christian commonwealth, and neither has immorality, whether debauchery or consorting with the devil.[122] In this perspective religious toleration could only be seen as 'a truly diabolical dogma' to use the words of the Calvinist leader Theodore Beza.[123] And his definition would have readily been subscribed to by Catholic churchmen, his archenemies.

The general attitude of religious intolerance was reinforced, in the confessional age, by the realization born of the horrors of religious warfare, that doctrinal divisions undermine the unity of the nation and the peace of society. As Martin Becanus, a Jesuit controversialist at the time of the Thirty Years War, put it, 'heretics disturb the Christian peace more than murderers, thieves and adulterers, and if the latter are justly punished by death, the same punishment ought to be meted out to the former'. Adam Stewart, a Presbyterian writing at about the same time on the evil of religious toleration, was equally convinced that the latter 'is dangerous to the State, [for it] may breed factions and divisions betwixt all persons of whatsover relation' and those divisions 'dissolve all naturall, civil, and domesticall bonds of societies'. A corollary of intolerance was that war against the heretics is morally justified. In 1579, in the midst of the French wars of religion, the Huguenot author of

122. The early modern state's preoccupation with religious uniformity as a condition of its internal cohesion has been highlighted by Wolfgang Reinhard, 'Confessionalizzazione forzata? Prolegomeni ad una teoria dell'eta confessionale', *AISIG* 7 (1982), pp. 13–37. The pursuit of religious uniformity by church and state on both sides of the confessional divide is thoroughly documented by R. Po-Chia Hsia, *Social Discipline in the Reformation: Central Europe 1550–1750*, Routledge 1989; although dealing only with the German states, the book is indispensable for understanding the climate of intolerance prevailing then in Europe. And so is Henry Kamen's *The Rise of Toleration*, McGraw Hill, New York and Toronto 1972, especially chs 3, 6 and 8.

123. Quotation in Kamen, *The Rise of Toleration*, p. 80. Writing in the early sixteenth century, the Catholic Gaspare Contarini was no less drastic: 'There is no more deadly plague . . . than heresy, for while it undermines the foundations of faith, it also overturns the commonwealth' (quoted in Paolo Prodi, 'The Structure and Organization of the Church in Renaissance Venice: Suggestions for Research' in *Renaissance Venice*, ed. J.R. Hale, Faber and Faber 1973, p. 413).

the celebrated political tract *Vindiciae contra Tyrannos* had no doubts about the legitimacy of taking arms against Catholic forces: in his words, 'those who fall in that holy war are no less martyrs than those who suffer the cross for religion's sake'. In 1620, at the time of the Bohemian insurrection that touched off the Thirty Years War, a Jesuit tract intended to incite Catholic troops against the Calvinist rebels assured them that they were fighting a truly holy war, for heresy was like a cancer and the source of discord, conflict and war.[124] Throughout Europe, then, intolerance, coercion and repression of religious ideas were approved and encouraged by churchmen as much as by statesmen and, because of the political implications of religious dissent, by the latter even more vehemently than by the former. If to churchmen heresy and ungodly conduct were to be prosecuted as offences against the true faith, to early modern governments their suppression was deemed necessary for preserving social tranquillity. What has been called the 'confessional age' viewed religious conformity as essential to a well-run polity and only exceptionally was the coexistence of different churches tolerated for reasons of expediency, as was done in France between 1598 and 1685. In general, the confessional state was so keen on combatting and eradicating religious dissenters that it undertook to do so whenever church authorities proved less than zealous in the prosecution of error or too lenient in punishing the errant. Such had been the case in the early sixteenth century when the government of Milan had loudly complained of the negligence of the clergy in suppressing the infiltration of Lutheran ideas; later in the century it was the Venetian government that took the initiative in prosecuting Anabaptists; and even in the early seventeenth century when the Venetian Republic found itself at loggerheads with the Papacy and was more inclined than ever to curb the power of the Roman Inquisition, the principle that religious dissent should not be tolerated was never called into question. It is all the more striking to hear, later in the century, Pope Innocent XI (1676–89) openly deplore Louis XIV's use of force against the Huguenots on grounds that conversion should not be the work of armed apostles, since Christ himself 'did not use this method to convert the world'.[125]

124. Becanus' words, the quotation from *Vindiciae* and a paraphrase of the 1620 tract are in Francesco Gui, *I Gesuiti e la rivoluzione boema. Alle origini della guerra dei Trent'Anni*, Franco Angeli, Milan 1989, pp. 16, 298 and 349; Adam Stewart's in John M. Murphy, 'John Goodwin and His Initial Campaign for Religious Toleration', unpublished M.A. thesis, University of Wisconsin at Madison 1993, p. 71.
125. Prosperi, 'Per la storia dell'Inquisizione', p. 58, and Borromeo, 'Contributo allo studio dell'Inquisizione', p. 234. The Venetian government at times accused the Inquisition of excessive leniency in dealing with religious dissenters ('the evil species of men that follow the new opinions in religion'): Brian Pullan, *The Jews of Europe and the Inquisition of Venice 1550–1670*, Blackwell 1983, p. 18. On Innocent XI see Ludwig von Pastor, *History of the Popes from the Close of the Middle Ages*, transl. Ernest Graf, vol. 32, Kegan Paul 1938, p. 341.

In this general context of intolerance the Inquisition's (and/or the state's) primary concern had been to prevent the infiltration of Protestant ideas into Italy; but after about 1580, once that threat had been largely eliminated, the Inquisition's main focus shifted to other forms of deviance from orthodoxy and right conduct, notably to philosophical or scientific ideas (such as Averroism, pantheism, atomism and the heliocentric theory) that had nothing to do with Protestantism, but were considered contrary to Catholic doctrine. Attention was also increasingly trained on forms of mysticism, such as Quietism or the 'simulation of holiness', that bypassed the Church's sacramental system, as well as various kinds of immorality, from blasphemy to the priest's abuse of confession for the purpose of seduction. Above all, the Inquisition investigated and prosecuted superstition, magic and witchcraft.

Reference has already been made to the action taken against Quietism and clerical immorality, and more will be said in a later chapter about the condemnation of philosophical and scientific ideas. Right now we must focus on what became, if we are to judge from the partial evidence available today, the Inquisition's major concern in the seventeenth century, namely the prosecution of individuals accused of engaging in 'magical arts', a term that covered a variety of practices – from necromancy to various 'superstitions', from some forms of astrology to diabolical witchcraft. In contrast with the previous century when heresy trials had formed the bulk of the Inquisition's work, in the seventeenth century it was the magical arts that held pride of place in its records.[126]

Even pretty harmless superstitions, such as the use of blessed candles for allegedly therapeutic purposes, were frowned upon by the Inquisition as forms of magic which, inasmuch as they turned religious objects into talismans or charms, competed with and might even replace genuine religious faith.[127] But, of course, the greatest vigilance and severity were reserved for those practices that involved black magic, that is to say the invocation of the devil for achieving illicit personal advantage or causing physical harm to people, crops or cattle. Witches were persons who were suspected of having

126. The shift from the persecution of heresy to that of magic, superstition and clerical misconduct is borne out by what data are available for a number of local Inquisition tribunals: see John Tedeschi, *The Prosecution of Heresy. Collected Studies on the Inquisition in Early Modern Italy*, Medieval and Renaissance Texts and Studies, Binghamton, N.Y. 1991, pp. 94 and 105–8 and Zardin, 'L'ultimo periodo spagnolo', p. 584. There is a large and growing body of literature on 'simulation of holiness or sainthood' (generally involving alleged visions, ecstasies, miracles and prophesying), for which now see Gabriella Zarri, ed., *Finzione e santità tra medioevo ed età moderna*, Rosenberg and Sellier, Turin 1991.

127. Instances of healing rituals and of love magic in O'Neil, 'Magical Healing', pp. 94 and 97; Adriano Prosperi, 'Vicari dell'Inquisizione fiorentina alla metà del Seicento. Note d'archivio', *AISIG* 8 (1982), p. 303; and Guido Ruggiero, ' "Più che la vita caro": onore, matrimonio e reputazione femminile nel tardo Cinquecento', *QS* 66 (1987), pp. 753–75.

made a pact with the devil and, as a result, of being endowed with occult evil powers. Insofar as they were followers and agents of Satan, they were regarded as enemies of the true religion as well as of society, and were, therefore, treated on a par with heretics, their diabolical allegiance being viewed as 'a sort of Christianity turned inside out'.[128]

The repression of magic in general and of witchcraft in particular was not a peculiarity of the Roman Inquisition nor was it a distinctly Catholic phenomenon. The witch-craze was, in fact, a European phenomenon which engulfed both Protestant and Catholic countries, with peaks of ferocity being reached in the 1590s, the 1630s and the 1660s. Responsible for an estimated 100,000 executions in the whole of Europe over two centuries or so, the campaign against witchcraft greatly varied in intensity from country to country, with Germany (both Lutheran and Catholic), Switzerland, Scotland, Languedoc, Lorraine and later on Poland and Sweden leading in the number of executions, while both Spain and Italy, the heartlands of the Inquisition, saw surprisingly few of them, except in border areas along the Pyrenees and the Alps.[129]

The reasons why witchcraft became such a collective obsession in the Europe of the Renaissance and the Reformation are still a matter of much speculation and debate[130] – and so is the question of why Italy in particular was largely spared the horrors of the great witch hunt. After all, Italian theologians and magistrates were as familiar as their northern counterparts with the theory of diabolical influences that had been formulated in the late fifteenth century, and apparently they never entertained serious doubts about its validity. And yet, only in rare cases did the Roman Inquisition inflict the death penalty on convicted witches, and nothing in the annals of Italian history even remotely compares to the blood-stained record of the Canton of Vaud, Switzerland where 90 per cent of witch trials resulted in executions, or of Scotland where 1,350 witches were burnt at the stake out of 2,300 who were brought to trial between 1560 and 1700.[131]

The main reason for the relative leniency of the Roman Inquisition is to be found in the way that tribunal operated. As John Tedeschi has demonstrated, the Italian inquisitors were no fanatics out on a rampage; rather, they by and large were conscientious judges who approached the denunciations brought

128. Delumeau, *Catholicism*, p. 174. On the Inquisitors' understanding of what constituted diabolical magic see Tedeschi, *The Prosecution of Heresy*, p. 233, and Geoffrey Scarre, *Witchcraft and Magic in Sixteenth and Seventeenth-Century Europe*, Humanities Press International, Atlantic Highlands, N.J. 1987, pp. 3–6.

129. Scarre, *Witchcraft*, pp. 19–24.

130. A review of the debate in Scarre, *Witchcraft*, pp. 30–54. Scarre himself rejects the views that the witch hunt was a response to natural calamities, a weapon in confessional or social conflicts, or an instrument of social control, and argues instead (convincingly, I believe) that it resulted from the authorities' sincere belief that witchcraft represented 'a destructive onslaught of the great enemy of God and of mankind'.

131. Michele Cassese, 'L'interpretazione protestante' in *La religione popolare*, p. 170.

before their court with a meticulous respect for legal procedures and for the law of proof. In dealing with witches, they took great pains in establishing the fact that a *maleficium* had actually been perpetrated and often dismissed charges which they considered unsubstantiated; they did not admit in evidence charges brought by personal enemies of the defendant; before accepting at face value an accusation of witchcraft, they first tried to determine whether the harm allegedly caused by a witch could be explained by a physician on the basis of some natural cause; and they ruled out the use of suggestive or leading questions in the course of the trial. With these safeguards in place, it is not surprising that a good number of cases were simply dismissed. But even when a verdict of guilt was pronounced, first offenders usually got off with a short prison sentence.[132]

The Roman Inquisition thus played a major role in curbing the persecution of witches. Yet, one wonders whether some of the credit for this should not also go to the Italian people. True enough, in early modern Italy, notably in the Alpine region, the popular fear and hatred of witches could at times turn into mass hysteria and result in the crowd's demand for swift and exemplary justice.[133] So much so, in fact, that the Holy Office in Rome often had to remind its representatives in the provinces of their duty to protect indicted or convicted witches from lynching mobs.[134] Yet one can doubt that even so powerful an agency as the Inquisition could have long and consistently adhered to a policy of moderation had public opinion been swept by a tidal wave of uncontrollable hysteria as apparently happened in other parts of Europe. Actually, there is little evidence that explosions of popular fury against witches were either frequent or widely spread in Italy; and one is led to believe that the obsession with and fear of witchcraft were not a major component of Italian popular culture. If this be true, then the question is why. To my knowledge there is no ready answer to that question, but at least two hypotheses come to mind. One is based on the fact that the practice of 'good' or 'white' magic – another, but less worrisome target of the Inquisition – was widespread in early modern Italy. Insofar as white magic intends to make use of occult forces to achieve a good result such as curing a disease or

---

132. Tedeschi, *The Prosecution of Heresy*, pp. 131–40, 150 and 154. On the relative leniency of the Inquisition tribunals see also Ginzburg, *The Night Battles*, pp. 112, 126, 131, 133, and 142; Anne J. Schutte, 'I processi dell'Inquisizione veneziana nel Seicento: la femminilizzazione dell'eresia' in *L'Inquisizione romana in Italia*, p. 167; Giovanna Paolin, 'Inquisitori e confessori nel Seicento in Friuli', pp. 182–3 of the same vol.; O'Neil, 'Magical Healing', pp. 106–7; Nicholas Davidson, 'The Inquisition and the Italian Jews' in *Inquisition and Society in Early Modern Europe*, ed. Stephen Haliczer, Croom Helm 1987, pp. 20 and 37; and Mario Rosa, 'La Chiesa e la città' in *Storia di Prato*, vol. 2, ed. Elena Fasano Guarini, Le Monnier, Prato 1986, p. 555.

133. Instances of mass hysteria in Luigi Fumi, 'L'Inquisizione romana e lo Stato di Milano. Saggi di ricerche nell'Archivio di Stato', *Archivio Storico Lombardo*, 4th ser., 13 (1910), p. 101 (against witches) and pp. 369–70 (against heretics).

134. Tedeschi, *The Prosecution of Heresy*, pp. 237–8.

recovering a lost object, it embodies a belief in a benevolent, if mysterious, nature and is thus likely to provide a sense of assurance capable of countering or assuaging the fear of diabolical influences. Another and perhaps more plausible hypothesis is provided by one of the distinctive features of Italian popular religion in the age of the Counter-Reformation, namely the cult of saints with its proliferation of shrines, relics, and miraculous icons. A world peopled with patron saints and sacred objects could not but be perceived as a place where the individual and the community are not alone in the face of suffering and calamities, but rather as an ultimately benign place where the devil's snares could be avoided and the witch's spells could be neutralized with the help of heavenly guardians; and since the saints people venerated and prayed to were, after all, themselves human beings who had vanquished the devil, the devout could feel confident that they, too, would be able to do the same. Further research will have to decide whether either of these two hypotheses has any merit. What is certain, at any rate, is the role of the Inquisition in restraining whatever hostility there was in the popular mind against witches by applying strict legal standards to their prosecution. This moderating role, by the way, was not always appreciated by secular authorities: as Paolo Sarpi noted, Venetian law required that 'maleficient witchcraft be punished by the [the state's] magistrates, because ecclesiastical penalties are no adequate chastisement for so great a crime'.[135]

The Inquisition exhibited the same attention to and respect for legal procedures and for rigorous standards of proof when dealing with other offences that came under its jurisdiction, whether heresy, clerical immorality, or simulated holiness (*finzione di santità*). In all cases it applied safeguards to protect the rights of the defendant, and those safeguards were often far ahead of those then in use in secular courts. The Inquisition, for instance, did not admit in evidence anonymous denunciations or unsworn testimony; it instructed its officials to proceed only with great caution before making an arrest, for it acknowledged that 'the mere fact of incarceration [by order of the Inquisition] brings notable infamy to the accused'; it granted the defendant the right to ask for a change of venue if there were grounds for suspecting that the local inquisitor was biased against him or her; it recognized the defendant's right to be assisted by counsel and provided 'public defenders' to the indigent; throughout the trial the defendant's and the prosecutor's every word was meticulously recorded to ensure that no leading questions were being asked; the accused had a right to read the depositions (although not to know the identity) of prosecution witnesses and to rebut them in writing; and in formulating its verdict the court took into account, as secular courts seldom did, extenuating circumstances such as the defendant's level of education, emotional or mental state, and age. Finally, the Inquisition, in keeping with

---

135. Quotation in Tedeschi, *The Prosecution of Heresy*, p. 211. The Inquisition's leniency toward sorcerers and witches was denounced by the Spanish governor of Milan in 1611 and again in 1620 as encouraging the spread of witchcraft (Fumi, 'L'Inquisizione romana', pp. 115 and 117).

the rules laid down by Pius IV in 1562, normally absolved heretics who were first offenders and showed signs of genuine remorse for their errors. In short, writes the Inquisition's foremost scholar, 'it may not be an exaggeration to claim that in several respects the Holy Office was a pioneer in judicial reform'.[136]

If this last comment sounds paradoxical, it is because we almost instinctively associate the Inquisition with torture, long prison sentences, and burnings at the stake. Here again, however, recent scholarship has done much to dispel misconceptions and exaggerations. No one denies that the Inquisition, like any court of law in early modern continental Europe, did resort, in some cases, to judicial torture in order to obtain full confession of guilt or proof of complicity. Yet, according to the law of proof generally accepted at the time, torture was never routinely applied as a quick way of extracting a guilty plea from the accused. Rather, it was intended as a means of achieving certainty when only circumstantial evidence (as opposed to the direct sworn testimony of at least two eyewitnesses) was available and the defendant denied all charges; under these, but only under these, circumstances medieval and early modern courts would not convict unless the defendant confessed under torture and subsequently confirmed his or her confession.[137] Absurd and inhumane though the logic of the system looks to us, it was generally followed by the courts with only a few isolated voices being raised in the seventeenth century against it.[138]

The Inquisition thus adopted the accepted law of proof and used torture in cases where the jurisprudence of the time called for it. Yet, unlike criminal courts, it excluded its use on pregnant women, the aged, the disabled and children under fourteen; the duration of torture was shorter than when imposed by a criminal court and the pain inflicted was milder; finally, if the defendant did not confess his guilt under torture, he or she was generally set free. This last provision would seem rather ludicrous were it not for the fact that 'in an astonishing number of cases involving both men and women [torture] did not produce admissions of guilt'.[139]

136. Tedeschi, *The Prosecution of Heresy*, pp. 8 and 132–40.
137. John H. Langbein, *Torture and the Law of Proof. Europe and England in the Ancien Regime*, University of Chicago Press 1976, ch. 1. The 1594 case of a midwife who, after confessing under torture to the charge of diabolical witchcraft, later retracted and was acquitted has been admirably reconstructed by Silvia Mantini, 'Gostanza da Libbiano, guaritrice e strega' in *Rinascimento al femminile* ed. Ottavia Niccoli, Laterza, Rome-Bari 1991, pp. 143–62.
138. Piero Fiorelli, *La tortura giudiziaria nel diritto comune*, Giuffrè, Milan 1954, vol. 2, pp. 222–41, discusses sixteenth- and seventeenth-century opponents of torture, notably the German Jesuits Adam Tanner and Frederic von Spee. Torture was also denounced by the utopian writer Ludovico Agostini on grounds that 'the pain of the strappado and of other instruments of torture is generally greater than anything the defendant would have to endure if he confessed to the crime of which he is charged' (quoted in Luigi Firpo, *Lo Stato ideale della Controriforma: Ludovico Agostini*, Laterza, Bari 1957, p. 288).
139. Tedeschi, *The Prosecution of Heresy*, pp. 141–5.

The same pattern of relative leniency that characterized the use of torture by the Inquisition is discernible in the sentences it inflicted. These ranged from the requirement that the person convicted perform some acts of devotion and of penance to the humiliation of a public recantation, to house arrest, incarceration, service in the galleys and, lastly, the death penalty. In practice, however, the actual sentence served was milder than what court papers indicate: 'perpetual imprisonment', for instance, seldom amounted to more than a three-year term and was often commuted to house arrest. Capital punishment was inflicted only in the case of the most serious offences, such as apostasy, heresy, diabolical witchcraft, or the desecration of altars, and only when the defendant remained obstinate and refused to be reconciled with the Church, or when he or she had experienced a previous formal conviction. How often this happened is hard to say, but what partial evidence we have suggests that only in a small percentage of trials was execution the tragic outcome. For instance, out of roughly 200 sentences handed down by provincial inquisitorial courts in Italy in 1580–82 only four carried the death penalty; in Venice, from 1547 to 1583, of 774 individuals charged with heresy 199 were found guilty and of these twelve were executed; of one thousand defendants brought before the Inquisition in Aquileia from the mid-sixteenth to the mid-seventeenth century only four were sent to the stake; and in Friuli no witchcraft trial resulted in death for the offender.[140]

How should one assess the Inquisition's record as regards capital punishment? From the vantage point of our time the answer is not in doubt: even the execution of one individual for his or her beliefs is one too many. It would be anachronistic, however, to measure the early modern centuries by a yardstick that even the most decent people in those centuries would have found utterly incomprehensible: to them, as we have seen, any grave offence against religious faith, including witchcraft, deserved at least the same treatment as any major crime against fellow human beings. The Inquisition's record must thus be placed in the context of the time and compared with that of other agencies which dealt with religious dissent or witchcraft. With no assistance from the Roman Inquisition nearly three hundred Protestants were sent to the stake during the five-year reign of the Catholic Queen Mary Tudor; during the much longer reign of her Protestant successor Elizabeth nearly two hundred Catholics met the same fate and so did twenty-four more (along with some anti-Trinitarians) under James I. If in Calvinist Geneva only one heretic (Michael Servetus) was ever executed, between 1540 and 1620 sixty-eight witches were, and, as mentioned earlier, thousands of them went to the stake

---

140. Tedeschi, *The Prosecution of Heresy*, pp. 103–4; also John Martin, 'Per un'analisi quantitativa dell'Inquisizione veneziana' in *L'Inquisizione romana in Italia*, p. 143. No complete data are available for Rome. Romolo Quazza, *Preponderanza spagnola (1559–1700)*, Vallardi, Milan 1950, pp. 237–50, has identified some fifty executions for either heresy or witchcraft between 1559 and 1605, against only three during the next forty years.

in Europe at large.[141] In a relative sense, then, one can say that the Inquisition was no more repressive or cruel, and probably less so, than most other courts of law (ecclesiastical or secular) throughout Europe that were entrusted with the defence of right doctrine and right conduct.

What did repression (primarily, but not solely, at the hands of the Inquisition) achieve in Italy? It certainly succeeded in eliminating the threat of Protestantism from across the Alps: by the 1580s Protestant groups no longer represented a serious probem in the peninsula, as shown by the rapid decline in the number of cases involving Lutherans, Calvinists or Anabaptists brought before the Inquisition in those areas, at any rate, for which the relevant information has survived or is accessible.[142] Over and against this record of 'success', however, stand the limited results achieved, as will be seen in a later chapter, in suppressing philosophical and scientific ideas considered dangerous to the faith; there also stands the failure to convert or destroy the Waldensian communities (numbering perhaps 15,000 people) located since the late Middle Ages in valleys west of Turin.[143] Fiercely independent and prepared to take up arms in defence of their faith as well as of their communal autonomy, the Waldensians had been repeatedly subjected to intense campaigns of indoctrination by Catholic preachers during the sixteenth century; in 1602 and again in 1618 the duke of Savoy had stepped in to break their resistance by threatening deportation to all those who refused conversion. While some success was achieved in the area around Saluzzo, the Waldensians held their ground in the Valle Pellice near Pinerolo. Full-scale military campaigns were staged in 1655 and 1663, but to no avail; in 1685–86 a massive attack was mounted by Duke Vittorio Amedeo II at the request of the French king Louis XIV and with the intervention of French troops alongside the Savoyard army. Attacked from two sides, outnumbered and outgunned by their enemies, their ranks depleted by death in combat, deportation or flight abroad, by 1686 the Waldensians of Piedmont seemed on the verge of total obliteration. But three years later a remnant of a thousand men led by Henry Arnaud managed to fight their way back into their homeland in what came to be known as 'the Glorious Return' and to establish a stronghold capable of fending off the combined onslaught of Savoyard and French forces. The Waldensians were assisted in their struggle by the fact that the relationship between the duke of Savoy and the Sun King was beginning to sour as the former was now secretly trying to distance himself from his domineering ally and was preparing to join the newly formed coalition (the

---

141. Kamen, *The Rise of Toleration*, pp. 117 and 161–2; Joseph Lecler, *Histoire de la tolérance au siècle de la Réforme*, Aubier, Paris 1955, vol. 2, pp. 308–13 and 350–5; and Cassese, 'L'interpretazione protestante', p. 170.

142. See note 126 above.

143. For what follows see Giorgio Spini, 'Italy after the Thirty Years War' in *New Cambridge Modern History*, vol. 5, ed. F.L. Carsten, Cambridge University Press 1961, pp. 460–1 and 472; Geoffrey Symcox, *Victor Amadeus II. Absolutism in the Savoyard State, 1675–1730*, Thames and Hudson 1983, pp. 91–114; and Erba, *La Chiesa sabauda*, pp. 394–9.

League of Augsburg) against France. This the duke did in 1690 after securing the support of both the Waldensians and Spain for driving the French forces out of Piedmont; once this was achieved he issued an edict that restored the right of the Waldensians to practice their religion undisturbed.

The Waldensians' astonishing resilience and ultimate survival in the seventeenth century stands in sharp contrast to the elimination of all other Protestant groups in the peninsula during the previous century. Political circumstances, notably the duke of Savoy's switch of alliances, no doubt helped rescue the Waldensians at a decisive moment of their history. But their long record of resistance from the early sixteenth to the late seventeenth century reflects the fact that they had long formed tightly knit communities with a strong tradition of self-government, a jealous sense of their autonomy, and a capability to defend themselves, by force of arms if necessary, in their mountains; the fact that in the 1530s they had subscribed to the Swiss Reformed Church's creed had diluted neither their 'native', deeply rooted sense of identity nor their fierce attachment to home rule. By contrast, the Italian followers of Luther and Calvin never formed more than small, scattered conventicles that lacked the support of a larger community; as such, they could be plucked out one by one, as it were, by the hand of the state or of the Inquisition unless they managed, as many of them did, to escape abroad.

In the climate of intolerance that came to pervade Italy as well as Europe in the 'confessional age' another religious minority, the Jews, was bound to attract the attention and the disapproval of ecclesiastical and secular authorities. Their goal was either to drive out entirely the dissident group or, if it was to be tolerated as a distinct community, to isolate it in such a way that it would not 'contaminate' or 'pollute' the rest of society with unorthodox beliefs and rituals.[144] In sixteenth- and seventeenth-century Italy this climate of hostility and intolerance was something new, for until the late Middle Ages Jews in Italy had enjoyed greater freedom than elsewhere in Europe and had been active and at times prominent in the economic and cultural life of the country.[145] The sixteenth century, however, heralded a general hardening of attitudes toward the Jews and spawned legislation aimed at their suppression or marginalization. This was especially true in Spanish-dominated Naples, Sicily and Sardinia from which Jews were expelled *en masse* as early as 1510 in keeping with the policy already in force in Spain itself.[146] A few years later

144. Davidson, 'The Inquisition and the Italian Jews', p. 25 has called attention to the fear that regular, friendly contacts with Jews might lead some Christians to view Judaism as 'an alternative system of beliefs' and would thus insinuate doubts about Christianity.

145. Attilio Milano, *Storia degli Ebrei in Italia*, Einaudi, Turin 1963, pp. 150–60; Jonathan I. Israel, *European Jewry in the Age of Mercantilism, 1550–1750*, Clarendon Press 1985, pp. 15 and 72. On the medieval Papacy's tolerant attitude toward Jews see Edward A. Synan, *The Popes and the Jews in the Middle Ages*, Macmillan, New York 1967. I am indebted to Professor William J. Courtenay for bringing this important work to my attention.

146. Israel, *European Jewry*, p. 7.

the Venetian Republic, while allowing Jews to settle permanently in Venice, confined them to an enclosed, cramped district (the ghetto) where they were expected to make their home in rented houses and from which they were not allowed to absent themselves after dark. Intended as it was both to forestall the 'contamination' of Christianity with Judaism and to encourage conversion from Judaism by dangling before the Jews the prospect of leaving behind the hardships and the humiliations of the ghetto,[147] the Venetian model of segregation was soon widely imitated: even the Papacy adopted it in spite of the fact that traditionally it had been the 'foremost protector' of the Jews in western Europe and as late as the 1540s and early 1550s had made increasingly generous concessions in the hope of attracting to the seaport of Ancona Jews who had been expelled from the Spanish dominions. In 1555 the intransigent Paul IV (1555–59) ordered their internment in all the towns of the Papal States and imposed humiliating restrictions on their economic activities. Under his successor Pius IV (1559–65) a more lenient policy prevailed, but harsher measures were introduced by Pius V (1566–72): he ordered the expulsion of Jews from all papal towns, Rome and Ancona excepted. In the next century this policy was mitigated somewhat and a number of towns were reopened to them.[148] In other Italian states, too, intolerance toward the Jews was rife in the late sixteenth century: in 1565 Philip II king of Spain decided to expel the Jews from the State of Milan, but the objections of local authorities who depended heavily on loans from Jewish bankers succeeded in stalling the royal decree for thirty years; only in 1597 was the decree of expulsion carried out and nearly 900 families were forced to leave.[149] In Tuscany internment in the ghetto was imposed in the 1560s; in Piedmont outright expulsion was decreed, although not strictly enforced, at about the same time. There were exceptions to this general climate of hostility: the duke of Mantua, for one, welcomed Jews to his small state; on their part, the grand dukes of Tuscany not only encouraged them to settle in Leghorn, the seaport they were striving to transform into a major international entrepôt, but exempted those who did come there from all the restrictions and disabilities that were in force in the other towns of their dominions.[150]

In the seventeenth century the policy of segregating the Jews remained basically unchanged, except in Leghorn, and so did the rationale behind it, namely that contacts with Jews must be strictly limited to insulate Christians from Jewish religious influence, and that the disabilities imposed on Jews might hasten their conversion. At the same time one notices in the seventeenth century a shift away from the harsh, uncompromising attitudes of the previous century. One main reason for the shift was the pragmatic

147. Pullan, *The Jews of Europe*, pp. 151–70.
148. Milano, *Storia degli Ebrei*, pp. 245–60.
149. Renata Segre, *Gli Ebrei lombardi in età spagnola. Storia di un'espulsione*, Accademia delle scienze, Turin 1973.
150. Milano, *Storia degli Ebrei*, pp. 262–301.

recognition by some Italian rulers, whether popes, grand dukes or doges, of the crucial, indeed irreplaceable role Jews could play in international trade thanks to the expertise they had acquired over the centuries in that area and to their connections with other Jewish communities in Europe (notably in Holland and Poland) and in the Ottoman Empire. The Medici grand dukes were well aware of that when they encouraged Jews to come to Leghorn, and so were the popes when, in granting permission for Jews to settle in such key trading centres as Ancona, Pesaro and Senigallia, they explicitly acknowledged their role in the trade between Italy and the eastern Mediterranean. Likewise the Venetian Republic, as it felt threatened by Ancona's competition, took the unprecedented step of giving its own Jews the right to trade in the Levant – a privilege previously reserved to, and jealously guarded by, its patricians and citizens. Not to be outdone, in 1652 Carlo Emanuele II, duke of Savoy, in an effort to build up the fortunes of his only outlet to the sea, expressly invited Jewish merchants from Holland and from North Africa to settle in Nice.[151] The long-term effect of this mercantilist pragmatism was the survival and growth in a select number of towns of large and dynamic Jewish communities which in spite of segregation inevitably interacted with gentile society. In Venice the Jewish community more than doubled in size in the first half of the seventeenth century; in Leghorn the growth was fourfold; no precise figures are available for Ancona, Pesaro and Senigallia, but we know that they all harboured substantial Jewish communities.[152] The original goal of eliminating or rigidly isolating a religious minority that refused to be pressured, cajoled or intimidated into conformity thus gave way, at least in part, to utilitarian considerations. Segregation, to be sure, continued to be the norm (except in Leghorn), but paradoxically it may have defeated one of its main purposes, namely that of pressuring Jews to convert, because it helped preserve the distinctive culture and the sense of identity of Italian Jewry and thus made assimilation in the larger community all the more unlikely.[153]

Repression was probably more successful in curbing superstitions and magical practices than it was in suppressing either the Waldensians or the Jews, although in these areas of popular culture education and persuasion, whether through catechisms, sermons, schools or the confessional, may have played as important a role as the punishment of errants.[154] Not that various forms of magic disappeared altogether: as late as 1694 the diocesan synod convened in Naples by Cardinal Cantelmo felt it necessary to threaten with excommunication 'witches, magicians, and necromancers who invoke the

151. Milano, *Storia degli Ebrei*, pp. 298–9; Israel, *European Jewry*, pp. 113–80; and Benjamin C.I. Ravid, *Economics and Toleration in Seventeenth-Century Europe: The Background and Context of the 'Discorso' of Simone Luzzatto*, American Academy of Jewish Research, Jerusalem 1977.
152. Israel, *European Jewry*, p. 113.
153. Israel, *European Jewry*, pp. 73–90; and Pullan, *The Jews of Europe*, p. 154.
154. Paolin, 'Inquisitori e confessori', pp. 175–87; and Martin, 'Per un'analisi quantitativa', p. 143.

demons to win someone's love, to stir up hatred, or to discover hidden treasures'. Nonetheless the steady decline in the number of cases of magic and witchcraft tried before the Neapolitan episcopal court, from 125 in the first decade of the seventeenth century to 25 in the last, suggests that the problem was receding or interest in controlling it was waning.[155] It is more difficult to assess the impact of repression on clerical immorality, dereliction of duty, absenteeism and the often scandalous behaviour of monks and nuns. The most that can be said is that, while abuses and misconduct did not entirely disappear, while lay meddling in the life of the clergy through various forms of patronage remained strong, and while papal nepotism reached high levels in the first half of the century, especially during Urban VIII's pontificate, nonetheless, as mentioned earlier in this chapter, standards of clerical conduct did improve overall in the second half at the time of the so-called 'Tridentine revival'.

To round off our survey of repressive measures in Counter-Reformation Italy mention must be made of the censorship of books. The first step in that direction had been taken in 1549 with the publication of the first in a long series of Indexes of Forbidden Books; then, in 1571, the Congregation of the Index was established as an agency of the Roman Curia whose specific mandate was to identify, in cooperation with the Inquisition, books deemed dangerous to the faith and to review manuscripts of Catholic authors in order to determine their orthodoxy prior to publication. Censorship has generally been viewed as an effective instrument in the hands of the Church with dire consequences for Italy's intellectual development in early modern times. It has been blamed for cutting off Italian culture from that of the rest of Europe, for forcing it into a straitjacket of conformism, and, in the end, for having a deadening impact on creativity and free inquiry.[156] Once again, however, it is well to remember that censorship was confined neither to the Catholic Church nor to Italy, but was a common practice on both sides of the confessional divide and was advocated and enforced by both church and state.[157] Even

155. Lopez, *Clero, eresia e magia*, pp. 153 (Cantelmo's threats) and 162 (number of trials); also, Ginzburg, 'Folklore, magia e religione', p. 660.
156. Antonio Rotondò, 'La censura ecclesiastica e la cultura' in *SIE Documenti*, vol. 5 (1973), pp. 1404 and 1407. For a critique of this view, see Tedeschi, pp. 338–45.
157. The Venetian government's insistence that any book must have its approval as well as the Church's before it could be printed led to prolongued quarrels between the two powers (see Paul F. Grendler, *The Roman Inquisition and the Venetian Press, 1540–1605*, Princeton University Press 1977); for the period after 1605 see Mario Infelise, 'A proposito di imprimatur. Una controversia giurisdizionale di fine Seicento tra Venezia e Roma' in *Studi veneti offerti a Gaetano Cozzi*, Il Cardo, Vicenza 1992, pp. 287–99. State and church censorship overlapped and competed in the State of Milan as well (Kevin M. Stevens, 'Printing and Politics: Carlo Borromeo and the Seminary Press of Milan' in *Stampa, libri e letture a Milano nell'età di Carlo Borromeo*, ed. Nicola Rasponi and Angelo Turchini, Vita e Pensiero, Milan 1992, pp. 106–7. On censorship in Protestant countries, see Hsia, *Social Discipline*, pp. 24 and 117.

someone as critical of the Papacy and of its meddling in the life of states as Paolo Sarpi had no hesitation in upholding the legitimacy and indeed the necessity of censorship, if not by the Church, most certainly by the state. 'The matter of books', he wrote,'may seem of small importance, for only words are involved; but from those words come the opinions of the world that cause factions, seditions and ultimately wars. They are words indeed, but [words] can draw armies in their wake.'[158] One must also bear in mind, in the light of recent studies, that censorship in Italy was no iron curtain capable of effectively insulating Italian culture from the winds of change blowing north of the Alps. It is revealing in this respect that in a letter addressed to provincial inquisitors in 1614 Cardinal Bellarmine expressed grave concern about the persistent and widespread circulation throughout Europe of 'infected and pernicious books' and called the inquisitors to redouble their vigilance so that 'at least Italy' would be spared this 'plague of books'.[159] His sense of alarm suggests that nearly half a century after the creation of the Congregation of the Index censorship did not provide adequate protection against heterorthodox literature. Nor were his worries unwarranted, for we now know that, one way or another, heretical books did seep into Italy often hidden in bundles of merchandise from Protestant countries or as special editions in which the original front matter had been replaced with one featuring a false (and innocent-looking) title and a false place of publication. As will be seen in a later chapter, it was thanks to a clandestine, but vigorous book trade that the writings of the 'libertines', replete with ferocious anticlerical invective, circulated widely in seventeenth-century Italy; besides, the fact that Italian translations of unorthodox books were printed abroad strongly suggests that there was a market for them in Italy.[160] All in all, it would seem that the elaborate censorship machine set up in 1571 largely failed to achieve its goal.

158. Quotation in Rotondò, 'La censura', p. 1473.
159. Ibid., p. 1399.
160. In addition to Tedeschi, *The Prosecution of Heresy*, pp. 335–8, see Peyronel Rambaldi, 'La Controriforma', pp. 80–1; and Benzoni, 'Intellettuali e Controriforma', p. 135. Rodolfo Savelli, 'Tra Machiavelli e S. Giorgio. Cultura giuspolitica e dibattito istituzionale a Genova nel Cinque-Seicento' in *Finanze e ragion di Stato in Italia e Germania nella prima età moderna*, ed. Aldo De Maddalena and Hermann Kellenbenz, Mulino, Bologna 1984, pp. 249–52, records the somewhat surprising 1647 publication in Genoa (in a cultural environment seemingly under Jesuit control) of a book on politics that savaged the Jesuits for their alleged 'fraudulent' practices. Paolin, 'Inquisitori e confessori', pp. 183–4, speaks of libertine books that 'flooded' Venice and Udine around the mid-seventeenth century and of the Inquisition's leniency towards those charged with owning and reading them. John Hedley Brooke, *Science and Religion. Some Historical Perspectives*, Cambridge University Press 1991, p. 108, observes that Italian scholars were not cut off by the Index from European culture and that prohibited books, notably books of science, 'entered private libraries where they could be consulted by those prepared to break the rules in the interest of learning'.

Some twenty years ago Jean Delumeau concluded his discussion of the Counter-Reformation period in Italian history with the startling and unconventional statement that seventeenth-century Italy 'was one of the freest countries in Europe' and adduced as evidence such diverse facts as that fewer heretics and witches were burnt at the stake than elsewhere and that artists did not feel constrained in their rendition of pagan subjects; the fact also that Venice refused to deliver Paolo Sarpi into papal hands and that the country at large continued to harbour a great many libertines and atheists.[161] Since then, as we have seen, more evidence has surfaced that indicates that the machinery of repression assembled by the Counter-Reformation Papacy proved far less effective and less severe than had traditionally been supposed: the relative leniency of the Inquisition is a case in point and so is the wide circulation of 'prohibited' books. We shall see that resistance to papal claims was not confined to the Venetian Republic and that Italian culture was not cast into a rigid mould of blind conformity, but retained a good deal of originality and creativity. Nor can one say that the religious future of the country was inexorably shaped by dint of coercion and repression. One is rather led to conclude that that future owed more to the enduring work of education and persuasion that was at the heart of the Catholic reform. Its fruits were the persistent religious fervour of the popular masses, the Catholic loyalty of much of the cultural elite, even of those who suffered at the hands of church zealots, the diffusion among the laity of more personal, more intimate forms of piety, and, lastly, the impressive array of charitable institutions run for the most part by lay men and women.[162] No amount of coercion could have achieved that much.

161. Delumeau, *L'Italie de Botticelli à Bonaparte*, Colin, Paris 1974, pp. 275–6.
162. Salmann, 'Le Catholicisme triomphant', p. 283; Paolo Prodi, 'Riforma cattolica e Controriforma' in *Nuove questioni di storia moderna*, Marzorati, Milan 1964, vol. 1, p. 405; and Hsia, *Social Discipline*, p. 89.

CHAPTER FIVE

Church and state

The Church that emerged from the Council of Trent – revitalized, more militant, and fully determined not only to contain and, if possible, to roll back the Protestant tide, but also to set its own house in order and to reshape society according to its own moral standards – had to depend on the cooperation of the confessional state for implementing its vast programme. On their part, secular governments, in their efforts to strengthen their hold on the various components of society and to avoid civil strife generated by religious divisions, had an obvious interest in safeguarding the religious unity of their respective countries, and this meant supporting the established Church as it strove to stamp out religious dissent and to correct the most flagrant forms of clerical misconduct. Yet, for all those shared goals and common interests, the alliance of throne and altar was bound to experience strains and even temporary breakdowns, not because the religious allegiance of the several Italian rulers was ever in doubt, but because the Church's determination to pursue its own programme in full autonomy inevitably ran into the state's equally strong determination to assert a measure of control over ecclesiastical institutions, properties and personnel, a control it considered essential for its own consolidation.[1]

For the post-Tridentine Church (and for the Papacy which had assumed a leading role in carrying out the programme of reform laid out at Trent) a main goal was to reassert its 'liberty' from the encroachment or the tutelage of the secular state as a pre-condition of its own effectiveness. This meant, first and

1. The inevitable tension between the Counter-Reformation Church and the rising absolute state in spite of their shared commitment to religious unity has often been noted in the literature. See, for instance, Gregorio Penco, *Storia della Chiesa in Italia*, vol. 2, Jaca Books, Milan 1976, pp. 21–2; A.D. Wright, 'Relations between Church and State: Catholic Developments in Spanish-ruled Italy of the Counter-Reformation', *History of European Ideas* 9 (1988), p. 385; Paolo Prodi, 'Controriforma e/o Riforma cattolica: superamento di vecchi dilemmi nei nuovi panorami storiografici', *Roemische Historische Mitteilungen* 31 (1989), p. 230; and Wolfgang Reinhard, 'Reformation, Counter-Reformation and the Early Modern State: A Reassessment', *Catholic Historical Review* 75 (1989), pp. 400–2.

foremost, the right to select and police its own personnel, from bishop to parish priest to monk; it also meant the exercise of jurisdiction over the laity not only in cases of heresy or simony (areas readily conceded by the state), but also in 'mixed cases' involving crimes (such as blasphemy, adultery, bigamy, usury and perjury) that were punishable under both canon law and civil law, or in cases involving lay encroachment on church property. It also meant claiming or reclaiming for the clergy immunity from taxation and from the jurisdiction of secular courts; finally, it meant contesting the state's right to give (or to deny) its approval (*exequatur*) to church legislation and directives before they could be formally made public and enforced.

The Council of Trent had been keenly aware of the importance of reaffirming the principle of 'ecclesiastical liberty' *vis-à-vis* the state and, as will be recalled, an attempt had been made in the final hours of the Council to enact a decree known as the 'reform of the princes' that would spell out the rights of the Church as well as the penalties rulers would incur for violating those rights. In the face of French and Medici opposition the draft of the decree had to be, if not entirely dropped, at least transformed into a 'harmless admonition' in which the rights of the Church were 'recommended to the princes for observance and protection', but with no mention of penalties for those who infringed them.[2] In 1568, five years after the closing of the Council, however, Pope Pius V, confronted with Philip II's refusal to allow the publication and the implementation of the Council's decrees in their entirety in Spain and its dependencies, issued a revised and expanded version of the bull *In coena Domini*, a papal document which, since late medieval times, was to be read every year from all pulpits on Maundy Thursday: it enumerated a series of possible violations of ecclesiastical liberty at the hands of laymen and automatically subjected transgressors to excommunication. Subsequent pontiffs were to reaffirm *In coena Domini* over and over again, and in 1623 Urban VIII went so far as to set up a permanent committee of cardinals charged with monitoring its application.[3]

Opposition to *In coena Domini* was spirited from the start, with Spain and the Venetian Republic in the lead among the states that resisted its publication. What made the papal document so obnoxious to secular governments was the fact that it ran counter to long-standing policies most European governments had unilaterally adopted since the fifteenth century taking advantage of the eclipse of papal authority at the time or to policies that were based on concessions granted by the Papacy itself in that same

2. Hubert Jedin, *Crisis and Closure at the Council of Trent. A Retrospective View from the Second Vatican Council*, transl. N.D. Smith, Sheed and Ward 1967, pp. 129–32. The text of the decree titled 'The rights of the Church are recommended to the princes for observance and protection' in H.J. Schroeder, *Canons and Decrees of the Council of Trent. Original Text with English translation*, Herder, St Louis, Mo. 1941, p. 251.

3. Ludwig von Pastor, *History of the Popes from the Close of the Middle Ages*, transl. Ernest Graf, vol. 18, Kegan Paul 1929, pp. 35–58 and vol. 29, pp. 171–5.

period as it tried to forge alliances with various governments in order to win their support in its struggle against the centrifugal forces of conciliarism. Whether unilaterally or through negotiations, by the early sixteenth century Catholic rulers in Europe had acquired a broad measure of patronage over church appointments, had managed to extend the jurisdiction of secular courts over members of the clergy and even over cases of heresy that had traditionally been handled by church courts, and had asserted a measure of control over church property in their respective dominions. The Spanish monarchy had been especially successful in this respect and had gone so far as to create its own Inquisition fully under royal control. In this way not only could governments use ecclesiastical appointments (with the revenues attached to them) as rewards for loyal servants and to divert at least some of the wealth of the Church to their own advantage; they had also, and more importantly, managed to ensure that most church personnel were loyal to them and willing to inculcate in their subjects the religious and moral duty to obey and serve the state, for as the political writer Giovanni Botero put it in the late sixteenth century, 'no law is more favourable to princes than the Christian law, for it submits to them not only the bodies and the means [i.e. the wealth] of their subjects, but their souls and consciences as well, and binds not just their hands, but their feelings and thoughts too'. These sentiments, needless to say, were not confined to Catholic Italy but were common currency in Europe during the confessional age. In the mid-seventeenth century they were voiced by a German Lutheran writer in these terms: 'One religion in one country binds together the minds of the subjects among themselves and with their superiors more than anything else.'[4]

So crucial to internal peace and to the cohesion of the state was the religious unity of their subjects that lay authorities took an active interest in the preservation of religious orthodoxy and church discipline. Actually, long before church authorities took stringent measures to combat heresy and clerical misconduct, governments had already taken steps in that direction. In the 1530s and 1540s, at a time, that is, when Milan had no resident archbishop, the Spanish governors and the Senate repeatedly intervened to prosecute heretics, to ban dangerous books, and to curb immorality in a number of monasteries, for in their eyes heresy and clerical misconduct were tantamount to 'sedition'.[5] In Venice, from the 1550s, the dreaded Council of Ten worked hand in hand with the Inquisition to stamp out heretical infiltrations and in subsequent years three Venetian magistrates always took part in the Inquisition's proceedings. The Venetian Doge Nicolo' Da Ponte (1578–85), no friend of the Roman Curia, boasted to be 'a fierce prosecutor of heretics' and at the opening of the seventeenth century Paolo Sarpi himself,

---

4. Quotations in Reinhard, 'Reformation, Counter-Reformation', p. 403.
5. Federico Chabod, *Lo Stato e la vita religiosa a Milano nell'epoca di Carlo V* (1938), new edn, Einaudi, Turin 1971, pp. 236–7, 244, 247, 249, 364–8; Luigi Fumi, 'L'Inquisizione romana e lo Stato di Milano. Saggio di ricerche nell'Archivio di Stato', *Archivio Storico Lombardo* 13 (1910), pp. 341, 360.

for all his opposition to the Papacy, expressed satisfaction that 'by God's grace there are no heretics in this city' and had no doubts as to the government's right (and indeed duty) to prosecute heresy and censor the press.[6] Even in Macerata, a town under papal rule, it was the city fathers rather than the absentee bishop who, in the early sixteenth century, had taken it upon themselves to monitor the behaviour of monks and nuns, to provide for the upkeep of church buildings and to ensure the decorum of religious services.[7] In short, far from moving in the direction of complete neutrality in religious matters, early modern states identified themselves with the cause of religion, closely watched and to a large extent controlled the clergy, and took a keen interest in preserving orthodoxy. As Fulgenzio Micanzio, a churchman himself and an advisor of the Venetian government on church matters, put it in 1639, 'the concern over religion and its purity is shared by the Prince and the Prelate alike, for they both have to answer to the Divine Majesty for their people'.[8]

After Trent, as the Catholic Church strove to recover ground it had lost to the state, the stage was set for a confrontation between 'two absolutisms', to use Jean Delumeau's apt expression: the absolutism of the state seeking religious uniformity, cohesion, and unquestionable loyalty among its subjects, and the absolutism of a Church now determined to assert its independence from lay tutelage and to influence the lives of the faithful, both clerics and lay people, in an effort to carry out its programme of reform.[9] Under the circumstances, it is hardly surprising that the history of the Italian states in the age of the Counter-Reformation is strewn with frictions and quarrels with the Church, their frequency and intensity varying, of course, from state to state. They were minimal in the Grand Duchy of Tuscany, for the Medici rulers owed in part to the Papacy their return to power in 1530 and their elevation to the rank of grand dukes in 1569. Accordingly, they consistently strove to keep on good terms with Rome and to accommodate its demands as regards the jurisdiction of ecclesiastical courts, clerical immunity from taxation, the publication of papal decrees (including the controversial bull *In coena Domini*) in their dominions, and the steady expansion of the landholdings of

6. Gaetano Cozzi, 'Venezia nello scenario europeo' in Gaetano Cozzi, Michael Knapton and Giovanni Scarabello, *La Repubblica di Venezia nell'età moderna. Dal 1517 alla fine della Repubblica*, UTET, Turin 1992, pp. 36–7. On Doge Da Ponte see Aldo Stella, *Chiesa e Stato nelle relazioni dei nunzi pontifici a Venezia. Ricerche sul giurisdizionalismo veneziano dal XVI al XVIII secolo*, Biblioteca Apostolica Vaticana, Vatican City 1964, p. 14; Sarpi's quotation in John Martin, 'L'Inquisizione romana e la criminalizzazione del dissenso religioso a Venezia all'inizio dell'eta moderna', *QS* 66 (1987), p. 794.

7. Daniela Moltedo, 'Aspetti dell'applicazione della Controriforma in una diocesi dello Stato pontificio: Macerata', *QS* 15 (1970), pp. 817–21.

8. Quotation in Fabrizio Andreella, 'Una partita a tre: la Repubblica di Venezia e le devozioni popolari attraverso i consulti di Fulgenzio Micanzio' in *Studi veneti offerti a Gaetano Cozzi*, Il Cardo, Vicenza 1992, p. 254.

9. Jean Delumeau, *L'Italie de Botticelli à Bonaparte*, Colin, Paris 1974, p. 205.

the Church. The Medici's was a consistent policy dictated by their need to safeguard their legitimacy under the mantle of papal protection and to assert a measure of independence against Spanish claims and pressures. In return for their unwavering loyalty to the Holy See, for two centuries the Medici grand dukes enjoyed a great deal of leeway in nominating to vacant bishoprics in Tuscany individuals whom they considered politically 'safe' and willing to support their rulers against both foreign pretenders and internal critics of the regime. Further rewards of this close alliance between throne and altar included the right the grand dukes enjoyed, with Rome's blessing, of raising a limited, but substantial amount of revenue from church property in Tuscany, and the virtual assurance that at each generation one member of the Medici family would be raised to the cardinalate, with the result that the rulers of Tuscany were always in a position to influence papal policies and, more importantly, papal elections: Paul V in 1605, Urban VIII in 1623, Innocent X in 1644 and Alexander VII in 1655 all owed their election, in part, to the support and electioneering of a Medici cardinal. And yet, even such cosy alliance and cooperation at times showed signs of strain, notably on the issue of the Inquisition: Grand Duke Francesco I (1574–85), for instance, succeeded over Rome's objections in disbanding the Crocesignati, a lay association charged with assisting the Roman Inquisition in the detection and suppression of heresy and, in practice, operating as a sort of private police force. Francesco's successors, on their part, occasionally supported the bishops' complaints against Inquisition officials appointed by Rome who allegedly undermined their own authority. These, however, were minor skirmishes that did not really call into question the Medici's close relationship with the Papacy.[10]

Few other Italian states entertained such amicable rapport. One of them was the small Republic of Genoa with a nearly unblemished record of loyalty to Rome, a loyalty that manifested itself in 1606–7 when the Republic not only squarely sided with the Papacy in the celebrated quarrel with Venice, but went so far as to repeal all laws that had been enacted over the years for curbing the growth of church property.[11] By contrast, another small republic, that of Lucca, always had a combative and fiercely independent stance *vis-à-vis* the Papacy. Unlike neighbouring Tuscany where individuals suspected of harbouring unorthodox ideas were given no quarter, Lucca was

10. A.D. Wright, 'Why the "Venetian" Interdict?', *English Historical Review* 89 (1974), pp. 541–4. For a fuller analysis of the Medici's relationship with Rome see Furio Diaz, *Il Granducato di Toscana. I Medici*, UTET, Turin 1976, pp. 186–97 and 235–81. The subject of taxation of the Church in Tuscany is covered by Roberto Bizzocchi, 'Politica fiscale e immunità ecclesiastica nella Toscana medicea fra Repubblica e Granducato (secoli XV–XVIII)' in *Fisco, religione, stato nell'età confessionale*, ed. Hermann Kellenbenz and Paolo Prodi, Mulino, Bologna 1989, pp. 355–85. On tensions between the grand dukes and the Inquisition see, in addition to Diaz, p. 277, Adriano Prosperi, 'Vicari dell'Inquisizione fiorentina alla metà del Seicento. Note d'archivio', *AISIG* 8 (1982), pp. 277–80.

11. Claudio Costantini, *La Repubblica di Genova nell'età moderna*, UTET, Turin 1978, p. 543.

repeatedly accused of tolerating heretics within its walls. Another issue that pitted the small republic against Rome was whether the local bishop had the right (in the name of ecclesiastical 'immunity') to have his own armed guard and to use force, if needed, without the prior permission of the city magistrates. In 1640 a bloody incident involving a member of the bishop's guard led to the man's arrest; in retaliation the bishop left Lucca after excommunicating the city fathers and placing the whole Republic under an interdict, that is to say ordering the suspension of all religious services and the closing of all churches until the Republic gave in. Lucca, however, did not give in and after prolonged negotiations the interdict was lifted and the bishop resigned.[12] The whole incident would be no more than a mere footnote in the history of seventeenth-century Italy were it not for the fact that it illustrates how limited, after all, was the Papacy's power even toward a miniscule state such as Lucca – and this in an age when the Counter-Reformation Papacy is supposed to have had untrammelled power over Italian affairs.

IN THE SAVOYARD STATE

How limited that power was is revealed even more clearly by the conflicts that pitted Rome against the major Italian states: Piedmont-Savoy, the Spanish dominions in Naples, Sicily and Milan, and, above all, the Venetian Republic. In the Savoyard state a special concession (an 'indult') granted in 1457 by a beleaguered Papacy to Duke Ludovico of Savoy for his cooperation in the cause of church unity had made all major ecclesiastical appointments contingent on the duke's approval (*placet*) and had thus ensured to him and his successors a virtual stranglehold on the life of the Church within his dominions. During the sixteenth century Rome had tried over and over again to reassert its control in a frontier area that was crucial to its programme of reform and had argued that the concession had been made to Duke Ludovico personally, not to his successors. The privilege enjoyed by the House of Savoy, however, was too precious to be relinquished without a fight, and indeed such forceful rulers as Emanuele Filiberto (1553–80) and Carlo Emanuele I (1580–1630), busy as they were at rebuilding their state along absolutist lines, adamantly refused to surrender it and, in fact, after interminable legal battles and diplomatic negotiations, succeeded in securing its confirmation.[13]

Another source of conflict between a ruling dynasty bent on state-building and a Papacy determined to assert its 'liberty' was the publication of the

12. Rita Mazzei, 'La questione dell'Interdetto a Lucca nel secolo XVII', *Rivista Storica Italiana* 85 (1973), pp. 167–82.
13. Achille Erba, *La Chiesa sabauda tra Cinque e Seicento. Ortodossia tridentina, gallicanesimo savoiardo e assolutismo ducale (1580–1630)*, Herder, Rome 1979, pp. 73–5 and 122–34.

decrees of the Council of Trent. Prodded by the high courts (*parlements*) of Savoy and Piedmont, the dukes at first opposed the publication; in 1573 they consented to it subject, however, to a crucial restriction, namely that 'the rights and privileges formerly granted by the Holy See as well as the [state's] jurisdiction in mixed cases will be fully safeguarded'. An uncompromising stand, indeed, and one that elicited from the papal nuncio the caustic comment that the Savoyard and Piedmontese *parlements* 'want to be popes'.[14]

The rulers of Piedmont-Savoy were no doubt in a strong position when bargaining with Rome and resisting its claims, for their dominions lay perilously close to Geneva and the Swiss Confederates and thus their loyalty to the Catholic faith was essential for preventing Protestant inroads south of the Alps. All the more so as in Piedmont itself, as will be recalled, there lived a small Protestant minority (the Waldensians) that proved impervious to all efforts at conversion. Therefore, not only must the Papacy refrain from pressing too far the cause of 'ecclesiastical liberty', for doing so might result in an irreparable break and open the floodgates to Protestantism; the Papacy must also support the dukes of Savoy whenever they took legal or military measures (as they did in 1655 and again in 1688–92) against the Waldensians, even though those measures were motivated by reason of state rather than religious zeal. Conversely, when political expediency dictated to the dukes a policy of limited toleration toward the Waldensians and of *rapprochement* with Protestant Europe, relations with the Papacy soured. Such was the case in 1694 when Vittorio Amedeo II, under pressure from the English king William III whose help he needed in his struggle against Louis XIV, revised his earlier policy of suppression of the Waldensians and issued a decree of toleration. In retaliation for the loud protests of the Papacy the duke began to tamper with clerical privileges and immunities, claimed his right to the revenues of vacant bishoprics and went so far as to threaten the abolition of the Inquisition in his dominions. The quarrel would fester to the end of his reign in 1730, and in the meantime Vittorio Amedeo exercised nearly total authority over church affairs; in 1703 he defined his authority to do so by invoking the divine theory of monarchy and using terms that were strikingly similar to those used by Louis XIV, his nemesis, in defending against Rome his control over the Gallican (French) Church: 'The ecclesiastical and the secular powers', said the duke, 'derive equally from the authority of God ... The secular power ... is subordinate [to the Church] only in purely spiritual matters.'[15]

---

14. Ibid., pp. 33–7 and 54–61 (the nuncio's words are on p. 60).
15. Geoffrey Symcox, *Victor Amadeus II. Absolutism in the Savoyard State, 1675–1730*, Thames & Hudson 1983, pp. 114 and 127–33 (quotation on p. 129).

IN THE SPANISH DOMINIONS

The Spanish rulers of Sicily, Naples and Milan would have approved, although perhaps not dared to utter, those blunt words, for they shared an equally exalted notion of their God-given mission as Christian monarchs and felt responsible for the spiritual as well as for the material welfare of their subjects. They, too, were determined, for political no less than for ideological reasons, to control the life of the Church in their dominions, yielding to papal authority only on strictly doctrinal matters. In Spain itself the Habsburg monarchs enjoyed a position few Catholic rulers could equal: in 1523 the crown had secured from the Papacy the right to appoint to all bishoprics in Spain; appeals from Spanish church courts to Rome had been ruled out; in Castile one-third of all church tithes went into the royal coffers and the crown levied other taxes on a theoretically tax-exempt clergy; and, lastly, the crown also ran its own Inquisition, entirely distinct and independent from its Roman counterpart.[16] 'Ecclesiastical affairs', it has been said, 'were more fully dominated in Spain than in any other contemporary kingdom of Europe.'[17] Nor would Spanish kings, for all their unquestionable loyalty to the Catholic faith, hesitate to stand up to the Papacy when their control over church affairs was at stake. Philip II, in particular, had had his share of quarrels with Rome over the Spanish Inquisition, the disposition of the revenues of vacant bishoprics, the publication in Spain of the Tridentine decrees insofar as they encroached on the royal prerogative, and his right to veto all papal pronouncements before they took effect in Spain.[18]

In Spain's Italian dominions church–state relationships were no carbon copy of those in Spain itself and, as will be seen, varied a great deal from place to place. In all of them, however, conditions were ripe for tensions and confrontations. The Kingdom of Sicily was the one Italian dominion where the Spanish crown held a position of clear domination over the Church, much as it did in Spain. From a legal standpoint that position rested on a privilege granted in 1098 by the pope to the Norman ruler of Sicily, Count Roger, in recognition of his efforts against the Infidels. The papal document was said to have bestowed upon Roger and his successors the awesome title of 'papal legate' in Sicily. This meant that the rulers of the island had the right to make all ecclesiastical appointments, to give (or deny) clearance to papal pronouncements before they could be validly enacted in Sicily, and to exercise supreme judicial authority over all church matters through a high court of justice known as Monarchia Sicula whose decisions could not be appealed to Rome. 'Through the Monarchia', it has been said, 'the Sicilian

---

16. John H. Elliott, *Imperial Spain 1469–1716*, Arnold 1963, pp. 91–6, 222, 242 and 244.
17. Stanley G. Payne, *A History of Spain and Portugal*, University of Wisconsin Press, Madison 1973, vol. 1, p. 218.
18. John Lynch, 'Philip II and the Papacy', *Transactions of the Royal Historical Society*, 5th ser., 2 (1961), pp. 23–42.

Church became nearly as independent from Rome as the English Church [under Henry VIII',[19] and that independence was further enhanced by the fact that in Sicily, unlike in the other Spanish dominions in Italy, the Spanish rather than the Roman Inquisition held sway. The peculiar status of the Sicilian Church had long been tolerated, however reluctantly, by Rome. After the Council of Trent, however, the Papacy began to question the extensive powers of the crown in the island and to raise doubts about the validity of the original grant, for the Tridentine programme of reform required an episcopate answerable to Rome rather than to the government, as well as Rome's right to issue decrees and directives without government approval – two conditions that could not be realized as long as Monarchia Sicula was in effect. Predictably, as the Papacy demanded the repeal or at least the curtailment of the latter tensions mounted. They reached a climax in 1605 when the eminent church historian Cardinal Caesar Baronius published the eleventh volume of his authoritative *Annales ecclesiastici* which included, at the pope's request, a detailed and critical analysis of the whole issue. Baronius questioned the authenticy of Urban II's grant at least in the form currently used by Spanish authorities and vigorously upheld full papal authority over church matters in Sicily. Reaction from Madrid was swift: Baronius's volume was banned from all Spanish dominions – an unprecedented measure since it targeted a work written by a cardinal at the request of the pope himself. In 1610 Madrid went a step further and ordered all copies of the book that had managed to slip into Spanish-controlled territory to be confiscated, and the order remained in force in subsequent years in spite of pressures and complaints from Rome.[20] Further tension developed in 1629 when the Sicilian bishops, in a rare show of independence from the crown to which they owed their appointment, protested against the way Monarchia Sicula interfered with their pastoral work and undermined their efforts at implementing the Tridentine decrees. In reply the government issued so-called 'letters of safeguard': anyone who could persuade the high court that a bishop was his personal enemy and was thus prejudiced against him would be exempted from his jurisdiction.[21]

In the end the crown emerged the winner in these battles with Rome: the firm grip of the crown on the Sicilian Church remained in place till the end of Spanish rule and even beyond. Only in 1867 was Monarchia Sicula formally abolished.[22] But what is remarkable in the whole story is that, for all the

19. Helmut G. Koenigsberger, *The Government of Sicily under Philip II of Spain. A Study in the Practice of Empire*, Staples Press 1951, pp. 147 and 144–9 (for a discussion of *Monarchia Sicula*).
20. Cyriac K. Pullapilly, *Caesar Baronius, Counter-Reformation Historian*, University of Notre Dame Press, Notre Dame, Ind. 1975, pp. 105–9; Agostino Borromeo, 'Il Cardinale Cesare Baronio e la corona spagnola' in *Baronio storico e la Controriforma*, Centro di Studi Sorani V. Patriarca, Sora 1982, pp. 111–17 and 151–65.
21. Pastor, *History of the Popes*, vol. 29, p. 187.
22. Pullapilly, *Caesar Baronius*, p. 109.

tensions and mutual recriminations between church and state, no final irreparable break was ever contemplated by either side. One reason for this is that it would have been as inconceivable for the Spanish monarchs, unwavering as they were in their Catholic allegiance, to break ties with Rome as it would have been for the Papacy to forgo the support of the greatest Catholic power in Europe, especially in the age of the Thirty Years War when the religious future of Europe seemed to be in the balance. Another reason may have been that the city of Rome, with its teeming population of nearly 100,000 souls, was totally dependent on Sicilian grain for its survival. A complete break with Spain might have jeopardized the food supply. The two powers, while struggling for hegemony, thus needed each other and had to coexist no matter how difficult that coexistence might prove.[23]

While in Sicily the king's writ took precedence over the pope's, in the neighbouring Kingdom of Naples positions were reversed: for here the crown could not appeal to a broad grant of authority over church matters as in Sicily; on the contrary, it found itself, from the start, in a somewhat subordinate position *vis-à-vis* the Papacy, for in strictly legal terms the kings of Naples had received their crown in the eleventh century as 'vassals' of the Papacy and the latter could thus claim a kind of suzerainty or tutelage over the southern kingdom. Moreover, after the Council of Trent the popes pressed that claim with renewed force in order to assert their control over ecclesiastical affairs. Predictably, Spain resisted their efforts and the upshot was a prolonged tug-of-war between the two powers, with no clear winner. In the process, one might add, a growing Erastian tradition formed in Naples, as it did not in Sicily, for the city's jurists, magistrates and viceroys resented papal interference and the assumption of subordination it implied and (invoking, as other governments did at the time, the divine right theory of monarchy) vigorously argued in favour of greater government control over church affairs.[24] The increasing rancour between the two sides over the issue of Naples's vassalage is illustrated by an otherwise trivial incident that took place in 1643, when Urban VIII, then engaged in a military campaign against the small Duchy of Castro, called upon the Neapolitan nobility, in typical, if anachronistic, feudal terms, to join the papal army as his loyal vassals. The Spanish viceroy at once reacted by enjoining any nobleman from answering

23. Flavio Rurale, 'Stato e Chiesa nell'Italia spagnola: un dibattito aperto', *Cheiron* 17–18 (1992), pp. 360 and 364, has emphasized the political considerations that called for cooperation between the Papacy and Spain. Wright, 'Relations between Church and State', p. 387, has called attention to the issue of the food supply.
24. On Naples's peculiar position *vis-à-vis* the Papacy as a source of endless tensions see Giuseppe Galasso, *Il Mezzogiorno nella storia d'Italia*, LeMonnier, Florence 1977, pp. 237–8, and Mario Rosa, 'La Chiesa meridionale nell'età della Controriforma' in *SIE Annali* 9 (1986), pp. 295–6. For appeals to the divine right theory of monarchy, see Vittor Ivo Comparato, *Uffici e società a Napoli (1600–1647). Aspetti dell'ideologia del magistrato nell'età moderna*, Olschki, Florence 1974, pp. 185–90.

the pope's call to arms and bluntly asserted that the Kingdom of Naples 'is not a fief of the Church, but a free state'.[25]

Behind the issue of vassalage, however, lay a number of more practical and more sensitive issues that were likely to spawn endless tensions and quarrels. In the Kingdom of Naples, for one thing, the choice of candidates to episcopal sees escaped royal control. Accordingly, the crown could not fully depend on the bishops' loyalty and docility and might even find them inclined to work against government policies as apparently was the case in 1647, at the time of the Masaniello revolt, when the then archbishop of Naples Ascanio Filomarino was 'generally viewed as supporting the popular cause'. Nor could the loyalty of his predecessors be taken for granted either: in 1613 Philip III, after instructing a new viceroy 'to support and protect ecclesiastical authority', added that, in the event of any prelate failing to prove cooperative, he should be treated as 'an enemy of the public peace'.[26] No less important in generating tensions between church and state was the exceptionally broad measure of immunity, from both secular jurisdiction and taxation, enjoyed by the clergy. Even though it is probably an exaggeration to speak of the Neapolitan clergy as enjoying total immunity from the fiscal demands of the state, there is little doubt that its immunity was greater than in any other Italian state at the time.[27] So much so, in fact, that in 1671, when Neapolitan authorities were pleading with Rome (in vain, as it turned out) for a reduction in the number of exemptions enjoyed by the clergy as a way of broadening the tax base and relieving the pressure on the laity, even the archbishop of Naples supported the authorities' pleas and acknowledged in a report to the Roman Curia that 'in Naples ... at nearly every step one finds churches, convents, chapels and countless religious houses enjoying immunity [from taxation]'.[28]

A large measure of exemption from royal taxation, by the way, did not mean that the Neapolitan clergy enjoyed its revenues scot free, for those revenues were burdened, far more heavily than anywhere else, by sundry types of taxes due to the papal treasury.[29] In addition, as will be recalled, dioceses and monasteries often had to bear the heavy burden of 'pensions' payable to dignitaries in the Roman Curia. All in all, it has been estimated that in the mid-seventeenth century roughly 25 per cent of all episcopal revenues in the Kingdom of Naples were funnelled to Rome. Under the circumstances,

25. Pasquale Lopez, *Riforma cattolica e vita religiosa a Napoli dalla fine del Cinquecento ai primi anni del Settecento*, Istituto Editoriale del Mezzogiorno, Naples and Rome 1964, pp. 54–6.
26. Ibid., pp. 49, 55 and 57.
27. Aurelio Musi, 'Fisco, religione e Stato nel Mezzogiorno d'Italia (secoli XVI–XVII) in *Fisco, religione, Stato nell'età confessionale*, pp. 428–9.
28. Quotation in Romeo De Maio, *Società e vita religiosa a Napoli nell'età moderna (1656–1799)*, Edizioni Scientifiche Italiane, Naples 1971, p. 89; pp. 88–91 provide a good review of the immunity issue in the last quarter of the century.
29. Giovanni Muto, 'Il Regno di Napoli sotto la dominazione spagnola' in *SSI*, vol. 11, p. 267.

it is understandable that the government in Naples tried to stem the annual outflow of monies to Rome and to divert at least some of it to its own generally depleted coffers, but to no avail, for the Papacy, always in dire need of money, and especially so during the Thirty Years War and during the war against the Turks later in the century, was not prepared to forgo one of its major sources of revenue. Only occasionally did the Spanish government manage to extract temporary concessions from the Holy See and thus to reduce the drain of currency to Rome. In the main, however, clerical immunity from taxation and papal claims on church revenue persisted and remained at the centre of the tensions between Rome and Naples.[30]

Church–state relations could also become strained over issues of jurisdiction or when the two powers competed for the allegiance of the people. At the turn of the century Archbishop Alfonso Gesualdo (1596–1603) clashed with the Spanish viceroy when he ordered some monks to move out of the female convent where they had taken up residence in clear violation of the Tridentine decrees; the viceroy objected on grounds that the convent was a 'royal chaplaincy' and, as such, lay outside the archbishop's jurisdiction. In 1633 another archbishop took issue with the viceroy over the right of sanctuary claimed by two knights of Malta who were sought for murder, but had managed to escape arrest by taking refuge in the town of Benevento, a papal enclave in the Kingdom of Naples. Thereupon the viceroy had laid siege to the town; on his part, the pope had threatened to place the whole kingdom under an interdict, but eventually the quarrel was patched up through negotiations.[31] Nearly thirty years later a new jurisdictional squabble broke out when a lay servant in the archbishop's household murdered the pregnant wife of a man with whom he was having an argument. The culprit had been arrested on the spot and arraigned in the city's high court, the Vicaria. The archbishop, however, demanded that he be handed over to his own tribunal on the grounds that, as a church employee, he fell under ecclesiatical jurisdiction. As the judges of the Vicaria refused to comply, they were promptly excommunicated. Undaunted, they went on with the trial and, in the end, had the defendant executed on the public square, while the government, in retaliation for the judges' excommunication, expelled the archbishop's vicar general from Naples, threw in jail two of the archbishop's nephews, and confiscated part of his financial assets. After laborious negotiations the quarrel was settled with a compromise: the archbishop lifted the excommunication in exchange for the release of his nephews and the restitution of his money, but the vicar general's expulsion was upheld, much to the secular authorities' satisfaction. Even greater satisfaction must have been felt in 1661 when the Neapolitan nobility was able to persuade the viceroy to expel the head of the Naples office of the Roman Inquisition who had been accused of causing serious harm to the reputation and honour of a

30. Musi, 'Fisco, religione e Stato', pp. 434–51, and Galasso, *Il Mezzogiorno*, pp. 241–6.
31. Lopez, *Riforma cattolica*, pp. 50–4.

nobleman when he had him arrested on charges of possessing a heretical book. This new success emboldened the Neapolitan authorities to go further: alleging a 1547 papal concession, they demanded that from now on all inquisitorial matters be handled by the archbishop with the assistance of lay magistrates rather than by an official of the Roman Inquisition. Their demand did not imply a rejection of church authority over ideas or beliefs *per se*; it reflected a desire to eliminate any outside interference in the religious affairs of the realm. This time, however, the Papacy prevailed as the Spanish viceroy sided with it, probably because in the city fathers' request he sensed a dangerous trend toward home rule on the part of his Neapolitan subjects, and this could some day turn against Spain itself.[32]

The issue of who should be in charge of prosecuting heretics surfaced again in the 1690s in connection with the celebrated 'trial of the atheists', of individuals, that is, accused of subscribing to a materialistic philosophy and thus of denying the very foundations of Christianity. The strictly religious aspects of the trial are discussed elsewhere in this book. Here we wish to call attention to its significance as a final church–state confrontation in seventeenth-century Naples. Upon the arrest of the suspects at the hands of the Inquisition the city council challenged the legality of the latter's action, arguing that the arrests had been carried out without the formal authorization of the secular magistrates and that, at any rate, the proper authority in the case was the archbishop and not the Roman Inquisition. Duly impressed by the city's spirited reaction, the viceroy threw his support behind its request and ordered the inquisitor to leave the country and the accused to be transferred to the archbishop's jail. After years of squabbling and after it raised the spectre of a papal interdict, Rome yielded, but at the same time managed to uphold its legal rights by the face-saving device of declaring that the archbishop would indeed preside over the trial, but as delegate ('commissary') of the Roman Inquisition. It was under these somewhat ambiguous terms that the trial was allowed to proceed.[33]

All these quarrels and controversies would be of little more than antiquarian interest were it not for the fact that they all illustrate the peculiar nature of church–state relationships in the Kingdom of Naples, caught as it was between the competing claims of papal suzerainty, Spanish domination and local autonomy. It is probably anachronistic to see in those quarrels and especially in the one surrounding the trial of the atheists early manifestations of a genuinely modern secular spirit against clerical domination, if by that it is implied that the Neapolitan ruling elite advocated freedom of thought and denied the Church's right to repress religious dissent. In fact, no one at the time was ready to question that right; what the city magistrates and officials were asserting, in the true spirit of the confessional age, was that secular authorities have as much of a stake in the religious unity of the country as

32. Giuseppe Galasso, *Napoli spagnola dopo Masaniello. Politica, cultura, società*, Sansoni, Florence 1982, pp. 59–68.
33. Ibid., pp. 443–73.

Rome does and, therefore, are entitled to a major role in the defence and preservation of that unity.

In the State of Milan the Spanish monarchy found itself in a stronger position *vis-à-vis* the local church than in the Kingdom of Naples. Unencumbered by any claim of papal suzerainty, the State of Milan boasted since the time of the Visconti and Sforza dukes a long tradition of lay control over church affairs. Not only had the dukes asserted in the fourteenth and fifteenth centuries their right to determine the limits of clerical immunity from taxation and to enforce discipline and good administration on monastic houses and confraternities; they had also consistently exercised the right to approve or reject papal appointments to high church office; under their rule, moreover, cases that normally would be handled by church courts, such as usury and even heresy, had been brought within the purview of lay courts and notably, in the early sixteenth century, of the powerful Milan Senate with no right of appeal to Rome.[34] In annexing Milan to his already vast Italian dominions, Emperor Charles V had thus inherited an impressive authority over the Milanese Church, an authority which he did not hesitate to use, through the governor and the Senate, against papal interference as well as against the spread of Lutheran ideas and clerical misconduct – all tasks made easier by the weakness of the Renaissance Papacy and the absence of a resident bishop in Milan from 1497 to 1550.[35]

Yet, ironically enough, it was in Milan that, in the second half of the sixteenth century, the Church was able to recover much lost ground and to reassert its 'liberty' to a far greater degree than in any other Spanish possession.[36] One reason for this comeback was the extraordinary personality of Archbishop Carlo Borromeo who held the Milanese see from 1565 to 1584. Borromeo, as will be recalled, was a leading figure of the post-Tridentine Church, the champion of the latter's programme of reform and a model bishop whose prestige and reputation reached well beyond the boundaries of his large diocese. His irreprehensible, ascetic conduct, his unswerving loyalty to Rome in spite of occasional disagreements, and his total commitment to the reform of the clergy were matched by his fearless determination to reassert the autonomy of the Church against what he regarded as unacceptable state meddling. That determination led him into a series of dramatic confrontations with the Spanish governor of Milan and with the Senate.[37] One issue was the

34. The standard work on the subject is still Luigi Prosdocimi, *Il diritto ecclesiastico dello Stato di Milano dall'inizio della signoria viscontea al periodo tridentino (secoli XIII–XVI)*, Edizioni dell'Arte, Milan 1941.

35. Federico Chabod, *Lo Stato e la vita religiosa a Milano nell'epoca di Carlo V*, Einaudi, Turin 1971, pp. 236–7 and 281–3.

36. Gauro Coppola, 'Fisco, finanza e religione: lo Stato di Milano da Carlo a Federigo' in *Fisco, religione, Stato*, pp. 293–354, has provided an excellent discussion of the topic, especially on the issue of ecclesiastical immunity from taxation.

37. In addition to Prosdocimi, *Il diritto ecclesiastico*, pp. 291–3 and 312–14, see Mario Bendiscioli, 'Politica, amministrazione e religione nell'età dei Borromei' in *Storia di Milano*, vol. 10, Fondazione Treccani degli Alfieri, Milan 1960, pp. 204–54;

right of the archbishop to use his own police force rather than deferring to the secular arm in apprehending a layman accused of adultery (a 'mixed' crime); another issue that put him at odds with the civil authority was his ban on public dancing during holy days – a ban the Spanish governor strongly opposed; a third source of contention was his decision to publicize the bull *In coena Domini*. These and other confrontations had their moments of high drama as when Borromeo excommunicated the entire Senate and the Spanish governor himself, an action that led one exasperated governor to dub the archbishop 'the greatest rebel Your Majesty ever had [*el mayor rebelde que nunca V.M. ha tenido*]'.[38] If a complete break between church and state was averted at that time, it is because Pope Gregory XIII (1572–85) interposed himself in the quarrel and urged moderation on both sides, but also because Borromeo was able to persuade Philip II that his intent was strictly religious and in no way intended to undermine the king's rights and prerogatives. On his part the Spanish king may have realized that to take on an archbishop whom the populace venerated for his integrity and his dedication to the poor was bad politics in a frontier area such as the State of Milan where foreign meddling could never be totally discounted.

Carlo Borromeo did not have in the seventeenth century successors of quite the same calibre; nonetheless the legacy of independence and assertiveness *vis-à-vis* the state which he left to the Milanese Church did not easily die out. Accordingly, tensions and conflicts surfaced again, especially during the episcopate of such forceful prelates as Federico Borromeo (1595–1630), Alfonso Litta (1652–79) and Federico Visconti (1681–93).[39] Issues such as the clergy's immunity from taxation, the crown's right to approve various church appointments and to investigate the finances of charitable institutions, all produced tensions and dissensions. By and large the Milanese Church, while making concessions on lesser points, emerged from those contests with its rights virtually intact, just as its mentor and model St Charles

Paolo Prodi, 'San Carlo Borromeo e le trattative tra Gregorio XIII e Filippo II sulla giurisdizione ecclesiastica', *Rivista di Storia della Chiesa in Italia* 11 (1957), pp. 195–240; and Agostino Borromeo, 'Le controversie giurisdizionali tra potere laico e potere ecclesiastico nella Milano spagnola sul finire del Cinquecento' in *Atti dell'Accademia di San Carlo*, Milan 1981, pp. 43–89.

38. Quotation in Giorgio Politi, *Aristocrazia e potere politico nella Cremona di Filippo II*, SugarCo, Milan 1976, p. 15.

39. On this period, see E. Cattaneo, 'La religione a Milano nell'età della Controriforma' in *Storia di Milano*, vol. 11, pp. 309–16, and Agostino Borromeo, 'La Chiesa milanese del Seicento e la Corte di Madrid' in *'Millan the Great'. Milano nelle brume del Seicento*, CARIPLO, Milan 1989, pp. 93–108. On Archbishop Litta and his quarrels with Spanish authorities, see Silvia Grassi and Alberto Grohmann, 'La Segreteria di Stato di Sua Santità e la Milano dell'età barocca', pp. 274–5 in the same volume. A conflict on whether the government or the archbishop had the right to investigate the finances of lay confraternities broke out again in the 1680s (Gianvittorio Signorotto, 'Milano e la Lombardia sotto gli Spagnoli' in *SSI*, vol. 11, pp. 216–17).

would have wanted. And again the crown's willingness not to press its claims too far may have reflected its concern not to antagonize public opinion in a province that more than once in the course of the century was turned into a battlefield where Spanish and French forces were locked in combat. To Spain the loyalty of the State of Milan was essential and an open conflict with the Church might have undermined that loyalty, something a member of the Spanish Council of State had in mind when in 1632 he spoke of 'the authority which the archbishops of that Church have acquired and of the respect and obedience they enjoy'.[40] Even when the Spanish government scored a victory as it did in 1663–64 against Archbishop Litta after a bitter clash over a fugitive from the law who had sought sanctuary in a local church, it had to tread cautiously and negotiate rather than force a showdown, for, as a foreign diplomat observed at the time, 'the populace worships the archbishop [and] he has declared himself to be ready, following the example of St Charles, to defend the rights of the Church to the last of his days'.[41]

IN THE VENETIAN REPUBLIC

Of all the many quarrels between church and state in seventeenth-century Italy none has had as much resonance, both among contemporaries in and outside the country and among later historians, as the one between the Venetian Republic and the Papacy culminating in the celebrated papal interdict of 1606. The quarrel itself was neither unique nor were the issues involved totally novel. Relations between church and state, as we just saw, were often tense in several Italian states at the time, and those between Venice and the Papacy, in particular, had shown signs of strain long before 1606.[42] In 1510, for instance, the Republic, after suffering military defeat at the hands of the League of Cambrai led by Pope Julius II, had been deprived of the right to nominate to vacant bishoprics in her mainland dominions, and this had left a bitter aftertaste; for the rest of the century Venice had tried, in vain as it turned out, to have that right restored. The popes' unyielding attitude on this point had been especially galling to the proud Republic of St Mark, because other governments, notably those of France and Spain, continued to enjoy in their respective realms the very right that was being denied to Venice. In 1510 Venice had also been stripped of the right to raise

40. Quotation in Borromeo, 'La Chiesa milanese', p. 97.
41. State Archives, Florence, *Mediceo* 3201, dispatch from Milan, 14 Nov. 1663.
42. For what follows I have relied on Cozzi, 'Venezia nello scenario europeo', pp. 19–22 and 71–9; Paolo Prodi, 'The Structure and Organisation of the Church in Renaissance Venice: Suggestions for Research' in *Renaissance Venice*, ed. J.R. Hale, Faber and Faber 1973, pp. 412–17; Stella, *Chiesa e Stato*, pp. 46–52; and Giuseppe Del Torre, 'La politica ecclesiastica della Repubblica di Venezia nell'età moderna: la fiscalità' in *Fisco, religione, Stato*, pp. 389–417. The papal nuncio's remark quoted below is from Stella, p. 46.

taxes (*decime*) on the clergy and although over the years Rome had given its approval to such levies on a temporary basis in times of emergency, dependence on papal benevolence rankled as a humiliation. In addition to jurisdictional issues (such as control over the patriarchate of Aquileia, the inspection of monastic houses by a delegate of the Holy See, and the right of papal ships to navigate freely in the Adriatic) there had been others that over the years had given rise to tensions and recriminations: one was the censorship of books by Roman authorities, an especially sensitive issue in a city like Venice which harboured a flourishing printing industry; another was whether the Republic's nominee to the patriarchate of Venice ought to submit to a formal 'examination' in Rome to ascertain his doctrinal and moral qualifications. Relations with Rome had become especially tense in 1569 following Venice's refusal to allow the publication of the bull *In coena Domini* in its dominions, a refusal which the papal nuncio had denounced as being 'close to a schism' and as 'a first step towards heresy'. From the 1580s, when leadership in the Venetian Republic had passed into the hands of the 'young', a group of patricians who were determined to free the Republic from what they considered papal meddling in its internal affairs, relations with Rome had further deteriorated, notably as a result of the Venetian government's decision in 1589 to recognize, in open defiance of Rome, Henry IV (still a Protestant) as the legitimate king of France.

The crisis of 1606 had thus been building for quite some time, but was triggered by the enactment in 1604–5 of two Venetian statutes, one making the foundation of new churches, monastic houses and charitable institutions subject to government approval; the other forbidding the conveyance of real estate property, whether by sale, donation or bequest, to members of the clergy unless it had been authorized by the state.[43] The two statutes reflected a growing concern, on the part of Venetian authorities, over the loss of revenue resulting from the transfer of more and more land into ecclesiastical hands, for land so transferred would enjoy at least partial exemption from taxation. As a government document put it in 1605, 'if [more] lay properties were allowed to go to the clergy, there is no doubt that in a short time all of them would end up in their hands ... and the taxes borne by our subjects, being assessed on a lesser amount of property, would become intolerable and

43. On the Interdict crisis see Gaetano Cozzi, *Il doge Nicolò Contarini. Ricerche sul patriziato veneziano agli inizi del Seicento*, Istituto per la Collaborazione culturale, Venice and Rome 1958, ch. 3, and by the same author 'Venezia dal rinascimento all'età barocca' in *Storia di Venezia*, vol. 6, ed. G. Cozzi and Paolo Prodi, Istituto dell'Enciclopedia Italiana, Rome 1994, pp. 82–90. Also: William J. Bouwsma, *Venice and the Defense of Republican Liberty. Renaissance Values in the Age of the Counter-Reformation*, University of California Press, Berkeley 1968, chs 7 and 8. A short account in Frederic C. Lane, *Venice. A Maritime Republic*, Johns Hopkins University Press, Baltimore 1973, pp. 394–8; Luigi Salvatorelli, 'Venezia, Paolo V e Fra Paolo' in *La civiltà veneziana nell'età barocca*, Sansoni, Florence 1959, pp. 67–95, is still valuable for understanding the resonance of the Venetian Interdict in Europe.

the Prince [i.e. the government] would lose a great deal of revenue which is the true lifeblood of the state'.[44] The Papacy, on its part, saw in the new legislation a violation of the 'liberty' of the Church, denounced it as such, and demanded its immediate repeal. As tensions between the two powers mounted, the arrest, on orders of the Council of Ten, of two Venetian priests charged with common crimes and its refusal to hand them over to a church court were interpreted in Rome as a blatant act of defiance that could not be allowed to stand lest it create a dangerous precedent for other countries to follow. Pope Paul V thus decided to meet the challenge head-on in the hope of forcing the proud Republic to yield. The international situation seemed to be favourable for an all-out confrontation: Henry IV king of France, recently reconciled with the Church, was in no mood, for all his long-standing friendship with Venice, to rush to the latter's support, for this might cast doubt on the sincerity of his conversion to Catholicism; as for Venice's staunchest supporter, James I king of England, he was too far away to be of any real help to the Republic. At the same time the Papacy could count on the sympathetic attitude of Spain, for the latter, having just blockaded the Valtelline, thus cutting the main link between the Venetian Republic and her Swiss allies (the Grisons), was only too willing to support any papal action likely to create trouble for the Venetians. Last but not least, Venice was faced at the time with a severe economic recession and a badly strained budget and thus might not be prepared to resist papal demands for long. But quite apart from the international situation, Paul V had every reason for wanting to make the quarrel with Venice a test case of his own authority: the city of St Mark lay close to the Protestant lands and harboured a good many Protestants who were attracted to it for commercial reasons or as students at the University of Padua; there was genuine fear in Rome that Venice might serve as a Protestant bridgehead in Italy and that the recent ascendancy of the 'young' with their determination to oppose papal interference in the affairs of the Republic made that fear all the more real. Accordingly, Paul V issued two statements, one condemning and demanding the repeal of the two statutes and the other requesting that the two indicted clerics be turned over to a church tribunal. After a series of inconclusive negotiations, on 17 April 1606 Paul V issued an ultimatum: the Venetian Senate would be excommunicated and the whole territory of the Republic would be placed under papal interdict unless within twenty-four days Venice repealed the two statutes and handed over the two clerics to papal authorities. Undaunted, Venice rejected the ultimatum with a formal *protesto* and denounced it as a violation of 'every form of natural law and of what Holy Scripture, the doctrine of the Church Fathers and Canon Law teach' and, as such, 'null and of no validity at all'. Diplomatic relations with the Holy See were then severed and Rome made good on its threats. In response the Venetian Senate ordered all clergy, under

44. Quotation in Ivana Pederzani, *Venezia e lo 'Stado de Terraferma'. Il governo delle comunita nel territorio bergamasco (secoli XV–XVIII)*, Vita e Pensiero, Milan 1992, p. 319.

severe penalties, to ignore the papal interdict and to keep all churches open and functioning. Compliance with the government's orders was nearly unanimous: only the Jesuits, the Capuchins and the Theatines sided with the pope and were promptly expelled from Venetian territory and their properties declared forfeit; a small number of priests who followed their example were jailed.

The impasse thus reached in 1606 between two equally intransigent 'absolutisms', however, was resolved within a year as both sides had an interest in finding a way out of it: Venice because the break with the Papacy, if prolonged, might result in serious diplomatic complications and even war with Spain, but also, and perhaps more ominously, because it might exacerbate the discontent that already simmered in the mainland possessions against the government;[45] the Papacy, because a Venetian schism raised the prospect of massive Protestant infiltrations in Italy. The two major European powers – France and Spain – favoured a reconciliation, too, for a drawn-out conflict between Rome and Venice could well force them to take sides, with grave risks for the political stability of the Italian peninsula and even of Europe, a prospect neither nation cherished at the time. In the event, it was France that mediated a face-saving compromise: Venice was persuaded to hand over the two clerics to the French ambassador who, in turn, would deliver them into papal hands; on the other hand, the legislation concerning church property remained in force; the Capuchins and the Theatines were allowed to return, but the Jesuits were not; the pope lifted the interdict and absolved the Republic, but at the latter's insistence, the absolution was not formally announced in a public ceremony, as this would have been an admission of guilt on Venice's part. The compromise, it should be noted, did not split gains and losses evenly between the contenders: of the two it was Venice that came out ahead and emerged with its prestige virtually intact, for it had asserted and retained the right to regulate church property and to expel a religious order (the Jesuits) most closely identified with papal authority, while at the same time avoiding the humiliation of surrendering the two indicted clerics directly to papal authorities. The Papacy, on its part, suffered a thinly veiled defeat and was forced to recognize that its chief weapons – excommunication and interdict – had been blunted in the confrontation. As the Curia ruefully put it in its instructions to a nuncio in 1621,

those spiritual weapons that were resorted to by Pope Paul V in the defence of ecclesiastical liberty against the Venetian Republic ... were believed by upright people to produce good results; yet from them evil consequences have in fact come, because from that time ecclesiastical jurisdiction and discipline as well as respect for the Pope and the Apostolic See have received, not without danger for the Catholic faith itself, so many grave injuries that, instead of gain and redress, we have suffered no small losses.

45. Cozzi, 'Venezia nello scenario europeo', pp. 149–50.

And the nuncio was urged to act with the utmost tact and moderation in his dealings with Venetian authorities, to look the other way in the face of abuses, and to avoid further confrontations, especially in matters of jurisdiction.[46] In Venice, however, or rather among those members of the government who had been in the forefront of resistance to papal claims, the compromise of 1607 was perceived as only a partial victory, for it had left unresolved a number of controversial issues and had fallen short of their hope for a Republic totally free from papal tutelage in ecclesiastical matters. To achieve complete freedom would have implied the establishment of a 'national', that is to say schismatic, Church, and this was an option which some of the most fervent defenders of Venetian liberty may have contemplated, but which, if adopted, would have rent the Venetian state asunder, for not only did the Papacy still enjoy the support of a considerable portion of the patriciate itself, but in the populace at large and especially in the mainland dominions where loyalty to Rome still ran strong, an open break with the Papacy would have likely caused unrest, if not outright rebellion.[47] As Paolo Sarpi put it, 'controversies [with Rome] never reach the point of a rupture, because the Republic, on its part, has been and is resolved not to upset the public peace'.[48] The Venetian ruling elite, in other words, had to take popular sentiment into account when dealing with the Papacy.

The Interdict crisis ushered in a long period of uneasy coexistence during which occasional disagreements and frictions were generally followed by *ad hoc* compromises. To these we shall return presently, but not before we look at the broader significance of the crisis itself and at the wide resonance it had both in Italy and abroad. To outsiders looking on it was much more than watching a relatively small, albeit pivotal, Italian state taking enormous risks in its defiance of the highest religious authority in Christendom; nor was it just a question of waiting for the outcome of a conflict that could have far-reaching consequences for the religious policies of other Italian states and for the balance of power in Italy. The Interdict crisis attracted international attention also because it generated, as other similar crises did not, a debate in which the conflicting claims of church and state were articulated in such a way as to transcend the narrow boundaries of the Venetian case.[49] In other words, the Interdict crisis put squarely on the table the ideological dilemma created by the clash of two absolutisms in the confessional age. That debate was largely the work of two of the best theological and legal minds Italy could offer at the time: on the Venetian side stood Paolo Sarpi, theologian, jurist and historian, a man of vast learning and a formidable polemicist; on the

46. Stella, *Chiesa e Stato*, p. 75. The above quotation is on pp. 73–4.
47. Cozzi, 'Venezia nello scenario europeo', pp. 91, 148–50, and 155.
48. Quotation in Bouwsma, *Venice*, p. 484.
49. A.D. Wright, 'The Venetian View of Church and State: Catholic Erastianism?', *Studi Secenteschi* 19 (1978), pp. 75–106, has rightly stressed the similarities between the Venetian government's attitude towards the Papacy and the attitude of other Catholic states such as France and Spain; hence the latter's interest in the outcome of the crisis.

papal side was Cardinal Robert Bellarmine, Jesuit theologian and controversialist of international stature, equally learned and combative.[50] While sharing a common adherence to Catholic dogma, the two contenders (along with lesser participants in the debate such as Fulgenzio Micanzio and Giacomo Menochio on the Venetian side, and Cesare Baronius and Tommaso Campanella on the papal side) held diametrically opposing views not only on the nature of civil and religious authority, but also on the very nature of political society as well as of the Church. At the heart of the debate was the question of whether the state has the authority to legislate and to enforce legislation in ecclesiastical and moral matters, and whether that authority is subject to being appealed to, or can be superseded by, that of the Papacy whenever the latter deems that the rights of religion have been infringed. To Sarpi the answer was not in doubt as it was not, by and large, to most Catholic governments who had refused to accept the decrees of the Council of Trent in their entirety and the bull *In coena Domini* precisely on grounds that they restricted their own authority. Sarpi thus articulated a widespread sentiment when he argued that secular authority cannot, except in strictly spiritual matters (read: dogmatic pronouncements), be subject to any outside limitations. Indeed he denied to the Church any coercive power, the use of force being, he thought, the sole prerogative of the state even in matters of religious practice and of moral conduct.[51] To buttress his argument he, too, appealed to the divine right theory of monarchy or, rather, the divine right theory of government since it applied to republics as well as to monarchies. In 1608 he explained that 'God has instituted two governments in the world, the spiritual and the temporal, each of them supreme and independent from the other' and that rulers are 'vicars of God in temporal things' so that 'where public tranquility and civil life are involved all men, including ecclesiastics, are subject to the prince'.[52] But Sarpi, as Paolo Prodi has noted, also appealed to the living Venetian tradition that saw the doge, like a latter-day Constantine or Justinian, as a quasi-priestly figure, as both *princeps in republica* and *princeps in ecclesia*. This sacred character of the head of state he construed to mean that the Venetian government had the right and indeed the duty to monitor and to judge clerical conduct and to ensure the religious welfare of the people, for 'it received this power from God at its birth'.[53] From these premises it followed that secular governments are accountable to God alone,

50. The debate and the battle of the books it generated are discussed in great detail by Bouwsma, *Venice*, ch. 8.
51. On Sarpi's notion of the Church as a purely spiritual community of believers with no coercive powers see Salvatorelli, 'Venezia, Paolo V', pp. 89–90; and Gaetano Cozzi, 'Paolo Sarpi' in *Storia della Letteratura italiana*, vol. 5, Garzanti, Milan 1967, pp. 437–9.
52. Quotation in Bouwsma, *Venice*, p. 540. Elsewhere Sarpi stated that 'the prince is established by God and rules with divine authority, and his subjects are bound in conscience to obey him' (quoted by Antonio Rotondò, 'La censura ecclesiastica e la cultura' in *SIE*, vol. 5 (1973), p. 1474).
53. Prodi, 'The Stucture and Organization of the Church', pp. 410–13.

not to the Papacy – a notion that was widely held by Catholic governments at that time. To give but one example, in 1614 the French theologian Edmond Richer expressed it in very clear terms at the meeting of the Estates General when he explained the crown's refusal to give legal standing to the Tridentine decrees in France: 'there is no earthly power, whether spiritual or temporal, that has any right over the king's realm to the detriment of the sacred persons of our monarchs'.[54] To say that governments held their authority directly from God did not mean that they had received it through some miraculous intervention from Heaven, but rather that, according to the law of nature established by the Creator, government is an inescapable necessity for society and is willed by God himself, the creator of nature. In practice, the divine right theory could serve two purposes, both crucial to the legitimization of the early modern state: in a general way, by asserting that rulers are accountable only to God, it ruled out active resistance to the state and thus provided the best safeguard against sedition and anarchy; in Catholic countries, as the examples of Venice and France indicate, it also gave legitimacy to the confessional state's claims that it could regulate church affairs, insofar as they affected the welfare of the country, without papal interference.[55]

Defenders of 'ecclesiastical liberty' – of the right, that is, of the Church to act as a self-governing, sovereign body entitled to choose and police its own personnel, to hold property that was exempt from secular exactions and limitations, to judge and, if need be, to impose legal penalties on lay people insofar as they broke ecclesiastical or moral laws – denied their adversaries' basic premise, namely that governments are by divine right and argued instead that, according to natural law, men, as Bellarmine put it, 'are born free and cannot be subjected to a fellowman's authority unless it be by some legitimate title such as election, succession or other'.[56] In so arguing Bellarmine and a majority of Catholic political theorists in his time did not necessarily advocate a representative form of government, let alone a democratic one; rather, Bellarmine rejected his opponents' notion that the authority of the state, being divinely sanctioned, can never be questioned, resisted or subjected to any outside control.[57] More importantly, in the context of the Interdict crisis, Bellarmine, while denying the 'sacred' character of the

54. Quotation in Jean Delumeau, *Catholicism between Luther and Voltaire. A New View of the Counter-Reformation*, transl. Jeremy Moiser, Burns & Oates 1977, p. 26.
55. Johann P. Sommerville, *Politics and Ideology in England, 1603–40*, Longman 1986, pp. 12, 34, and 47–8. For what precedes I have heavily relied on his penetrating analysis of the divine right theory in a European perspective.
56. Quotation in Francesco Gui, *I Gesuiti e la rivoluzione boema. Alle origini della guerra dei Trent'anni*, Franco Angeli, Milan 1989, p. 26. Gui, pp. 26–7, underlines the fact that the Catholic natural law theory of government made it possible for its supporters not to feel irrevocably bound to any specific form of government or to any particular dynasty.
57. Sommerville, *Politics and Ideology*, pp. 59–63, for an analysis of the Catholic natural law theory and its rejection of democracy.

state, asserted that only the Church, grounded as it is in God's revealed word, is of divine origin and is thus superior to man-made governments; although it cannot and should not dictate to secular rulers how to run their countries, it can intervene whenever spiritual values and the liberty of the Church are at stake. Known as the pope's 'indirect power', this limited right of intervention could easily be stretched so as to give the pope the final word on any controversial issue, and that is one reason why it was denounced by Sarpi, Richer and James I – the more strongly so as it was difficult to draw the line where 'indirect power' stopped, just as it was difficult for the advocate of the divine right theory of government to separate the purely spiritual from the temporal.[58] Bellarmine's theory also caused alarm because it seemed to countenance the right of resistance and even of armed rebellion against the state, for if indeed authority had originally rested with the community and had subsequently been transferred to a king, emperor or doge by common consent and under certain conditions, then it followed that the community could reclaim that authority whenever the ruler violated those conditions. Not surprisingly and rather ironically, Bellarmine and other Catholic theologians of his time were often lumped with their worst adversaries, the Calvinists and notably the Puritans, as being instigators of sedition and anarchy[59] – a charge Bellarmine felt bound to reject in the strongest terms as when he wrote, in response to James I: 'I did not say . . . that the authority of kings derives directly from the people . . . What I did say . . . is that the authority of kings is not directly derived from God in the same way the authority of the pope is', and then went on to reassure his critics that his intent was 'to impress on men's minds that kings are subject to the pope, not to the people, from which subjection neither seditions nor rebellions are to be feared'.[60] This reassurance was unlikely to assuage the misgivings of Catholic rulers who after Trent, as we have seen, were increasingly wary of papal intervention in their affairs. To them, as to their Protestant counterparts, only a theory that rooted their authority firmly in a divine mandate could provide an iron-clad guarantee against any challenge from below or from the Papacy.

Underlying the debate between divine right theorists and the supporters of papal supremacy (albeit in the less extreme form of 'indirect power') lay two diametrically opposed concepts of society and of the role of the Church in society. Sarpi envisaged society in terms of specific, historically defined political communities, each with its own distinctive and closely intertwined civic and religious traditions and institutions, each self-contained and

58. Gennaro Barbuto, 'Il "Principe" di Bellarmino' in *Bellarmino e la Controriforma*, ed. Romeo De Maio *et al.*, Centro di Studi Sorani V. Patriarca, Sora 1990, pp. 152–3; and Sommerville, *Politics and Ideology*, pp. 190–6.
59. Sommerville, *Politics and Ideology*, pp. 44–5, 202 and 208; Domenico Ferraro, 'Bellarmino, Suarez, Giacomo I e la polemica sulle origini del potere politico' in *Bellarmino e la Controriforma*, p. 198; and Barbuto, 'Il "Principe" di Bellarmino', pp. 160 and 177.
60. Quotation in Barbuto, p. 175.

autonomous and, as such, authorized freely to legislate even on matters pertaining to the local Church; to him the universal Church was not a supranational institution endowed with coercive powers and entitled to impose its laws on the several local Churches, but rather the purely spiritual community of all true believers.[61] Like his contemporary Campanella, Bellarmine, by contrast, thought in terms of Catholic universalism, that is to say of one all-embracing human community ideally united under the authority of one temporal and one spiritual leader; his paradigm was the *respublica christiana* as conceived and dreamed of in medieval times. Since, in practice, that unity had given way to a multiplicity of nations often at odds or at war with one another, he looked upon the Papacy as the only remaining sign of a lost unity and the only remaining arbitrator between states.[62] The two perspectives, Sarpi's and Bellarmine's, could not be farther apart and it is no wonder that the two sides seemed, more often than not, to argue past each other.[63]

Bellarmine's perspective looks somewhat unrealistic, not to say anachronistic, in the light of the Papacy's declining role in international affairs and of the national states' growing assertiveness. It is nonetheless worth our attention, for it reveals one important facet of the spirit of the Counter-Reformation: behind the mundane quarrels over church property and ecclesiastical jurisdiction lay, at least among the most selfless and genuinely religious advocates of papal authority (and Bellarmine was most certainly one of them), a sincere concern for the common good and a belief that the Church, speaking through the pope, could contribute to the common good by acting, as it were, as the conscience of the state. In a revealing passage of his work *De officio principis christiani* (1619) where he discussed the moral duties of a Christian prince, Bellarmine wrote:

There are not a few princes who, although very pious and righteous in their private lives, ignore the sins of the chief ministers who run the state, while the poor are oppressed, court decisions are perverted, and the lowly subjects are scandalized; ignorance [of such evils] is no excuse before God . . . [The prince] must, in fact, seriously consider who his ministers are and inquire into how they behave.[64]

61. Salvatorelli, 'Venezia, Paolo V', pp. 89–90; and Bouwsma, *Venice*, p. 545.
62. Ferraro, 'Bellarmino, Suarez', pp. 212–16. Paolo Prodi, *The Papal Prince. One Body and Two Souls: the Papal Monarchy in Early Modern Europe*, transl. Susan Hawkins, Cambridge University Press 1987, pp. 178–9, has called attention to the gradual shift that occurred in the late sixteenth century from the medieval notion of the pope's spiritual and temporal supremacy over Christendom to that of the pope as 'mediator' between Catholic governments. On Campanella's universalism see Luigi Firpo, *Lo Stato ideale della Controriforma. Ludovico Agostini*, Laterza, Bari 1957, pp. 324–6.
63. A balanced assessment of the whole controversy in Eric Cochrane, *Italy 1530–1630*, ed. Julius Kirshner, Longman 1988, pp. 262–3.
64. Quotation in Barbuto, 'Il "Principe" di Bellarmino', p. 127.

Bellarmine went on to argue that the prince is bound in conscience to compensate his subjects for the material and moral harm they may have suffered at the hands of evil government officials, and apparently he had in mind the harm caused both by excessive taxes and various forms of harassment. Nor was his the isolated voice of a saintly prelate: the notorious bull *In coena Domini* had denounced as oppressive, and therefore immoral, the exorbitant taxes imposed on the poor and, much to the rulers' chagrin, had thus interposed papal authority between them and their subjects.[65]

The Interdict controversy had concluded, as will be recalled, with an uneasy and lopsided compromise. All the books and tracts it had spawned had certainly clarified, but had failed to reconcile, the two opposing views. The upshot was that in Venice as in other Italian states the tug-of-war went on, albeit without the high drama and the resonance of the 1606 crisis. On a number of points the Venetian Republic held its ground to the end of the century, and continued to subject all papal pronouncements to its approval before they could be considered valid in its dominions; it continued as well to keep a close watch on the Inquisition's proceedings, to prosecute clerics charged with criminal offences or with disloyalty toward the government, and to regulate and impose limitations on ecclesiastical property.[66] There were times when tensions reached high levels as they did in 1607 in connection with the attempted assassination of Paolo Sarpi and on the eve of the Thirty Years War when Venice seemed more and more inclined to support the Protestant cause in Germany as the only way to resist Habsburg hegemony in Europe, while the Papacy was trying to muster all Catholic forces in an attempt to break the back of Protestantism; and again in 1629 when the Republic objected to the papal choice for the episcopal see of Padua; or in the 1650s when a quarrel broke out with the Inquisition over the Pelagini dissidents in Brescia and another was triggered by Rome's demand that Venice lift the ban on the officially sanctioned *History of the Council of Trent* by Cardinal Sforza Pallavicino, a book Venetian authorities considered 'contrary to the public service and hostile to the person of Father Paolo [Sarpi]'.[67] There were no clear winners or losers in any of those quarrels, for the Venetian patriciate was often divided unto itself and therefore vacillating, and the Papacy was not inclined to run the risk of another all-out

65. That the pope must act as defender of the common man against excessive taxation by rapacious rulers was a recurring theme in Catholic teaching and was embedded in *In coena Domini*. Government opposition to the latter largely hinged on that point (Prodi, 'Introduzione' in *Fisco, religione, Stato nell'età confessionale*, pp. 17–19).

66. Bouwsma, *Venice*, pp. 495–6; Cozzi, 'Venezia nello scenario europeo', p. 91; and A.D. Wright, 'Bellarmine, Baronius and Federico Borromeo' in *Bellarmino e la Controriforma*, pp. 340–6.

67. Bouwsma, pp. 486–97 and 539; Wright, 'Why the Venetian Interdict?', pp. 539–40; Gui, *I Gesuiti*, p. 73; Gianvittorio Signorotto, *Inquisitori e mistici nel Seicento italiano. L'eresia di Santa Pelagia*, Mulino, Bologna 1989, pp. 142–6; and Cozzi, 'Venezia nello scenario europeo', p. 163.

confrontation. Compromise was generally the outcome, but tensions lingered. Only when Venice became involved in the long and costly war for the defence of Crete against the Turks (1645–69) was there a temporary *détente*, for Venice needed the financial support of the Papacy and the latter, consistent with its policy of containment of the Ottoman Empire, had every reason to support the Venetian Republic to the hilt. Even then, however, the two powers bargained hard before reaching an agreement: the Papacy insisted on the repeal of the infamous statutes of 1604–5 and on the readmission of the Jesuit order as the price of its support; after prolonged negotiations Venice granted the latter point in 1657, but remained unyielding on the former.[68] Less than ten years later the relationship between the two powers seemed to have soured once again over the Republic's old claim to subject clerics to the jurisdiction of secular courts. The papal nuncio at that time voiced his displeasure in terms that echoed those used sixty years earlier: he lamented the arrogance of the patriciate *vis-à-vis* Rome 'whose supremacy they cannot suffer' and denounced them for 'claiming that their authority derives directly from God'. Interestingly, however, his recommendation that severe penalties be once again imposed on the proud Republic was quietly ignored in Rome.[69] In 1689 there was a temporary sense of euphoria when a Venetian cardinal, Pietro Ottoboni, was elected pope as Alexander VIII, but after his brief pontificate (1689–91) frictions resumed, so much so that in 1699 the Venetian Senate passed a statute that excluded from any government position anyone with relations employed in the papal diplomatic service.

Taken as a whole, the history of church–state relations in seventeenth-century Italy appears, for all its local variations, dominated by deadlock. Neither side was willing to yield ground or had the means to force the other to do so. Both sides, moreover, had much to lose from an all-out confrontation. The Spanish crown, for one, could not afford to push its claims over church affairs in Milan, Naples or Sicily to the breaking point, for to do so would have undermined its image and its role as the leading Catholic power and might have fed anti-Spanish sentiment among its Italian subjects. Nor could Venice afford an irreparable break with Rome, for such a break would have been likely to enhance the role of Spain in the affairs of the peninsula as the champion of Catholicism against the errant Republic. As for the Papacy, it too had very good reasons for avoiding a rupture with the major Italian states, for it needed peace and a measure of harmony in the peninsula if it was to concentrate its efforts and resources on the struggle against Protestantism north of the Alps. Yet it would be simplistic to conclude that because deadlock characterized church–state relations the whole thing was an exercise in futility or a mere cover for purely political or economic interests. Actually, beneath it all was the issue of whether secular rulers have a 'sacral' character that entitles them a large measure of control over religious matters, and whether the Papacy has the right to impose its will on those

68. Cozzi, pp. 155–63.
69. Stella, *Chiesa e Stato*, pp. 78–80.

rulers when, in its view, religious values are at stake. The issue was not resolved in the seventeenth century and would not be resolved until the state shed its 'confessional' posture and assumed one of neutrality toward religion, and until the Papacy renounced not so much its right to pass moral judgement on the policies and actions of governments, but its claim to enforce its judgement on recalcitrant governments with the use of force if need be. These changes, of course, were still far in the future. Meanwhile, however, the tensions and conflicts of the seventeenth century laid the groundwork for two important developments: one, as Paolo Prodi has noted in connection with the Venetian Interdict crisis, was that the Papacy, by denying the state any religious authority, unwittingly promoted a new and purely secular view of the state itself;[70] another was the emerging separation between a secular and a religious sphere, and this separation would, in the long run, give rise to the modern notion that 'no state can claim a final authority on the conscience of any man'.[71]

70. Paolo Prodi, 'Chiesa e società' in *Storia di Venezia*, vol. 6, p. 330.
71. Francis Oakley, *Kingship and the Gods. The Western Apostasy*, University of St Thomas, Houston, Tex. 1968, p. 49.

CHAPTER SIX

Culture

When compared to that of the late Middle Ages and of the Renaissance the culture of seventeenth-century Italy looks, at first sight, anticlimactic as few, if any, names of artists, poets and writers from that century come to mind who can match those of painters like Giotto, Botticelli or Raphael, of architects like Brunelleschi or Palladio, and of poets who can even remotely approach the stature of a Dante or a Petrarch. One is thus left with the impression that by the late sixteenth century the creativity of the previous three centuries or so had spent itself and that Italian culture was now incapable of keeping alive the dazzling legacy of the past. It is an impression which, until not long ago, was also accepted orthodoxy: the Seicento was portrayed as a time of intellectual and artistic decadence, a time when the Baroque style (in the sense of a search for the outlandish, for the bizarre, for whatever can 'thrill, amaze and entertain' rather than truly inspire and elevate) allegedly transformed Italian culture into a hollow exercise in artificiality, ostentation or, at best, sheer virtuosity. As for the reasons behind this decadence, they were variously found in an oppressive foreign domination, in religious conformism and repression, or in a sclerotic social order.[1]

There is some truth in this indictment, as will be seen, but in recent years it has been increasingly questioned or at least modified in various ways. For one thing, art historians have rehabilitated the Baroque style in the visual arts and in architecture by stressing its original contribution to a new in-depth perception of space and its ability to impart a dynamic quality to the human figure and to architectural structures in contrast to the more linear, more classical approach of Renaissance art. For another thing, literary critics have uncovered some hidden treasures in the literature of the period, notably bold

---

1. Francesco De Sanctis, *History of Italian Literature* (1870–71) transl. Joan Redfern, Basic Books, New York 1959, vol. 2, pp. 620–36; Benedetto Croce, *Storia dell'età barocca in Italia*, 2nd edn, Laterza, Bari 1946, pp. 25–33. A recent, equally critical view of Baroque culture with emphasis on the 'servility' of Italian intellectuals is found in Gino Benzoni, *Gli affanni della cultura. Intellettuali e potere nell'Italia della Controriforma*, Feltrinelli, Milan 1978.

attempts at breaking with an ossified stylistic tradition in poetry and in the theatre, at questioning the excessive, almost servile reverence for the Greek and Latin classics exhibited by Renaissance humanists, and at developing new literary genres such as fiction and travel narratives. Lastly, and more importantly, scholars have given fresh emphasis to those areas, such as music and science, from which medieval and Renaissance culture had been largely absent and where, by contrast, the seventeenth century made some of its most original and lasting contributions. In the end what we now have is a mixed picture of light and shade or, as H.G. Koenigsberger put it in a seminal essay written as early as 1960, a picture of 'shift' rather than of unmitigated decadence.[2]

THE ARTS[3]

In painting the originality of Baroque artists, their ability to innovate on Renaissance models were heralded by the monumental canvasses which Michelangelo Merisi (1573–1610), better known as Caravaggio from his native town in Lombardy, painted in Rome, a city that was becoming a premier magnet for artists from Italy and indeed from Europe thanks to the lavish patronage of popes, cardinals and members of the local nobility.[4] Caravaggio boldly broke with tradition by adopting a 'naturalistic' approach even when dealing with religious subjects: in his paintings the figures are drawn straight from contemporary life as he could observe it in the streets and taverns of Rome rather than from some idealized and somewhat remote world. He also departed from tradition (and in so doing influenced generations of artists both in Italy and abroad) in the way he played with light and shadow to impart a

2. H.G. Koenigsberger, 'Decadence or Shift? Changes in the Civilization of Italy and Europe in the Sixteenth and Seventeenth Centuries' (1960) reprinted in his *Estates and Revolutions. Essays in Early Modern European History*, Cornell University Press, Ithaca, N.Y. 1971, pp. 278–97. Other revisionist interpretations include Jean Delumeau, *L'Italie de Botticelli à Bonaparte*, Colin, Paris 1974, pp. 249–75; Alberto Asor Rosa, *Il Seicento. La nuova scienza e la crisi del Barocco*, Laterza, Bari 1974, vol. 1, pp. 3, 16–18, 30–6; Roberto Alonge, 'Letteratura e spettacolo nel Seicento', in *SSI*, vol. 11, p. 463; and Brendan Dooley, 'Introduction' to his *Italy in the Baroque. Selected Readings*, Garland Publishing, Hamden, Conn. 1995, pp. 1–21. This anthology offers a fine selection of less well-known yet important literary and scientific texts in English translation.

3. Unless otherwise indicated, this section is based on H.W. Jason with Dora Jane Jason, *History of Art. A Survey of the Major Visual Arts from the Dawn of History to the Present*, Prentice Hall, Englewood Cliffs, N. J. 1971, pp. 405–19.

4. On patronage in Rome see Francis Haskell, *Patrons and Painters. A Study in the Relations Between Italian Art and Society in the Age of the Baroque*, Chatto and Windus 1963, especially ch. 2 (on papal patronage in the first half of the century) and ch. 7 (on European patronage in the second half).

189

dynamic, dramatic quality to the scenes he portrayed. His contemporary Annibale Carracci from Bologna (1560–1609) did not quite equal him in terms of originality and boldness, nor, for that matter, did any other seventeenth-century Italian painter. Carracci, however, was an artist of considerable talents and vision who made his mark, notably in the ceiling frescoes of the Farnese palace in Rome, by creating the illusion of endless space as a setting for his rendition of mythological stories (*The Loves of the Classical Gods*). He could also, like Caravaggio, portray in a naturalistic vein vivid scenes from everyday life.

Caravaggio's legacy of naturalism and the consummate use of chiaroscuro found its foremost expression in the work of a woman artist, Artemisia Gentileschi (1593–1652).[5] The daughter and pupil of the distinguished, if somewhat conventional painter Orazio Gentileschi, she spent the better part of her life in Rome (with shorter stays in Florence, London and Naples) and is remembered not only because, in an age so steeped in misogynist prejudice that women were seldom encouraged or allowed to pursue a career as professional artists, she rose to prominence and could boast a French queen, an English monarch and a grand duke of Tuscany among her patrons, but also because she produced canvasses (notably those celebrating heroines such as Judith, Lucretia and Cleopatra) of unquestionable dramatic force, sheer pictorial beauty and uncompromising realism.

Alongside and in sharp contrast to Caravaggesque naturalism Baroque Rome also saw the development of another school of painting that found its inspiration in the notion that the artist should not merely imitate nature, but should idealize it as earlier 'classicists' had done. In this spirit the Bolognese Guido Reni (1575–1642) decorated the Casino Rospigliosi with a graceful *Aurora* in which he achieved stunning effects in terms of sheer luminosity. Giovanni Francesco Barbieri, known as Guercino, (1591–1666) went a step further by combining luminosity with the striking dynamism of figures who seem to be driven by winds. His example was emulated and surpassed by two other artists who also worked in Rome and produced what are possibly the most breath-taking ceiling frescoes of the entire century: Giovanni Battista Gaulli (1639–1709) with his *Triumph of the Name of Jesus* in the Il Gesù church, and Pietro Da Cortona (1596–1669) with his *Glorification of the Reign of Urban VIII* in the Barberini palace. In both of them an illusion of light-filled, limitless space is created whereby the figures (and, one dare say, the viewers themselves) are drawn into an irresistible ascending movement.

Among the many artists who flocked to Rome in the later part of the seventeenth century was the Neapolitan Salvator Rosa (1615–73).[6] Painter, actor, musician and poet, he stands out not only on account of his astonishing versatility, but also because he, unlike most of his peers, exhibited a fierce

---

5. Mary D. Garrard, *Artemisia Gentileschi. The Image of the Female Hero in Italian Baroque Art*, Princeton University Press, Princeton, N. J. 1989, provides an exhaustive study of a long neglected artist.
6. See Jonathan Scott, *Salvator Rosa. His Life and Times*, Yale University Press, New Haven and London 1995.

sense of independence, going so far as refusing to attach himself to any one patron or to paint on commission unless he was moved by his own inspiration. For all that, he achieved an enormous reputation in his lifetime and was wooed (unsuccessfully as it turned out) by Cardinal Mazarin, the French prime minister, by Louis XIV and by Queen Christina of Sweden. As an artist, he was admired in his own time and even more so in the eighteenth century both in Italy and abroad primarily for his landscapes which rivalled those produced by northern European artists such as Nicholas Poussin and Claude Lorrain. Drawing in part his inspiration from them, he was the first Italian painter to devote whole canvasses to landscapes rather than using them as mere backdrops for his subjects. And magnificent landscapes they are: with their abrupt precipices, threatening cliffs and storm-battered trees, they all project a new appreciation of the sheer beauty of wilderness. It is on their account that Rosa has been called 'proto-romantic'.

Baroque sculpture at its best broke new ground, too. Its achievements are epitomized in the work of Gianlorenzo Bernini (1598–1680), another artist who was called upon to contribute, in many ways as will be seen, to the splendour of the papal city. His *David* and his *Ecstasy of St Theresa* are perhaps the two finest achievements of Italian Baroque sculpture. The former stands in sharp contrast to the static, somewhat aloof *David* Michelangelo had sculpted a century or so earlier, for it embodies motion and emotion to an unprecedented degree. In the more famous, but not necessarily greater *Ecstasy*, the figures of the saint and of the angel are bathed in light and appear as if they were suspended in a supernatural space and the illusionistic effect is truly remarkable. Yet the saint's facial expression and the abandonment of her body reflect truly human feelings – that blend of pain and 'infinite sweetness' which the great Spanish mystic herself had described in her autobiography.

Besides being a superb sculptor Bernini was also a great architect, indeed the greatest in seventeenth-century Italy. His reputation in this area rests on his contributions to the completion of St Peter's basilica, both inside and outside. For its interior decoration he designed the colossal, hundred-foot-high bronze canopy over the main altar with its four spiral-shaped columns as well as the altar of the throne of St Peter at the end of the basilica. In both, architecture and sculpture are blended to achieve spectacular results, although the modern viewer, while standing in awe and admiration before such astonishing feats of art and craftsmanship, may well find them overly ornate and even extravagant and as representing no real improvement over the more subdued, more restrained and, in the end, more elegant altars of the Renaissance period. The same viewer, however, is unlikely to harbour similar reservations toward the majestic St Peter's square designed by Bernini in the 1620s, certainly the most widely known and admired achievement of this most versatile artist who could be a flamboyant decorator inside the basilica and a controlled classicist architect outside it. In conjunction with Carlo Maderno's (1556–1629) recently completed façade where ingeniously spaced pilasters and columns seem to converge and to draw people toward the basilica's central portal, Bernini's oval square with its magnificent four-row-deep colonnade dramatically expressed the all-embracing universality of a rejuvenated Church with the Papacy at its centre (Bernini himself described his colonnade as 'the motherly arms of the Church') besides serving as a majestic stage for outdoor processions and religious celebrations.

The design of St Peter's square brought to the fore architectural elements that had made sporadic appearances even in the sixteenth century at the hands of Vignola, but were to become central to Baroque architecture: the oval plan and the curved surface. It would be left to Francesco Borromini (1599–1680), a reclusive, neurotic, but immensely talented man who for a time served as one of Bernini's chief assistants at the St Peter's construction site, to adopt these new elements and make them integral parts of the Baroque architectural language. Not only did he design an oval plan for the church of San Carlo alle Quattro Fontane in Rome, but he also designed its outside walls as an intricate succession of concave and convex surfaces that make the whole structure look as if it had been formed 'not of stone, but of a pliant substance set in motion by an energetic space'.[7]

What has been called 'animated architecture' earned Borromini a vast reputation and inspired countless architects both in Italy and abroad in the late seventeenth and early eighteenth centuries. Among them Guarino Guarini (1624–83) stands out not only for his originality, but also as the man who first transplanted the Baroque style to the city of Turin in Piedmont. A remarkably gifted and versatile priest who was a mathematician and a philosopher in addition to being an architect, Guarini adopted Bernini's 'undulating' formula for the elegant, all-brick façade of the Carignano palace; in the 1660s, for the chapel of the Holy Shroud, he designed an extraordinary cupola of pointed profile that was inspired by, but went well beyond, Borromini's dome in the church of S. Ivo alla Sapienza built in Rome some twenty years earlier.

POETRY AND THE THEATRE

While there is much to admire in the arts and the architecture of the seventeenth century, the same cannot be said, by and large, of literature. The field of poetry looks especially barren and De Sanctis's and Croce's stigmatization of Italian Baroque poetry as sheer verbal artifice and virtuosity devoid of genuine inspiration is still accepted today, at least in part, by many literary critics. Although the leading poet of the period, Giambattista Marino (1569–1625), achieved enormous popularity in his lifetime and for much of the century both in his native country and abroad,[8] few people today are

7. Isabelle Hyman, 'The Baroque' in Marvin Trachtenberg and Isabelle Hyman, *Architecture from Pre-History to Post-Modernism. The Western Tradition*, Prentice Hall, Englewood Cliffs, N.J. 1986, p. 346.
8. Asor Rosa, *Il Seicento*, p. 17.

likely to read, let alone enjoy, his endless metaphors, puns, ornate imagery, alliterations, onomatopoeias, lush imagery, and above all the sheer quantity of words he devoted to topics that would have benefited from a much lighter touch. *Adone*, the poem which he considered his masterpiece and earned him the applause of his contemporaries, was nearly twenty-five years in the making and eventually ran to an astonishing 40,984 verses supposedly devoted to retelling the touching, but fairly simple mythological tale of the love between Venus and Adonis. The poem is replete with interminable descriptions of landscapes, animals, flowers, and festivities, and is frequently interrupted by other fables only remotely linked to the main plot.[9] A well-known example of Marino's verbosity is his digression on the contest between the nightingale and the lute player to which he devoted no less than 200 verses.[10] Such feats of verbal opulence may well have made his reputation at the time, but are unlikely to appeal to and truly move a modern reader. Marino can no doubt dazzle his audience with the wealth of descriptive details, with his encyclopedic knowledge of plants and animals and precious stones, and with his astonishing erudition in terms of classical mythology and literature, but as one literary critic has noted, he is ultimately insensitive and indifferent to genuine human emotions whether of ecstasy or of anguish.[11]

Nonetheless, for all his limitations, Marino cannot be lightly dismissed as a hollow relic of the past, for, in fact, as recent scholarship has argued, he occupies a significant place in the annals of Italian culture. For one thing, he must be credited with overturning an ossified literary tradition that all too often consisted of the servile imitation of Petrarch or blind adherence to the precepts of Aristotelian poetics; and he must also be credited with replacing the stereotyped, disembodied feminine images dear to Petrarch's late imitators with more sensuous, flesh-and-blood ones.[12] For another, Marino's poetry reflects some of the most distinctive ideas of the time: the necessity of sense perceptions for a true understanding of nature, the exaltation of the experimental method and of technological progress, the glorification (found in *Adone*) of inventors, mythological or real, from Prometheus to Gutenberg, to his contemporary Galileo. In short, it has been said, one should not ignore 'the new and energizing contribution his poetry made to the culture of the seventeenth century'.[13]

9. On Marino see Giovanni Getto, *Barocco in prosa e poesia*, Rizzoli, Milan 1969, pp. 13–54, who defines *Adonis* as 'a true encyclopedia aimed at covering all that man can know' (p. 51). See also Alberto Asor Rosa, *Sintesi di storia della letteratura italiana*, Nuova Italia, Florence 1972, pp. 207–9 and *Il Seicento*, pp. 430–1.
10. An English translation of the 'contest' is available in Paschal C. Viglionese, *Italian Writers of the Seventeenth and Eighteenth Centuries*, McFarland, Jefferson, N.C. 1988, pp. 44–9.
11. Getto, *Barocco*, p. 50.
12. Alonge, 'Letteratura', pp. 466–8.
13. Paul Renucci, 'La cultura. Il Seicento' in *SIE*, vol. 2 (1973), pp. 1381–7 and 1414–16.

Marino was not alone in challenging venerable literary traditions and in extolling modern achievements. Traiano Boccalini (1556–1613) used his satyrical talents in *Ragguagli di Parnaso* against the stale repetition of the precepts of Aristotelian rhetoric and the artificiality of the Petrarchists.[14] Tommaso Campanella (1568–1639) proudly wrote that in his own age 'the art of navigation, the art of printing, the use of the magnet, astronomy, clocks, artillery, the telescope and other inventions are by far superior to the most wonderful achievements of the Greeks, the Jews and the Romans'.[15] The monk Secondo Lancillotti (1583–1643), too, reacted vigorously against the unconditional admiration of the Ancients and against the notion that the culture of his time represented a decline from the glories of the classical age: in a book with the transparent title of *Today, or the world neither worse nor more calamitous than the past* (1623) he fired one of the earliest salvos in the *querelle* of the Ancients and the Modern that was to loom so large in seventeenth-century culture, especially in French culture.[16]

For all that, the classics could still serve as literary models and inspire some genuine poetry as shown by Gabriello Chiabrera (1552–1638) and by Fulvio Testi (1593–1646). They both avoided Marino's flamboyant style and overt hedonism, and opted instead for more restrained literary forms taking as their models the ancient Greek and Latin poets, notably Pindar and Horace. Their ideal was elegance and decorum, their target was the moral corruption and the political servitude they saw around them. Their poetry, however, ended up being too imitative and somewhat contrived, and while they deserve our respect for upholding (much against the prevailing mood of their own age) high standards of style and of substance, they ultimately fail to captivate our attention and to engage our emotions.[17]

Not so the poetry of Campanella and Salvator Rosa (1615–73). The former is chiefly remembered as a philosopher, political reformer and religious writer, but during his long captivity in a Naples prison he composed a number of poems that are remarkable for the depth and sincerity of the feelings they embody – anguish and hope, outraged protest and religious acceptance.[18] Rosa, the artist, was also the author of seven satirical poems each aimed at a specific aspect of contemporary culture and society. In language that at times could be blunt and acerbic, he denounced the horrors of war and the sufferings of the poor, and ridiculed the hollowness of Marinist

14. Luigi Firpo, 'Boccalini, Traiano', in *Dizionario biografico degli Italiani*, vol. 11, Istituto dell'Enciclopedia Italiana, Rome 1969, pp. 10–19; and Asor Rosa, *Il Seicento*, vol. 1, p. 86.
15. Leandro Perini, 'Gli utopisti: delusioni della realtà, sogni dell'avvenire' in *SIE Annali* 4 (1981), p. 316.
16. Sergio Bertelli, *Ribelli, libertini e ortodossi nella storiografia barocca*, Nuova Italia, Florence 1973, pp. 185–91; Renucci, 'La cultura', p. 1388. On Baroque culture in general as an effort to break with tradition see Alonge, 'Letteratura', pp. 464–5.
17. Asor Rosa, *Sintesi*, pp. 209–10.
18. Claudio Varese, 'Teatro, prosa, poesia' in *Storia della Letteratura italiana*, vol. 5, Garzanti, Milan 1967 (henceforth cited as *Storia Garzanti*), pp. 899–903.

poetry. Campanella's and Rosa's, however, were isolated voices in an age when verbal virtuosity and the ostentation of encyclopedic knowledge were more highly prized than the sincere expression of genuine emotions.

Much the same applies to the theatre. Baroque Italy, like the rest of Europe, loved the theatre and its towns, large and small, enjoyed a 'frenetic succession' of comedies, tragedies, pastoral dramas, allegorical and mythological plays; it was then that theatres, in the sense of permanent structures exclusively devoted to stage performances, were first built and that the elevated stage, as we know it, with a curtain, moveable wings and backgrounds was first adopted. It was then, too, that theatrical performances were first opened to a paying public rather than only to invited guests as had been the case in Renaissance courts. For all this, virtually the entire (and enormous) theatrical output of the century has not survived the test of time and is now generally forgotten. There were, however, a few remarkable exceptions: the tragedies of Federico Della Valle (1560–1638) and of Carlo de' Dottori (1618–80) have been rediscovered and rehabilitated in our own time after nearly three centuries of undeserved oblivion. And rightly so, for both playwrights achieved literary greatness in their tragedies. Their tormented sense of human frailty, of the ambiguities of the human condition; their portrayal of overwhelming passion (whether hatred, arrogance or lust) and of redeeming virtue; their analysis of individuals torn between conflicting loyalties – all these ring true in *Judit* and *Reina di Scozia* by Della Valle and in *Aristodemo* by de' Dottori in spite of a style that is often weighed down (in true Baroque fashion) by hyperbole and theatricality.[19]

Unlike tragedies no seventeenth-century comedies have come down that can elicit in us either interest or enjoyment. Even the *commedia dell'arte* (staged performances without a script in which professional actors wearing the mask of stock characters improvised on the basis of only a rough outline) after a promising start early in the century and considerable comic potential in terms of spontaneity and originality, soon degenerated into sheer buffoonery.[20]

MUSIC

Far more original and enduring was another form of theatre – the opera – in which script and music meshed in a new and immensely successful symbiosis. In the opera, however, it was music rather than the spoken word that took pride of place and it is its music that to this day delights audiences, while the script serves as mere support for it and is totally subordinated to the melodies.[21] Not surprisingly, we still remember and celebrate the name of, let us say, Claudio Monteverdi (1567–1643), the composer of such operatic

19. Alonge, 'Letteratura', pp. 475–6 and 479.
20. Ibid., pp. 477–83.
21. Ibid., p. 485.

masterpieces as *Orpheus* (1607) and *The Coronation of Poppea* (1642), but most of us would be hard put to recognize the names of the authors of the two librettos, Alessandro Striggi and Giovan Francesco Busenello, respectively.

The opera had its beginnings in Florence in the last quarter of the sixteenth century with a group of men of letters and practising musicians (foremost among them Vincenzo Galilei, Galileo's father) known as the Camerata de' Bardi, and its earliest examples were Jacopo Peri's *Daphne* (1597) and Emilio De' Cavalieri's *Representation of Soul and Body* first performed in Rome in 1600. What was distinctive about the opera (known at first as *melodramma* or as *favola in musica*) was its combination of theatrical performance with music: singers were at the same time actors, enunciating the words of the libretto in long solo recitatives in such a way as to express to their audience all the shades of emotion embedded in the drama. In the course of time the increasingly elaborate scenic apparatus and the use of a growing number of instruments (notably violins) added to the representational and emotional power of the opera: in 1645 John Evelyn, the English traveller and diarist, could write from Venice that the opera he had attended was 'doubtless one of the most magnificent and expenseful diversions the wit of man can invent'.[22] And a modern historian has written that the opera was 'a whole new language, an original way of expressing passions and feelings' and so well attuned to the temper of the age of the Baroque that 'the whole of Europe followed Italy's lead'.[23]

The opera, however, was but one of the new forms of musical expression created in the seventeenth century. At the hands of Giacomo Carissimi (1605–74) the *oratorio* provided church audiences with a parallel form of spectacle; Alessandro Scarlatti (1660–1725), in addition to composing over one hundred operas, developed and perfected the *cantata* for solo voice accompanied by a number of instruments; Arcangelo Corelli (1653–1713), on his part, concentrated on purely instrumental musical compositions, notably the *sonata* and the *concerto grosso*, thus paving the way to the great composers of the next century, Antonio Vivaldi and Domenico Scarlatti.

As anyone even superficially acquainted with Baroque music will readily agree, concertos and sonatas, operas and oratorios are as many glories of seventeenth-century Italian culture and possibly one of its richest legacies. As Koenigsberger has said in arguing that Italian culture did not so much decline as shift in the seventeenth century, music was 'perhaps the most revolutionary shift in Italian creative activity'.[24] In the words of Alberto Asor Rosa music represented 'an alternative to literature'.[25] As to why music came to

22. Quotation in Arthur Jacobs, *A Short History of Western Music*, Penguin 1972, p. 97. Ch. 7 of this book provides a fine survey of the origins and development of the opera. For a more recent and fuller discussion see the two essays on music by Franco Bezza in *SSI*, vol. 11, pp. 511–40 and vol. 12, pp. 435–61.
23. Delumeau, *L'Italie*, p. 273.
24. Koenigsberger, 'Decadence or Shift?', p. 286.
25. Asor Rosa, *Sintesi*, p. 213.

overshadow literature and particularly poetry, and why the former still moves and delights us while the latter is largely forgotten, this is an intriguing question for which there is probably no clear answer. Over a century ago De Sanctis, after noticing at the close of his discussion of seventeenth-century Italian literature that 'as literature was dying . . . music was being born', went on to assert that 'once words had lost their reason for existing . . . they retired from the field, giving place to music and song'.[26] As an explanation this does not go very far, as there is no obvious reason why music ought to have filled the void left by a dying literature. Koenigsberger, on his part, has suggested (without, however, claiming to have proved conclusively) that there may be a link between the extraordinary development of music throughout Europe from the seventeenth century onward and the growing secularization of European civilization; music, in his view, gradually came to fill the 'emotional void' left by the declining power of religion over people's minds and hearts.[27] There is an element of truth in this argument, especially as regards the eighteenth and nineteenth centuries, when indeed agnosticism and even outright unbelief spread among large sections of the public and yet some of the finest church music was produced. It is not implausible to think that even today Handel's *Messiah* or other masterworks of church music speak to the emotions of the non-believer not only on account of their intrinsic beauty, but also on account of the religiosity that resonates through them and is likely to evoke a kind of nostalgic echo in the soul of the listener. On the other hand, the link between music and secularization does not seem to fit the late sixteenth century and the Baroque age, an age that was still intensely and militantly religious in spite of isolated undercurrents of scepticism and unbelief. As a matter of fact, churchmen of that time, as Koenigsberger himself has noted, saw in music a powerful means for stimulating religious devotion, and we have no reason to assume that a St Filippo Neri in the late sixteenth century or the Italian Jesuits in the seventeenth century promoted oratorios and sung masses as a way of filling an emotional void. It would rather seem that so long as religious sentiment remained strong, as it did in the confessional age, music was seen as a natural component of public worship and an additional source of inspiration, just as it was seen as an indispensable vehicle for expressing emotions in the secular sphere.

HISTORIOGRAPHY

Traditionally, the verdict on seventeenth-century Italian historiography has hardly been more charitable than that on poetry. Unlike the Renaissance

26. De Sanctis, *History of Italian Literature*, vol. 2, pp. 710–11.
27. H.G. Koenigsberger, 'Music and Religion in Early Modern European History' (1971) reprinted in his *Politicians and Virtuosi. Essays in Early Modern History*, Hambledon Press 1986, pp. 179–210.

historians, from Flavio Biondo and Leonardo Bruni in the fifteenth century to Machiavelli and Guicciardini in the sixteenth, who had tried to detect the deeper forces behind the rise and fall of nations, their counterparts in the Baroque age – it was charged – trained their attention on the day-to-day intrigues and backstage manoeuvres of rulers and courtiers, on their personal foibles and petty rivalries, and their works degenerated into collections of titillating gossip in ways that were more suitable to journalists than to serious students of the past.[28] In recent years this verdict has been revised in some important respects. Sergio Bertelli has convincingly argued that it is somewhat unfair to judge seventeenth-century historiography by the standards of the Renaissance period, 'because the frankly political perspective of a Machiavelli or a Guicciardini and their passionate interest in the vicissitudes of states gradually, and not surprisingly, gave way after the coming of the Protestant Reformation and the onset of the Counter-Reformation to a new outlook characterized by a paramount concern over religious history. Given this shift of focus, the best minds, the most serious scholarship were channelled into religious rather than political history, while the latter was left to what today would be called news reporters.[29]

Among church historians pride of place belongs to Cardinal Caesar Baronius (1538–1607), the Oratorian scholar who, as will be recalled, played an important role in the controversies between the Papacy and the governments of Sicily and Venice. He was the author of the monumental *Annales ecclesiatici* in twelve in-folio volumes published between 1588 and 1607 as a response to the equally monumental *Ecclesiastica historia* (better known as the *Magdeburg Centuries*) by Lutheran scholar Flacius Illyricus. The *Annales* were meant to vindicate the legitimacy of papal authority and of the decrees of the Council of Trent against Protestant attacks by methodically assembling original sources bearing on the history of the Church, thus setting new standards of scholarly erudition for church historians.[30] Paolo Sarpi's famous *History of the Council of Trent* (published in London in 1619) provides another (and quite different) example of a major historical work devoted to a religious subject. He wrote in an overtly partisan vein, his aim being that of exposing the manoeuvres of the Papacy as it strove to assert its supremacy over the entire Church, a process which, in his view, negated the true nature of the Church as an evangelical community free of political ambitions, built on consensus rather than command, and committed to

28. Croce, *Storia dell'età barocca*, pp. 106–15; and Benzoni, *Gli affanni della cultura*, pp. 109–14.

29. Sergio Bertelli, 'Storiografi, eruditi, antiquari e politici' in *Storia Garzanti*, pp. 321–3 (for a critique of Croce) and pp. 386–7 (for the shift from political to church history). Giorgio Spini, 'Historiography: the Art of History in the Italian Counter-Reformation' in *The Late Italian Renaissance, 1525–1630*, ed. Eric Cochrane, Harper, New York 1970, pp. 91–133, is especially valuable for his discussion of theories of history.

30. Bertelli, *Ribelli*, pp. 64–9; and Eric Cochrane, *Historians and Historiography in the Italian Renaissance*, University of Chicago Press 1981, pp. 457–63.

poverty. The result was a merciless analysis of backstage politics, but one that ignored the genuine achievements of the Council in the area of dogmatic definitions, ecclesiastical discipline and the reform of long-standing abuses.[31] Another and unintended result was to prompt the Jesuit Pietro Sforza Pallavicini, a distinguished and prolific writer, to undertake his own *History of the Council of Trent* (1656–57) as a refutation of Sarpi's and as an impassioned defence of the Council and the Papacy. This was no mere diatribe, but a serious, if ideologically slanted, historical work, for, in order to counter Sarpi's argument, the Jesuit historian had to marshal all available documentary evidence (and he had more of it at his disposal than Sarpi had had forty years earlier), combining, as Baronius had done before, advocacy with meticulous scholarship.

The same painstaking study of primary sources was at the root of a new field of scholarship, Christian archeology. The path, once again, was opened by Baronius with his *Martyrologium Romanum* (1584). In its wake there developed a new interest in the early Christian centuries and a need was increasingly felt for rigorous studies, such as Antonio Bosio's *Roma sotterranea* (1632) and Ferdinando Ughelli's *Italia sacra* (9 vols, 1643–62), that would do for the early Church what Renaissance humanists had done for pagan antiquity. Not all the historical scholarship of the Counter-Reformation, however, was of the same calibre as Baronius's or Bosio's: as the century wore on it was also applied to the study of the history of religious orders and either turned into sheer antiquarianism or was used as ammunition in what has been called 'the battle of the saints against the saints', in quarrels, that is, that often amounted to little more than popularity contests between religious orders.[32] But in the end there is no denying the impressive contributions made by church historians and archeologists of the Counter-Reformation to the progress of historical methodology and the critical use of original sources. In this way those scholars paved the way for a later generation of historians to apply the same rigorous approach to the study of political, legal and cultural history, a study that was to find in such eighteenth-century scholars as Ludovico Antonio Muratori (1672–1750) and Girolamo Tiraboschi (1731–94) its most distinguished practitioners.[33]

In the seventeenth century political historians, as mentioned earlier, all too often confined themselves to reporting real or alleged courtly intrigues and scandals as well as to trying to penetrate the innermost recesses of princely minds, as yellow journalists rather than scholars.[34] For the best of them, however, the label 'journalist' may, in fact, turn out to be a badge of honour,

31. Gaetano Cozzi, 'Paolo Sarpi' in *Storia Garzanti*, pp. 445 and 453–60; Bertelli, *Ribelli*, pp. 94–5 and 107–8; and Cochrane, *Historians*, pp. 472–8.
32. Bertelli, *Ribelli*, pp. 109–14 (on Sforza Pallavicino) and pp. 70, 77, 84, 91, 120 (on antiquarians and on religious orders).
33. Bertelli, *Ribelli*, pp. 117–39; and Benzoni, *Gli affanni*, pp. 203–19.
34. Chief among them was the scandal-monger Gregorio Leti (1630–1701), author of a three-volume *The State Secrets of the Princes of Europe* (1673–76). On him see Bertelli, *Ribelli*, pp. 182–4 and p. 208 below.

for they must be credited with initiating the practice of reporting the news as we know it: they wrote as eyewitnesses or on the basis of direct contacts with the protagonists of current or recent events, and their works are still considered important sources for our understanding of those events. Arrigo Caterino Davila (1576–1631), for instance, grew up in France the son of an Italian gentleman at the court of Catherine de' Medici and lived through and fought in the final stages of the French wars of religion before his return to his native Padua in 1599. There he entered a career as a civil servant of the Venetian Republic. His *Historia delle guerre civili di Francia* (1630) is based on first-hand knowledge of events and personalities. Sceptical about the religious claims of both sides (Catholic and Huguenot), Davila vividly portrayed the French wars of religion mainly as a struggle between noble factions for the control of the royal government and, within limits, is still a rich source of information for a troubled period of French history. What Davila did for the French wars of religion Guido Bentivoglio (1577–1644) did for the revolt of the Netherlands against Spain. As papal nuncio in the Spanish Low Countries from 1607 to 1615, he had a chance to acquire first-hand knowledge of that country and to meet personalities who had played a role in or had witnessed the long-drawn-out struggle between Calvinists and Catholics. Somewhat surprisingly for a papal diplomat and future cardinal, in his *Historia delle guerre di Fiandra* (1632–39) he seems utterly indifferent to the religious divisions that had rent the Netherlands asunder, his main focus being strictly political. The civil wars that erupted in several European countries in the 1640s found a brilliant reporter in Maiolino Bisaccioni (1582–1663) whose adventurous career as a mercenary soldier, government official and diplomat took him all over Europe and provided him with a wealth of first-hand information for his grand opus, the *Historia delle guerre civili di questi ultimi tempi* published in Venice in 1653–55. Girolamo Brusoni (c. 1614–c. 1686), on his part, filled over one thousand in-folio pages with a year-by-year narrative of Italian events from 1627 to 1680, based in part on his own personal experiences. Vittorio Siri (1608–85) devoted the fifteen volumes of his *Mercurio politico* to a chronicle of European political events from 1635 to 1655 and was rewarded for his labours by being appointed later in life 'royal historiographer' in France.[35]

TRAVEL LITERATURE

The interest in contemporary politics was paralleled by that in distant and exotic lands. Italy could boast a long tradition in this area, going back to Marco Polo's account of his travels through Asia in the late thirteenth century and those produced by Italian explorers such as Amerigo Vespucci and

35. On Davila, Bentivoglio, Bisaccioni and Brusoni see Croce, *Storia dell'età barocca*, pp. 122–32; Bertelli, *Ribelli*, pp. 199–213; and Asor Rosa, *Il Seicento*, pp. 114–20.

Antonio Pigafetta in the sixteenth century. The seventeenth century continued
to produce travel narratives and descriptions of remote countries, not so
much, however, at the hands of professional navigators and explorers, but
rather of missionaries and freelance wanderers.[36] Among the former the Jesuit
Matteo Ricci stands out with his remarkable account of the introduction of
Christianity in China where he lived from 1582 to 1610: in a straightforward,
somewhat lacklustre style he offered an unprecedented and highly
sympathetic inside view of Chinese society, religion and culture. Among the
wanderers one finds the Florentine merchant Francesco Carletti who left for a
slaving voyage to West Africa and America in 1591 and then 'out of curiosity
to see the world' proceeded to India and Japan. On his return to Italy in 1606
he wrote a vivid, matter-of-fact account of his 'journey around the globe'. On
his part, the wealthy Roman nobleman Pietro Della Valle, declaring himself
'sick and tired' of a life spent among the 'delicacies' of high society, embarked
in 1614 on a journey to the Middle East and to India in order to satisfy his
curiosity about the great civilizations of Asia. After twelve years of wandering
he returned to Rome and wrote thousands of pages (eventually published in
four tomes between 1650 and 1663) aiming, as he put it, 'at the truth pure and
simple . . . without any pretence of literary virtuosity'. The result was a richly
textured account full of penetrating observations on the culture and ways of
the countries he visited. Curiosity was also what prompted Francesco Negri, a
learned priest from Ravenna, to set out in 1663 on a three-year journey
through the Scandinavian countries; at the end of his travels he wrote a
Nordic Journey that was published in 1700, two years after his death. The
purpose of his journey was, in his words, 'to observe the diversity of that
beautiful [nordic] world', a diversity that included the customs and way of life
of the Lapps whom he greatly admired for living 'according to the true laws of
nature'.

What is remarkable about this travel literature is that, in spite of the
sometimes enormous size of the travellers' accounts, it did find its way to the
printing press and thus reflects the presence of a reading public eager to learn
about distant lands and cultures. Nor were books the only sources capable of
assuaging the public's curiosity: the proliferation of private collections of
'curiosities' ranging from fossils to exotic plants and animals, to artifacts from
non-European countries was an expression of the same interest in things new
and strange that was so much part of Baroque culture.

BOOKS OF ADVICE

The same attention to the concrete, the factual, the specific that was at the
root of antiquarianism, political journalism, travel literature and, one might

36. What follows is based on Ezio Raimondi, 'Scienziati e viaggiatori' in *Storia
Garzanti*, pp. 242–302.

add, casuistry also gave rise to a new literary genre known as *precettistica* that aimed at providing advice and guidance to people in all walks of life, from cardinals and statesmen to merchants and husbandmen, so as to enable them to conduct themselves appropriately in all circumstances.[37] Out of that vast literature hardly any book has survived the test of time. One that has is *Della dissimulazione onesta* (On Honest Dissembling) written in 1641 by Torquato Accetto, an indifferent poet, but a subtle observer of the human condition in a troubled age. In his little book of advice he argued that 'dissembling' (by which he meant the ability to conceal one's opinions and emotions when to reveal them might cause harm to oneself or to others) is indispensable if one is to protect one's own privacy and to withstand the injustice visited on one by other people or by misfortune.[38] Dissembling, he further argued in a rather moving, melancholy mood, ought to be practiced toward ourselves too, in the sense that occasionally and for brief periods we should erase from our minds the memory of our misfortune and 'entertain some pleasurable thoughts so as not to be always engrossed in the object of our miseries'. This, he wrote, 'is an honest deception, for it is a mild form of oblivion that offers respite to those who suffer . . . a form of sleep for our weary thoughts'.[39] At the root of this kind of advice was a perception of life as a pilgrimage full of sorrows to be borne and of dangers to be avoided as best one can – and concealing our true feelings may at times be the best survival strategy. In other words, Accetto's message was not one of hypocrisy or duplicity aimed at manipulating others for personal gain as the title of his book might suggest at first; rather it was a message addressed to those who endure evils that cannot be avoided, as many could certainly not be avoided in a country devastated by wars and epidemics and oppressed by overbearing rulers and rapacious tax collectors.[40]

37. The search for specificity and concreteness as a defining feature of Italian Baroque culture has been underlined by Asor Rosa, *Il Seicento*, pp. 9 and 20. On casuistry as a manifestation of this, see Alonge, 'Letteratura', p. 465. On 'precettistica', Croce, *Storia dell'età barocca*, pp. 137–51 still provides the best discussion.
38. An English translation in Dooley, *Italy in the Baroque*, pp. 368–84. It should be noted that Accetto drew a distinction between *simulazione* and *dissimulazione*: in the former one simulates something that does not exist (and is thus a form of fraud); in the latter one conceals something that exists (and is thus a form of prudence). On this point see Asor Rosa, *Il Seicento*, pp. 96–105.
39. Quotation in Croce, *Storia dell'età barocca*, p. 158.
40. Rosario Villari, *Elogio della dissimulazione. La lotta politica nel Seicento*, Laterza, Bari 1987, pp. 17–30, has interpreted the practice of dissembling (as advocated by Accetto and, among others, by Sarpi) as a strategy of opposition and protest indispensable in the prevailing climate of repression, a strategy that 'helps explain . . . why new ideas and plans of reform continued to circulate in spite of the great religious divisions and of political obstacles' (p. 18).

POLITICAL THEORY

Not everyone at the time shared Accetto's melancholy resignation. Actually, in the early part of the century quite a lot was written, in a more sanguine vein, on how to reform society from the ground up and many of those blueprints for reform took the form of descriptions of imaginary cities or republics – a literary genre which could boast a glorious ancestry from Plato's *Republic* in ancient times to Thomas More's *Utopia* in the early sixteenth century.[41] More's work had been translated into Italian in 1548 and in the second half of the century had inspired a number of writers to produce their own 'utopias', notably Francesco Doni, its translator, the Platonist philosopher Francesco Patrizi and other lesser authors, each with his own prescription for radical social change. In a class by himself, however, stands Tommaso Campanella, the author of *La città del Sole* (The City of the Sun) written in 1602. Here was the work of a man who had played a leading role in 1599 in a conspiracy in his native Calabria for the overthrow of Spanish rule and the launching of a social revolution against an oppressive feudal regime. The book itself was written in prison where Campanella spent thirty-one years after being convicted of both high treason and heresy; it was, in the words of Luigi Firpo, 'a meditation on a beautiful dream that had failed' and, at the same time, an attempt at fixing on paper the high hopes, the millenarian expectations Campanella had harboured in his mind for a return to a golden age and for a cosmic regeneration based on Christian universalism.[42] Not surprisingly, *The City of the Sun* offers a revolutionary plan for transforming, and not just reforming, society along egalitarian and clearly utopian lines. Later in life its author shifted from this grand utopian vision and, without ever abandoning his hope for a universal community embracing all humanity, advocated the creation of a Christian polity under the joint rule of the pope and the king of Spain as the only way, in his view, for ensuring peace and justice for the entire human race. When this, too, proved to be a chimera as Europe sank deeper and deeper into the horrors of the Thirty Years War, the Spanish monarchy declined and Campanella lost the temporary favour shown to him by Pope Urban VIII between 1629 and 1634, he fled to France and pinned on that nation his final and fragile hope for a universal monarchy.

Even as Campanella was formulating his grand vision of a model society, the utopian genre was already moving in a different direction. Among political theorists of the early seventeenth century one notices a growing dislike for radical utopian plans which were viewed as impractical and therefore unattainable. Aristotle, with his emphasis on a 'mixed' constitution in which

---

41. Full coverage of the subject in Rodolfo De Mattei, *Il pensiero politico italiano nell'età della Controriforma*, vol. 2, Ricciardi, Milan and Naples 1984; and in Perini, 'Gli utopisti', pp. 303–413.
42. Luigi Firpo, *Lo Stato ideale della Controriforma. Ludovico Agostini*, Laterza, Bari 1957, pp. 307–29; and Asor Rosa, *Il Seicento*, pp. 181–3, 206–8 and 231–2.

monarchical, aristocratic and popular forces all had a role to play and with his defence of the indispensable function of private property in ensuring good order and fostering industry, came to be preferred to Plato; in keeping with the spirit of the Counter-Reformation and its insistence on social justice, their main goal was now to correct social evils, especially the glaring economic inequalities they saw all around, rather than to alter radically the entire socio-economic system; accordingly, the leitmotif was not complete equality or the abolition of private property as in earlier utopias, but a less skewed distribution of wealth and the establishment of a welfare system and of strong social discipline as preconditions of social harmony.[43] In his *Repubblica immaginaria* Lodovico Agostini (1536–1609) described in great detail a city built at public expense according to a rational, geometric plan; a city where prices were as strictly regulated as was public entertainment; where usurers and speculators were outlawed and a system of rationing was rigorously enforced; where government was in the hands of an aristocracy of merit, but with checks and balances to prevent the abuse of power. The ultimate goal for him was a society where no one was either destitute or excessively wealthy, basic needs were provided by the state and the highest standards of moral conduct were expected of all citizens – in short, a society that closely reflected the Counter-Reformation vision of a Christian polity. The same concern for a limited measure of equality, the same rejection of greed as the root cause of discord and strife are present in two other utopias of that time, *La repubblica regia* by Fabio Albergati (1538–1606) and *La repubblica di Evandria* by Ludovico Zuccolo (1568–1630). While rejecting communism, both went to great pains to formulate laws that were intended to prevent the excessive concentration of wealth into a few hands and both lay great emphasis on education and social discipline as means of creating harmony among the citizens of an ideal commonwealth. Whether these less radical utopias were any more attainable than More's or Campanella's is, of course, open to doubt, but they must be remembered as evidence of a persisting awareness of social ills and economic inequalities in early seventeenth-century Italy and of a desire 'to reform the world toward true Christian living' which, as will be recalled, was at the heart of the Catholic revival and was manifesting itself, in a piecemeal fashion, in the proliferation of lay confraternities and other charitable institutions.

Drawing up plans for model communities, however, was only one, and not the major, concern of political theorists in the age of the Baroque. Even more prominent in their writings was a theme they had inherited from the Renaissance: the relationship between reason of state and the moral law, between politics and ethics. Machiavelli had solved the dilemma by unequivocally upholding the demands of politics as fully legitimate even when they run counter to the claims of morality. In the intensely religious

---

43. In addition to Firpo's work just cited with its full reconstruction of Agostini's political theory, see De Mattei, *Il pensiero politico*, vol. 2, pp. 249–304, especially for Zuccolo's ideas.

climate of the Counter-Reformation, however, his amoralism was unacceptable and a host of writers undertook the difficult task of trying to reconcile politics and morality, for, as Croce put it, 'they were sensitive, as Machiavelli had not been, to the difficulties, the anguish, the doubts' generated by that conflict, and even though none of them had the intellectual stature of Machiavelli, their writings represent a 'higher stage' in the debate he had opened in that they were keenly aware that the moral conscience cannot be simply brushed aside or ignored.[44]

The solutions offered to the dilemma ranged from the outright condemnation of any form of political conduct that does not square with the principles of Christian morality (a position defended by the distinguished Jesuit theologian, diplomat and poligraph Antonio Possevino [1533–1611]) to the carefully nuanced compromise proposed by Giovanni Botero (1544–1617), a priest who served as secretary to both Carlo and Federico Borromeo. For Botero, a keen analyst of the geographic, economic and institutional factors that lie behind the world of politics, reason of state must be based on the virtue of prudence in the sense of the search of that which is both useful to the state and morally good, in contrast to cunning which seeks only what is expedient. For him prudence must be flexible enough to make room for the complexities of politics, but in saying so he ultimately left the old dilemma unresolved. In the early seventeenth century several other writers (Ludovico Settala, Virgilio Malvezzi, Fabiano Strada among them) confronted the nagging issue, but possibly the most original of them all was Zuccolo, the author, in addition to his description of an ideal republic referred to earlier, of a small book on reason of state (1621) in which he provided a more radical solution to the old dilemma, and one that was widely adopted both in Italy and abroad: 'to act according to reason of state', he wrote, 'means to act according to the essence or form of the state one wishes to preserve or establish'; accordingly, 'if the form of the republic is good, so will the reason of state that pertains to it, and if the form of the republic is bad, we will call unjust the reason of state that is used to support it'; in other words, reason of state is morally as good or as bad as the kind of government it is made to serve. This was a return to Machiavellian utilitarianism, to the view, that is, that the end justifies the means, but with the added caveat that the end pursued must be morally good.[45]

By mid-century both the search for the ideal state and the debate over reason of state had exhausted themselves and attention shifted to other issues. Under the influence of Hugo Grotius's natural law theory Italian jurists and political writers, especially in the Kingdom of Naples, increasingly focused on individual rights as opposed to feudal privilege and on statutory as opposed

44. Croce, *Storia dell'età barocca*, p. 89.
45. The whole debate about reason of state was magisterially presented by Croce, pp. 76–98, and later historians have, in the main, adopted his conclusions: e.g. Romolo Quazza, *Preponderanza spagnola (1559–1700)*, Vallardi, Milan 1950, p. 16; Vittorio De Caprariis, 'Il Seicento' in *Storia d'Italia*, UTET, Turin 1959, vol. 2, pp. 599–600; and Delumeau, *L'Italie*, pp. 209–12.

to customary law, the latter being denounced more and more as the main obstacle to any project of judicial and administrative reform based on rational principles. These, however, were but the beginnings of a trend that would fully develop only in the next century.[46]

PHILOSOPHERS AND LIBERTINES

Seventeenth-century Italy did not produce philosophical minds comparable to those of the Cinquecento – the Paduan Aristotelian Pietro Pomponazzi (1462–1525), the naturalist philosophers Girolamo Cardano (1501–76) and Bernardino Telesio (1509–88), the neo-Platonist Francesco Patrizi (1529–97), or the towering and tragic figure of Giordano Bruno (1548–1600).[47] After them there was little in the way of original philosophical speculation, with the notable exception of Tommaso Campanella whose life straddled the two centuries and whose intellectual journey took him from the naturalism of Telesio, the rejection of Scholasticism and a sharp critique of traditional religion to an attempted reconciliation of modern thought and a rejuvenated Catholic orthodoxy freed from its Aristotelian moorings. Those sixteenth-century philosophers had all, to various degrees, ran afoul of church authorities: Pomponazzi had been condemned on account of his denial of the immortality of the soul, Telesio because of his naturalism that seemed to border on all-out materialism, Patrizi for his critique of the Aristotelian tradition as interpreted by Scholasticism. Bruno had been tried for heresy and burnt at the stake in Rome in 1600 for his denial of the Trinity, of transubstantiation and of the divine origin of Christianity as well as for his assertion that the latter represented the corruption of an earlier, undefiled religion which he associated with ancient Egypt. Campanella, too, suffered at the hands of the Inquisition, although the life sentence he received in 1599 and which kept him in prison for thirty-one years until he was pardoned by Pope Urban VIII resulted both from charges of heresy and from his leading role in the conspiracy to overthrow Spanish rule in Calabria.[48]

The legacy of Renaissance philosophy, insofar as it represented a departure from, or even an outright rejection of, Catholic orthodoxy and proposed a purely rational, naturalistic worldview, did not vanish after 1600, but was kept

46. Salvo Mastellone, *Francesco D'Andrea politico e giurista (1648–1698). L'ascesa del ceto civile*, Olschki, Florence 1969, pp. 8–9 and 44.

47. On Renaissance philosophers see Paul Oskar Kristeller, *Eight Philosophers of the Italian Renaissance*, Stanford University Press 1964; Luigi Firpo, 'The Flowering and Withering of Speculative Philosophy. Italian Philosophy and the Counter-Reformation: the Condemnation of Francesc Patrizi' (1950) reprinted in *The Late Italian Renaissance*, pp. 266–84; and Michele Ciliberto, *Giordano Bruno*, Laterza, Bari 1990.

48. Luigi Firpo, 'Campanella Tommaso' in *Dizionario Biografico degli Italiani*, vol. 17, pp. 372–401.

alive, in spite of the Church's efforts at suppression, by the so-called 'libertines' (often loosely referred to as 'atheists').[49] None of them can even remotely measure up, in terms of originality and breadth of vision, to the sixteenth-century thinkers from whom they drew their inspiration, and their writings are largely and deservedly forgotten. They must be mentioned, at least briefly, if for no other reason than they demonstrate the survival in Counter-Reformation Italy of a strong heterodox undercurrent which ecclesiastical repression failed to stamp out. The presence of the libertines, in other words, requires that we take with a grain of salt the conventional view according to which, under the watchful eye of the Roman Inquisition, any expression of dissent was promptly and effectively silenced and Italian culture was cast in a rigid mould of total conformity and blind acquiescence.[50] In discussing libertinism it is also well to bear in mind that it did not represent a marginal and barely perceptible underground phenomenon. On the contrary, foreign visitors did not fail to notice the conspicuous presence of libertines among Italian intellectuals: the French writer Gabriel Naudé, a libertine himself who lived in Italy in the 1630s, reported that the country 'is full of libertines, of atheists, of individuals who believe in nothing',[51] and although the word 'full' is clearly a hyperbole, the existence of a widespread unorthodox counter-culture is beyond doubt. And apparently it was still alive and conspicuous a century later, if an English visitor could write that many Italians 'are tempted to throw off tradition all at once: [they] assert the eternity of the world; deny the government of Providence; and . . . renounce the God of Nature'.[52] Those unorthodox ideas were not new; they were the legacy of a long philosophical tradition that went back to the late Middle Ages and the Renaissance and identified God with nature, denied that the world had been created and that the soul was immortal, and often dismissed all religions as frauds perpetrated by impostors to keep the rabble quiet. Given these premises, the libertines scoffed at religious beliefs as mere superstitions, ridiculed the Church, championed moral relativism, and postured as an enlightened elite whose views the common people, steeped as they were in ignorance and credulity, could not (and should not) share.[53] A corollary of

---

49. The classic work on the subject is Giorgio Spini, *Ricerca dei libertini. La teoria dell'impostura delle religioni nel Seicento italiano* (1950), revised edn, Nuova Italia, Florence 1983. What follows is largely based on it. A recent, excellent overview is by Nicholas Davidson, 'Unbelief and Atheists in Italy, 1500–1700' in *Atheism from the Reformation to the Enlightenment*, ed. Michael Hunter and David Hutton, Clarendon Press 1992, pp. 55–85. Although not dealing specifically with Italian libertinism Tullio Gregory, *Theophrastus redivivus. Erudizione e ateismo nel Seicento*, Morano, Naples 1979, is also very useful.

50. This point has been duly noted by Spini, *Ricerca dei libertini*, pp. 9 and 205; Bertelli, *Ribelli*, p. 194; and Delumeau, *L'Italie*, pp. 275–6.

51. Quotation in Delumeau, *L'Italie*, p. 276.

52. Quotation in Davidson, 'Unbelief and Atheists', p. 56.

53. Gregory, *Theophrastus redivivus*, pp. 185–7 has highlighted the 'aristocratic conservatism' of the libertines and their profound contempt for the popular masses.

their rejection of all religious beliefs was that one religion was as good as any other and, therefore, all of them ought to be tolerated not so much, it should be noted, in the name of freedom of conscience, but because they assumed that some form, any form of religion was necessary for legitimizing political authority in the eyes of the plebs, thus ensuring the social peace.

Among the many Italian libertines a few stand out, if not for the originality of their ideas, at least for the considerable resonance their writings had at home and abroad. Giulio Cesare Vanini (1585–1619) is an early example: a defrocked Carmelite monk who fled to England, converted to Anglicanism and then moved to France after a feigned reconciliation with the Catholic Church, he was the author of philosophical works in which he expounded a frankly materialistic view of the cosmos and of man, denied creation and mocked all religions as the fabrications of power-hungry political leaders; in the end he paid for his views with his life at the hands of the French Parlement of Toulouse. Libertinism of a far less sophisticated sort was that of Ferrante Pallavicino (1615–44), a nobleman from Piacenza who, after a short stint as a monk, attended the University of Padua, still a hotbed of heterodox Aristotelianism, and then moved to Venice where he joined the Academy of the Unknown (Accademia degli Incogniti), possibly the most important and uninhibited gathering of Italian libertines in the first half of the century. In Venice he earned a living by producing an avalanche of cheap novels that mixed cynicism and obscenities with scurrilous attacks on religion. Hounded by the Inquisition, he was briefly incarcerated on orders of the papal nuncio, but was soon released at the request of the Venetian Senate in whose ranks he had many friends and admirers. His troubles, however, were just starting: after publishing some acrimonious satires in which he savaged Pope Urban VIII and his Barberini nephews, he was persuaded by an undercover agent of the papal government to go to France, supposedly to be welcomed and rewarded by the prime minister Richelieu himself. In fact, he was led, unbeknownst to him, to the papal enclave of Avignon where he was tried (probably on charges of lèse-majesté) and executed. His friend, biographer, fellow Incognito, prolific novelist and historian Girolamo Brusoni was more fortunate: after a short stay in prison, he was set free thanks to the intercession of influential Venetian friends, mended his ways and ended up writing works of impeccable orthodoxy and devotion to the Church.

Outside Venice a libertine who enjoyed enormous fame both in Italy and abroad was Gregorio Leti (1630–1701), the scion of a family of prelates and high-ranking officials. After years spent moving from town to town in Italy and after coming into contact with the Incogniti in Venice, Leti settled in Geneva, Switzerland and converted to Calvinism, most certainly out of convenience rather than conviction. There he wrote numerous erotic novels of the cheapest sort, but also, and more importantly for his reputation, produced a steady stream of books and pamphlets in which he exposed real or alleged scandals in the various courts of Europe and in which he gave vent, whenever possible, to his rabid anticlericalism. Forced to leave Geneva in 1679 on account of some unflattering comments he had made about

Calvinism in his *Life of Philip II*, he moved to France first and then to England. His stay in that country was cut short following the publication of a book in which he exposed some amorous indiscretions by members of the royal family. He spent most of his remaining years in Amsterdam churning out his venomous invectives.

With Pallavicino and Leti we have drifted a long way from philosophy. Yet there is a tenuous link between their writings, even at their most shallow and vulgar, and some of the heterodox strands of Renaissance philosophy, for it is from the latter that those writers borrowed and adapted, in however superficial and even distorted form, their assumptions about religion as fraud, the mortality of the soul and, to a lesser extent, their moral relativism. But it would be a mistake to conclude that in seventeenth-century Italy libertinism represented all that was left in terms of philosophical interests or that Italian culture was deaf to the philosophical ideas then being debated north of the Alps. For, in fact, genuine interest in philosophy did enjoy a revival in the second half of the century, notably in Naples among the educated elite (largely recruited from the *ceto civile* or liberal professions) as it came into contact with the works of René Descartes and Pierre Gassendi in the field of philosophy proper, and of Hugo Grotius and Samuel Pufendorf in the field of jurisprudence and natural law theory.[54] Much of the credit for exposing the Neapolitan intelligentsia to new ideas from across the Alps belongs to Tommaso Cornelio (1614–84), a distinguished mathematician and physician who had been trained under two foremost students of Galileo, Evangelista Torricelli and Bonaventura Cavalieri, and had enthusiastically embraced the new experimental method in the natural sciences. Called upon in 1649 to teach medicine at the University of Naples, he brought along a library well stocked with the most significant philosophical and scientific works recently published in France and England. A group of like-minded men soon gathered around Cornelio to discuss and debate the new ideas, particularly Descartes's rationalism and Gassendi's atomistic philosophy, and to criticize the Aristotelianism then prevailing in academic quarters. In the course of time the learned group came to include some of the best minds Naples could offer – from Bishop Giovanni Caramuel (1606–82), a friend of Descartes, to the distinguished jurist Francesco D'Andrea (1625–98), to the physician and literary critic Leonardo di Capua (1617–95), to the celebrated attorney Giuseppe Valletta (1636–1714) who built a remarkable private library and opened it to the public. Together and under the patronage of a prominent nobleman, Andrea Concublet Marquess of Arena, in 1663 they formed the Accademia degli Investiganti (Academy of the Inquirers), one of the few academies of the century that did not indulge in the mere exercise of rhetorical talent or in idle debates on vacuous topics that were so fashionable at the time, and instead discussed the new philosophical and scientific ideas then current in Europe, with a predilection for Gassendi's and Descartes's – a predilection that was tempered, however, by the belief that all scientific

54. Croce, *Storia dell'età barocca*, pp. 211–27.

conclusions are only probable and, as such, always open to revision in light of new findings. It was that group, too, that, by embracing the notion of natural law as something that is based on reason alone and is, therefore, entitled to supersede customary, feudal and ecclesiastical law, paved the way to the legal reforms and the battles against the Roman Curia that were to loom so large in the Kingdom of Naples during the eighteenth century.[55]

From about 1650 to the 1680s the intellectual circle that gathered around Cornelio was left undisturbed by church authorities in spite of its overt anti-Aristotelianism and its advocacy of 'freedom of inquiry'.[56] In the 1680s, however, as a more rigorist climate (the 'Tridentine revival') set in the Church, the terms 'libertine' and 'atheist' came to be used interchangeably in Neapolitan ecclesiastical circles to brand anyone who subscribed or was suspected to subscribe to Gassendi's and Descartes's theories, notably their mechanistic view of the cosmos as consisting of atoms or corpuscules; their Aristotelian critics assumed that such theories inevitably led to a denial of the universe as God's creation and of the Catholic dogma of the Real Presence in the Eucharist resulting from transubstantiation. As the latter concept rested on the Aristotelian notions of substance and accident which atomism denied, there was understandable concern among theologians that the spread of atomism would undermine faith in the Real Presence. Little wonder, then, that the mechanistic and atomistic views of the universe came under attack early on. Galileo himself, as will be seen, had briefly come under a cloud of suspicion on this score. On his part, Descartes was vigorously criticized by Antoine Arnauld, one of the foremost Jansenist theologians in seventeenth-century France, precisely because his corpuscular theory of matter seemed to deny transubstantiation – a charge Descartes tried to counter, apparently with little success. In 1663, long after his death, his *Meditations on First Philosophy* were placed on the Index of Prohibited Books in Rome and in 1671 the teaching of Cartesianism was excluded from the curriculum of the University of Paris.[57] For all this, Descartes's ideas, and to a lesser extent Gassendi's,

55. The vibrant cultural climate in Naples at this time is discussed by Pasquale Lopez, *Riforma cattolica e vita religiosa e culturale a Napoli dalla fine del Cinquecento ai primi anni del Settecento*, Istituto Editoriale del Mezzogiorno, Naples and Rome 1964, pp. 142–57; Mastellone, *Francesco D'Andrea*, pp. 42–3, 97, and 107–20; Ugo Baldini, 'La scuola galileiana' in *SIE Annali* 3 (1980), p. 456; Maurizio Torrini, 'L'Accademia degli Investiganti. Napoli 1663–70', *QS* 48 (1981), pp. 845–83; and Giuseppe Galasso, *Napoli spagnola dopo Masaniello. Politica, cultura, società*, Sansoni, Florence 1982, pp. 85–120 and 391–424.
56. Spini, *Ricerca dei libertini*, p. 333 calls this 'a sort of tacit armistice' between theologians and philosophers. The expression 'freedom of inquiry' (*libertà nello investigare*) was used by Di Capua (Mastellone, *Francesco D'Andrea*, p. 168).
57. John H. Brooke, *Science and Religion. Some Historical Perspectives*, Cambridge University Press, 1991, p. 142; William B. Ashworth Jr., 'Catholicism and Early Modern Science' in *God and Nature. Historical Essays on the Encounter between Christianity and Science*, ed. David C. Lindberg and Ronald L. Numbers, University of California Press, Berkeley 1986, pp. 140 and 151–2.

continued to be discussed in Italy, particularly in Naples and in Florence, causing alarm in some church quarters. In 1671 Rome had voiced its concern over reports that in Naples 'there are some who, in order to flaunt their talents, promote certain philosophical ideas of someone named Renato de Cartes who has revived the ancient Greeks' opinions concerning atoms' and declared those ideas to be 'pernicious'.[58] In the 1680s D'Andrea himself, who had written in defence of Di Capua's scientific work against a Jesuit theologian, was variously denounced, in spite of his well-known piety, as a libertine, an atheist, a rebel and even a 'new Masaniello'.[59] Rumours began to circulate that a number of 'young men' were embracing atomism and were questioning the existence of God and the immortality of the soul. Things came to a head in 1688 when an otherwise obscure lawyer, Francesco Paolo Mannuzzi, formally denounced before the office of the Inquisition in Naples several individuals (among them the distinguished mathematician Giacinto De Cristofaro) alleging that they all belonged to the 'impious Epicurean sect' – another code word for libertinism or atheism.[60] Not until 1691 were the accused formally charged and incarcerated and only then did the celebrated 'trial of the atheists' get under way. It was going to drag on until 1697, mainly because the proceedings were repeatedly suspended (while the defendants sat in prison) for months in a row as the Neapolitan civil authorities quarrelled with Rome over whether a judge appointed by the Inquisition or the archbishop of Naples had jurisdiction over the case.[61] In the end the court found De Cristofaro 'vehemently suspect of heresy', that is to say it convicted him of having held heretical ideas, albeit without evil intent. He was asked to recant (which he did) and sentenced (like Galileo some sixty years earlier) to house arrest. By seventeenth-century standards it was a mild sentence indeed: in that same year, in Presbyterian Scotland, Thomas Aikenhead, a twenty-year-old university student, was convicted by a secular court of much the same offences as De Cristofaro (ridiculing Scripture, denying the divinity of Christ, and asserting the eternity of the universe). Even though he expressed remorse and blamed his errors on 'some atheistical books' (and these probably included Pomponazzi's and Vanini's writings), he was executed within a week of sentencing.[62]

The Naples trial of the atheists, it has been written, was 'the first confrontation between the modern genuinely secular spirit . . . and clerical

58. Quotation in Spini, *Ricerca dei libertini*, p. 348 n. See also Lopez, *Riforma cattolica*, pp. 158–9.

59. Mastellone, *Francesco D'Andrea*, pp. 10 and 170–3.

60. A detailed reconstruction of the whole affair has been provided by Luciano Osbat, *L'Inquisizione a Napoli. Il processo agli ateisti, 1688–1697*, Edizioni di Storia e Letteratura, Rome 1974.

61. On the quarrel as to who had jurisdiction over the case see Galasso, *Napoli spagnola*, pp. 445–70.

62. Michael Hunter, ' "Aikenhead the Atheist": the Context and Consequences of Articulate Irreligion in the Late Seventeenth Century' in *Atheism from the Reformation*, pp. 221–54.

obscurantism'; church authorities 'had no doubts about the true nature of that culture and the harmful influence which, from their point of view, it could have on the very drive for renewal then under way in the Church'.[63] This, however, is unconvincing. True enough, the trial was perceived in some quarters at the time as a warning against all those who, like the Investiganti, rejected Aristotelianism in favour of Descartes's and Gassendi's philosophy. Yet, the actual charges brought against De Cristofaro indicate that the new philosophical ideas were not the Inquisition's prime targets. De Cristofaro was accused of denying the existence of God, the divinity of Christ, the immortality of the soul, papal authority, and of 'holding that there had been other men before Adam'.[64] Basically these were all views that had long formed the core of Renaissance naturalism and even more so of seventeenth-century libertinism and those views had been repeatedly condemned over the previous two centuries; no self-respecting ecclesiastical court could have failed to condemn them as heresy when they resurfaced in Naples in the 1680s. At the same time it is remarkable that nothing was said in their verdict about Descartes's rationalism or Gassendi's atomism except for a brief reference to 'men being made of atoms like other animals'. Moreover, neither D'Andrea nor Valletta, who, loyal and devout Catholics though they were, had shared De Cristofaro's interest in French philosophy, were ever formally charged or silenced in spite of the virulent attacks levelled at them by staunch defenders of Aristotelianism. As a matter of fact, after the trial the circle of intellectuals that gathered around these two men continued to thrive and it was in its midst that young Giambattista Vico (1688–1744), the leading philosophical mind of eighteenth-century Italy, was soon to find inspiration and encouragement. What is even more remarkable is that Cartesianism continued to be studied and discussed, for its scientific implications, by the most serious among the Jesuits of Naples, in spite of the intemperate diatribes of some of their confrères,[65] and that in 1695 Archbishop Cantelmo, the very prelate who had presided over the trial of the atheists, appointed to a chair in the Naples seminary the learned priest Carlo Giuseppe Majello, a friend of Valletta and an admirer of Descartes. Not only did Cantelmo shield him from his detractors and keep him on the seminary faculty, but after Cantelmo's death, Majello was appointed prefect of the Vatican Library.[66] In short, the trial of the atheists must be seen not so much as the first confrontation between the Church and an emerging modern culture, but rather as the epilogue of the long-drawn-out battle between the Church and Italian libertinism.

63. Galasso, *Napoli spagnola*, p. 443.
64. The text of the charges in Osbat, *L'Inquisizione a Napoli*, p. 243.
65. Romeo De Maio, *Società e vita religiosa a Napoli nell'età moderna (1656–1799)*, Edizioni Scientifiche Italiane, Naples 1971, pp. 74–7 and 124–5.
66. On Cantelmo's reform of the curriculum see De Maio, *Società evita religiosa*, p. 65. On Maiello and other churchmen sympathetic to Cartesianism, see Lopez, *Riforma cattolica*, pp. 203–22.

CHAPTER SEVEN

Science

If seventeenth-century Italian culture was rather barren in the area of philosophy proper, it was not due to intellectual torpor, but because some of the best minds at the time trained their attention on 'natural philosophy', on what we now call science. And even though their investigations raised some fundamental epistemological and metaphysical issues, Italian scientists did not pursue those issues in a systematic way, but focused instead on the study of natural phenomena.

The shift from philosophy to science[1] is perhaps best illustrated by comparing two intellectual giants, one (Giordano Bruno) epitomizing the achievements of the Renaissance philosophy of nature, the other (Galileo Galilei) the new interest in science. Superficially, there are similarities between the two, for both repudiated traditional Aristotelian–Ptolemaic cosmology in favour of Copernicanism and both ran afoul of the Inquisition. The differences, however, outweigh the similarities: Bruno was condemned not for his support of Copernicus's heliocentric theory, but for his assertion of the eternity and infinity of the cosmos, for his identification of God with the 'soul of the universe', for his denial of the divinity of Christ and for his denunciation of Christianity as a degenerate form of religion.[2] Galileo, on the other hand, was condemned for having 'held and defended' the Copernican theory in violation of a 1616 ruling by the Inquisition that the theory was contrary to Scripture. More significantly, Bruno adopted Copernicanism not because it offered a better explanation of methodically observed phenomena, but because it somehow fitted his mystical and naturalistic vision of an infinite universe in which all celestial bodies, the earth included, are living creatures

1. The shift was noted by Benedetto Croce, *Storia dell'età barocca in Italia*, 2nd edn, Laterza, Bari 1935, p. 485: while lamenting the decadence of Italian culture in general (including philosophy), Croce saw in the pursuit of the natural sciences 'the only living source of intellectual and moral uplift' left to the country.
2. Giorgio Spini, *Ricerca dei libertini. La teoria dell'impostura delle religioni nel Seicento italiano*, 2nd edn, Nuova Italia, Florence 1983, pp. 80–1; and Michele Ciliberto, *Giordano Bruno*, Laterza, Bari 1990, pp. 59 (on Bruno's criticism of some aspects of Copernicanism) and 264 (for the charges levelled at Bruno).

in constant motion. Galileo, by contrast, embraced the new heliocentric cosmology because, in his view, it provided the best explanation of astronomical phenomena, but did not incorporate it into an overarching philosophical theory. And one must add that, unlike Bruno, he remained a loyal Catholic to the end of his life.

GALILEO'S SCIENCE

Galileo was born in Pisa in 1564, the son of Vincenzo Galilei, a distinguished musician who had made some important contributions to musical theory as well as to the rise of new musical forms that foreshadowed the opera. At his father's request, in 1581 Galileo registered as a medical student at the University of Pisa, but left for Florence four years later without completing his degree. It was in Florence that the mathematician and court tutor Ostilio Ricci (1540–1603) introduced him to the study of Euclid's geometry and Archimedes's mechanics and thus laid the groundwork for Galileo's lifelong commitment to the mathematical and experimental approach to science. His earliest original contribution in that field (influenced no doubt by his study of Archimedes) was the invention in 1586 of a hydrostatic balance for the measurement of the specific weight of objects; this was followed the next year by an important study on the centre of gravity of parabolic conic figures. On the strength of these early accomplishments and thanks to the help of influential patrons he was appointed in 1589 to the chair of mathematics at Pisa. It was a poorly paid and unglamorous position, for mathematics was regarded as definitely inferior to such prestigious academic disciplines as philosophy, theology or the law. While at Pisa, Galileo taught courses on Euclid's geometry, Ptolemaic astronomy and Aristotelian physics, notably the theory of motion. Even though most of his teaching at the time followed traditional lines, Galileo began to entertain doubts about some of Aristotle's basic conclusions, such as the notion that the earth cannot possibly rotate on its axis because this would involve an 'unnatural' motion. His reading at that time of Copernicus's great work *On the Revolutions of the Celestial Spheres* (1543) may have further encouraged him to question the Aristotelian view of the immobility and centrality of the earth in the universe, to consider the possibility that the sun rather than the earth is at the centre of the universe, and to attempt to find (as Copernicus had not done) a physical proof for it.[3] All of which did not endear him to his Aristotelian colleagues and may have been one main reason why he applied for a position at the University of Padua whose faculty he joined in 1592 as professor of mathematics.

3. Annibale Fantoli, *Galileo. For Copernicanism and for the Church*, transl. George V. Coyne S.J., Vatican Observatory Publications, Vatican City 1994, p. 55. Paul Oskar Kristeller, *Eight Philosophers of the Italian Renaissance*, Stanford University Press 1964, p. 138, has raised the possibility that Galileo was influenced by Bruno's cosmology.

Padua was at the time a prestigious institution, renowned for its schools of medicine and of philosophy. The latter was dominated by the distinguished philosopher Cesare Cremonini (1550–1631), a representative of the Paduan tradition of Averroistic Aristotelianism that was quite distinct from, and in many respects opposed to, the Thomistic tradition (which the Council of Trent had consecrated as the official philosophy of the Church) in that it rejected, on strictly rational grounds, the notions of the creation of the world and of the immortality of the soul. Shortly before Galileo's arrival, the University of Padua had also had on its faculty another eminent Aristotelian, Jacopo Zabarella (1533–89), who had advocated the use of the inductive method based on empirical observations for the study of natural philosophy, and Galileo would one day acknowledge his debt to Zabarella's methodology. In Padua he also came into contact with other intellectual currents, for the city boasted, as no other Italian city did at the time, a climate of relative cultural tolerance and a cosmopolitan openness made possible, and in fact promoted, by the Venetian Republic whose government was then dominated, as will be recalled, by the so-called 'young', by a faction, that is, that advocated closer ties with France and even with Protestant countries in order to offset Spanish (and papal) hegemony in Italy. During his eighteen-year tenure at Padua Galileo thus became part of a lively cultural milieu where he made friends (and often engaged in spirited debates) with intellectuals as diverse as the Aristotelian Cremonini, the Jesuit Platonist Antonio Possevino, the combative friar Paolo Sarpi, and briefly met the two foremost champions of the Counter-Reformation, Cardinals Bellarmine and Baronius when they visited the town.[4] In 1595 Galileo turned his attention to the study of the tides and concluded that they could only be explained as the mechanical result of the two motions of the earth (rotation on its axis and revolution around the sun) proposed by Copernicus half a century earlier. Although this mechanical explanation of the tides was wrong, it marked the start of Galileo's 'conversion' to heliocentrism at least in the sense that he considered it more probable than the geocentric theory.[5] For some years yet, however, astronomy and cosmology were not going to be Galileo's overriding interests, as the study of motion continued to occupy his mind: in those years he achieved some major breakthroughs (notably as regards the pendulum, the

4. The intellectual milieu at Padua and its influence on Galileo is discussed by Gaetano Cozzi, 'Galileo Galilei, Paolo Sarpi e la società veneziana' in his *Paolo Sarpi tra Venezia e l'Europa*, Einaudi, Turin 1979, pp. 135–60. Roberto Maiocchi, 'La rivoluzione scientifica del Seicento' in *SSI*, vol. 11, pp. 440–3, stresses the intellectual debt Galileo owed both to Aristotelianism and to Platonism. On Zabarella's inductive methodology see P.O. Kristeller, *Renaissance Thought: The Classic, Scholastic and Humanist Strains*, Harper and Row, New York 1961, p. 38. On Cremonini's unorthodox Aristotelianism, Fantoli, *Galileo*, pp. 51 and 91.
5. Stillman Drake, *Galileo*, Oxford University Press 1980, p. 29. Fantoli, *Galileo*, p. 64 notes that until 1595 Galileo had considered the Copernican system only more probable than the geocentric system and that his adherence to the former had been only tentative.

law of free-falling bodies and the law of inertia) that ran counter to the generally accepted principles of Aristotelian physics.

Astronomy attracted Galileo's attention again in 1604, when a *nova* was sighted in the sky by several observers. According to Aristotelian principles no such thing as a 'new star' could possibly exist, for, by definition, the heavens, being perfect, are also unchanging; change is possible only in the sublunar world, that is to say on or near the earth. *Novae*, in this view, must be explained not as astronomical, but as meteorological phenomena located in the sublunar atmosphere. Galileo, on his part, argued, on the basis of careful observations and measurements of angles, that the nova was indeed a true star. This was his first public confrontation with Aristotelian cosmology and it led to a lively debate with his friend and colleague Cremonini who defended the traditional distinction between terrestrial matter and celestial substance (the 'quintessence') and argued that ordinary rules of measurement do not apply to the vast distances of the heavens.

The debate over the nova was still a temporary diversion in Galileo's main work which continued to be focused on motion until 1609. In that year, however, he heard from his friend and fellow scientist Sarpi of the recent invention in Holland of a marvellous new optical instrument, the spyglass (shortly to be re-named telescope) that made distant objects appear closer. Galileo at once had one such instrument made for himself and trained it toward the night sky. In December 1609 he detected mountains and craters on the surface of the moon (an observation that dealt another blow to the Aristotelian notion of the perfection of celestial bodies) and found that the Milky Way consisted of innumerable stars rather than of dense ether as previously assumed. A month later he discovered four satellites revolving around the planet Jupiter – a finding that disproved the notion that all celestial bodies circle the motionless hub of the cosmos, that is the earth. In March 1610 he presented his discoveries in the *Sidereal Messenger*, a book that generated enormous excitement among the educated public, but also elicited the negative reaction of most 'natural philosophers', such as Cremonini, who dismissed Galileo's observations as optical illusions produced by his lenses. Even after Jesuit astronomers, having obtained a telescope of their own, were able to confirm Galileo's observations, strong reservations persisted as to what to make of them – so entrenched was the belief that the moon must be perfectly spherical and its surface smooth.

The *Sidereal Messenger*, however, had raised its author to such a level of celebrity that he was soon offered a prestigious appointment, free of teaching responsibilities, as court mathematician and philosopher by the grand duke of Tuscany, Cosimo II.[6] It was in Florence that Galileo made another crucial

6. The role of Medici and (later) papal patronage in Galileo's scientific career is analysed by Mario Biagioli, *Galileo Courtier*, University of Chicago Press, Chicago 1993. While providing valuable insights on a largely neglected aspect of the story, Biagioli has gone too far in arguing that the patron–client relationship was a major factor in determining the course of Galileo's scientific work. For a critique of Biagioli, see Fantoli, *Galileo*, p. 146, and Michael H. Schank, 'Galileo's Day in

discovery, that of the moon-like phases of the planet Venus. This showed conclusively that Venus revolved around the sun rather than around the earth as traditionally assumed, but did not provide final proof of the validity of the heliocentric system, for the phases of Venus could be accommodated equally well in the geocentric cosmological model proposed by the great Danish astronomer Tycho Brahe (1546–1601), a model in which the planets revolve around the sun and the sun revolves with them around a motionless earth. In 1611 Galileo journeyed to Rome and received a hero's welcome at the hands of the Jesuit astronomers of the Collegio Romano (the Jesuit university), of several cardinals and of the prestigious Lincei (the Lynx-Eyed) Academy, a learned society established in 1603 under the patronage of Prince Federico Cesi and dedicated to the promotion of new ideas, notably in the sciences, and inspired by a desire (not uncommon at the time, as will be recalled) to reject 'the authority of this or that ancient writer' in favour of 'reading the book of the universe'.[7] All this admiration for Galileo's astronomical work, it should be noted, did not reflect any widespread adherence to the new heliocentric cosmology: actually, most members of the intelligentsia of the time apparently either did not grasp all the implications of Galileo's discoveries or assumed, as was common at the time, that astronomy, however useful for mapping or predicting the movements of heavenly bodies, had little to do with the 'real' structure of the heavens – the latter being the province of the natural philosopher rather than of the astronomer. Whatever the case, it is revealing that a priest friend of Galileo's, Paolo Gualdo, informed him in the spring of 1611 that 'as to the matter of the Earth turning around, I have found hitherto no philosopher or astrologer who is willing to subscribe to the opinion of Your Honour, and much less would a theologian want to do so'; he went on to say that 'the contrary opinion is held by everyone' and prophetically warned Galileo of the risks that an outright endorsement of the Copernican system might entail.[8]

Upon his return to Florence Galileo became involved in a debate with some Aristotelian philosophers over the nature and causes of flotation and out of the debate came a new book of his, the *Discourse on Bodies in Water* (1612), a book that was an immediate success and sold two editions in one year. His next achievement, the *Letter on Sunspots* published in Rome the following year under the auspices of the Lincei Academy, represents a turning point in his life not so much because, on the basis of systematic observations and measurements of the daily movements of sunspots, he was able to prove

Court', *Journal for the History of Astronomy* 25 (1994), pp. 236–43.

7. On the Lincei Academy, see Ezio Raimondi, 'Scienziati e viaggiatori' in *Storia della Letteratura italiana*, ed. Emilio Cecchi and Natalino Sapegno, vol. 5: *Il Seicento*, Garzanti, Milan 1967, p. 230. Jean-Michel Gardair, 'I Lincei: i soggetti, i luoghi, le attività', *QS* 48 (1981), pp. 763–88 has emphasized the dilettante approach to science of most of its members, Cesi and Galileo being notable exceptions.
8. Quotation in Fantoli, *Galileo*, p. 117.

that the spots themselves are actually on the sun's surface and that the sun rotates around its axis, but because it was in that book that for the first time he openly and unequivocally endorsed the Copernican system and was drawn, much against his will, into a theological debate.

The first salvo in that debate was fired late in 1613 at the court of Christina of Lorraine, grand duchess dowager of Tuscany. She had invited a number of academics from the University of Pisa to a reception in the course of which she asked one of them, the Benedictine monk Benedetto Castelli, a student of Galileo's and now professor of mathematics, to explain and discuss Galileo's latest astronomical discoveries. It was then that one of the guests, Cosimo Boscaglia, professor of philosophy and a strict Aristotelian, made the point that Copernicanism must be wrong for it contradicted certain passages in the Bible that refer to the stability of the earth and to the motion of the sun. Castelli replied that strictly scientific matters ought to be discussed on their own merits rather than on the basis of a literalist reading of the Bible; shortly afterwards he sent Galileo an account of the incident. Galileo responded with a long *Letter to Castelli*,[9] in which he fully endorsed his former student's viewpoint and elaborated on it by arguing that the biblical authors, when dealing with matters not pertinent to salvation, used either metaphorical expressions or the language used by ordinary people in everyday life as their purpose was not to teach science; scientists, by contrast, must proceed on the basis of 'sense experiences and cogent demonstrations'. In other words, Galileo drew a sharp distinction between the religious message of the Bible and the findings of science (the former being the province of the theologian, the latter of the scientist) and concluded that no contradiction need exist between the two. In saying so he no doubt felt confident that the debate had been settled, the more so as he could find in St Augustine and in Thomas Aquinas solid precedents for his position, since both had warned against linking religious faith to matters or theories that had no relevance to salvation.[10]

The debate, however, far from being settled, was just starting. In 1614 a young Dominican named Tommaso Caccini, who held the chair of Scripture at the Florence cathedral and, like most Dominicans at the time held to very traditional positions in philosophy and theology, preached a fiery sermon in Florence in which he excoriated the 'mathematicians' of the Galileist persuasion for spreading ideas contrary to Scripture. The sermon shocked those in and outside Florence who held Galileo in high esteem and influential voices were raised demanding an apology from Caccini's superiors. But one of Caccini's confrères, Father Lorini, kept up the attack, deeply disturbed as

9. Translations of the *Letter* are available in Maurice A. Finocchiaro, *The Galileo Affair. A Documentary History*, University of California Press, Berkeley 1989, pp. 49–55, and in Richard J. Blackwell, *Galileo, Bellarmine and the Bible*, University of Notre Dame Press, Notre Dame, Ind. 1991, pp. 195–201.
10. On this point see Mario D'Addio, *Considerazioni sui processi a Galileo*, Herder, Rome 1985, pp. 23–6.

he was that a mere mathematician had dared to discuss theological questions: in February 1615 he submitted a copy of the *Letter to Castelli* to the Inquisition in Rome for examination.[11] The response from that quarter was that the letter was theologically unexceptionable and the case was closed – or so it seemed at the time. Galileo, on his part, must have felt so confident that his rejection of a literalist exegesis based on the distinction between religious truth and scientific truth was fully acceptable and that his scientific work could proceed without obstructions from church authorities, that in 1615 he circulated an expanded version of his letter to Castelli and addressed it to Grand Duchess Christina. His intent was not to persuade church authorities formally to endorse Copernicanism (or, for that matter, any other cosmology), but rather to persuade them not to take sides in a strictly scientific debate. Only in this way, he felt, would the Church be spared the embarrassment of opposing a scientific theory that some day might prove to be true, for this would discredit the Church itself – or, as Blaise Pascal was to put it some forty years later, would 'render our religion contemptible'.[12]

At the time he wrote his letter to the grand duchess Galileo's confidence must have been reinforced by the recent publication of a *Letter Concerning the Opinion of the Pythagoreans and Copernicus About the Mobility of the Earth and The Stability of the Sun* by the respected theologian Paolo Antonio Foscarini.[13] It was meant to demonstrate that 'that opinion agrees with, and is reconciled with, the passages of Sacred Scripture and theological propositions which are commonly adduced against it'. Foscarini fully concurred with Galileo's view that biblical passages that merely describe natural phenomena rather than convey religious truths do so by using ordinary language and are not intended 'to instruct us in the truths of the secrets of nature': the latter are the proper province of scientific investigation while only matters pertaining to faith and morals are to be decided by the Church in its teaching capacity. He then engaged in a close analysis of controversial passages in the Bible to prove that they were not incompatible with Copernicanism. Although he professed neutrality toward the two competing cosmologies (Ptolemaic and Copernican), he claimed that the latter was at least as probable as the former, and indeed seemed to suggest that it was more so.

11. The fact that Galileo's early accusers were Dominican friars was no mere accident: at the time they formed the more conservative wing of the Church, whereas the Jesuits (at least until 1616) stood for greater openness toward the new science and, in fact, made significant contributions to it. The differences and rivalries between the two orders is analysed by Rivka Feldhay, *Galileo and the Church. Political Inquisition or Critical Dialogue?*, Cambridge University Press 1995, pp. 37–44, and pp. 240–52 for the Jesuits' admiration for and support of Galileo's early discoveries.
12. A translation of the letter to Christina in Finocchiaro, *The Galileo Affair*, pp. 87–119. Pascal's quotation in Carl J. Friedrich, *The Age of the Baroque 1610–1660*, Harper and Row, New York 1962, p. 100.
13. A translation of Foscarini's letter in Blackwell, *Galileo, Bellarmine*, pp. 217–51.

219

Galileo's optimism in the likelihood that the Church would not stand in the way of the new cosmology was not shared by many, not even by his closest friends. From Venice Giovanni Sagredo and Paolo Sarpi, both strongly critical of Aristotelian physics and Ptolemaic astronomy, had advised him as early as 1612 to pursue his scientific work quietly and without publicity lest 'the truth might run into difficulties'.[14] From Rome another friend, Monsignor Giovanni Ciampoli, relayed to him in February 1615 that two influential cardinals, Maffeo Barberini (the future Pope Urban VIII) and Roberto Bellarmine, much as they admired him, urged caution and advised him 'not to exceed the limits of physics and mathematics, because the explication of the Scriptures is restricted to theologians'.[15] The Florentine ambassador in Rome was more blunt: 'this is no place . . . to bring and defend new doctrines', for the pope 'cannot stand all these novelties' and 'there are monks and others that are ill disposed toward him [Galileo]'.[16] And the ambassador was right, for since the publication of the *Sidereal Messenger* in 1610 opposition to Galileo had been gaining steam, especially among professors of natural philosophy. In Bologna opposition was led by Giovanni Antonio Magini; in Pisa by Ludovico delle Colombe, the author of treatise *Against the Motion of the Earth* (1611) in which he not only questioned Copernicanism on philosophical (Aristotelian) grounds, but also raised the stakes by arguing that it contradicted the literal sense of the Bible as generally understood by the Church. Meanwhile in Florence opposition to Galileo continued unabated at the hands of the Dominicans Caccini and Lorini with Copernicanism being increasingly branded as heretical.[17]

Faced with so much opposition and more or less overt insinuations that he was a heretic, late in 1615 Galileo decided, much against the advice of his friends and of the Florentine ambassador to Rome, to journey to the Eternal City there to plead his case with the highest church authorities. He was well received both by high-ranking members of the papal Curia and by the Jesuit scientists of the Collegio Romano, and was offered every opportunity to debate the new astronomy with various groups of specialists as well as before large lay audiences. He dazzled them all with his command of science, his dialectical brilliance and his effective use of sarcasm against his opponents. The results of his visit, however, turned out be the very opposite of what he had anticipated: precisely because his performance had generated so much interest and excitement, it had also caused growing anxiety among the more

14. Cozzi, 'Galileo Galilei', pp. 199–200 and 207.
15. Quotation in Blackwell, *Galileo, Bellarmine*, p. 74.
16. Quotation in Alberto Asor Rosa, *Il Seicento: la Nuova Scienza e la crisi del Barocco*, vol. 1, Laterza, Bari 1974, p. 465. See also Giorgio de Santillana, *The Crime of Galileo*, University of Chicago Press 1959, p. 119.
17. Blackwell, *Galileo, Bellarmine*, pp. 59–63; and Robert S. Westman, 'The Copernicans and the Churches' in *God and Nature. Historical Essays on the Encounter between Christianity and Science*, ed. David C. Lindberg and Ronald L. Numbers, University of California Press, Berkeley 1986, p. 99.

conservative church leaders.[18] Galileo, on his part, made a last-ditch effort to salvage his position: he asked a friendly Cardinal Orsini to submit to Pope Paul V what he considered the conclusive proof of the validity of the heliocentric system, namely his theory of the tides. It was a tactical mistake: far from being convinced, the pope was alarmed and turned the whole matter over to the Inquisition requesting a formal review of the Copernican system.[19] The response came on 23 February 1616: the proposition that the sun is at rest at the centre of the universe was declared 'foolish and absurd in philosophy [i.e. from a scientific standpoint] and formally heretical inasmuch as it expressely contradicts the doctrine of Holy Scripture'; the proposition that the earth is not the centre of the universe was said to deserve 'the same censure in philosophy' and to be 'at least erroneous in faith'; as such, neither proposition could be 'defended or held'. On 5 March the Congregation of the Index issued a decree which, after declaring the heliocentric theory 'false and altogether opposed to Holy Scripture', condemned Foscarini's *Letter* outright, but merely proscribed Copernicus's book 'until it be amended'. The different treatment of the two works is revealing: by condemning the former without appeal the Congregation was sending a clear signal to the effect that any attempt at reconciling heliocentrism with Scripture would not be tolerated, presumably because such a reconciliation would imply a rejection of the literalist reading of biblical texts; on the other hand, by merely suspending Copernicus's work pending some unspecified correction, the Congregation (probably under the moderating influence of Cardinal Barberini, Galileo's friend and future pope) left the door open to the admissibility of Copernicanism as a legitimate computational construct for astronomers to use.[20]

Neither the Inquisition nor the Congregation of the Index had mentioned Galileo in their rulings, but Paul V himself had already instructed Bellarmine to meet with Galileo in order to notify him of the Inquisition's finding and to warn him not to defend or hold the Copernican theory. We know that the meeting took place on 26 February, but what was actually said is far from clear and is still a matter of scholarly controversy. The reason for the controversy is that there are two different versions of the event. One is provided in a short statement written by Bellarmine himself at Galileo's

18. De Santillana, *The Crime of Galileo*, p. 115, comments: 'it remained Galileo's fate through life to create an excitement and consensus around him which had little to do with real understanding. His tragedy was an excess of gifts.' See also Fantoli, *Galileo*, pp. 194–8, and Brendan Dooley, 'Processo a Galileo', *Belfagor* 51 (1996), pp. 1–21.

19. Jerome J. Langford, *Galileo, Science and the Church*, revised edn, foreword by Stillman Drake, University of Michigan Press, Ann Arbor 1971, p. 87. The key documents relating to Galileo's troubles with the Inquisition are available in English in Finocchiaro, *The Galileo Affair*.

20. On Barberini's moderating role, see de Santillana, *The Crime of Galileo*, p. 123; and Fantoli, *Galileo*, p. 239 who points out that the term 'heretical' does not appear in the decree of the Congregation of the Index.

request as the latter, before leaving Rome, wanted to put an end to rumours that he had been asked to recant his heliocentric views and had received a penalty for his past endorsement of them. In his statement the cardinal explicitly denied those 'calumnious rumours' and stated that 'only the declaration [of the Inquisition] had been read to him which states that the doctrine of Copernicus . . . is contrary to Holy Scripture and therefore cannot be defended or held'. The other version is given in an unsigned minute of the meeting between the two men, a minute that surfaced in Galileo's file at the time of his trial in 1633. According to that minute, Galileo, in the presence of three other Inquisition officials, was 'admonished by the Cardinal [Bellarmine] of the error of the aforesaid [Copernican] opinion and [told] that he should abandon it'; and 'subsequently and immediately' he was ordered 'to relinquish altogether . . . said opinion . . . nor henceforth to hold, teach or defend it in any way either verbally or in writing. Otherwise proceedings would be taken against him by the Holy Office. The said Galileo acquiesced in this ruling and promised to obey it.'[21] The fact that the minute bears neither Bellarmine's nor Galileo's signature has led a number of scholars to question its authenticity and to speculate that it is a later forgery planted in Galileo's file to nail him on the charge of having transgressed a formal injunction of the Inquisition. Others have upheld its authenticity and have ascribed its defective form to carelessness rather than malice or fraud. Others yet have argued more plausibly that the document had been routinely drafted before the meeting took place to be used only in the event Galileo did not readily heed Bellarmine's admonition and a sterner injunction would then be needed. Since such was not the case, the draft of the minute was left unsigned and should have been thrown away, but somehow was kept in the file even though it had no legal standing whatsoever. Finally, it has been suggested that the minute was drafted at the meeting by a lesser official of the Inquisition who objected to the moderate tone of Bellarmine's warning to Galileo; the cardinal, however, rejected this uncalled-for intervention of one of his subordinates and thus declined to sign the document.[22]

The scholarly debate is still on and is not likely to be resolved any time soon. But what really matters is that, regardless of what happened at the meeting, in 1616 the Catholic Church declared the heliocentric system philosophically false and theologically unacceptable. Such a pronouncement strikes us as nearly incomprehensible not only because we know (even though most of us would be hard put to demonstrate) that the cosmos is heliocentric rather than geocentric, but also because the Church itself, however belatedly, would one day recognize the blunder of 1616 by

21. The texts of the two documents are in Langford, *Galileo*, pp. 92–3 and 102, and Finocchiaro, *The Galileo Affair*, pp. 148 and 153.
22. The most recent discussion of the several interpretations is in Fantoli, *Galileo*, pp. 203–6 and 236–7. Fantoli himself endorses as 'the most plausible' the interpretation of Guido Morpurgo-Tagliabue, *I processi di Galileo e l'epistemologia*, Edizioni di Comunità, Milan 1963, pp. 14–25, according to whom Bellarmine declined to sign the document prepared by a lesser official of the Inquisition.

removing Copernicus's book from the Index (1757), by officially lifting the stigma of heresy from the heliocentric theory (1820) and eventually by endorsing Galileo's and Foscarini's interpretation of the relevant biblical passages as speaking in ordinary rather than scientific language (1893).[23] The historian's task, however, is to try to understand what has been called the 'aberration' of 1616.[24] Why did it happen? Why in 1616, a good seventy years after the publication of Copernicus's book?

To assume that the church leadership at the time was dominated by benighted fanatics who were a priori hostile to the new science will not do. After all, the opposition to Copernicanism in Rome included competent and even distinguished astronomers like the Jesuits Clavius and Grienberger who were very much abreast of, and had themselves contributed significantly to, the latest scientific advances; it included an eminent theologian like Bellarmine who, although not a scientist, kept well informed of the latest developments and had not hesitated to reject key elements of the Aristotelian–Ptolemaic cosmology, notably the solid, crystalline spheres, the perfect circularity of planetary orbits and the venerable notion of the incorruptibility of the supralunar world;[25] and it included a highly educated prelate like Maffeo Barberini, the lavish patron of scholars and artists. Their opposition to Copernicanism is certainly baffling, but cannot simply be ascribed to sheer obscurantism or fanaticism. Rather, it must be viewed as reflecting, in part, the climate of defensiveness then prevailing in a Church that was still reeling under the impact of the Protestant Reformation. The rejection of Copernicanism was obviously motivated by a fear that the new astronomy cast doubts on the inerrancy of the Bible as traditionally interpreted by the Church and thus on the Church's teaching authority; a fear also that departure from a strictly literalist exegesis might lend credence to Protestant charges that the Catholic Church took liberties with the sacred text. Accordingly, they fell back, defensively, on uncompromising, literalist exegetical standards such as the Church itself had never adopted in the past. To Foscarini's distinction between biblical statements that pertain to 'faith and morals' and must be accepted at face value, and passages that merely describe phenomena or events that have no bearing on salvation, Bellarmine opposed the view that each and every word in the Bible must be held literally true by the mere fact that it is part of the sacred text.[26]

23. D'Addio, *Considerazioni*, pp. 114–18.
24. Blackwell, *Galileo, Bellarmine*, p. 84.
25. George V. Coyne, 'Bellarmino e la nuova astronomia nell'età della Controriforma' in *Bellarmino e la Controriforma*, cd. Romeo De Maio *et al.*, Centro di Studi Sorani, Sora 1990, pp. 573–8; Paola De Falco, 'Bellarmino e la scienza' in the same vol., pp. 545–8; and Ugo Baldini, *'Legem impone subactis'. Studi su filosofia e scienza dei Gesuiti in Italia, 1540–1632*, Bulzoni, Rome 1992, pp. 286, 295–8, and 321. On Clavius see now the exhaustive study by James M. Lattis, *Between Copernicus and Galileo. Christoph Clavius and the Collapse of Ptolemaic Cosmology*, University of Chicago Press, 1994.
26. On the climate of defensiveness prevailing in the Catholic Church at the time see

But this defensive posture and the literalist exegesis that it engendered do not explain everything. It is hardly conceivable that highly educated, intelligent churchmen would have taken such an intransigent stance had they not been confident of having the consensus of the scientific and philosophical community on their side; confident also that the geocentric cosmology (or its modified, geo-heliocentric version proposed by Tycho Brahe) was fully defensible on rational, scientific grounds. Had this not been the case the risk of discrediting the very institution they represented and defended would have been too great for them to take. It is significant that Bellarmine, in his reply to Foscarini, had envisaged the possibility that some day 'a true demonstration [might] be produced that the sun stands at the centre of the universe', in which case, he conceded, one would have to reinterpret Scripture to accommodate the new cosmology. But he had added, apparently with complete assurance: 'I do not believe that there is such demonstration'.[27] Nor was Bellarmine's an isolated opinion. In a critique of Foscarini's *Letter* an unidentified theologian referred to the geocentric theory as 'the most common opinion of almost all astronomers' and a friend of Galileo's informed him in 1612 that 'as to the matter of the earth turning round, I have found hitherto no philosopher or astrologer [*sic*] willing to subscribe to it'.[28] As David C. Lindberg has remarked, if Bellarmine had polled all European astronomers on the relative merits of the heliocentric and the geocentric systems, the former 'would have lost by a landslide'.[29] All the more easily so as by 1600 those who upheld an earth-centred view of the universe could find comfort in Tycho's cosmology – an astronomical model, one ought to point out, that dispensed with the solid spheres of the Aristotelian cosmos and was compatible with all the most recent astronomical observations, including Galileo's.[30] Under the circumstances, the acceptance of Copernicanism, insofar as it contradicted common sense experience and could not yet be demonstrated with incontrovertible physical proofs, required a 'feat of the imagination', an intellectual leap few individuals were prepared to take.[31] All the fewer, in fact, as a number of objections raised against heliocentrism since it was first contemplated in the days of the Greeks (the absence of a stellar

---

William R. Shea, 'Galileo and the Church' in *God and Nature*, p. 119; and Susanna Peyronel Rambaldi, 'La Controriforma' in *SSI*, vol. 11, p. 55, who quotes Antonio Possevino's description of the Catholic Church as a 'beleaguered citadel assailed by Turks, heretics and Jews. On Bellarmine's exegesis, Blackwell, *Galileo, Bellarmine*, pp. 103–6. And on the Jesuits' retreat from their earlier support of Galileo, Feldhay, *Galileo and the Church*, pp. 253 and 271.

27. Bellarmine's *Letter to Foscarini* in Blackwell, *Galileo, Bellarmine*, pp. 265–7.
28. Ibid., p. 254.
29. David C. Lindberg, 'The "Age-Old Conflict" between Christianity and Science Reconsidered', *University of Wisconsin Letters and Science Magazine* 4 (1987), p. 15.
30. Baldini, '*Legem impone subactis*', pp. 311–13 and 330–1.
31. John H. Brooke, *Science and Religion. Some Historical Perspectives*, Cambridge University Press 1991, p. 84.

parallax and the fact that, if the earth rotated, it would leave everything behind) were still a long way from being satisfactorily answered. Lastly, the geocentric system fitted in with the still widely accepted Aristotelian physics, notably with the notion that the earth being intrinsically 'heavy' must also be at rest at the centre of the cosmos. To replace it in the scientists' mind with a whole new physics would inevitably take more than the few years that separate Galileo's discoveries in 1610 and the Inquisition's ruling of 1616.[32]

A further reason why Galileo's discoveries, even as they made helio-centrism appear more and more plausible, failed to shake the prevailing adherence to the old cosmology was the notion, widely accepted by philosophers at the time, that even if an astronomical model satisfactorily accounted for observed phenomena (if 'it saved the appearances'), it did not follow that it thereby provided a true picture of what the universe was really like. That picture, it was assumed, had to be based on 'natural philosophy', a discipline distinct from and indeed superior to astronomy and, in its Aristotelian version, concerned with the essence of things, their intrinsic qualities, their final causes. From that perspective astronomy was seen as a branch of mathematics and geometry, indispensable no doubt for computational purposes such as the prediction of eclipses or the establishment of a calendar, but of little use for determining the actual fabric of the heavens.[33] This is why over the centuries Aristotle's view of the universe as a nest of concentric transparent spheres each carrying a celestial body on its back had coexisted with a complex system of epicycles, deferents, equants and eccentrics that 'saved the appearances', but could not be squared with the solid spheres of Aristotelian cosmology. This is also why in the late sixteenth century, when Pope Gregory XIII ordered the reform of the calendar, the Jesuit astronomers entrusted with the job had used the Copernican model since it facilitated their computations, but had not for a moment thought of endorsing it as the true representation of the universe. The separation of astronomy from cosmology thus made it possible for Galileo's best educated and most open-minded opponents (Bellarmine among them) to acknowledge the validity of his astronomical discoveries without, however, discarding the geocentric system, if not in its Aristotelian form, at least in its Tychonic variant: they could confidently argue that Galileo's

32. Dorothy Stimson, *The Gradual Acceptance of the Copernican Theory of the Universe*, Peter Smith, Gloucester, Mass. 1972 (1st edn 1917), pp. 45–96, shows how, irrespective of religious considerations, the old cosmology continued to find supporters well into the seventeenth century. The reasons why Aristotelian physics and cosmology were widely accepted until Newton's time are discussed in Stephen Toulmin and June Goodfield, *The Fabric of the Heavens. The Development of Astronomy and Dynamics*, Harper, New York 1961, pp. 92–3 and 116–26. A lucid discussion of the objections against the heliocentric theory then current among scientists in Finocchiaro, *The Galileo Affair*, pp. 18–25.

33. On the separation of astronomy from cosmology, dating back to Ptolemy (2nd century AD) see Toulmin and Goodfield, *The Fabric of the Heavens*, pp. 135–45, and also Westman, 'The Copernicans', p. 78.

heliocentric conclusions were legitimate mathematical 'hypotheses' (in the sense of computational models) capable of 'saving the appearances' better than other models, but could not be taken as proofs that the earth is really in motion.[34] It was a curious and ultimately fragile compromise and one that Galileo vehemently rejected, convinced as he was that physics and mathematics are inseparable and that, as he put it, a true 'astronomer-philosopher' must 'investigate ... the true constitution of the universe, because that constitution is true and real and cannot possibly be otherwise'.[35] In other words, for Galileo astronomy could and indeed must lead to absolute certitude, whereas to his opponents certitude could be reached only deductively from a knowledge of the essence and the final cause of a given object.[36] The only demonstration that would have convinced them of the truth of the heliocentric system would have been one based on a physics totally different from Aristotle's, but in 1616 such physics was only beginning to emerge. Under the circumstances, it has been said, the two sides in the dispute did not so much clash as 'passed by each other wholly without contact'.[37]

And yet, even though one can understand why, given their pre-suppositions, Galileo's opponents could not take his heliocentric cosmology as a true representation of the universe, it is still puzzling that they chose to condemn it rather than prudently suspend judgement on the whole issue; all the more puzzling in that Bellarmine himself, as will be recalled, had not ruled out the possibility of a reinterpretation of Scripture should a convincing 'physical' proof of the Copernican system be forthcoming in the future. The answer seems to be, as Ugo Baldini has written, that Bellarmine 'believed that, if science could not choose in a definitive way between various theoretical alternatives, the choice could be made with the help of another tool [of knowledge], and he found it in a rigorous biblical literalism'.[38]

At any rate the 1616 decree of the Inquisition and the injunction allegedly served on Galileo seemed to close the debate once and for all and to preclude any further attempt on his part 'to hold and defend' Copernicanism

34. The scholastic distinction between 'true demonstrations' that explain effects by their causes and 'hypotheses' that work their way from effects to causes, and Galileo's rejection of that distinction are discussed in Morpurgo-Tagliabue, *I processi di Galileo*, pp. 28–51. In his reply to Foscarini Bellarmine had made it clear that the 'hypothetical' acceptance of Copernicanism 'presents no risk', but offering it as a true description of the cosmos would be wrong (Baldini, *'Legem impone'*, pp. 325–6). For Bellarmine 'hypothesis' thus meant a merely computational device; Galileo, by contrast, understood it as a tentative explanation awaiting verification (D'Addio, *Considerazioni*, p. 45, and Blackwell, *Galileo, Bellarmine*, p. 85).
35. Quotation in D'Addio, p. 45.
36. This point is stressed by Westman, 'The Copernicans', p. 99.
37. Richard S. Westfall, *Essays on the Trial of Galileo*, Vatican Observatory Publications, Vatican City 1989, p. 21.
38. Baldini, *'Legem impone'*, p. 329.

as a true representation of the cosmos. All that he was still permitted to do was to discuss (*tractare*) the heliocentric theory 'hypothetically'; the distinction between astronomical hypothesis and physical reality so dear to Bellarmine and the Scholastics thus meant that scientific research could proceed undisturbed provided it made no claims to physical certitude.[39] Or, as Monsignor Piero Dini, a friend of Galileo's, put it: 'One can write as a mathematician, and under the form of hypothesis . . . one can write freely'.[40]

After his return to Florence in 1616 Galileo was resigned to keep quiet on the issue of Copernicanism and devoted himself once again to the study of motion and of a new practical method for determining longitude at sea. But the burning issue of cosmology would not go away. In 1618 three comets were sighted creating enormous popular excitement and trepidation, but also re-opening among astronomers a debate about the true nature of those apparitions. The Jesuit scientists at the Collegio Romano led by Orazio Grassi, a distinguished mathematician and architect, issued a report in which they endorsed Tycho Brahe's view that comets were not to be considered atmospheric phenomena as traditional astronomy had maintained, but genuine planets that circled the sun and, along with it, the earth. Needless to say, not everyone agreed and friends in high places asked Galileo for an opinion. This he provided indirectly in the form of a *Discourse on Comets* written by one of his students. In it the Tychonic theory of comets was rejected, a rejection the Jesuits interpreted as an attack on their reputation as scientists. Grassi counter-attacked with a book, *Libra astronomica*; Galileo replied with his own *The Assayer* (1623) – and the relationship between him and the Jesuits was permanently soured. Ironically, on the question of the comets Galileo defended the old Aristotelian view against his adversaries' Tychonic and, as it turned out, more accurate theory. At the same time, in that book he forcefully argued in favour of a science based on direct empirical observations and on rigorous measurements rather than on the uncritical acceptance of the authority of the Ancients. The book of the universe – he proclaimed in a celebrated passage with obvious philosophical implications – 'is written in the language of mathematics . . . without which it is humanly impossible to understand a single word of it'; mathematics must thus be used in lieu of the 'sympathy', 'antipathy', and 'occult properties' and other such terms dear to philosophers. In that same book he also drew a distinction between sense perceptions and external physical phenomena and argued that the former 'are no more than mere names' and that 'they reside only in our

39. Morpurgo-Tagliabue, *I processi di Galileo*, pp. 26–7, has pointed out that, probably at Bellarmine's request, the original injunction 'not to teach, defend or discuss' was reformulated as 'not to hold, teach or defend', thus allowing Galileo to pursue his heliocentric model as a computational device or, in Bellarmine's terminology, as a 'hypothesis'; and that in his statement of 26 May 1616 Bellarmine went a step further and dropped the word 'teach', thus implying that Galileo was free to lecture on Copernicanism, albeit in purely 'hypothetical' terms.

consciousness', and he implicitly endorsed a corpuscular or atomistic concept of matter that denied key elements in the physics of Aristotle, notably the concepts of substance and accident[41] – and this, as the anonymous author of a theological opinion pointed out at the time, could have serious implications for the doctrine of transubstantiation in the Eucharist.[42]

Just as Galileo was completing *The Assayer* his friend and admirer Maffeo Barberini was elected pope as Urban VIII. His election was at once interpreted as signalling the dawn of a new cultural age in which the chilling decree of 1616 might be rescinded and the new science given the green light. Accordingly, *The Assayer* was promptly sent to press and dedicated by the Lincei Academy to the new pontiff; Galileo himself journeyed to Rome to pay him his respects and to raise with him the possibility of the Church lifting the ban on Copernicanism. Even though Urban VIII did not commit himself to a change of policy and held firm to the view that the heliocentric theory must be treated as a mere hypothesis or calculating device, the six long and very cordial meetings Galileo had with him led the Florentine scientist to conclude that the time was propitious for further, if cautious, discussions of the heliocentric theory. His optimism was encouraged by influential members of the new papal entourage – men such as Cardinals Zollern and Boncompagni, the Dominican Niccolò Riccardi soon to be put in charge of the Index, the pope's secretary Monsignor Ciampoli, and Tommaso Campanella whom the pope himself had ordered released from prison. Equally encouraging was the fact, promptly relayed to Galileo, that a denunciation of his latest work submitted to the Inquisition by 'a devout soul' on grounds that it defended the Copernican theory had been shelved after the book itself had been examined by a theologian and duly cleared inasmuch as the theory was presented as a mere astronomical 'hypothesis' or computational model.

To Galileo, then, the time seemed ripe for a full-scale discussion of the relative merits of the two rival cosmologies (the Aristotelian–Ptolemaic and the Copernican) and in 1625 he began to work on a book on that controversial subject in the hope that he could prove once and for all the truth of Copernicanism not so much on the basis of his own astronomical observations (which by now he had realized not to be fully conclusive), but on the basis of mechanical evidence that would undermine the very foundations of Aristotelian physics. That evidence he thought he had found in his study of tides, for he believed that tides could be accounted for only as the result of the earth's combined motions of rotation around its axis and revolution around the sun. If Galileo's theory of the tides had proved correct, it has been written, 'it would have struck at the heart' of Bellarmine's and the Jesuit astronomers' position. In fact, the theory was incorrect (and was criticized as such even then) and thus a conclusive proof in favour of heliocentrism continued to be lacking.[43]

41. Quotations in Drake, *Galileo*, p. 70.
42. See note 47 below.
43. Baldini, '*Legem impone*', pp. 319–20 and 336 n.51 (for quotation). On p. 337 Baldini notes that, in granting approval to the publication of the *Dialogue*, Urban VIII

The new book, written in the form of a dialogue or debate between a supporter of the old cosmology and a supporter of the new, was completed in 1630 and Galileo himself brought the manuscript to Rome in order to secure from the Congregation of the Index, now headed by Riccardi, the necessary authorization to publish (*imprimatur*). Riccardi granted it subject to minor changes in the text aimed at stressing the purely hypothetical nature of the heliocentric theory.[44] Having thus cleared this hurdle, the celebrated *Dialogue of the Two World Systems* came off the press in February 1632 and, as expected, created a sensation in Italy and abroad.

THE TRIAL

Yet not even the official stamp of approval of the Congregation of the Index could shield Galileo from the attacks of his adversaries – first among them the Jesuits, but also the officials of the Inquisition who may have resented, in what looks like an 'inter-agency squabble', the fact that the Congregation had acted without consulting them. But possibly the greatest source of hostility to the book lay in the fact that, although the *Dialogue* purported to be an impartial presentation of the two systems, it was the Copernican system that in the end came out on top: the argument from the tides, which Urban VIII himself had wanted omitted from the book, was there to provide, in Galileo's view, conclusive proof of the validity of the new theory. To make things worse, Simplicius, the fictional defender of the old cosmology, was portrayed in the dialogue as a presumptuous simpleton and subjected to relentless ridicule ('I must tell you that I laughed my heart out when I came across Signor Simplicio', wrote one of Galileo's friends[45]), a ridicule that by implication extended to all the opponents of Copernicanism. Some of them apparently insinuated that the figure of Simplicius was intended to lampoon Urban VIII himself, for toward the end of the *Dialogue* Galileo (most likely without realizing the folly of his action) had put in Simplicius's mouth an argument especially dear to the pope, namely that no matter how compelling the scientific arguments in favour of one system could be it was still impossible for the human mind to attain complete certitude, for God in his omnipotence could have obtained the same results in some other way.[46]

---

had requested that the chapter on tides be omitted. Galileo did not comply and this may well have cost him the pope's support.

44. On the negotiations with Riccardi see D'Addio, *Considerazioni*, pp. 71–2.
45. Quotation in D'Addio, p. 73.
46. Much has been written about Urban's argument. It has been dismissed as 'captious' by Ludovico Geymonat, *Galileo Galilei: A Biographical Inquiry into His Philosophy of Science*, transl. Stillman Drake, McGraw Hill, New York 1965, p. 113; Morpurgo-Tagliabue, *I processi di Galileo*, pp. 103–5, has stressed its roots in medieval Scholasticism's distrust of human reason and has written that Descartes's *Discourse on Method* was 'a reply to Urban's argumernt'; D'Addio,

To Urban VIII, then, the *Dialogue* was a violation of the 1616 decree in that it actually presented Copernicanism as a true physical theory rather than as a 'mathematical hypothesis'. He was also incensed by what he regarded as Galileo's duplicity in pretending that he had merely discussed Copernicanism 'hypothetically' while, in fact, he had introduced physical arguments in its favour; and he may have felt personally offended as a theologian in the character of Simplicius. Accordingly, in the summer of 1632 he ordered all copies withdrawn from circulation and instructed the Inquisition to conduct a formal investigation of the book's orthodoxy. But he may have had other reasons for departing from his earlier support of the new science, reasons that had little to do with cosmology or theology. In 1632, in the wake of Gustav Adolphus's intervention in the Thirty Years War, the military situation in Germany had rapidly deteriorated for the Catholic forces. Consequently, Urban's policy of supporting France (and indirectly her Protestant allies) as a way of preventing a Habsburg hegemony in Europe came increasingly under attack. In March of that year the Spanish Cardinal Borgia, speaking for his government, had openly accused the pope of favouring the Protestant cause and had gone so far as to raise the spectre of the convocation of a general council that would judge the pope's conduct and orthodoxy. Under the circumstances, it is possible that Urban sensed that any show of support for or even leniency toward Galileo would play into his critics' hands and that only an intransigent stand on the issue of Copernicanism could put to rest all insinuations that he, the pope, was 'soft' on heresy.[47]

Considerazioni, pp. 42–6, has presented the argument as an answer to the old theological problem of the relationship between God's omnipotence and man's limitations, a problem Galileo apparently ignored; Baldini, '*Legem impone*', p. 317, has noticed 'a surprising similarity' between Urban's argument and the modern notion that scientific theories must be viewed as no more than provisional conjectures always capable of being proven false as new observations become available.

47. In his highly controversial book, *Galileo Heretic*, transl. Raymond Rosenthal, Princeton University Press 1987 (originally published in 1983), Pietro Redondi has argued, largely on the basis of an unsigned document he discovered in the archives of the Holy Office in Rome, that Copernicanism was not the real reason why Galileo was put on trial. In that newly discovered document Galileo was denounced for his endorsement in *The Assayer* (1623) of the theory of atomism or corpuscularism, a theory his accuser found especially dangerous, indeed heretical, in that it undermined the doctrine of transubstantiation which the Council of Trent had formally adopted in defining the dogma of the Real Presence in the Eucharist. According to Redondi, the anonymous author of the document was the Jesuit Orazio Grassi, Galileo's staunch opponent; his denunciation could have provided the more conservative faction in the Roman Curia with powerful ammunition both against the new science and against Urban VIII who had long supported it. To avoid the embarrassment of having his friend and protégé tried for Eucharistic heresy as well as in order to appease the growing conservative opposition, Urban VIII ordered Galileo to be tried on the charge of defending Copernicanism, a charge far less serious, according to Redondi, than the one

Whatever the pope's motives may have been, by the summer of 1632 the machinery of the Inquisition had been set in motion. At once Galileo's friends and the government of Tuscany tried to defuse the crisis by suggesting that a new sanitized version of the *Dialogue* be published. The respected physicist and papal mathematician Fr. Castelli, on his part, discreetly (and prophetically) warned church officials of the dire consequences a condemnation of Galileo's book might have for the reputation of the Church, because, as he put it not without a touch of irony, the Church 'can forbid men to write, but cannot make the earth either stand still or move'; besides, he added, whether it does or does not move 'matters nothing as far as the salvation of souls is concerned'.[48] Even among Jesuit scientists opinions were divided: much to his credit and to his colleagues' dismay Fr. Grassi expressed a favourable view of the Copernican system and advocated a purely scientific discussion of its merits. And we know that even among the judges of the Inquisition there were at least two cardinals who were sympathetic toward Galileo.[49] Urban VIII, however, remained adamant and in September 1632 Galileo was summoned to come to Rome to answer charges.

Galileo arrived in Rome in February 1633, but was made to wait two months before appearing before the court, apparently because his judges were divided as to what exactly those charges were. After all, had not the *Dialogue* been vetted and approved by the appropriate authorities? The first court hearing took place on 22 April and to the charge of having held, defended and taught the Copernican theory Galileo answered that, in keeping with the 1616 ruling of the Inquisition and with Bellarmine's warning, he had presented it 'purely as a hypothesis' and had, in fact, refuted it. As a line of defence, it would not do, for the theologians who had examined the *Dialogue* had already concluded that it represented an all-out effort at validating the heliocentric theory; Galileo's disclaimer thus smacked of insincerity and

lodged by Grassi. In this view, then, Galileo's trial was a mere smokescreen meant to shield the pope's reputation. Although brilliantly argued and *per se* not implausible, Redondi's thesis is largely conjectural and has been rejected by a number of foremost Galileo scholars. The most detailed critique has been by Vincenzo Ferrone and Massimo Firpo in their long essay 'Galileo tra inquisitori e microstorici', *Rivista storica italiana* 97 (1985), pp. 177–238 (English version in *Journal of Modern History* 58 [1986], pp. 485–524). Redondi's reply and his two critics' rejoinder are in the same volume of *Rivista storica italiana*, pp. 934–68. Other reviews are by Bruno Basile in *Rivista di storia e letteratura religiosa*, 20 (1984), pp. 510–20; Guido Morpurgo-Tagliabue in *Rivista di storia della filosofia*, NS 39 (1984), pp. 741–50; Edward A. Gosselin in *American Historical Review* 91 (1986), pp. 1232–3; William S. Shea in *Isis* 79 (1988), pp. 348–50. See also Maurice A. Finocchiaro, 'Recent Interpretations of the Galileo Affair' in *Science and Religion*, ed. Anne Baumer and Manfred Buttner, Brockmeyer, Bochum 1989, pp. 110–18; Richard S. Westfall, 'Galileo Heretic: Problems, as they appear to me, with Redondi's book', *History of Science* 26 (1988), pp. 399–415; and Blackwell, *Galileo, Bellarmine*, pp. 155–6.

48. Quotation in D'Addio, *Considerazioni*, p. 92.
49. Ibid., pp. 94 and 96.

ultimately aggravated his position in the eyes of his accusers. At this point, in an attempt to spare the old, frail scientist the humiliation of a formal trial and condemnation, the Commissary of the Inquisition, Vincenzo Maculano, tried to reach an out-of-court settlement: Galileo would confess to him that, out of 'vainglory' and 'inadvertence', he had gone too far in presenting arguments in support of Copernicanism, thus departing from a purely hypothetical format and violating Bellarmine's order; in return for confessing his error Galileo would receive a mild penance and the whole matter would be closed. Possibly out of sheer exhaustion Galileo accepted Maculano's extrajudicial plan, signed his confession and even offered to add a chapter to his *Dialogue* with a refutation of the arguments in support of Copernicanism. In the end, however, the more intransigent view prevailed among the judges: on 22 June 1633, after Galileo pleaded guilty to the charge of having 'held and defended' the Copernican theory in violation of the injunction he had received in 1616, the court found him 'vehemently suspected of heresy', required him to make a solemn recantation in which he 'abjured, cursed and detested [his] errors and heresies', and sentenced him to indefinite imprisonment at the pleasure of the court.[50]

The whole tragic story was marked by indecision and ambiguity. We saw that Galileo's judges hesitated beween an extrajudicial settlement that would have merely involved a mild penance and possibly a revision of the *Dialogue* and an outright condemnation for heresy, albeit in the somewhat milder form of 'supicion of heresy'.[51] Three of the ten cardinals who sat on the court were not present at the time of sentencing and did not sign the verdict, possibly as a way of expressing their dissent. Nor was the verdict issued in the pope's name, but only in the Inquisition's (*in forma communi*, i.e. not infallible) – a circumstance that was quickly interpreted at the time (notably by Descartes, Gassendi and Mersenne) as an indication that the condemnation of the heliocentric theory was no 'article of faith'.[52] Lastly, the harsh sentence of life imprisonment was immediately commuted to house arrest: for the rest of his life Galileo was confined to his own home in Arcetri outside Florence and allowed, under certain restrictions, to have visits and to pursue his scientific work. It was there that before his death in 1642 he wrote his masterpiece, the *Discourse of Two New Sciences*, a work devoted to dynamics and mechanics that did not discuss the forbidden subject of Copernicanism, but, in fact, reinforced the foundations on which it rested. As for the sentence inflicted on Galileo, it represented, as the eminent Catholic philosopher Jacques Maritain once wrote, a flagrant 'abuse of power': given their own presuppositions, Galileo's judges could have legitimately enjoined him not to defend or teach a doctrine they regarded as contrary to the faith; they could have even imposed

---

50. For the most recent reconstruction of events see Fantoli, *Galileo*, pp. 400–24.
51. In the Inquisition's terminology 'suspicion of heresy' meant that, while there was no doubt that the defendant had committed a certain act, there was no proof of evil intent. I am indebted to Dr John Tedeschi for this clarification.
52. D'Addio, *Considerazioni*, p. 113 n.116.

some penalty for having done so in his book, but they should not have made him swear that he 'cursed and detested' something he knew to be true: this was 'violence done to his conscience'.[53]

GALILEO'S LEGACY

From the mid-eighteenth century, in the climate of the Enlightenment, Galileo's condemnation by the Inquisition has often been interpreted as evidence of an irreconcilable conflict between the Church amd modern science, and Galileo has often been hailed as a forerunner of modern secularism and as a martyr of free thought. But this is an anachronistic reading of past events, and one that Galileo himself, his closest followers such as Castelli and Cavalieri (both of them churchmen in good standing) and Catholic scientists like Descartes and Pascal would have rejected as absurd: to them science and faith, far from being incompatible, could and should be harmonized if only church authorities would abandon an increasingly discredited, pagan philosophy (Aristotelianism) and a literalist exegesis that had little basis in the tradition of the Church. The conflict, it has been written, 'was not between science and Christianity, but within Christianity (between opposing theories of biblical interpretation, the one liberal, the other conservative) and within science (between proponents of the major cosmologies)'.[54]

Nonetheless the outcome of that conflict as epitomized by the 1633 verdict was bound to influence subsequent scientific developments in Catholic countries and especially in Italy. To be sure, the old view that after Galileo's condemnation all scientific work there came under a cloud and was systematically discouraged, if not totally banned, and that, as John Milton reported after visiting Galileo in Arcetri, the 'tyranny' of the Inquisition had 'dampened the glory of Italian wits'[55] has been laid to rest by recent scholarship.[56] In its place we now have a more nuanced and far more complex picture of Italian science after 1633. On its dark side is the fact that the heliocentric theory was now off-limits for Catholic scientists or, at best, could be cautiously discussed as a mere computational model – with the

53. Jacques Maritain, *On the Church of Christ. The Person of the Church and Her Personnel*, transl. Joseph W. Evans, University of Notre Dame Press, Notre Dame, Ind. 1973, p. 208. See also Fantoli, *Galileo*, pp. 426–7 for an equally trenchant, if somewhat different, critique of the verdict.
54. Lindberg, 'The "Age-Old Conflict"', p. 15. See also Ugo Baldini, 'L'attività scientifica nel primo Settecento' in *SIE Annali* 3 (1980), pp. 513–14.
55. Quotation in Shea, 'Galileo and the Church', p. 132.
56. Ugo Baldini, 'La scuola galileiana' in *SIE Annali* 3 (1980), pp. 437–8 and 450–1; William B. Ashworth, Jr., 'Catholicism and Early Modern Science' in *God and Nature*, pp. 152–3; and Roberto Maiocchi, 'La rivoluzione scientifica nel Seicento' in *SSI*, vol. 11, pp. 449–53.

result that in Catholic Italy progress in astrophysics was very limited after 1633. And the same can be said of the corpuscular or atomistic theory of matter, a subject increasingly frowned upon in Rome. On the bright side stands, first of all, the fact that no other scientist was prosecuted by the Inquisition and very few books on science were placed on the Index, so much so that Galileo's condemnation has been called, not without reason, a 'tragic aberration'.[57] Nor did church authorities raise any objections to the publication of Galileo's last work in Holland and to its wide circulation in Italy.[58] On the bright side there is also the fact that after 1633 important and original scientific work did not come to a halt, but was carried on for the rest of the century with sometimes brilliant results, if not in astrophysics, certainly in other fields, some of which had been largely unexplored before.

Much of the credit for the scientific advances of the mid and late seventeenth century belongs to a small group of men generally known as Galileo's 'pupils', although only one of them had been formally trained by him.[59] The oldest among them was the Benedictine monk Benedetto Castelli (1577–1643), the recipient of the famous letter of 1613 who held the chair of mathematics at Pisa first and then at Rome. He was famous in his time primarily on account of his work in hydrodynamics, but his research interests ranged widely and included astronomy, thermodynamics and optics. Castelli must also be remembered as the teacher of some leading scientists of the mid-seventeenth century. One was Bonaventura Cavalieri (1598–1647), a member of the Gesuati order of friars, who was appointed to the chair of mathematics at Bologna on Galileo's recommendation and made a name for himself as the creator of the 'method of indivisibles' for the calculation of areas and volumes, a method that foreshadowed the invention of modern calculus by Newton and Leibniz later in the century. Although primarily interested in pure mathematics, around 1640 Cavalieri also lectured on astronomical systems – Ptolemaic, Tychonic and Copernican. The fact that he did so in Bologna, a town in the Papal States, is worth noticing as evidence that even there it was still possible to study and teach about the Copernican system, albeit as a 'hypothesis'. Another celebrity among Castelli's students was Evangelista Torricelli (1608–47): he served as Galileo's assistant at Arcetri and after the old master's death succeeded him as court mathematician in Florence. He perfected and systematized Galileo's mechanics and after 1642 came to be regarded as the standard-bearer of the Galilean school. His most original work focused on atmospheric pressure which led him to the invention of the barometer and to the empirical demonstration of the existence of the vacuum, something that had been denied by Aristotelian physics. Last, but by no means least, among Castelli's students was Giovanni Alfonso Borelli (1608–79), professor of mathematics first at Pisa and then at

57. Brooke, *Science and Religion*, p. 108.
58. Fantoli, *Galileo*, p. 465.
59. Baldini, 'La scuola galileiana', pp. 393–424; and Michael Segre, *In the Wake of Galileo*, Rutgers University Press, New Brunswick, N.J. 1991.

Messina.[60] The leading figure in the 'second Galilean generation', he is remarkable both for the originality and the range of his investigations: as an astronomer, in 1665 he published an important work on comets and the following year one on the orbits of Jupiter's satellites (which Galileo had first sighted and named the 'Medicean planets' in honour of his patrons) which he used as a proxy for the solar system, thus avoiding the risk of being branded a Copernican and yet assembling important new data that one day Newton would use for his own study of the solar system. Borelli also initiated the scientific study of volcanoes and investigated the causes of epidemic disease rejecting the astrological explanations still current at the time and replacing them with a corpuscular theory of contagion. Lastly, in his *On the Motion of Animals* (1680–81) he drew on both physiology and mechanics to study the functioning of muscles and to analyse the complex processes involved in animal motion.

Borelli's interest in the natural sciences was no isolated phenomenon in the second half of the century. Actually, it was precisely in that area that some Italian scientists excelled and achieved international reputation. Two names, in particular, stand out here: Francesco Redi (1626–97) and Marcello Malpighi (1628–94).[61] The former is chiefly remembered for his refutation, based on carefully designed experiments, of the time-honoured theory of the spontaneous generation of plants and insects. Building on the work of William Harvey, Malpighi, on his part, made decisive contributions to the study of the circulation of the blood, notably with his discovery of capillary vessels; he also pioneered, with his microscopic observations of various organs and tissues, in the study of embryology and histology.

These leading scientists (and a plethora of lesser ones) all subscribed to Galileo's call for a science grounded in experimentation rather than in a priori assumptions. But the same emphasis on experimentation inspired another group of scientists who certainly did not want to be seen as followers of the great Florentine master and who were not prepared to give up Aristotelian science, namely the Jesuits.[62] This may seem, at first sight, rather paradoxical, but it must be recalled that the Jesuits had a long and distinguished record as students of science, and especially of mathematics and astronomy, that went back to the days of Fathers Clavius, Grienberger and Grassi; one must also bear in mind that the Jesuits prided themselves with running some of the

60. On Borelli, in addition to Baldini's and Segre's works, see A. Rupert Hall, *The Revolution in Science 1500–1750*, Longman 1983, pp. 167–8 and 301–2; and Giuseppe Giarrizzo, 'La Sicilia dal Cinquecento all'Unità' in Vincenzo D'Alessandro and G. Giarrizzo, *La Sicilia dal Vespro all'Unità*, UTET, Turin 1989, pp. 326–30.

61. Baldini, 'L'attività scientifica', pp. 501–4; and Hall, *The Revolution in Science*, pp. 163–4, 172, and 337–9.

62. Gabriele Baroncini, 'L'insegnamento della filosofia naturale nei collegi italiani dei Gesuiti (1610–1670): un esempio di nuovo aristotelismo' in *La 'ratio studiorum'. Modelli culturali e pratiche educative dei Gesuiti in Italia fra Cinque e Seicento*, ed. Gian Paolo Brizzi, Bulzoni, Rome 1981, pp. 163–215.

finest schools in Europe, and insofar as those schools were meant to train the future elites (military officers, government officials, members of the liberal professions) they had to make room in their curricula for mathematics and the sciences as indispensable prerequisites for the study of practical subjects such as geography, navigation, surveying, civil engineering and so on. Moreover, in order to ensure the reputation of their schools the Jesuits felt that they must keep abreast of the latest scientific developments and, if possible, contribute themselves to those developments.[63] And, in fact, a number of Jesuit scientists did so contribute by embracing with zest Galileo's call for experimentation. In the first half of the century Niccolò Cabeo (1585–1650) discovered and studied electrostatic attraction; Christopher Scheiner (1575–1650), a German Jesuit who taught for years at the Collegio Romano, engaged in a spirited and at times acrimonious debate with Galileo and may have had a hand in formulating charges against him, made important observations of sunspots, discovered the refraction of light in the eye and how images form on the retina. At mid-century Giovanni Battista Riccioli (1598–1671) wrote one of the most comprehensive and thorough surveys of cosmology then available anywhere, the *Almagestum Novum* (1651), a fifth of which was devoted to a sympathetic and indeed admiring discussion of the Copernican system as a valuable 'hypothesis'. Together with his fellow Jesuit Francesco Grimaldi (himself a distinguished student of optics whose theory of diffraction fore-shadowed Newton's) he also completed a systematic mapping of the moon surface, produced the best study of the pendulum before Huygens's and was the first accurately to measure the rate of acceleration of free-falling bodies. In 1684 his confrère Paolo Casati published an extensive and authoritative treatise on mechanics in which he openly acknowledged his debt to Galileo.[64]

For all its undeniable merits, however, the work of Jesuit scientists suffered from serious constraints, especially in the areas of cosmology and of the structure of matter, for in those areas they had to contend, as a matter of religious obedience, with the Church's condemnation of heliocentrism on the one hand and with the incompatibility of corpuscularism or atomism with Aristotelian physics on the other. As a result they engaged in an intellectual balancing act as they bravely (but vainly) tried to accommodate the old and the new science. As far as cosmology was concerned, they felt free, with a clear conscience, to lecture and write about the heliocentric system, but always insisting that it was only a useful computational device and not a true, or even probable, representation of what the cosmos was really like. By endorsing the Tychonic system they could maintain the centrality and stability of the earth, while discarding the by now discredited Aristotelian planetary spheres and the notion of the incorruptibility of the heavens. When it came to atomism, Jesuit scientists were torn between the increasingly persuasive explanation it provided for such phenomena as rarefaction, condensation or

63. Brooke, *Science and Religion*, pp. 108–9.
64. Baldini, 'L'attività scientifica', pp. 516–17 and 522–3.

heat, and the challenge it represented to Aristotelian physics in general and to the doctrine of transubstantiation in particular. The solution they adopted as scientists was, once again, a compromise: on the one hand, in their research and teaching they made a limited use of atomism when discussing specific phenomena of the inorganic world, but at the same time rejected it as a general theory of matter. The upshot of all this, it has been said, was a 'new Aristotelianism', a curious blend of old and new and often conflicting ideas, that enabled Jesuit scientists to move toward the new frontiers of knowledge without abandoning their philosophical and theological moorings. The payoff, as we just saw, was a good deal of first-rate scientific work; the price was a reluctance to formulate broad new theories and to confront squarely some fundamental questions which the new science posed to religion.[65] Only in the mid-eighteenth century would the Jesuits abandon their balancing act, embrace the new science, and even contribute to the repeal of the anti-Copernican decree of 1616.[66]

Even though work in the sciences in general continued to be carried out till the end of the century, historians have often noted a contrast between the golden days of Galileo, Castelli, Cavalieri and Torricelli, and the far less impressive record of the last quarter of the century when scientists all too often devoted an inordinate amount of energy to 'curious' experiments and shied away from broader issues of theory. Jesuit science, in particular, has been singled out as a prime example of this unhappy trend and as proof that the trend itself was chiefly caused by the chilling impact that Galileo's condemnation presumably had on Italian scientists in general. In recent years, however, this interpretation has come under severe criticism.[67] It has been pointed out that the influence of ecclesiastical repression and censorship has been overestimated: the only area of science to be seriously affected was cosmology, and yet even there some excellent work was carried out (as it was by Borelli) so long as one avoided an open endorsement of Copernicanism; the latter, as we have seen, continued to be discussed and taught, albeit behind the fig leaf of 'hypothesis', even in Jesuit schools; and books on atomism, notably the works of Gassendi, freely circulated in Italy in the later part of the century.[68]

Other factors were no doubt responsible for the decline of scientific research. One was the growing and ultimately nearly exclusive interest in one

---

65. On the eclecticism of Jesuit scientists see Ashworth, 'Catholicism and Early Modern Science', pp. 155–7; Baroncini, 'L'insegnamento', pp. 176–8 and 179–83 has stressed the fact that the Tychonic system embraced by the Jesuits 'endorsed Copernicus' astronomy while rejecting his cosmology and that, while atomism was adopted as an explanation of specific inorganic phenomena, Aristotelian hylomorphism was retained to explain changes of an organic nature.
66. Baldini, 'L'attività scientifica', pp. 526–9.
67. See note 56 above.
68. Nicholas Davidson, 'Unbelief and Atheists in Italy, 1500–1700' in *Atheism from the Reformation to the Enlightenment*, ed. Michael Hunter and David Hutton, Clarendon Press 1992, p. 62.

aspect of Galileo's legacy, experimentation, to the detriment of bold, overarching theories. Early signs of the new trend are visible in the celebrated Accademia del Cimento, a select group of nine top-notch scientists (Borelli, Redi and Vincenzo Viviani, Galileo's first biographer, among them) gathered under the patronage of Leopold de' Medici, the grand duke's brother, between 1657 and 1667. Even in that group the design of experiments, notably on atmospheric pressure, heat and magnetism, and their careful description and recording took precedence over the formulation of general scientific laws. The Cimento's cautious, strictly experimental approach to nature may well have reflected, to some extent, its Medici patron's fear that the discussion of scientific theories might cause problems with church authorities;[69] but it was also due to two reasons of a quite different nature. One was that, unlike astronomy and mechanics, the new areas of physics that were being investigated did not at the time easily lend themselves to quantification and therefore could not yet be brought under general laws. The other reason was that even in fields such as astronomy and mechanics where a mathematical approach would have been appropriate and especially fruitful, Italian scientists were handicapped, relative to their fellow scientists north of the Alps, by their lack of familiarity with the latest developments in algebra and analytical geometry or their unwillingness to use those new tools in their research. Surprisingly, to the end of the century Italian scientists seem to have been insensitive, much as Galileo had been, to the potential role these new developments could play in the progress of science and remained loyal to Galileo's reliance on Euclidean geometry as the basic investigative tool[70] – an instance perhaps of how veneration for a great master can turn into a somewhat ossified legacy.

The Cimento Academy lasted only ten years and had no successor in Tuscany, probably because of the climate of narrow conservatism and religious intolerance that prevailed in the Grand Duchy during the long reign of Cosimo III (1670–1723). The legacy of the Cimento, however, lived on outside Tuscany. The publication in 1667 by its versatile secretary Lorenzo Magalotti of its members' scientific experiments under the title of *Examples of Natural Experiments Performed in the Academy of Cimento* served as a model for other scientific academies to follow and to emulate, and indeed a number of them sprang up and prospered from the 1660s, notably in Naples, Rome, Bologna and Siena.[71] None of them became as prestigious and widely known as the Cimento had been during a short, glamorous decade, but they all contributed to keeping alive an interest in experimental science, that was to bear rich fruits in the next century.

69. Paolo Galluzzi, 'L'Accademia del Cimento: "gusti" del principe, filosofia e ideologia dell'esperimento', *QS* 48 (1981), pp. 788–844.
70. Baldini, 'La scuola galileiana', pp. 410 and 442–3.
71. Luigi Besana, 'Le accademie e l'organizzazione del sapere' in *SSI*, vol. 11, pp. 460–2.

Appendix: Tables of succession

1. Popes
Clement VIII (Ippolito Aldobrandini)	1592–1605
Leo XI (Alessandro Ottaviano de' Medici)	1605
Paul V (Camillo Borghese)	1605–1621
Gregory XV (Alessandro Ludovisi)	1621–1623
Urban VIII (Maffeo Barberini)	1623–1644
Innocent X (Giambattista Pamphili)	1644–1655
Alexander VII (Fabio Chigi)	1655–1667
Clement IX (Giulio Rospigliosi)	1667–1669
Clement X (Emilio Altieri)	1670–1676
Innocent XI (Benedetto Odescalchi)	1676–1689
Alexander VIII (Pietro Ottoboni)	1689–1691
Innocent XII (Antonio Pignetelli)	1691–1700

2. Kings of Spain (and of Naples, Sicily, Sardinia and Milan)
Philip III of Habsburg	1598–1621
Philip IV	1621–1665
Carlos II	1665–1700

3. Grand Dukes of Tuscany
Ferdinando I de' Medici	1587–1609
Cosimo II	1609–1621
Ferdinando II	1621–1670
Cosimo III	1670–1723

4. Dukes of Savoy and Piedmont
Carlo Emanuele I	1580–1630
Vittorio Amedeo I	1630–1637
Regency	1637–1648
Carlo Emanuele II	1648–1675
Regency	1675–1684
Vittorio Amedeo II	1684–1730

5. Dukes of Mantua and Monferrato
Vincenzo I Gonzaga	1587–1612
Francesco II	1612
Ferdinando II	1612–1626
Vincenzo II	1626–1627
Carlo I Gonzaga-Nevers	1627–1637
Regency	1637–1647
Carlo II	1647–1665
Regency	1665–1669
Ferdinando Carlo	1669–1707

6. Dukes of Modena
Cesare d'Este	1597–1628
Alfonso III	1628–1629
Francesco I	1629–1657
Alfonso IV	1657–1662
Francesco II	1662–1694
Rinaldo	1694–1737

7. Dukes of Parma
Ranuccio I Farnese	1592–1622
Odoardo	1622–1646
Ranuccio II	1646–1694
Francesco	1694–1727

Index